Juvenile Delinquency and the Limits of Western
Influence, 1850–2000

Palgrave Studies in the History of Childhood

Series Editors: George Rousseau, University of Oxford and Laurence Brockliss, University of Oxford

Palgrave Studies in the History of Childhood is the first of its kind to historicise childhood in the English-speaking world; at present no historical series on children/childhood exists, despite burgeoning areas within Child Studies. The series aims to act both as a forum for publishing works in the history of childhood and a mechanism for consolidating the identity and attraction of the new discipline

Editorial Board: Jo Boyden, University of Oxford, Matthew Grenby, Newcastle University, Heather Montgomery, Open University, Nicholas Orme, Exeter University, Lyndal Roper, University of Oxford, Sally Shuttleworth, University of Oxford Lindsay Smith, Sussex University, Nando Sigona, Birmingham University

Titles include:

Heather Ellis (*editor*)
JUVENILE DELINQUENCY AND THE LIMITS OF WESTERN INFLUENCE,
1850–2000

Hilary Marland
HEALTH AND GIRLHOOD IN BRITAIN, 1874–1920

Heidi Morrison
CHILDHOOD AND COLONIAL MODERNITY IN EGYPT

George Rousseau
CHILDREN AND SEXUALITY
From the Greeks to the Great War

Lucy Underwood
CHILDHOOD AND RELIGIOUS DISSENT IN POST-REFORMATION ENGLAND

Karen Vallgårda
IMPERIAL CHILDHOODS AND CHRISTIAN MISSION
Education and Emotions in South India and Denmark

Stephen Wagg and Jane Pilcher (*editors*)
THATCHER'S GRANDCHILDREN
Politics and Childhood in the Twenty-First Century

Palgrave Studies in the History of Childhood
Series Standing Order ISBN 978–1–137–30555–8 (Hardback)
978–1–137–40240–0 (Paperback)
(*outside North America only*)

You can receive future titles in this series as they are published by placing a standing order. Please contact your bookseller or, in case of difficulty, write to us at the address below with your name and address, the title of the series and the ISBNs quoted above.

Customer Services Department, Macmillan Distribution Ltd, Houndmills, Basingstoke, Hampshire RG21 6XS, England

Juvenile Delinquency and the Limits of Western Influence, 1850–2000

Edited by

Heather Ellis
Senior Lecturer in History of Education, Liverpool Hope University, UK

First published 2014 by
PALGRAVE MACMILLAN

Palgrave Macmillan in the UK is an imprint of Macmillan Publishers Limited,
registered in England, company number 785998, of Houndmills, Basingstoke,
Hampshire RG21 6XS.

Palgrave Macmillan in the US is a division of St Martin's Press LLC,
175 Fifth Avenue, New York, NY 10010.

Palgrave Macmillan is the global academic imprint of the above companies
and has companies and representatives throughout the world.

Palgrave® and Macmillan® are registered trademarks in the United States,
the United Kingdom, Europe and other countries.

ISBN 978–1–137–34951–4

This book is printed on paper suitable for recycling and made from fully
managed and sustained forest sources. Logging, pulping and manufacturing
processes are expected to conform to the environmental regulations of the
country of origin.

A catalogue record for this book is available from the British Library.

Library of Congress Cataloging-in-Publication Data
Juvenile delinquency and the limits of Western influence, 1850–2000 / edited
    by Heather Ellis.
        pages cm. — (Palgrave studies in the history of childhood)
    Summary: "Juvenile Delinquency and the Limits of Western Influence, 1850–2000
    brings together a wide range of case studies from across the globe, written by
    some of the leading scholars in the field, to explore the complex ways in which
    historical understandings of childhood and juvenile delinquency have been
    constructed in a global context. The book highlights the continued entanglement
    of historical descriptions of the development of juvenile justice systems in other
    parts of the world with narratives of Western colonialism and the persistence of
    notions of a cultural divide between East and West. It also stresses the need to
    combine theoretical insights from traditional comparative history with new global
    history approaches. In doing so, the case studies examined in the volume reveal
    the significant limitations to the influence of Western ideas about juvenile
    delinquency in other parts of the world, as well as the important degree to which
    Western understandings of delinquency were also constructed in a transnational
    context" — Provided by publisher.
    ISBN 978–1–137–34951–4 (hardback)
    1. Juvenile delinquency—History—19th century. 2. Juvenile delinquency—
    History—20th century.   I. Ellis, Heather, editor.
    HV9065.J88 2014
    364.3609′04—dc23   2014019322

Contents

Part IV Cold War Contexts

Part V Juvenile Delinquency and the Post-War State

Acknowledgements

The editor would firstly like to thank the contributors for all their hard work and help with putting this volume together over the last two and a half years. All of the chapters included here began life as conference papers at a two-day event titled "Juvenile Delinquency in the 19th and 20th Centuries: East-West Perspectives" organized at the Centre for British Studies, Humboldt-Universität zu Berlin, on 12 and 13 March 2011. I would very much like to thank the Fritz-Thyssen-Stiftung in Cologne, who awarded me a grant of €10,000 which allowed me to organize the conference and cover the travel and accommodation costs of speakers from a wide range of countries. I owe additional thanks to the Leverhulme Trust's "China's War with Japan" Project, which also helped to sponsor the initial conference which was co-organized with Lily Chang.

My thanks also go to the academic and administrative staff of the Centre for British Studies, which hosted the conference and provided invaluable administrative and organizational support in the run-up to the event and during the conference itself. I am also grateful to the other conference participants whose papers are not included in this edited volume. Their research stimulated many interesting discussions which influenced the way this volume has been written and organized and reminded us of what an active and innovative field of study the history of juvenile delinquency has become. Finally, I would like to express my gratitude to the team at Palgrave Macmillan, who have supported me through the various stages of production, in particular Jenny McCall and Holly Tyler. In addition, I would like to thank the series editors, Laurence Brockliss and George Rousseau, for their interest, help and support as the volume was put together.

Contributors

Sarah Bornhorst is currently scientific assistant at the German Historical Museum in Berlin. She gained her PhD in 2008 under the supervision of Prof. Dr Andreas Wirsching at the University of Augsburg, Germany. Her doctoral thesis examined juvenile delinquency in the context of First-World-War Germany and appeared as a monograph in 2010 titled *Selbstversorger: Jugendkriminalität während des Ersten Weltkriegs im Landgerichtsbezirk Ulm* (Konflikte und Kultur – Historische Perspektiven 19).

Kate Bradley has been Lecturer in Social History and Social Policy at the University of Kent's School of Social Policy, Sociology and Social Research since 2007. Before this, she was an ESRC Postdoctoral Fellow at the Centre for Contemporary British History at the Institute of Historical Research, University of London. She completed her PhD, which was funded by the Leverhulme Trust, at the Centre for Contemporary British History, Institute of Historical Research, University of London, between 2002 and 2006. Her current research interests focus on the relationship between juvenile crime and the welfare state in post-war Britain.

Miroslava Chávez-García is Associate Professor and Chair of the Chicana/o Studies Program at the University of California, Davis. She received her doctorate in history from the University of California at Los Angeles in 1998 and has published a book and several articles on gender, patriarchy and the law in nineteenth-century California. Her current research interests and publications focus on youth, juvenile justice, race and science in early twentieth-century California reform schools. Currently, she teaches courses on Chicana/o history, Latina/o history, race and juvenile justice, US–Mexico border relations and research methodologies.

Nazan Çiçek is Assistant Professor in the Faculty of Political Sciences at the University of Ankara. She completed her PhD at the School of Oriental and African Studies, University of London in 2006. She is the author of *The Young Ottomans: Turkish Critics of the Eastern Question in the Late Nineteenth Century* (2010). She has also published articles on the political and intellectual history of the Ottoman Empire and Turkish Republic in several journals, including *Middle Eastern Studies* and *Études Balkaniques*.

Amrit Dev Kaur Khalsa is currently Project Manager for Leiden Global, an initiative of Leiden University to develop Global and Area Studies in Leiden. In 2011–2012 she was Lecturer in History at Leiden University, where she completed her PhD in modern European colonial history in 2010. Her doctoral project focused on forced re-education policies for juvenile delinquents in the Netherlands Indies (now Indonesia), and she uses this topic to show the interaction between a "modernizing" Dutch colonial state and the growth of a "colonial civil society" between approximately 1890 and 1945.

Heather Ellis is Senior Lecturer in History of Education at Liverpool Hope University. Before this, she was Lecturer and Researcher in British History at the Centre for British Studies, Humboldt-Universität zu Berlin. She holds a DPhil in history from Balliol College, Oxford. A monograph based on her doctoral thesis, entitled *Generational Conflict and University Reform: Oxford in the Age of Revolution*, was published in 2012. She edited a special issue of *Social Justice: A Journal of Crime, Conflict and World Order* in December 2011 entitled "Juvenile Delinquency, Modernity and the State". She is co-editor (with Ulrike Kirchberger) of *Anglo-German Scholarly Networks in the Long Nineteenth Century* (Brill 2014) and has published widely on the history of masculinity, generational identity and the history of childhood.

Barak Kushner is Senior Lecturer in Modern Japanese History in the Faculty of Asian and Middle Eastern Studies at the University of Cambridge. He holds a PhD in history from Princeton University. He was recently awarded a 2012 British Academy Mid-Career Fellowship which he will use to complete his book on Japanese War Crimes Trials in China. In the summer of 2008 he was a visiting scholar at Nanjing University (China) and during 2009 he was a visiting scholar at Waseda University (Japan). He was a 2008 Abe Fellow and conducted research concerning "Cold War Propaganda in East Asia and Historical Memory".

Howard Lupovitch is Director of the Cohn-Haddow Center for Jewish Studies and Associate Professor of History at Wayne State University. He obtained his PhD from Columbia University in 1996. He is a specialist in the history of Hungarian Jews and the Jews of the Habsburg Monarchy, and the urban Jewish experience. His current research interests include a history of the Jews of Budapest, the Neolog Movement, ennobled Jews and Hungarian-Jewish Immigration to North America with a particular focus on attitudes toward juvenile crime.

Nina Mackert is Lecturer and Researcher in the Department of North American History at the University of Erfurt, Germany. She is currently working as part of a research team on a project entitled "Das essende Subjekt: Eine Geschichte des Politischen in den USA vom 19. bis zum 21. Jahrhundert" (The Eating Subject: A History of the Political in the USA from the 19th to the 21st Century). She obtained her PhD in history in 2012 from the University of Erfurt. Her doctoral dissertation examined juvenile delinquency as a social and political problem in the US between the 1940s and 1960s.

Stephanie Olsen is currently a postdoctoral researcher at the Max Planck Center for the History of Emotions in Berlin, Germany. She obtained her PhD in history from McGill University in 2009. Her current research project is titled "Emotional Manhood: Adolescence, Informal Education and the Male Citizen in Britain, 1880–1914". She has published a number of articles on the informal education of boys in the nineteenth century, the history of masculinity and the history of childhood.

Gleb Tsipursky is Assistant Professor of History at the Ohio State University. He gained his PhD in history in 2011 from the University of North Carolina at Chapel Hill. He teaches courses on modern European and global history. His research is in the field of modern Russian and Eurasian history, with a particular interest in socialist modernity, youth, consumption, popular culture, emotions, the Cold War, crime, violence and social controls. He is the author of a monograph entitled *Having Fun in the Thaw: Youth Initiative Clubs in the Post-Stalin Years* (2012).

1
Introduction: Constructing Juvenile Delinquency in a Global Context

Heather Ellis

East–West divisions

The division between East and West has been one of the most important structuring principles used to make sense of the world both today and in the past. Historically, it has been most commonly applied by individuals and groups who have identified with the West and has been used to denote a particular geopolitical relationship, between the West as the stronger, superior partner and the weaker, dependent East.[1] Insofar as transfers of legal ideas and institutions have been considered by historians in the context of East–West divisions, they have mostly been seen as taking place from West to East, and tend to be interpreted within a discourse of imperial "improvement" and "civilization". In recent years (in particular, since the publication of Edward Said's *Orientalism*[2]), it has become popular to critique this division and to question how it came into being and what relation it bears to historical reality.[3] The East–West binary has been articulated in a variety of geopolitical contexts: within the continent of Europe, between Western imperial powers and their "Eastern" colonies and between the Western and Eastern hemispheres more broadly. In the post-war period, the East–West division was once again reinterpreted against the background of the Cold War to refer primarily to the division between the capitalist "free" West and the Soviet Communist East. Although this was a significant variation of the traditional East–West division, it should not be seen as a separate phenomenon, as it continued to bear the familiar imprint of "superior" West versus "inferior" East.[4]

Juvenile delinquency and the East–West division

Although perhaps not at first apparent, the East–West binary has been fundamental to the ways in which juvenile delinquency has been understood both by contemporary actors and scholars studying delinquency in the past. It is often identified as a profoundly Western problem. This is primarily due to the close association it enjoys with another idea with which the West is often coupled conceptually – modernity.[5] Scholars tend to link the appearance of juvenile delinquency as a social problem in western Europe and the US with the emergence of certain "processes of modernity" – industrialization, urbanization and the associated weakening of traditional social bonds and authority structures, in particular the separation of home and work. This link is frequently made even more specific by focusing attention on the nineteenth century in particular, during which the term "juvenile delinquency" first appeared and gained widespread usage in Britain. By contrast, the East (imagined variously as eastern Europe, the colonial East, the Far East or the Communist East) has often been seen to exhibit low levels of juvenile crime, which is explained either in terms of its pre-modern state (in the case of the colonial East or the Far East) or as a result of its rejection of "Western" modernity (in the case of the Communist East).[6] The relative strength of familial and community bonds and traditional structures of authority in the East are often stressed by contrast. Likewise, any signs of juvenile delinquency tend to be associated with the onset of "modernization processes", which, in turn, are seen as the result of "Western" influence.[7] The emergence of juvenile crime as a problem in the colonies of west European empires in the late nineteenth and early twentieth centuries has been interpreted in this way, as have similar developments in the non-colonial East, for example, in China. In the latter case, growing levels of youth crime are attributed to the influence of the West through trade, war, migration and other forms of contact.[8] In this oversimplified picture, the East is idealized as naïve, romantic, pre-modern and peaceful and is used as a foil to condemn the modern West as fallen, immoral and corrupt by comparison. Although the East would seem to emerge as the moral victor in representations like these, they are narratives created by Western nations in order to critique their own societies. They have in most cases little or nothing to do with the reality of life in whichever "East" is being discussed. In other narratives of juvenile delinquency involving the East–West division, the moral superiority of the West is stressed. Legal and institutional measures acknowledging and addressing juvenile crime are interpreted as a result of contact with the West and usually seen as progressive marks of "civilization". Once again, in such narratives the agency and importance of individuals and groups within the East are reduced, if not nullified.

Historians of juvenile delinquency and the East–West division

It is important to note that very few of the debates just mentioned involve historians. The vast majority of studies involving international, let alone intercontinental comparative studies of juvenile delinquency (which have become increasingly numerous in recent years) have been carried out by criminologists and sociologists.[9] Insofar as such works engage with a historical dimension at all, they tend to include at best a short historical overview, focused on a narrative of key legal and institutional developments in the last 50 or at most 100 years.[10] Although there have been isolated historical studies of juvenile delinquency in other parts of the world,[11] in general, historians have been reluctant to look outside of the West.[12] The standard work is a national study focused on the period from the mid-to-late nineteenth century to the present, which continues to assume a necessary link between juvenile delinquency, the West and processes of modernity. In this way, historians of juvenile delinquency have tended to produce narratives of Western superiority and Eastern dependence similar to those we have already examined.[13] They rarely ask important questions such as: can one speak of "juvenile delinquency" before the modern period, before the term itself was coined? What about older, non-Western ideas and assumptions about the behaviour of children and juveniles? How do imported Western ideas about juvenile delinquency interact with preexisting traditions? How completely were Western notions taken up in both colonial and non-colonial settings, and what were the reasons behind the different impact of Western ideas about juvenile delinquency in different parts of the world? Most importantly, such studies rarely ask, what *is* the Western notion of juvenile delinquency? Does it only exist in stereotype form outside the West, or can we really speak of one, coherent understanding of delinquency and of childhood, which underpins it, in the West itself?

The two-volume *History of Juvenile Delinquency: A Collection of Essays on Crime Committed by Young Offenders, in History and in Selected Countries*, edited by Priscilla F. Clement and Albert G. Hess and published between 1990 and 1993, at first appears to engage with precisely these questions. However, although countries such as Egypt and Japan are included, it is always with a focus on the successful exporting of Western ideas about juvenile crime. Older, pre-existing notions of childhood and juvenile delinquency and their interactions with imported Western ideas are not discussed. As Priscilla Clement explains in the introductory chapter,

> The parts of the world studied include the Near East, Western Europe, North America and Asia. However, the emphasis is on Western nations and on countries elsewhere in the world which have been particularly influenced by Western approaches to juvenile justice.[14]

This bias is arguably a side effect of the fact that this study is an exercise in traditional comparative rather than in transnational or global history. The writers do not seek to understand the ways in which understandings of childhood and delinquency were shaped by, and in, the very act of border-crossing, of cultural encounter. All cultural agency is located in the Western idea of delinquency; there seems to be an implicit assumption that this idea will subdue and ultimately replace pre-existing notions, which are not discussed in any detail. A more recent study, *Child Welfare and Social Action in the Nineteenth and Twentieth Centuries: International Perspectives*, published in 2001 and edited by Jon Lawrence and Pat Starkey, is entirely limited to countries traditionally seen as belonging to the West: Canada, Britain and America.[15]

Pamela Cox and Heather Shore's important edited volume *Becoming Delinquent*, which appeared in 2002, has moved the study of historical juvenile delinquency forward. Promisingly, they set themselves the aim of exploring how juvenile delinquency has varied "between and within states and across different periods of time".[16] The second aspect of this research question they go a considerable way toward achieving. They make a convincing case for arguing that many features of juvenile delinquency (panics about urban culture, poor parenting, dangerous pleasures, family breakdown, national fitness and future social stability) which historians have felt to be particularly characteristic of the nineteenth century can be found in earlier centuries, going back well into the early modern period.[17] Indeed, they argue against the popular idea that juvenile delinquency was "invented" in the early nineteenth century, despite this being the period in which the term came into use.[18] Building primarily on the work of Paul Griffiths, they argue convincingly that the early nineteenth-century discourse represents at most a "re-invention"[19] or reconceptualization of earlier understandings of juvenile crime, just one more "sequential stage in social commentaries on youth that evolved over time".[20] This is without doubt an important theoretical gain in work on historical delinquency as it provides an answer to one of the most important open questions – "can something exist without the power of prior definition"?[21] In his chapter in *Becoming Delinquent*, Paul Griffiths answers in the affirmative, describing delinquent youth as a transhistorical phenomenon, something which "can be found in all centuries".[22] The editor and contributors to this volume are in full agreement with this view of juvenile delinquency.

Arguably, though, Cox and Shore were somewhat less successful with regard to their first aim – to study how ideas of delinquency vary "between and within states". The chapters included focused mostly on the unit of the nation state and were limited to countries within western Europe. While such a survey is necessary and valuable, there are significant problems with restricting the geographical reach of the case studies in this way. Most importantly, as Cox and Shore themselves acknowledge, their study tends to emphasize similarity over difference and creates the impression of "a uniquely European construction or response to juvenile delinquency".[23] While the various chapters reveal some variations between the individual states, the editors nonetheless place considerable emphasis on the "many important parallels in different European communities' attempts to frame and to solve the question of delinquency".[24] They admit that by restricting their analysis to western Europe they "overlook vital developments in other parts of the world, not least Southern, Central and Eastern Europe, North America and European colonial societies".[25]

Although the volume is useful in extending backwards into the seventeenth century the period in which we see ideas of juvenile delinquency developing, it fails to say much about juvenile delinquency as it existed across space – not just about delinquency within different countries (although there is clearly a need for a wider geographical spread), but also about the ways in which Western ideas travelled to other cultural contexts via colonial and imperial systems, transnational migration for economic or political reasons, the spread of international media, magazines, television and the internet, and even more importantly, the differing degree to which Western understandings and assumptions about childhood and juvenile crime were adopted, rejected or adapted in different parts of the world. It is a basic theoretical assumption underpinning all the essays in this volume, that notions of juvenile delinquency, both in the West and in non-Western contexts, are constructed and understood within and through cross-cultural encounters and can only be made sense of by placing developments within a global frame. Looking at individual countries in isolation and comparing them alongside each other neglects the considerable extent to which cultural interactions and transfers were responsible for constructing understandings of juvenile delinquency in different parts of the world. A cross-border or cultural transfer model also allows for more interest and agency to be given to the parts of the world affected by Western ideas, for the strength of pre-existing notions to be realized and for the (often very real) limitations of Western influence in these areas to be appreciated.

By contrast, this collection is divided into five parts based on a combination of different geopolitical spaces and thematic concepts relevant to questions of historical juvenile delinquency. While the sections are divided into "Colonial Contexts", "Transnational Migration", "Juvenile Delinquency and War", "Cold War Contexts" and "The Post-war State", the terms "East" and "West" are also examined critically throughout. Multiple meanings of East and West are examined, and the validity of the terms themselves and the binary opposition they seek to establish is also questioned.

The first part explores the construction of the East–West relationship through the discourse of colonialism, with essays looking at the construction of moral and immoral boyhood in metropolitan Britain and colonial India in the late nineteenth century and the problems faced by the Netherlands Indies colonial administration in implementing juvenile justice in the early twentieth century. The second part looks at juvenile delinquency and transnational migration, placing the emphasis on movement across boundaries (both national and cultural) and seeking to move beyond the tendency to think in fixed categories of East and West. Here, the importance of cross-cultural movement in establishing and contesting meanings of juvenile delinquency and crime is examined in two very different, yet mutually illuminating case studies of Jewish communities in late nineteenth-century Budapest and Latino youth gangs in late twentieth and early twenty-first century Spain. In both cases, the complexity of ideas and assumptions about childhood and the meaning of delinquency within particular transnational communities is highlighted, as is the degree to which some sections of those communities adapt "foreign" ideas about juvenile delinquency much more readily than others. The third part focuses on the relationship between juvenile crime and war in an early twentieth-century context, with essays looking at the experience of young offenders in Germany's courts against the background of the First World War and the reconceptualization of the relationship between juvenile delinquency and the state in East Asia within the context of the First and Second Sino-Japanese Wars. Both studies highlight the role of war as a transnational experience, resulting in acute cultural dislocation at home, and, as part of this, a fundamental rethinking of the function of traditionally conceived juvenile delinquency. The final two parts move forward in time to focus on the post-war period. The fourth part concentrates on the construction of East and West in the context of the Cold War and examines the implications of the opposition between capitalist West and Communist East for understandings of juvenile delinquency in Soviet Russia and white middle-class America. Although traditionally seen as belonging to the diametrically opposed binaries of East and West, both case studies reveal the complex ways in which ideas of childhood and youth crime in both societies were shaped by, and were indeed dependent on, the broader global context and transnational experience of the Cold War. The final part focuses on the relationship between juvenile delinquency and the post-war state in Britain and Turkey, two countries which, in different ways, struggled to define themselves within a world increasingly polarized between East and West. As Kate Bradley shows, the debate in Britain (traditionally seen as a purely internal conversation) about the apparent failure of the welfare state to reduce rates of juvenile crime was shaped within a wider global context of British imperial decline, rising immigration and decolonization. From this, and from other case studies (including those examining Cold War America, and Latino/a youth gangs in modern Spain), we see that ideas about juvenile delinquency and childhood in the West were equally dependent upon and shaped within a broader, global context as they were in countries like Turkey, discussed here by Nazan Çiçek, which have traditionally been viewed as caught between the global cultural poles of East and West.

Combining comparative and global history approaches

This volume does not set out to abandon the comparative in favour of a global history approach, but rather to combine the best of the two approaches. On the one hand, it aims to set before the reader ten case studies from different parts of the world, encompassing a geographical range wider than most existing historical studies of juvenile delinquency. Areas including the US, Soviet Russia, Hungary, Turkey, Spain, East Asia, British India and the Netherlands Indies are covered and comparison between these case studies is directly encouraged. On the other hand, where the volume seeks to move beyond traditional historical comparisons of juvenile delinquency is in stressing the vital role which cross-border encounters within a broader global context (whether within colonial systems, transnational migrations or international wars) played in shaping understandings of childhood and delinquency and, crucially, in determining the extent to which Western ideas were adopted, adapted or rejected in other parts of the world.

Integral to all chapters is an investigation into how ideas travel within and as part of these cross-border encounters. Thus, in the first part, which focuses on "Colonial Contexts", Stephanie Olsen's discussion of the informal moral education of boys in Britain and India in the late nineteenth century draws attention to the role of religious missionary societies in spreading British ideas about childhood and juvenile delinquency to India. Crucially, she argues against the view that ideas about juvenile delinquency and how to deal with it were simply transferred from metropole to colony. Instead, she points to the important ways in which notions from Britain coexisted and interacted with a range of ideas about childhood and youth violence among the indigenous population of British India in the late nineteenth and early twentieth century. Rather than interpreting concern about juvenile delinquency and campaigns to set up reformatories and similar institutions as evidence of the civilizing role of the British in India, Olsen argues that such moves reveal considerably more about the fears of the British regarding the stability of their empire in India. Moreover, she stresses that concern about juvenile crime in a colonial context must be seen in relation to similar fears regarding the disciplining of poor urban youth back in Britain. In particular, she highlights the discursive relationship between anxieties about the potential of working-class youth to rebel at home and concern at the growth of political resistance in India and support for independence.

Amrit Dev Kaur Khalsa's study of the indictment of juveniles before the formal court system in the Netherlands Indies in the early twentieth century similarly highlights the important role of charitable organizations like Pro Juventute, founded in the Netherlands, in transferring European understandings of childhood and delinquency to the Indies and the many barriers, both linguistic and cultural they met with which dramatically limited the adoption of Western ideas. She takes issue with the traditional narrative of youth justice systems as a boon of empire by focusing on the immense difficulties which Dutch judges faced in dealing with juvenile offenders from the indigenous communities in the Netherlands Indies. Judges were nearly always brought over from the Netherlands, staying in one location only a few years, and almost never speaking the local languages necessary to administer justice effectively;

as a consequence, they were unduly dependent upon indigenous assistants, clerks of the court, who sometimes had their own scores to settle and could not always be relied upon to deal with local young offenders fairly. Such problems, as Amrit Dev shows, led frequently to serious miscarriages of justice and the summary (and often unjustified) removal of boys as young as six or seven from their families to state reformatories where conditions were often harsh and unsanitary.

The chapters by Howard Lupovitch and Miroslava Chávez-García in the second part examine the role of transnational migration, primarily for social and economic reasons, in disseminating Western ideas and understandings of juvenile delinquency. For his case study, Howard Lupovitch chooses the culturally diverse city of Budapest in the second half of the nineteenth century, a city and a time, marked by extensive and complex migration patterns. Lupovitch focuses his analysis on the city's substantial Jewish population and argues that understandings of delinquency within this single community were so diverse as to be in no way reducible to the simple adoption of "Western" ideas. Although there was a widespread belief that juvenile crime was a peculiarly urban problem, the strategies employed to deal with delinquency reflected the diverse cultural and religious background of the Jewish community and highlight once more the importance of immigration and the transnational transfer of ideas. While some organizations which worked to combat the spread of juvenile crime among Jewish youth were indeed influenced by notions of child-rearing and moral education from western Europe (in particular, from France and Germany), others advocated more traditional responses including corporal punishment and incarceration which members of the community had brought with them from north-eastern Hungary, the Carpathians and elsewhere. Chávez-García draws similar attention to the important role of transnational economic migration, specifically recent waves of young Latino/a immigrants from the former Spanish colonies in Latin America, in reshaping notions of juvenile delinquency in contemporary Spain. In particular, she highlights the research over many years of Carles Feixa and his team, who have carried out extensive oral interviews with gang members and have established the crucial role which the move from Latin America to Spain and the associated separation from the family and environment of their childhood has had on the identity of young gang members in modern Spain. Chávez-García thus demonstrates the necessity of looking beyond and outside traditional categories of thought and identity when dealing with the nature and causes of juvenile crime. She likewise stresses the need to bring in discourses of ethnic and racial identity into historical delinquency analysis which have long been ignored or inadequately acknowledged in scholarly treatments of the subject.[26]

The chapters by Sarah Bornhorst and Barak Kushner in the third part of the volume explore the role of international war in the first part of the twentieth century in generating and facilitating the spread of new ideas about childhood and juvenile delinquency. Bornhorst links rising levels of youth crime and innovations in juvenile justice in southern Germany to pressures arising in the context of the international crisis of the First World War. She argues that it was against this background of social and political upheaval, when fears about national survival were at their height, that levels of juvenile crime increased and innovative steps were taken in the handling of young offenders. In particular, she focuses on what she terms the "conditioned amnesty", where juvenile criminals were spared a prison sentence if they agreed to join the army and fight on the front. Thus, what from one perspective could be seen as a "progressive" move, a turning away from a policy of youth incarceration, when studied in context is seen to be related to the peculiar conditions of national crisis, in particular to a desire to strengthen the German army against the background of war.

In the very different conditions of wartime Japan, Barak Kushner, in his study of East Asia as a region, stresses the relative unimportance of Western-derived notions of juvenile delinquency. He argues that assumptions about the tendency of adolescents to exhibit violent behaviour were widespread in East Asia and should not be linked to Western influence. He also challenges the focus of historians of juvenile delinquency on Western colonial empires, drawing attention instead to the imperial endeavours of China and Japan in the twentieth century. He shows how the association of youth with violence, exemplified, above all, in the state-supported travel of large numbers of young men to areas of imperial struggle, was viewed as something which might actually assist the imperial cause. In the case of Japan, what many in the West condemned as aggressive, destructive behaviours were viewed by Japanese and Chinese imperialists as necessary and valuable for the expansion of their respective empires. Likewise, Kushner suggests that in China and Japan the link (so frequently made in the West) between juvenile delinquency and processes of modernization was not simply challenged, but reversed, forming an important part of the wider drive to "overcome modernity" in both societies. Both chapters neatly illustrate the important point that one person's delinquent is another person's hero and that delinquency, like beauty, really does lie in the eye of the beholder.

The chapters by Nina Mackert and Gleb Tsipursky which make up the fourth part of the volume and explore "Cold War Contexts", demonstrate the vital role of Cold War discourse, in particular the ideological distinction between the Communist East and the liberal-capitalist West, in shaping ideas about childhood and delinquency in both the US and USSR. The media in one country functioned as a vital conduit for transferring images and ideas about young people and their cultural activities in the other and each saw the other as ideologically responsible, through the appeal they seemed to make to young people, for the perceived rise in juvenile delinquency at home. As both chapters show, governments on both sides as well as the wider public engaged enthusiastically and anxiously with media and state representations of delinquency in both societies and constructed their own notions and roles accordingly. Once again, both chapters engage closely with the limited success of the respective governments in imposing an acceptable notion of youth culture and behaviour upon their domestic populations. Communism remained attractive for many working- and middle-class youths in the US, as Nina Mackert stresses, and the Communist state's campaign against the so-called *stiliagi*, or style-obsessed Western-inspired youngsters in Soviet Russia was similarly unsuccessful, despite the mobilization of considerable resources.

Finally, the essays by Kate Bradley and Nazan Çiçek, which focus on Britain and Turkey respectively, both highlight the role of the post-war state in constructing ideas of juvenile delinquency. Kate Bradley makes the vital point that debates within Britain about the failure of youth crime to abate after the Second World War and the introduction of a comprehensive welfare state cannot be properly understood apart from wider discourses about a crisis of identity for Britain as it experienced the final breakdown of its empire. Similar fears about the stability of the empire in the late Victorian period also led to heightened concerns about the behaviour of British children, as Stephanie Olsen's chapter shows. Nazan Çiçek, in her chapter, demonstrates a similar discursive dependence on the wider global context, when examining the introduction of children's courts in post-war Turkey. Like the chapters by Stephanie Olsen, Amrit Dev Kaur Khalsa and Howard Lupovitch, Nazan Çiçek's chapter shows convincingly the extent to which, despite a superficially enthusiastic and self-conscious adoption of Western understandings of childhood and juvenile justice by the Turkish government, these ideas enjoyed only a very limited acceptance among the broader Turkish population, with pre-existing Turkish notions of childhood as differing only in degree rather than in nature from adulthood continuing to thrive. Çiçek carefully shows the ways in which juvenile courts were treated as a symbol of "Western civilization" by some within the Turkish elite, but were consciously rejected by many others as markers of neo-colonial power relationships.

As well as dealing with many areas traditionally left out of studies of historical juvenile delinquency including Japan, China, Korea, Soviet Russia, Latin America and Turkey, the majority of case studies employ categories of analysis other than the nation state, focusing rather on regions, both sub-national (Ulm in southern Germany[27]) and supra-national (East Asia[28]) colonies (India,[29] the Netherlands Indies[30]) and individual cities (Budapest[31]). Where the nation state is the focus of study, the analysis nonetheless concentrates on the role of broader cultural divisions (especially between East and West) in constructing ideas of and responses to juvenile delinquency and youth crime (Turkey[32] and the US[33]).

In order to avoid presenting ten self-contained case studies, which the reader is left to compare for him- or herself aided by a few pointers given in the introductory chapter, the contributors to this volume have been explicitly encouraged to explore the relevance of the international context and the role of transnational circulation and transfer of ideas about juvenile delinquency for their own particular case study. Such a focus is particularly important for questioning the traditional narratives of a monolithic ideal of childhood and juvenile justice in the West and their successful exporting to many parts of the non-Western world. Insofar as scholars have considered the transfer of ideas about juvenile delinquency across national boundaries, this has been mostly limited to the context of western European colonial empires. At best, such studies highlight only one form of transfer which played an important role; at worst, they can reinforce old ideas about the "progressive", "civilizing" values of western European empires by judging as positive the exporting of "modern" "Western" views of childhood and policies for dealing with youth crime.[34] Hence it is a crucial aim of the essays in this collection to ask how important (relative to other influences) Western (or, indeed, British, American, French or German) understandings of juvenile delinquency were outside of western Europe. This collection of essays does not seek to offer a comprehensive critique of the relationship between ideas of "the West" and constructions of juvenile delinquency. To do this it would have to take account of a much greater number and wider range of case studies than it does at present. It would also have to extend its chronological focus considerably, not just looking at the last two centuries, but reaching back into the early modern period and beyond. What it does hope to achieve, however, is to show through a number of well chosen and geographically wide-ranging case studies the potential of research which stresses the limitations of the influence of Western ideas about childhood and juvenile delinquency in other parts of the world. It also seeks to question the extent to which the countries traditionally making up the West possessed a single, coherent idea of childhood and juvenile justice constructed in isolation from the wider global and transnational context. In these ways it hopes to add to a growing body of research, begun with groundbreaking studies such as Said's *Orientalism* and taken forward most recently with work on the notion of "multiple modernities", which aims to decentre, to critique and to contextualize historically the importance of the West, to establish the real reach and limits of Western ideas.

While acknowledging that even the range of examples included here can only scratch the surface of the complex realities of youth crime in different parts of the world, this volume hopes to show the advantages of combining studies of juvenile delinquency in a wide range of geographical locations. In doing so it has sought to take up the challenge posed by Shore and Cox in *Becoming Delinquent*, namely to explore the ways in which juvenile delinquency has varied not only across time but also, and crucially, for this volume, across space. However tentative the conclusions are which may be drawn from the various case studies presented here, we are convinced that this emphasis upon geopolitical analysis will prove crucial in deepening our understanding of the ways in which juvenile delinquency has been constructed in the past.

Notes

1. For a work which identified the West with the history of humanity as a whole, see W.H. McNeill, *The Rise of the West: A History of the Human Community* (Chicago: University of Chicago Press, 1964).
2. E.W. Said, *Orientalism* (London: Routledge & Kegan Paul, 1978).
3. For works which have focused on deconstructing the West as a category of thought, see, for example, C. Mohanty, "Under Western Eyes: Feminist Scholarship and Colonial Discourses", *Feminist Review*, 30 (Autumn 1988), pp. 61–88; J. Goody, *The East in the West* (Cambridge: Cambridge University Press, 1996); I. Morris, *Why the West Rules – For Now: The Patterns of History and What They Reveal about the Future* (London: Profile Books, 2010); R. Bernstein, *The East, The West, and Sex: A History of Erotic Encounters* (New York: Knopf Doubleday Publishing Group, 2010).
4. For the altered significance of the East–West division in the context of the Cold War, see, for example, N.P. Ludlow (ed.), *European Integration and the Cold War: Ostpolitik-Westpolitik, 1965–1973* (Abingdon: Routledge, 2007);

G. Wettig, *Stalin and the Cold War in Europe: The Emergence and Development of East–West Conflict, 1939–1953* (Plymouth: Rowman and Littlefield Publishers, Inc., 2008); U.G. Poiger, *Jazz, Rock, and Rebels: Cold War Politics and American Culture in a Divided Germany* (London: University of California Press, 2000).

5. However, note the influential recent scholarship on "multiple modernities". See, for example, D. Sachsenmaier, "Multiple Modernities – The Concept and Its Potential", in D. Sachsenmaier, S.N. Eisenstadt and J. Riedel (eds), *Reflections on Multiple Modernities: European, Chinese, and Other Interpretations* (Boston: Brill, 2001), pp. 42–67; S.N. Eisenstadt, "Multiple Modernities", in S.N. Eisenstadt (ed.), *Multiple Modernities* (New Brunswick: Transaction Publishers, 2002), pp. 1–30.

6. See, for example, Ö. Özbay and Y.Z. Özcan, "A Test of Hirschi's Social Bonding Theory: Juvenile Delinquency in the High Schools of Ankara, Turkey", *International Journal of Offender Therapy and Comparative Criminology*, 50, 6 (December 2006), pp. 711–726; J. Junger-Tas, I.H. Marshall, D. Enzmann, M. Killias, M, Steketee and B. Gruszczynska (eds), *Juvenile Delinquency in Europe and Beyond: Results of the Second International Self-Report Delinquency Study* (London and Heidelberg: Springer, 2010), p. 274.

7. See, for example, A. Binder, G. Geis and D.D. Bruce, Jr., *Juvenile Delinquency: Historical, Cultural and Legal Perspectives*, 3rd edition (Cincinnati, OH: Anderson Publishing Co., 2000), pp. 389–403, especially p. 392: "Many scholars agree that the disruptions created by urbanization, industrialization, and the increasing role of Western forms of culture are helping to create an atmosphere encouraging what they see as Western styles of delinquency."

8. P.F. Clement and A.G. Hess (eds), *History of Juvenile Delinquency: A Collection of Essays on Crime Committed by Young Offenders, in History and in Selected Countries Vol. 1* (Aalen: Scientia Verlag, 1990), p. 8.

9. See, for example, J.A. Winterdyk (ed.), *Juvenile Justice Systems: International Perspectives* (Toronto, ON: Canadian Scholars' Press, 2002); M. Tonry and A.N. Droob, *Youth Crime and Youth Justice: Comparative and Cross-National Perspectives* (Chicago: University of Chicago Press, 2004); C.A. Hartjen and S. Priyadarsini, *Delinquency and Juvenile Justice: An International Bibliography* (Westport, CT: Praeger Publishers, 2004); J. Muncie and B. Goldson (eds), *Comparative Youth Justice* (Sage: London, 2006); C.A. Hartjen, *Youth Crime and Justice: A Global Inquiry* (New Brunswick: Rutgers University Press, 2008).

10. Heather Shore (with Pamela Cox), "Re-inventing the Juvenile Delinquent in Britain and Europe 1650–1950", in Pamela Cox and Heather Shore (eds), *Becoming Delinquent: British and European Youth, 1650–1950* (Aldershot: Ashgate, 2002), p. 1.

11. See, for example, D. Ambaras, *Bad Youth: Juvenile Delinquency and the Politics of Everyday Life in Modern Japan* (Berkeley: University of California Press, 2006); A.B. Kinney (ed.), *Chinese Views of Childhood* (Honolulu: University of Hawaii Press, 1995), especially, chapter 11 by M. Lupher, "Revolutionary Little Red Devils: The Social Psychology of Rebel Youth, 1966–1967", pp. 321–344; J. Iliffe, *The African Poor: A History* (Cambridge: Cambridge University Press, 1987); M. Weiner, *The Child and the State in India: Child Labor and Education Policy in Comparative Perspective* (Princeton: Princeton University Press, 1991).

12. For the history of juvenile delinquency in North America, see, for example, A.M. Platt, *The Child Savers: The Invention of Delinquency* (Chicago: University of Chicago Press, 1969); J.M. Hawes, *Children in Urban Society: Juvenile Delinquency in Nineteenth-Century America* (Oxford: Oxford University Press, 1971); J. Gilbert, *A Cycle of Outrage: America's Reaction to the Juvenile Delinquent in the 1950s* (Oxford: Oxford University Press, 1986); M.E. Odem, *Delinquent Daughters: Protecting, and Policing Adolescent Female Sexuality in the United States, 1885–1920* (London: University of North Carolina Press, 1995); K.W. Jones, *Taming the Troublesome Child: American Families, Child Guidance, and the Limits of Psychiatric Authority* (London: Harvard University Press, 1999); D.O. Carrigan, *Juvenile Delinquency in Canada: A History* (Toronto: Irwin Publishing, 1998); for the history of juvenile delinquency in individual European countries, see, for example, H. Shore, *Artful Dodgers; Youth and Crime in Early Nineteenth-Century London* (Woodbridge: Royal Historical Society, 1999); P. Horn, *Young Offenders: Juvenile Delinquency, 1700–2000* (Stroud: Amberley, 2010) (focused on the UK); S. Fishman, *The Battle for Children: World War II, Youth Crime, and Juvenile Justice in Twentieth-Century France* (London: Harvard University Press, 2002); E. Harvey, *Youth and Crime in Weimar Germany* (Oxford: Oxford University Press, 1994).
13. One of the contributors to this edited collection, Miroslava Chávez-García, has elsewhere referred to these scholars as "march of progress historians". See M. Chávez-García, "In Retrospect: Anthony M. Platt's The Child Savers: The Invention of Delinquency", *Reviews in American History*, 35, 3 (October 2007), p. 466.
14. Clement and Hess (eds), *History of Juvenile Delinquency*, p. 8.
15. J. Lawrence and P. Starkey (eds), *Child Welfare and Social Action in the Nineteenth and Twentieth Centuries: International Perspectives* (Liverpool: Liverpool University Press, 2001). For similar "international" comparative studies whose case studies are completely confined to countries traditionally considered part of the West, see, for example, C. Heywood, *A History of Childhood: Children and Childhood in the West* (Cambridge: Polity Press, 2001); M. Gleason, T. Myers, L. Paris and V. Strong-Boag (eds), *Lost Kids: Vulnerable Children and Youth in Twentieth-Century Canada and the United States* (Vancouver, BC: University of British Columbia Press, 2010); D. Oberwittler, "Changing Penal Responses to Juvenile Delinquency in Late Nineteenth and Early Twentieth Centuries: England and Germany Compared", *Comenius, wetenschappelijk forum voor opvoeding, onderwijs en cultuur*, 1, 16 (1994), pp. 7–25.
16. Shore (with Cox), "Re-inventing the Juvenile Delinquent in Britain and Europe 1650–1950", in Cox and Shore (eds), *Becoming Delinquent*, p. 1.
17. Ibid., p. 2.
18. M. May, "Innocence and Experience: The Evolution of the Concept of Juvenile Delinquency in the Mid-Nineteenth Century", *Victorian Studies*, 17 (1973), pp. 7–29; S. Margery, "The Invention of Juvenile Delinquency in Early Nineteenth-Century England", *Labour History*, 24 (1978), pp. 11–27; P. King and J. Noel, "The Origins of the 'Problem of Juvenile Delinquency': The Growth of Juvenile Prosecutions in London in the Late Eighteenth and Early Nineteenth Centuries", *Criminal Justice History*, 14 (1993), pp. 17–41; P. King, "The Rise of Juvenile Delinquency in England, 1780–1840: Changing

Patterns of Perception and Prosecution", *Past and Present* 160 (1998), pp. 116–166.

19. Shore (with Cox), "Re-inventing the Juvenile Delinquent in Britain and Europe 1650–1950", p. 6.
20. Paul Griffiths, "Juvenile Delinquency in Time", in Cox and Shore (eds), *Becoming Delinquent*, p. 23.
21. Ibid., p. 34.
22. Ibid., p. 33.
23. Shore (with Cox), "Re-inventing the Juvenile Delinquent in Britain and Europe 1650–1950", p. 2.
24. Ibid.
25. Ibid.
26. M. Chávez-García, "In Retrospect: Anthony M. Platt's The Child Savers: The Invention of Delinquency", *Reviews in American History*, 35, 3 (October 2007), p. 466.
27. See below Chapter 6 by Sarah Bornhorst.
28. See below Chapter 7 by Barak Kushner.
29. See below Chapter 2 Stephanie Olsen.
30. See below Chapter 3 by Amrit Dev Kaur Khalsa.
31. See below Chapter 4 by Howard Lupovitch.
32. See below Chapter 11 by Nazan Cicek.
33. See below Chapter 5 by Miroslava Chávez-García and Chapter 9 by Nina Mackert.
34. See, for example, the view taken by Priscilla F. Clement and Albert G. Hess, *History of Juvenile Delinquency Vol. 1*, p. 13 when summarizing the conclusions of the two essays which looked at the development of juvenile delinquency in modern non-Western contexts (Egypt and Russia):

    The juvenile reformatory spread with the influence of Western European countries: Badr-El-Din Ali demonstrates that Egypt established reformatories a year after becoming a colony of Britain in 1882, and Yoshir Tsiyimoto shows that Japan, anxious to gain the respect of Western nations also copied the British reformatory system in the 1880s.

Part I
Colonial Contexts

2
Adolescent Empire: Moral Dangers for Boys in Britain and India, c.1880–1914

Stephanie Olsen[1]

This chapter analyses the attempts of the British, through a common consensus about the correct path to civil manhood, to educate and build a moral empire. India in particular, the brightest jewel in the British crown and in many ways a testing ground for British policies in the wider empire as well as at home, is a crucial object of study. It served as a significant site of contestation and negotiation, defining important questions related to morality and gender and class (caste) norms and who was allowed to define them in religiously, socially and ethnically diverse locations, far from the metropole. This was especially true after the Rebellion of 1857, which provoked a rethinking of British social and religious policies in India to prevent further civilian disquiet and to change moral codes, in addition to the more concrete institutional and formal consequences usually cited, such as the termination of the East India Company's charter and the imposition of direct government of India from London under the Raj (1858–1947).[2] The more informal and indirect responses to the fallout from the Rebellion have remained rather neglected in comparison and are the focus of this chapter. These changes had a direct role to play in increasing efforts in education, with moral education at the centre. Growing nationalist sentiment among Indians also encouraged the British to emphasize moral education to keep the threat at bay. This chapter will compare the textual tactics used to reach British and Indian boys, showing the overlap and tensions in content and approaches. It will begin with a discussion of the profusion of periodicals and books during a publishing boom for British boys beginning around 1880 and the didactic and moral motivations for this large and targeted campaign. It will then show how British youth experts and some within the Indian context perceived the Indian boy in similar ways to his British counterpart and began a similar campaign, yet with important differences which even these experts acknowledged were difficult linguistic, cultural, religious and social (caste) obstacles. The sources used include the periodical literature of the most important evangelical and other religious societies in Britain and their missions in India; advice literature written by British authors specifically for either British or Indian boys; and metropolitan and colonial school and university commissions. The analysis enhances our understanding of the interplay of East/West in the construction of juvenile delinquents in an influential colonial context. This special attention to childhood and adolescence was clearly associated with citizenship (or subjecthood), in addition to ideals of individual character and morality. The recognition of boyhood and youth as distinct categories from manhood necessitated a moral education specific to boys. The child, and in particular the boy, was expected to play a major role in safeguarding civilization, and its pinnacle, Britain and its empire, in the present and in the future. Not only was he instructed on the moral path that would lead to the ideal of domesticated Christian fatherhood, but he was expected to shine, beacon-like, so as to influence his own parents for the better.[3] This in turn contributes to our understanding of how boys were raised to be future husbands and fathers. By such instruction the good citizen was made or lost. Looming in the background was the fear of the wayward adolescent, the delinquent, the "dangerous" boy who would become a societal threat as a man. The methods devised to combat or to prevent adolescent delinquency in colonial India represent, ultimately, an example of how Indian middle-class children "became, under the growing cultural impact of British rule, the arena in which the battle for the minds of men was fought between East and West, the old and the new, and the intrinsic and the imposed".[4]

In Britain, throughout the nineteenth century, childhood was increasingly seen as separate from adulthood, requiring special interventions and care. By the end of the century, adolescence was also carved out as a distinct, and dangerous, stage in the lifecycle and the British boy, no matter his social class, became the focus of intense attention.[5] His behaviour, his education and particularly his bad habits and the temptations he faced, aroused concern and seemed to demand active intervention at parental, institutional and governmental levels. Many organizations, both religious and secular, were especially concerned with juvenile drinking, smoking, masturbation and other bodily vices, and they made vigorous appeals against them.[6] Despite a lack of exact knowledge of its nature, duration or causes, many attempted to solve the "problem" of adolescence. Its deleterious effects, if left unchecked, seemed certain, obvious and odious. The loss of boys to the wrong path in their process of emerging as men threatened the national body and contributed to contemporary fears of national and imperial decline.[7] These campaigns led to a profusion of literature for boys, and to successful movements for social and legislative reform. Experts agreed that it was far better to prevent boys from becoming delinquent in the first place than to resort to punitive or controlling measures.

British understandings of the dangers of youth were transplanted and adapted in various colonial contexts. As will be shown in this chapter, this is especially true of India, where potential juvenile delinquency was coupled with the threat of political and social unrest and the problem of an increasingly educated and dissatisfied Anglicized Indian elite. British writers on juvenile moral conduct imported their understandings of the importance of the distinct categorization of childhood and youth, while making significant gestures toward the differences in the social and religious contexts between India and the metropole. While it was easy rhetorically to draw lines between the efforts to educate the urban poor and efforts to inculcate morality in the colonial "other" in India, these parallels fell apart in British efforts on the ground because of the social and gendered stratification of Indian communities.[8] The language of difference, both in positive and negative terms, was used to a far greater extent in India than it was in Britain, where the ideals of universal moral attributes and a universal boyhood were promoted. Under the Raj new educational opportunities, especially for the privileged, meant that the concept of adolescence, as a period between childhood and adulthood, also developed in India.[9] This idea was by no means universal in India, however, and was not as pronounced or developed as it had become in Britain by the early twentieth century. And with this somewhat fuzzier definition of adolescence came less exaggerated fears associated with this particular age group. Whereas in Britain the liminal period of adolescence became a "problem" and one of potential emotional and physical danger, these fears were less tied to this specific category in India, where there was a different, less stark and more ambiguous adult–child differentiation. An increasingly stark generational differentiation in Britain, largely brought about by urbanization and industrialization, was not shared in India, where "childhood" institutions, like schools or recreational groups, were still nascent, and where "adult" institutions, like work and marriage, were still commonplace among the young.

Formal, legal and judicial recognition of Indian children as distinct from adults mainly took place after the period covered in this chapter. Specific Children Acts were put in place by various provincial governments in the 1920s, allowing for the provision of separate courts, institutions and measures of protection for juveniles. These Children Acts were modelled after Western, specifically British, definitions and conceptions of children and their special need of protection. The UK Children Act of 1908 was especially influential. Other legal provisions for children were enacted after independence in 1947. Different states still have different age ranges for who is defined as a child under the law.[10] The Madras Children Act (1920), for example, created three clear age and legal categories: a child (under 14 years of age); a young person (between 14 and 18 years of age); and a youthful offender (anyone under 18 years old guilty of a crime).

There were, however, some laws relating specifically to Indian children before the 1920s. The Apprentices Act of 1850 was the first, followed by the Reformatory School Acts (1876, 1897). Along with the Indian Penal Code Act (1860) and the Code of Criminal Procedure (1898), juvenile delinquents, those between 12 and 18 years old, were increasingly put in reformatory schools, showing a shift toward a desire to reform, rather than simply to punish, delinquent youth.[11]

Scholars' focus has generally been on girls and legal issues related to sexuality and to early marriage, specifically with the Child Marriage Restraint Act (1929).[12] With some notable exceptions, discussion that focuses on boys is scant, yet the laws directed at juvenile delinquents related to males only.[13] According to Tapan Chakreborty, "From the legal point of view, delinquency is called a pattern of behavior which is disapproved of by the law. It is a very simple concept involving ungovernable, unmanageable or incorrigible behavior, running away from home and association with anti-social elements."[14] "Youthful offender", however, was a term far more frequently used than "juvenile delinquent" in historical sources. For example, in the Reformatory Schools Act, 1897, the term "youthful offender" was exclusively employed to denote a male of less than 15 years of age who had received a conviction punishable by imprisonment or transportation.

This chapter, however, has a different focus. There were prevalent terms other than juvenile offender/delinquent to describe unsuitable behaviour, which could be termed delinquency. The chapter is not so much concerned with the reformation of youth through formal penal means in the juvenile justice system, as is amply discussed in the case of the Netherlands Indies in Amrit Dev Kaur Khalsa's chapter, but rather with attempts to make moral reforms in youth, or to pre-empt having to make these reforms through education and religion. It was hoped that the boy who was morally and spiritually educated correctly, both formally and informally, would not fall into vice and crime. This way of approaching education and reform was often based on a particular understanding of childhood, resonating with the Western philosophical discussion of the *tabula rasa*. Though by no means uncontested in Britain, by the late nineteenth century there were distinct practical and educational precepts attached to this concept, which were transported to and adapted in India. Among British missionary societies, their associates in colonial government and education, and their Indian supporters, the problems related to male youth were posed in a Christian idiom and as a religious struggle. Their moral teachings for boys, and the ways they attempted to form the next generation of effective heads of families and good subjects, were largely conceived of in relation to male youth, no matter what their social class, in the metropole.

Britain: Train the child, save the man

In Britain, boys were informally educated, through the fictional stories in popular periodicals, to become responsible, moral men and caring fathers.[15] These qualities, regardless of the era's preoccupations with muscularity and imperial derring-do, were the key indicators of that quintessential *fin-de-siècle* measure of character: manliness. The prevalence of this sort of influence increased throughout the nineteenth century, and accelerated at a rapid pace with the boom in juvenile publishing and especially in popular periodicals in the last two decades of the century.[16] This effectively transported exhortations about morality and manliness beyond the public school elite to an increasingly literate readership across social classes. This moral fiction aimed at correcting the "immoral" fiction of penny dreadfuls and vice, as well as immorality in general. It was an especially important undertaking at the turn of the twentieth century when, as Martin Francis and John Tosh have outlined, a rapidly changing society – widening franchise, rapid industrialization, emergence of feminism and a sharpening distinction between home and work, private and public – provoked questions about the place of men in the family.[17]

In Britain, ideas of citizenship were linked up with ideas of juvenile education, mainly of boys. This in turn was linked to legislation and reform organizations, the home and paternal authority. Why were boys, and the building of their manly characters, so central to ideas of societal improvement and to the betterment of a growing male (enfranchised) citizenship? Similar rhetoric was used, in diverse realms, to describe what made a good boy, man and citizen, and conversely, what made a delinquent or immoral boy. The practical consensus on boyhood education and enculturation involved an understanding that the future of society and the nation depended on reaching children in time and that it was far easier and better "to train the child" than "to reclaim the man".[18]

The good citizen was presumed to be male. Manliness was the code that signified good citizenship. The right to vote and the capacity to defend the nation through military sacrifice were the nominal indicators of citizenship, but they were not enough to meet the criteria for full citizenship in cultural terms. It was the fostering of manly character that was vitally linked to a full definition of citizenship. To that end, disparate groups tended to agree on the importance of disseminating Christian values for the task of raising the nation's boys into manly, domesticated men and good fathers. The components of this consensus included positive exhortations related to morality, good conduct, politeness, religiosity and respect for family, and negative prohibitions regarding bad conduct and perceived vices such as drinking, smoking, gambling, masturbation and early romantic interests. The emphasis was placed on making sure that these bad habits were not even tried, rather than on reforming boys who had already strayed. This same view provided a focus on promoting goodness in potentially corruptible children, rather than on reforming their already corrupted parents. Some of these bad habits, like drinking, smoking, gambling and masturbation, were condemned as having disastrous effects on the body. Others, such as disobedience to adults (especially to parents) and a lack of piety or honesty, were bad habits of the spirit. These two sets of bad habits were mutually propagating. Bad influences, found in the home, the street, the gambling den or the pub, could either be the first step toward the moral and physical corruption of the young, or could lead to further degradation in those already indulging in bad habits.

The juvenile publishing industry had long recognized the influence fiction could have on its readers. As early as 1886 Edward Salmon, a journalist who wrote extensively on juvenile literature, had made the connection clear:

> It is impossible to overrate the importance of the influence of such a supply [of fiction] on the national character and culture. Mind, equally with body, will develop according to what it feeds on; and just

as the strength or weakness of a man's muscle depends on whether he leads a healthy or vicious life, so will the strength or weakness of his moral sense largely depend upon whether he reads in his youth that which is pure or that which is foul.[19]

To boys, stories became real; their thoughts, actions and moral sense were shaped by reading as much as by their contact with the world around them.[20] The juvenile papers maintained that reading could have a decisive impact on boys' development. While they had different motivations, they all recognized the importance of the boy to society, and in the words of one commentator, "to the character and well-being of the nation and the state".[21] Thus, in the late Victorian and Edwardian period, "frantic educational and religious dashes" were made at boys.[22] This urgency to reach boys was clearly seen by the Religious Tract Society (RTS). Earl Cairns, a supporter of numerous evangelical causes, was chair of the RTS's 84th anniversary meeting in 1883. He urged increased support to be "drawn from the home life and the young life of this country", so that the RTS could continue to influence the "life of our country in its most sacred and influential spheres". The maxim that followed was as clear as it was common: "Guard home and young life, and you take the best method of establishing religion and righteousness in the land. Keep these pure, and you purify the whole nation."[23] In great part this was to be accomplished by publishing uplifting periodicals and other reading material for the young and for families.

Children, and especially boys, were the incipient citizenry of a future Britain in a time preoccupied by worries about efficiency and racial decline, especially after the South African war. These were not merely concerns about the physical health of Britons, although popular fears of national degeneracy were indicated by the rise of eugenic ideas and figured prominently. Crucially, they were also concerned with the moral welfare of the population. This placed a powerful emphasis on children as the "hope of the race".[24] The purity of childhood served as an example to an unfit adult citizenry, whose shortcomings were seen as both physical and moral.

India: Overcoming the childish state

India had long been a cause of moral concern for British missionaries and colonial administrators, especially in the decades after the Rebellion of 1857. In the late nineteenth century, similar language to that used to understand boyhood "problems" at home was used to describe the

"problems" of Indian boys, and similar tactics were used in their informal moral and emotional education. Yet important differences remained between their education and that of their counterparts in the metropole. Whereas class was increasingly downplayed in British boys' moral fiction and advice literature, caste was acknowledged as an important factor in the Indian context, although it was usually presented as something deleterious to be overcome. Cultural transfer is evident in the ways in which tactics developed with British boys in mind were adapted in India, as in the ways that Christian moral messages were presented in texts for Indian boys belonging to other religions. Sometimes these tactics and messages were re-imported, in their changed form, back to the metropole. In one interesting example, a novel entitled *Faith and Victory: A Story of the Progress of Christianity in Bengal* (London, 1865) by Hannah Catherine Mullens, a Calcutta missionary, was loosely adapted for publication in Bengali, with many changes apparently to make it more palatable for the local population. It was then retranslated from Bengali back into English as *Prasanna and Kamini: The Story of a Young Hindu* (London, 1885), adapted for the RTS by J.H. Budden of Almorah, North India, with further amendments for an English-speaking audience.

Significantly, the export of boyhood ideals to India stopped short of encouraging a juvenile Indian citizenry; imperial subjecthood was stressed; representations of the superiority of British ideals of morality and education remained constant. While the colonial man was perceived as a child, the colonial child was seen as plastic and therefore malleable.[25] As Elizabeth Buettner has put it, "Indians could be depicted as analogous to children and Britons seen as parental – yet in a political and cultural as distinct from a biological sense."[26] If properly trained, this child could, in manhood, overcome the childish state of his adult predecessors. Worried that only poor Indians were becoming Christians for less than pure motives, British educators focused their efforts on wealthy or high-born Indians, who, it was thought, would influence their inferiors by their own moral example. Just as it was hoped that emerging British men would lead the way for the future of the race, so the imperial man – whether British, British-educated and Christian Indian – would serve as moral messenger in what was seen as an empire of emotional, moral and character control.

These ideals of informal education were exported to various colonial contexts and were pursued in British India with special vigour. British reactions to male youth and delinquency took on new dimensions in the context of the Raj.[27] How were British ideas of these issues, informed by understanding and prejudice at home, transplanted to, and transformed in, India? While I argue for near consensus in British boys' publications and organizations on how adolescent boys were to be morally educated, I see no such consensus in India, where there was a far greater diversity of language, belief and practice, as well as the imposition of British norms, which themselves were adopted, rejected or adapted. Many British religious and missionary organizations, and even British purity organizations like the White Cross League, tried to exert influence over young men through their work on the ground and through their publications.[28] I want to focus here on one component of this mosaic: the late nineteenth-century British RTS's efforts in India, and those of its Honorary Agent, Dr John Murdoch and Murdoch's own organization, the Christian Literature Society for India, which had linked societies in every region of India.[29]

Murdoch, the Religious Tract Society and the Christian Literature Society

In the nineteenth and early twentieth centuries, the RTS, founded in 1799 and still active as the Lutterworth Press, published in 44 languages in India and 22 languages in Bengal alone. It was dismayed by the educational policy of "our" Government in India and saw it as their "imperative duty to provide some clean, wholesome, interesting and profitable reading for the boys and young men of the great dependency".[30] It supported many endeavours to promote and distribute Christian literature in India, like that of the Lieutenant Governor of Bengal, Charles Elliott and the Director of Education Department of Bombay, who formed a pure literature society in the 1890s to counteract "the evils which were found to exist in the supply of books to the different school boys and college boys of Calcutta". They feared that enemies of the Raj and of Christianity were supplying boys with "publications of the lowest class, both immoral and depraved literature, and seditious and anti-social literature". All varieties of behaviour that could be classed as juvenile delinquency – that might lead to crime, murder, political upheaval – could be blamed on the supply of morally impure literature and on education. This impure reading matter also accounted for the tightening of sedition laws.[31]

Much of the RTS advice for Indian boys of the period was in a similar vein to the British literature. An example is John Murdoch's *The Training of Children for Indian Parents*,[32] which was already in its third edition in 1897, with a total of 8,000 copies printed. The training of children depended on the training of parents (especially fathers, as mothers were thought still too ignorant). For example, rule number one of Murdoch's basic rules for parents cautioned that "If children turn out badly, it does not arise from fate [implying this is what Hindu parents thought]; but, in nearly every case, from neglect or mismanagement on the part of the parents." The work dwelt on traditional British precepts like self-help, temperance and honesty, and "always do what is right". It echoed advice that could be found in the RTS's *Boy's Own Paper* or any number of other publications for British boys. Also, Murdoch made clear that parental responsibility followed from responsibility to God; the successful training of parents (especially fathers) depended on their own obedience to the heavenly Father.[33]

Murdoch's *The Indian Student's Manual*, first printed in 1875, went through several editions. His book for a similar audience, *The Indian Young Man in the Battle of Life* (1903), was also reprinted in several versions.[34] *The Indian Student's Manual* reveals many of the lessons on character, responsibility and morality that the British, missionary and non-missionary alike, wanted to impart. It is identical in its assumption that the adolescent stage is crucial on a lifelong path of right or wrong, or as Murdoch put it, that "the whole career of every person is greatly modified by the habits he formed in his youth".[35] Most of these lessons are also identical to ones produced for British youth of all classes in this era (and presumably the author mainly had them in mind). In fact, much of the book, Murdoch admits himself, is merely a compilation from British sources.[36] In order to mitigate the potential for future religious strife, the British government in India had developed a policy of religious neutrality for its colleges and a large part of this book, on "Religious Duties", was intended to be used by students to counteract this deficiency. There are even Christian prayers at the end, intended for daily use. The book includes many chapters that would have been familiar to British boys. There are prohibitions on smoking and drinking, for the sake of bodily health and force of character.[37] Gambling is similarly prohibited.[38] The section on "Moral Conduct" is predictably the biggest and most important.[39] But there are also chapters on caste, on the women of India, and in addition to a chapter on duty to country (ideas about mutual assistance between classes or castes, which one would easily find in a similar British book), there is a chapter on duty to government (obedience to the Raj). Murdoch elaborated on what he meant by this type of obedience in a chapter called "Patriotism, false and true" in his 1903 book for Indian boys.[40]

The necessity to teach morality to Indian boys was reinforced by educationalists in India. Writing in Poona in 1910, Percival Wren argued for the need for moral education in schools, either on a religious or what he called a "direct" or "indirect" moral-teaching basis. For the "direct" approach, it was essential to have teachers with an adequate moral tone themselves.[41] Similarly, *The Student's Moral Guide*, directed at students of all religions, maintained that "true education" should be moral in nature and that character education was paramount.[42] In *The Student's Moral Guide* and for many educationalists in India, as in Britain, nurture was far more important than nature for Indian boys, making them redeemable and plastic, with the ability to morally surpass their "inferior" inheritance, if they could be reached in time.

Murdoch believed in the possibility of universal moral attributes and a universal boyhood, yet the acquisition of these was dominated by distinctions of race and class. As he states: "Right and wrong, duty, and country, benevolence towards men and responsibility towards the unseen Power by which human action is guided and controlled – these are not ideal phrases. In all countries and ages they have retained their meaning."[43] Though he peppered his text with Indian and Hindu examples, most of his advice could have been found in any British boy's manual: truthfulness (which he says is a particular challenge for Indians), integrity, frugality, purity (of thought, deed and reading material), avoiding bad companions, temperance, industry, modesty and good manners, moral courage and virtue were all stressed. Also borrowed from the British model was the importance of home. Home duties, filial piety and fatherly responsibilities were to be cultivated in young Indian men. But in contrast to British books of this kind, there was also a section on "Duties to wife". Unlike young British men, many Indian students were presumed to be married. There is also a particularly condescending section on "The Hindu Family System", in which Murdoch states that "one great difference between Hindus and Englishmen is the marked spirit of independence possessed by the latter. Hindus are like a flock of sheep, moving in one body; Englishmen are more like lions which live alone or in couples." Needless to say, Murdoch's texts had a perceived civilizing role. He thought the British family superior and worthy of emulation.[44]

Educators were concerned that young Indian men with good British educations, the target audience of manuals like Murdoch's, and generally a desirable group, could also prove dangerous because of frustrations that they were not receiving the work and status that their education should have afforded them.[45] The Calcutta University Commission called them a "menace to good government", especially in Bengal where "the small educated class is alone vocal".[46] Though the government

adopted a policy of religious neutrality,[47] it encouraged religious organizations to set up their own colleges. In government colleges, though
no religious training was allowed, they recommended the implementation of moral training (already present in the colleges supported by
missionary societies) through a moral textbook,[48] and through a series
of lectures on "the duties of a man and a citizen".[49] This sort of moral
education had been implemented in British elementary schools in this
period, with mixed results and with a continuing debate on whether
moral education should be religious or secular in nature.[50]

For educators and missionaries, distributing the right sort of literature
to the "right sort" of boys and young men was thought to be crucial.[51]
In an article entitled "How India Must Be Saved", the Rev. F.B. Meyer
asked rhetorically: "Do you realise that in Madras scarcely a student
leaves the University without receiving a packet of infidel literature?"
He concluded that "this widespread dissemination of anti-Christian literature is one of the standing menaces of the English rule in India".[52]
The Calcutta Christian Tract and Book Society, for example, promoted
books like *Exposure of Hinduism*, which it judged "should be of real worth
to all who are engaged in the training of young men in schools and
colleges, and we would commend them to their notice".[53] Obviously,
only a small number of Indian boys could read English and an even
smaller number were Christian. Whereas in Britain the widespread dissemination of immoral literature was a cause for concern, the solution
to which was improving literature, in India immoral influences could
not easily be reduced to "dreadful" literature and the major problem
was getting a reforming message across at all to any but a few of the
most educated boys. The main goal of the Christian Literature Society,
of which John Murdoch was an agent, was to provide cheap and edifying Christian literature for the newly literate. In the 50 years following
its creation in 1858, the society published almost 4,000 publications and
almost 39 million copies in 21 languages, including many schoolbooks.
Murdoch's various guides for boys were repeatedly reprinted well into
the 1920s. The main goal of these publications was to get their moral
messages across, in whatever language (vernacular or English) possible.

Mission narratives

Missionary schools were popular in India in this period, both in urban
and rural settings. Families and students understood this education "to
be a form of welfare and social advancement which the colonial state
had largely failed to provide".[54] The schools reproduced Indian values

as well as British and Christian ones, emphasizing a system of morality and discipline (imagined to be universal) and traditional hierarchies. In Vidarbha, for example, training students in morality was a concern in school, but "the scholars were more influenced by their home surroundings, customs and social ethics than by their teachers". The solution was the creation of a "School Boy League of Honour", similar to many such leagues in Britain, with the goal of reforming the bodies and morals of boys and, in the process, society as a whole.[55] Traditional customs, for example related to sexuality and early marriage or to the care of the body, and traditional spiritual and religious beliefs continued to be in opposition to such attempts at developing British and Christian understandings of the moral and physical self. Perhaps more fundamentally, traditional ideas of the collective nature of the family and the community conflicted with British notions of self-cultivation in the individual.

The RTS also published many books for boys, which were either intended for an Indian market, usually inspired by the British writers' missionary experiences in India, or for a young British readership. Clearly, the books written about India for British children were intended to impart moral lessons, but probably more importantly, they were intended to muster support and money in Britain for the missionary cause. The object of one story about Hindu life in South India, written by an itinerant missionary, was for "young readers, to understand clearly the difficulties which Hindu children and young people have to surmount in order to become Christians".[56] Stories like "Anthony: The Brahmin Boy", in which Anthony wants to become a Christian but is thwarted by his ignorant and abusive Hindu father, reinforced this for British readers.[57] Another was promoted as making "a capital present to a boy whom it was desired to interest in his coloured brothers".[58] There was even a Bengali version of the famous British *Boy's Own Paper*, issued by the Calcutta Christian Tract and Book Society, with RTS material, and founded with similar aims as when the original *Boy's Own Paper* was founded in 1879. After its first year of publication, the Calcutta Society was printing 10,000 copies per month, with reprints of around 20,000 copies.[59]

One story, *Seed-Time and Harvest: A Tale of the Punjab*, published in several editions by the Christian Literature Society for India, is a good example of the often misguided ideals of the British Christian literature societies in India and of their fears for the future if young men failed to adopt their standards of morality.[60] The story's main character is Narain Das, a boy from a rich and influential Hindu family, who converts to

Christianity. The chapter "The Light of Home"[61] is the most important for its moral message, both in its illustration of an evangelical personal awakening and because of its emphasis, as in Britain, on family life. Often in British stories of this type, the son will guide the father, through his good example, to change his ways. In this story, Narain Das's father's conversion to Christianity takes place thanks to his son, but only after the crisis point of near death from depression over the loss of his son and from losing some of his riches.[62]

The character of Amrit Lal, Narain Das's friend and an educated university man belonging to the same high caste, provides the author with an opportunity to bring forward some of the arguments of the Hindu majority of that social group. "It is the manner of life I object to," he says. "I mean both the religious and social manner of life of the West. It is a rigid growth which can never take root in Indian soil." "Friend," Das replies, "I scarcely need remind you that the Lord Jesus was an Eastern; His teaching is suited to the allegorical mind of the East." The Indian "cry for civilization...is the secular name for Christianity...India is hungering, not for bread, but for the Word of God". In the Bible, the Eastern mind is to find all it needs. It would supply the wants, according to Das, of "the greatest intellect and the simplest child", in "both East and West". In the end, Narain Das's friend also converts.[63] Just as Christianity is shown to be universal for a young Indian and British readership, so are the ways to upright boyhood and manhood.

For British men like Murdoch, good character and morality were intertwined with Christian faith and the English language, though Murdoch of course also focused on Christian publishing in Indian languages. English and Christianity were to be the vehicles through which Indian boys would improve themselves, their colony and the British Empire as a whole. Murdoch and many others devoted their lives to furthering Christianity in India, with young men especially in mind, as they would be the ones to encourage further conversions in their own communities. As they saw it in India and in the metropole, true religion brought with it political order, but also individual morality and strong families, thereby combating the potential for delinquency at its roots. The most obvious similarity between efforts to educate and reform boys in Britain and India was the belief that Christian values would save boys from delinquency. The most obvious difference, of course, was that British boys in this period were raised within a broadly Christian culture. The religious training of Indian boys could not be taken for granted. Thus there was a vigorous campaign to demonstrate to Indians the benefits of Christianity. The Christian texts discussed in this chapter tried to combat the widespread idea that Christianity only appealed to the most down-and-out in Indian society, those most interested in food for their bodies rather than for their souls. Samuel Satyanatha, in his book for the Christian Literature Society for India, *Sketches of Indian Christians*, explains that the idea that Christianity was only successful among "the very lowest classes of India society" is simply false, and he gives examples of high-born Christian conversions.[64] Work that was done by foreigners and paid agents of the Missions would be much better done (and more accepted) by high-born native converts. Indeed, he argues, it was these high-caste converts who had "a great mission to fulfil" in demonstrating to their countrymen the change Christ had wrought in him:

> If by his life and conversation he can make it clear that conversion does not mean merely a change in dress, in food, in language and style of living, but a radical change of life, a thorough readjustment in standards of judgments, in motives and in conduct; if he can show what he has gained in self-control, in self-reverence, in charity, in meekness and in power to help others.[65]

There was much debate among the English, even those promoting Christianity, as to whether English or vernacular languages should be the medium of moral instruction. One British minister, recently returned from a tour of Mission inspection in India, said:

> I should like to plead for one moment the cause of educated young men in India, the English-reading, the English-speaking young men [...] I think I should like to read to you the words of a young student [...] He was one of those who shrink from giving a definite answer to the question, "Are you a Christian?" He writes: "I consider Hinduism to be a bundle of lies, superstitions, and abominations." Then he goes on to speak of Christ, and tells of a book that was given to him at college, and a copy of the New Testament, and how carefully he read those books over, and read others. [...]Then he closes by saying: "There is no religion in the world to be compared with Christianity and its divine Saviour." That is the condition of these young men.[66]

A "Bengali Gentleman", and not a Christian one is quoted as saying that: "If the world and infidelity have their literature in such abundance for our young people, religion and faith ought to have theirs also."[67]

The British did not pursue a policy of systematic mass education in India, unlike in Britain, where universal education was increasingly a given, starting with the Elementary Education Act of 1870. In India, therefore, the moral suasion of the educated elite was seen as paramount, as this would eventually lead to the moral education of the masses.[68] Some suggested that the British were more friends of the poor and uneducated than the Indian elite and went as far as to suggest the

> optional use of Roman, or Romanic, letters for Indian languages or dialects, so that, besides other advantages arising from their use, the many millions of poor, unlettered, unleisured peasants of that land [...] may have the opportunity of receiving the benefits we ourselves have derived from our Alphabet, our Bible and our Saviour.[69]

Since they were ignored by the general education system, the argument was that poor people should be taught to read the vernacular in Roman letters because they were being held down by the rich and educated Indians. This view was in direct opposition to the more prevalent idea of the trickle-down effect of morality from higher caste to lower. Education which led to low-caste social mobility, however, was criticized by newspapers in both Hindi and Urdu.[70]

Conclusion

In the words of the Madras Native Christian Association on the occasion of Murdoch's 50 year anniversary of service:

> This long period he [Murdoch] has spent in fostering Christian education by means of useful training institutions; in preparing an excellent series of educational text-books, permeated with the spirit of Christianity; in helping to purify the vernacular texts prescribed by the local University; in travelling through the length and breadth of this vast country with a view to promote the cause of healthy Christian literature; in producing in marvellous succession a long series of readable and compact treatises on religious, moral, economic and social subjects of great practical importance.[71]

Yet, after around 50 years of efforts, the Christian Literature Society did not have a glowing report of its progress, nor of the Indian population it was trying to "educate". Circulation of its publications was a real problem, which they blamed, especially in South India, on the "entire absence of any desire for self-culture" and they acknowledged that they had not found a type of "Christian literature which will 'take on'".[72] This lack of a desire for self-culture would have been especially odious for Murdoch and his peers, given the emphasis on self-help in his books and the long tradition of this form of education for young men in Britain.[73] Even without mass conversions, Murdoch could still claim success by pointing out the ways that "Hindu public opinion [was] being Christianised". Especially for those Christians concerned with the moral upbringing of boys, Murdoch thought the establishment of a *Hindu* Young Men's Association, in conjunction with the Christianizing of Indian opinion, should have provided some comfort.[74] But boys' proper moral education, and therefore the avoidance of delinquency, was still thought only to be found within Christianity.

The RTS, the Christian Literature Society and others like them recognized a problem with potential juvenile delinquency in India and tried to remedy it in the same way they did in Britain: through Christianity and reading material. Through their many periodicals, these organizations argued that this potential delinquency not only put the family and the wider community in peril, as it did in the metropole, but it also created the possibility of political instability. The long shadow of the Rebellion (1857) and growing nationalist sentiment served as excuses to double their efforts at education and conversion in India and at fundraising at home and in the settler colonies. It seems fair to conclude, therefore, in agreement with Ashis Nandy, that "children bore the brunt of conflicts precipitated by colonial politics, Westernized education and exogenous social institutions".[75] In Britain and in India the stakes of adolescence concerned the efficient maintenance of a paternal system. In Britain this included the citizen father as a central component of the paternal state. The British adolescent was to be saved through appropriate reading matter and fashioned into a fair citizen; the Indian adolescent, by a similar means, was to become politically inert: a dutiful and loyal subject. While it could be argued that this was not too far removed from the formal education that working-class children were receiving in the same period, the potential for active citizenship and the franchise remained elusive for Indian children, making their subjecthood more complete.[76]

Cultural transfer, however, is never a straightforward process that travels only in one direction. If Indian notions of childhood (which remained ill defined in this period) presented a striking contrast to the British, new ideas could nevertheless be employed to Indian ends. Nita

Kumar's suggestion that "no narrative of the child exists in modern India, perhaps because the child as a category has not been discovered or invented yet" can be challenged.[77] The process of lifecycle differentiation in India may have been slower, but a clearer notion of childhood did emerge as an important concern that was tied to a process of modernity both for Indian nationalists as well as for the Raj.[78] Some scholars see an idea of childhood in India as beginning in the colonial period along with the creation of an influential British-educated Indian middle class, but I would tentatively suggest that it coexisted alongside and sometimes merged with an idea of childhood that was rooted in indigenous traditions.[79] As Swapna Banerjee has shown, this concern for shaping the minds and hearts of future citizens through reading material was not limited to the British in India. Indian authors expressed similar ideas about childhood, good character and links to the nation in Indian languages, with different ends in mind from the British. The Bengali elite, for example, made concerted efforts to produce literature and periodicals for children and young people, realizing the potential value to the nation of cultivating youth and the potential danger of neglecting that task.[80] As Pradip Bose has noted, nineteenth- and early twentieth-century Bengalis began to stress character-building in children, as they should be "moulded in accordance with the future needs of the nation so that they could bring glory to it". According to Bose, childhood began to be defined as a distinct period in the lifecycle and children were defined as innocents in need of protection, but conversely, more pressure and guilt was placed on them, and parents were encouraged to apply discipline and reason in raising their children.[81] Dipesh Chakrabarty also sees nationalism at the heart of the redefinition of childhood in British Bengal, with Bengali authors, inspired by their British counterparts, linking morality to the idea of the strong family and nation, with the obvious correlation that immorality wrought dissipation.[82] The British therefore lost control, at least partially, of their attempts to modify citizen-building strategies at home into loyalty-inducing strategies in India. What served as good reading matter for the "problem" stage of youth was as good for the colony as it was for the metropole. If the nation and the citizen lay at the heart of metropolitan strategy, we should not be surprised to see the nation and the citizen also emerging as the ends of moral guidance for the Indian adolescent.

Notes

1. The author wishes to thank Margrit Pernau, Swapna Banerjee, Monika Freier, Rob Boddice and, of course, Heather Ellis for their helpful comments and

advice on this chapter. Some of the material in this chapter first appeared in Stephanie Olsen, *Juvenile Nation: Youth, Emotions and the Making of the Modern British Citizen, 1880–1914* (London: Bloomsbury, 2014).

2. There is a vast historiography on the Rebellion of 1857. See, for example, Biswamoy Pati (ed.), *The 1857 Rebellion* (New Delhi: Oxford University Press, 2007).

3. Stephanie Olsen, "The Authority of Motherhood in Question: Fatherhood and the Moral Education of Children in England, c. 1870–1900", *Women's History Review*, 18, 5 (November 2009), pp. 765–780.

4. Ashis Nandy, *Traditions, Tyranny and Utopias* (New Delhi: Oxford University Press, 1987), p. 66.

5. Harry Hendrick, *Images of Youth: Age, Class and the Male Youth Problem, 1880–1920* (Oxford: Clarendon Press, 1990); John Springhall, "Building Character in the British Boy: The Attempt to Extend Christian Manliness to Working-Class Adolescents, 1880–1914", in J.A. Mangan and James Walvin (eds), *Manliness and Morality: Middle-Class Masculinity in Britain and America, 1800–1940* (Manchester: Manchester University Press, 1987), pp. 52–74.

6. M.J.D. Roberts, *Making English Morals: Voluntary Association and Moral Reform in England, 1787–1886* (Cambridge: Cambridge University Press, 2004); John Welshman, "Images of Youth: The Issue of Juvenile Smoking, 1880–1914", *Addiction*, 91, 9 (1996), pp. 1379–1386; Lesley A. Hall, "Birds, Bees and General Embarrassment: Sex Education in Britain, from Social Purity to Section 28", in Richard Aldrich (ed.), *Public or Private Education?: Lessons from History* (London: Woburn, 2004), pp. 98–115.

7. Stephanie Olsen, "Towards the Modern Man: Edwardian Boyhood in the Juvenile Periodical Press", in Adrienne Gavin and Andrew Humphries (eds), *Childhood in Edwardian Fiction: Worlds Enough and Time* (New York: Palgrave Macmillan, 2009); John Neubauer, *The Fin-de-Siècle Culture of Adolescence* (New Haven: Yale University Press, 1992); John Springhall, *Coming of Age: Adolescence in Britain, 1860–1960* (Dublin: Gill and MacMillan, 1986); John Gillis, *Youth and History* (New York: Academic Press, 1974), pp. 13–17, 33–57. Adolescence studies were pioneered by G. Stanley Hall, *Adolescence: Its Psychology and Its Relations to Physiology, Anthropology, Sociology, Sex, Crime, Religion and Education*, 2 vols (New York: D. Appleton and Company, 1904).

8. For a discussion of how understandings of the racial other were used to define class in the metropole, see Susan Thorne, " 'The Conversion of Englishmen and the Conversion of the World Inseparable': Missionary Imperialism and the Language of Class, 1750–1850", in Frederick Cooper and Ann Laura Stoler (eds), *Tensions of Empire: Colonial Cultures in a Bourgeois World* (Berkeley: University of California Press, 1997).

9. Vasanthi Raman, "The Diverse Life-worlds of Indian Childhood", in Margrit Pernau, Imtiaz Ahmad and Helmut Reifeld (eds), *Family and Gender: Changing Values in Germany and India* (New Delhi: Sage, 2003), p. 93.

10. Tapan Chakreborty, "Juvenile Delinquency and Juvenile Justice in India", in John Winterdyke (ed.), *Juvenile Justice Systems: International Perspectives* (Toronto: Canadian Scholars' Press, 2002), p. 269.

11. For more information see Chakreborty, " 'Juvenile Delinquency and Juvenile Justice in India' and Jyotsna Shah, 'Welfare of Children under India Laws' ", in K.D. Gangade (ed.), *Social Legislation in India*, vol. 2 (Delhi: Concept Publishing, 1978), pp. 102–103, 106–108.

12. See especially the work of Ishita Pande, *Medicine, Race and Liberalism in British Bengal: Symptoms of Empire* (Abingdon: Routledge, 2010); " 'Listen to the Child': Law, Sex, and the Child Wife in Indian Historiography", *History Compass*, 11, 9 (2013), pp. 687–701.
13. Satadru Sen, *Colonial Childhoods: The Juvenile Periphery of India, 1850–1945* (London: Anthem Press, 2005); Ishita Pande, "Sorting Boys and Men: Unlawful Intercourse, Boy-Protection, and the Child Marriage Restraint Act in Colonial India", *The Journal of the History of Childhood and Youth*, 6, 2 (2013), pp. 332–358.
14. Chakreborty, "Juvenile Delinquency", p. 268.
15. Stephanie Olsen, "Daddy's Come Home: Evangelicalism, Fatherhood and Lessons for Boys in Late Nineteenth-Century Britain", *Fathering*, 5, 3 (2007), pp. 174–196.
16. This boom in periodicals for boys began with the RTS's *Boy's Own Paper* in 1879.
17. Martin Francis, "The Domestication of the Male? Recent Research on Nineteenth and Twentieth-century British Masculinity", *Historical Journal*, 45 (2002), pp. 637–652; John Tosh, "Manliness, Masculinities and the New Imperialism", in John Tosh, *Manliness and Masculinities in Nineteenth-Century Britain* (Harlow and New York: Pearson Longman, 2005); John Tosh, *A Man's Place: Masculinity and the Middle-Class Home in Victorian England* (New Haven: Yale University Press, 1999), esp. p. 196.
18. Lancashire and Cheshire Band of Hope Union, *Annual Reports* (1910), p. 42.
19. Edward Salmon, "What Boys Read", *Fortnightly Review*, 45 (February 1886), p. 248.
20. Ibid.
21. W. Scott King, "The Boy: What He Is and What Are We Going to Make of Him", *Sunday at Home* (1913), p. 818.
22. Ibid.
23. *The Religious Tract Society Record of Work at Home and Abroad*, no. 27 (June 1883), pp. 39–40.
24. Much more work is to be done on grassroots moral and religious movements of and for children. As a starting point, see Lilian Lewis Shiman, "The Band of Hope Movement: Respectable Recreation for Working-class Children", *Victorian Studies*, 17, 1 (1973), pp. 49–74.
25. See an interesting discussion of this duality in Sen, *Colonial Childhoods*.
26. Elizabeth Buettner, "Fatherhood Real, Imagined, Denied: British Men in Imperial India", in Trev Lynn Broughton and Helen Rogers (eds), *Gender and Fatherhood in the Nineteenth Century* (Houndmills: Palgrave MacMillan, 2007), p. 185.
27. Indian religious or cultural understandings of morality are not the focus here. See Shobna Nijhawan, "Civilizing Sisters: Writings on How to Save Women, Men, Society and the Nation", in Carey Watt and Michael Mann (eds), *From Improvement to Development. "Civilizing Missions" in Colonial and Post-colonial South Asia* (London and New York: Anthem Press, 2011), pp. 193–215; Margrit Pernau, "Maulawi Muhammad Zaka Ullah: Reflections of a Muslim Moralist on the Compatibility of Islam, Hinduism and Christianity", in C. Clémentin-Ojha (ed.), *Convictions*

religieuses et engagement en Asie du Sud depuis 1850 (Paris: École française d'Extrême-Orient), pp. 31–47.

28. White Cross League, *Annual Reports* (1910–1911), p. 19.

29. "Dr Murdoch's Jubilee", *Religious Tract Society Record*, March 1895, 4. Linked societies, for example, were the Calcutta, Punjab Religious Book Society; Gujarat Tract Society; North India Tract and Book Society; Ceylon Religious Tract Society. The name of the society, originally the Christian Vernacular Education Society, was shortened in 1891.

30. "A Bengali BOP", *Seed Time and Harvest* (March 1912), p. 16.

31. *Religious Tract Society Record* (March 1898), pp. 25–27.

32. John Murdoch, *The Training of Children for Indian Parents*, 3rd edition (London & Madras: Christian Literature Society for India, 1897).

33. Ibid., pp. 88–89.

34. John Murdoch, *The Indian Young Man in the Battle of Life: Hints to Students on Leaving College* (London & Madras: Christian Literature Society for India, 1903).

35. John Murdoch, *The Indian Student's Manual: Hints on Studies, Moral Conduct, Religious Duties and Success in Life* (Madras: Christian Vernacular Society, 1875), p. 1.

36. Ibid., pp. 1–2.

37. Ibid., p. 107.

38. Ibid., p. 108.

39. For an interesting discussion of how this moral education was thought to lead to a "moral crisis" for Indian students see Sanjay Seth, *Subject Lessons: The Western Education of Colonial India* (Durham: Duke University Press, 2007), pp. 47–78.

40. Murdoch, *The Indian Young Man in the Battle of Life.*

41. Percival Wren, *Indian School Organization: Management, Discipline, Tone and Equipment* (Bombay: Longmans, Green and Co., 1911), pp. 159–160.

42. Layman, *The Student's Moral Guide or A Hand-Book of Moral Instruction, on a Religious Basis: Adapted for the Use of Students of All Creeds* (Trichinopoly: St. Joseph's Industrial School Press, 1915), p. 3.

43. Murdoch, *Indian Student's Manual*, p. 113.

44. Ibid., p. 166.

45. Sudhir Chandra, "The Loyalty of Educated Indians to British Rule (1858–85)", in Sudhir Chandra, *Continuing Dilemmas, Understanding Social Consciousness* (Delhi: Tulika, 2002), pp. 18–28.

46. India, Calcutta University Commission. Vol I, Part I (1917–1919), p. 23.

47. India, Indian Education Commission, 1882. Calcutta: Superintendent of Government Printing, India (1883), p. 295.

48. Indian Education Commission, p. 205.

49. Ibid., p. 312.

50. Susannah Wright, "Citizenship, Moral Education and the English Elementary School", in Laurence Brockliss and Nicola Sheldon (eds), *Mass Education and the Limits of State Building* (Basingstoke: Palgrave Macmillan, 2012), pp. 21–45.

51. Samuel Satyanatha, *Sketches of Indian Christians* (London & Madras: Christian Literature Society for India, 1896), pp. xiii–xvii.

52. F.B. Meyer, "An Array of Facts", *Religious Tract Society Record* (June 1899), p. 86.
53. "Calcutta Christian Tract and Book Society", *Religious Tract Society Record* (December 1899), p. 175.
54. Hayden J.A. Bellenoit, "Missionary Education, Religion and Knowledge in India, c. 1880–1915", *Modern Asian Studies*, 41, 2 (2007), p. 389.
55. S. Shabbir, *History of Educational Development in Vidarbha from 1882 to 1923* (New Delhi: Northern Book Centre, 2005), pp. 280–281. The first significant backlash against British education in India and a declaration of a national and universal alternative, which represented Indian values and educational goals, was at the Calcutta Congress of 1906. This movement was short-lived, however, almost disappearing by the beginning of the First World War and only springing up again in the 1920s in Mohandas Gandhi's Non-Cooperation Movement. See J.P. Naik, *Educational Planning in India* (Bombay: Allied Publishers, 1965), p. 66.
56. "Chenna and his Friends, Hindu and Christian by Edwin Lewis", *Religious Tract Society Record* (September 1899), p. 160.
57. E.F. Elwin, *Stories of Indian Boys* (Oxford: A.R. Mowbray & Co., 1903), pp. 14–30.
58. "Nuru the Shepherd Boy by Rev. Arthur Le Feuvre", *Religious Tract Society Record* (December 1900), p. 165.
59. "Balak: The Bengali BOP", *Seed-Time and Harvest* (March 1913), p. 1.
60. A.D., *Seed-Time and Harvest: A Tale of the Punjab*, 2nd edition (London: Christian Literature Society for India, 1899).
61. Ibid., pp. 46–48.
62. Ibid., pp. 43–45.
63. Ibid., p. 48.
64. Samuel Satyanatha, *Sketches of Indian Christians* (London & Madras: Christian Literature Society for India, 1896), p. vii.
65. Ibid., pp. xiii–xvii.
66. G. Everard, *Religious Tract Society Record* (June 1892), pp. 62–63.
67. R. Wright Hay, "Testimony from Bengal", *Religious Tract Society Record* (June 1899), p. 89.
68. J.P. Naik, *Educational Planning in India*, p. 66. For an interesting discussion connecting Hindu nationalism, universal education and national efficiency in this period see Carey A. Watt, "Education for National Efficiency: Constructive Nationalism in North India, 1909–1916", *Modern Asian Studies*, 31, 2 (May 1997), pp. 339–374.
69. J. Knowles, *Our Duty to India and Indian Illiterates* (London & Madras: Christian Literature Society for India, 1910), p. 2.
70. Hayden J.A. Bellenoit, "Missionary Education, Religion and Knowledge in India, c. 1880–1915", *Modern Asian Studies*, 41, 2 (2007), p. 392.
71. J. Murdoch, "Dr Murdoch's Jubilee", *Religious Tract Society Record* (March 1895), p. 4.
72. *Christian Literature Society's Quarterly Bulletin*, IV, 3 (January 1910), p. 5.
73. Samuel Smiles, *Self-Help: With Illustrations of Character and Conduct* (London: John Murray, 1859).
74. "Dr Murdoch's Jubilee", *Religious Tract Society Record*, no. 74 (March 1895), p. 3.

75. Ashis Nandy, *Traditions, Tyranny and Utopias*. (Delhi: Oxford University Press, 1987), p. 66.
76. For an excellent discussion of British working-class subjecthood, loyalty and dutifulness in elementary schools, see especially Stephen Heathorn, *For Home, Country and Race: Constructing Gender, Class and Englishness in the Elementary School, 1880–1914* (Toronto: University of Toronto Press, 2000) and Susannah Wright, "Citizenship, Moral Education and the English Elementary School", in Brockliss and Sheldon (eds), *Mass Education and the Limits of State Building*, pp. 21–45.
77. Nita Kumar, "Provincialism in Modern India: The Multiple Narratives of Education and their Pain", *Modern Asian Studies*, 40, 2 (May 2006), p. 414.
78. See, for example, Swapna M. Banerjee, "Children's Literature in Nineteenth Century India: Some Reflections and Thoughts" in "Stories for Children, Histories of Childhood, *GRAAT*, 36 (2007), pp. 337–351.
79. Vasanthi Raman, "The Diverse Life-worlds of Indian Childhood", in Margrit Pernau, Imtiaz Ahmad and Helmut Reifeld (eds), *Family and Gender: Changing Values in Germany and India* (New Delhi: Sage, 2003), pp. 89–91.
80. Banerjee, "Children's Literature in Nineteenth Century India: Some Reflections and Thoughts", pp. 337–351.
81. Pradip Bose, "Sons of the Nation: Child Rearing in the New Family", in Partha Chatterjee (ed.), *Texts of Power: Emerging Disciplines in Colonial Bengal* (Minneapolis: University of Minnesota Press, 1995), pp. 118–119.
82. Dipesh Chakrabarty, "The Difference-Deferral of (a) Colonial Modernity: Public Debates on Domesticity in British Bengal", *History Workshop Journal*, 36 (1993), p. 6.

3

The Road to the Reformatory: (Mis-)communication in the Colonial Courts between Judges, Juveniles and Parents in the Netherlands Indies, 1900–1942

Amrit Dev Kaur Khalsa

At ten o'clock in the morning, on 24 April 1926, 12-year-old Peri entered the courtroom of Pematang Siantar, East Sumatra. He was accompanied by an indigenous policeman who told him to sit down on the floor, in front of the table of *Landrechter* J. de Kruyff. For Sumatran Peri it was a strange experience to suddenly sit in front of a Dutch judge and indigenous council members. He had come to the city alone for a pleasant excursion and with the permission of his father, and now he was sitting in court, charged with theft, while his father had no idea where he was.[1] Just behind him on the floor sat Siau Kim Tong, the 37-year-old Chinese shopkeeper who was the witness in his case.

The court was a place where different actors in colonial society came together and the setting in which judges had to decide if a juvenile defendant was innocent, would receive a simple punishment, or had to be re-educated. Sources show that this process was complicated and fraught with difficulties. This chapter looks at the Netherlands Indies' court system and its judges – as representatives of the colonial state – and analyses how the police, court officials, children and parents communicated with each other and why mistakes were made. Court records, clemency requests from parents and other judicial documents are used to offer a rare view of the way the Netherlands Indies' juvenile reform system worked at a micro level. The stories and behaviour of juvenile offenders in the court rooms and the requests and protests of their parents give a voice to usually "invisible" members of indigenous society and the way they interacted with representatives of the colonial government.[2] This in turn may provide us with an idea of the practical administration of justice in the colony and how social relations and cultural differences in colonial society affected it.

Juvenile court cases can likewise give us insight into the pressures and challenges judges faced, and show the limits of a formalistic way of thinking about the workings of the colonial government. We will discuss how judges discovered and dealt with their own mistakes, and look at the responses of other civil servants, the Supreme Court and the colonial government. As will become clear, the limits of both ethical and formalistic thinking prevented the colonial government from responding adequately to the practical problems of colonial rule.

The functioning of the colonial court system naturally is part of a much larger history of the development of the juvenile justice and forced re-education system in the Netherlands Indies in the twentieth century. In this so-called late colonial period ideas of "modern" government, developed in Europe and the US, were broadly applied to the colonies. The proactive efforts of the modern state are quite visible when it comes to the Netherlands Indies in the first half of the twentieth century, and these were instigated and supported by the emergence of a Dutch civilizing mission called the ethical policy (*ethische politiek*) around 1900. Its promises of "uplift" and "improvement" for the indigenous population changed the nature of colonial rule from outright and open profiteering to an arrangement that was intended to be – or at least to appear to be – beneficial for colonial subjects.[3]

The rhetoric of this "civilizing mission" justified the territorial expansion of Dutch rule in the archipelago and an expansion of government services and policies that touched almost all aspects of colonial society. The shift toward an emphasis on the "rescue" and "betterment" of indigenous juveniles was in line with this system of "moral" politics and a symptom of the changing colonial state. But its contrasting elements of coercion and force reveal that the growth of a more "social" state went hand-in-hand with a more invasive, ambitious and coercive colonial regime. European – and later indigenous – civil associations played a crucial role in spreading "ethical" and reformist ideas among those parts of the Indies' population that were located on the margins of society including, above all, juvenile delinquents and orphans.

Considering the limited number of indigenous and (Indo-)European children that were sentenced to re-education between 1918 and 1938 – approximately 4,500–5,000 out of a total population of almost 61 million in 1930 – it is safe to say that the whole venture had little social impact and mostly had moral and symbolic significance.[4] The moral significance that was attached to re-education policies was not peculiar to the Dutch colony; the French too, were very concerned with what they called "the *métis* problem" and established a system of reformatories for abandoned European-African children in their West African colony in about the same period. Considering there were only about 3,500–4,000 Africans "of European descent" in French West Africa in the first half of the twentieth century, out of a population of about 14.5 million, this too was a case of moral politics.[5] Consequently, the story of juvenile reform is one about the fears, hopes and ideas that drove the colonial government and European and indigenous civil society associations to start re-educating indigenous youth; and about the values and ideas they tried to instil in these youngsters during their incarceration.

When Judge De Kruyff started questioning Peri – which probably happened through a translator – the boy admitted right away that he had made a transgression. He could not really do much else, since he had been caught in the act two days earlier, when he had stolen a jacket from the shop window of Siau Kim Tong. Siau had stepped outside for a cup of coffee and when he returned to the shop he had seen a boy walk away with one of his jackets. He had caught the culprit himself and brought him to the police. During the court session Peri told the judge that he had stolen the jacket because he had run out of money and hoped to sell it for cash.[6]

It was not difficult for De Kruyff to decide that Peri was guilty of minor theft; as such, he could choose between different penalties for youngsters under the age of 16, such as a fine or a prison sentence, but he also had the option of sending the boy back to his parents or putting him under the care of the government for a term of "re-education". This last option was only supposed to be used if the juvenile had an undeniably criminal and corrupted character or if he was growing up in a criminal environment. De Kruyff chose to send Peri to a reformatory, so we assume he must have believed that either the boy or his living environment qualified as "corrupted" or "criminal".[7]

From the remaining records we cannot reconstruct exactly what De Kruyff believed or knew, but the chances are that Peri became a government pupil because his parents were not present during his trial. Maybe Peri had stated that he did not have any, or the judge believed that the parents were not doing a good job raising the boy. The idea was that children without guardians stood more risk of becoming "hardened criminals" because they would end up on the street again after a short prison sentence and resort to crime in order to survive. Judges did not just look at the nature of the crime but also at age and family circumstances to decide a proper sentence.[8] Even so, it was very difficult for judges to get a good idea of the background of the suspect. Pro Juventute (PJ) associations aimed to do background research into each case of juvenile crime and inform the judges, but they were often unable to find proper information especially about indigenous suspects.[9] This is one reason why children who did not really belong in the reformatory – even in the eyes of the judges – ended up there nevertheless.

PJ was a secular philanthropic association which played an important role in the transfer of ideas about juvenile behaviour and reform from the Netherlands (where it had operated since 1896) to the Indies.[10] The association emerged in Batavia in 1916 and was soon established in the major urban centres across Java and Sumatra. Its members came mostly from the European and partly from the indigenous, Chinese and Arabic elites and they saw it as their duty as citizens (or subjects) to work for the betterment of society, while promoting their own position at the same time. Both the government and the PJ associations tried to interest the indigenous community in working with them in the field of re-education. Not necessarily out of intercultural idealism, but out of practical necessity; they wanted to help children in the indigenous community and needed local supporters.

New ideas about juvenile crime spread to the Indies in the early twentieth century through books, newspapers and magazines, as well as through personal contacts. Government and judicial officials were educated in the Netherlands, and during their work in the Indies they went back on leave to their home country every few years. Boats to and from the Indies did not just carry people and suitcases, but ideas as well. Inspector Van Walsem, for example, was an official with the Justice Department who was responsible for overseeing juvenile re-education, and a vocal supporter of the new juvenile laws introduced in the Netherlands in 1901. He wanted similar laws for the Indies.[11] H.J. Boswijk, a judge who was the first chairman of PJ in Medan, Sumatra, was also influenced by "modern" ideas about juvenile criminal justice and severely criticized the penal code and judicial realities in the Indies, which (to his mind) lagged far behind Dutch laws. Boswijk turned to a meeting of the Dutch Association of Judges (*Nederlandse Vereniging van Rechters*) on 29 and 30 June 1917 to support his claim that it was necessary to establish special judges for trying juveniles in the Indies. As this chapter will show, this ideal was never put into practice in the colony.[12]

The different local branches of PJ in Batavia, Semarang, Malang, Soerabaja and Medan soon became an active, reliable and influential partner of the colonial state. The governing boards and social workers *avant la lettre* organized meetings and printed newsletters and magazines to inform the public about the perceived problem of juvenile crime and neglect. Some branches established temporary shelters for juveniles and the Soerabaja association founded the agricultural re-education colony in Klakah. Specially appointed and government sponsored PJ "social workers" went into neighbourhoods and homes to find delinquent, neglected or abused children.[13]

The causes of miscommunication between judges and children

While the case of Peri seemed simple enough, the ways of the colonial courts and the process of sentencing were inherently problematic because of the complex social relations in colonial society.[14] The majority of the colonial courts were presided over by Europeans but they mostly judged indigenous suspects, even in the 1930s when judges from among the indigenous population became more numerous. At the first meeting between a judge and an indigenous suspect the gap between their worlds became apparent right away. The judge sat sternly behind his table, dressed in a formal black gown with a white band.[15] Next to him sat the "respectable indigenous chiefs" – who served as council members – and the clerk of the court. The juvenile suspect, in contrast, entered bowing – *djongkokkend* – and was usually dressed in rags, underfed and suffering from ill health.[16] Suspects, witnesses and other parties had to sit down on the floor in front of the judges' table, so they had to look up to the judge and council. Most of the suspects did not know the role of the people behind the table, apart from perhaps the judge, who was easier to recognize. They were also unfamiliar with the content of the law and the ways in which the courts functioned.[17] Obviously children found themselves in an unequal situation vis-à-vis the judge because of the age difference as well. In the East Indies special juvenile courts did not exist and this added to the creation of an intimidating atmosphere that could hinder the judicial process.

For most juvenile suspects their appearance in the formalized world of the court was a surreal experience. The absence of parents and guardians exacerbated this. It was not written in the law or court procedures that parents or guardians had to be informed when their children were brought to trial. In 1931 a member of the Volkskraad, Mr. Soangkoepon, even asked the government if it was possible to include such a measure in the penal law.[18] But according to Attorney General R. Verheyen this was unnecessary; that parents had to be informed was "implicitly clear" from the various instructions regarding juvenile delinquents which his office had been sending to courts in the Indies over the years. To be on the safe side, however, he sent out another instruction to remind judges of the guidelines for prosecuting juvenile suspects.[19] It remained a difficult issue, however, because parents were often hard to locate. Sometimes they could not attend due to their work or the distance from their home, or because children told the police and judge that they had no family.

Another factor affecting court proceedings was that employees of the courts were infamous for influencing witnesses and suspects. The *djaksa* – indigenous prosecutor – had a bad reputation among most judges because he was known to unduly influence the judicial procedure. Because of his local background and linguistic knowledge he was usually able to communicate more directly with suspects and witnesses than the judge. He often had a different idea about right and wrong too; some *djaksa* were involved in local intrigues and power games and used trick questions and suggestions during the cross-examination. Legal historian Ab Massier describes a case in which the *djaksa* managed to convince both the suspect and the witnesses to confess to a murder that had never happened. After the verdict, the victim, supposedly dead, suddenly walked into the courtroom, which made it abundantly clear that the whole case was built on lies.[20] The judge had failed to notice any of this.

While judges did not trust the *djaksa*, they did not shy away from using their own means of intimidation in the courtroom. W. Boekhoudt, a former president of the *landraad* and council member of the Supreme Court, wrote that he immediately looked the defendant sternly in the eye when he entered the courtroom and kept doing so throughout the proceedings. This was meant to show "overconfident suspects" that they should not underestimate the judge. Boekhoudt also employed a stern voice as long as "a defendant continued his game of misleading the judge with fallacy". Boekhoudt felt that most defendants changed their attitude after a while and became susceptible to a "jovial chat".[21] He apparently felt confident that he was able to discern when defendants were lying and when they were honest, but our evidence from juvenile cases shows that he was probably overestimating himself. That both defendants and witnesses used false reasons and lied in court is a scenario that appears frequently in the writings of colonial court officials.

Contemporaries did not just blame this on the "character" or "culture" of the indigenous population; it was also an indication of frustration with the functioning of the colonial court system. The judicial process suffered from a huge cultural and linguistic divide, and most people involved were acutely aware of this.

C. Snouck Hurgronje, advisor on Native Affairs to the Colonial government, concluded in 1904 that a lack of understanding between the judge and defendant played the largest role in the "ineffectiveness, even unreliability of the European administration of justice over Natives".[22] This missing cultural and emotional connection was caused by many different factors. Until 1925, when the first indigenous judicial official was installed as judge of the *landraad*, all judges came from the Netherlands.[23] These Dutchmen had learned some Malay and sometimes Javanese during their studies in Holland, but they did not speak these languages fluently. "A judge who knew Javanese, let alone the local vernacular used by suspects and witnesses, was a great exception," according to historian C. Fasseur.[24] Because there were no official translators working at the courts the judges were thus dependent on the services of the clerk of the court or the *djaksa*. The judge would speak to them in Malay, and they would translate his words into the local language of the defendants and witnesses, then translate the answers back into Malay, which was, in any case, only the second language of the judge. Colonial administration of the law was a messy business. No wonder that court officials could greatly influence the proceedings; even with good intentions many of the nuances were lost in translation.[25]

Language was not the only weak link in the colonial court; the judge usually also had other handicaps that made it hard to penetrate the cases he had to preside over. He was often a loner within the court system, with his law degree and as a Dutch newcomer in colonial society. The clerks were usually Indo-European and the *djaksa* and other members of the court were indigenous. The judge would only live in a community for a few years before he would move on to a new assignment and another newcomer would take his place, while the other personnel stayed connected to the court and the community for most of their lives. Class and ethnic/racial divides between the different employees of the court and between court officials and community members also created potential miscommunications or bad feelings. Consequently, there was a significant chance that the judge did not understand much about what was happening in the community he was presiding over.[26] "His contacts with the native community are much too superficial and short lived to give him some of that indispensable understanding of what is happening in the community, and of the motives that influence the actions and utterances of individuals," summarized Snouck Hurgronje.[27]

During the formalistic and multilingual court proceedings judge and defendant struggled to understand each other. So much so that even judges who spoke fluent Malay and/or local languages did not speak with the indigenous defendants or witnesses directly: "Even if he knows the language well, nervous witnesses *never* understand a European, even if he says exactly the same thing as the Djaksa."[28] In this context it seems more understandable that defendants and witnesses often lied – or seemed to lie – in front of a judge; juvenile delinquents were no exception.

The reports of the re-educators in the reformatories confirm that many pupils denied the existence of parents or guardians in court and continued to do so during their first months in the reformatory. The 1919 report of the Semarang reformatory claimed that lying "was, without exaggeration, their second nature. Very few pupils are truthful or become more honest in the reformatory."[29] There were many examples of boys who lied in front of the judge:

> This is usually about their name, their parents, place of origin, etc. It happened regularly that lads who said their name was Sidin, later seemed to carry the name Karta; or that they said they were from Wonigiri but were actually from a completely different place; or that they claimed to have no parents or family, while later on their father and/or mother came to visit them in the institution.[30]

The director of the reformatory did not offer an explanation about the underlying reasons for lying but he did reflect on the difficulties in observing and judging the behaviour of the boys. His account of the chasm between educator and pupils is similar to Snouck Hurgronje's description of the divide between judge and defendant. Director De Haas felt it was very difficult to determine the mental state of his pupils. His tone is almost despairing when he exclaims that "the Eastern psyche" is really very different from the "Western" one: "Almost every pedagogue in the Indies, who has tried to penetrate the depths of the souls of his pupils, will agree with this remark."[31] If it was this difficult for educators to understand their pupils, when they stood in daily contact with the boys, it must have been significantly more challenging for a judge who was always pressed for time and who only met the defendant during a short court session.

Since many court cases were not well researched by the officials responsible for this – usually due to a lack of time but also because the officials involved might have their own reasons to bend the truth – there were serious consequences for defendants who were found to be lying or not giving correct information about their background.[32] The research and court related work of PJ might have corrected some of these problems, especially in the late 1920s and 1930s, when the organization became more experienced and influential. From their inception, PJ associations saw a role for themselves in all cases of juvenile delinquency and aimed to have a close working relationship with the court system.[33] After a few years each PJ association in the Indies had its own full-time civil servant, who was paid by the government, and who did the brunt of the organization's daily work. A large part of this work consisted of background research into juveniles who had been reported to the organization as "problem cases" or who had been caught by the authorities for misbehaviour and were scheduled to come before the court. In order to carry out research and check out possible problem cases "the association's arm reached deep into the darkest kampong to give a helping hand to the child in danger of falling down and perishing", PJ Batavia stated dramatically.[34]

A civil servant of PJ Medan described his work in detail in a report to the Justice Department. In the first six months of 1920 the organization was responsible for keeping an eye on 106 children who had already been placed in different reformatories and families. He also researched 25 new cases of "juvenile criminality, or neglect that can lead to criminal behavior". To do so he often had to pay more than one visit to the home of the child and he talked to parents (if available), family members, teachers, heads of the kampong, police and justice representatives, acquaintances and neighbours. "These visits had to be conducted by daylight and in the evening, depending on the circumstances, usually in far-out kampongs and outskirts, a few times even outside of the city. They [...] take a lot of time, stamina and experience." The Pro Juvenutute worker also met with the juveniles a few times, to establish their mental and physical condition. The board of the association discussed all cases weekly and then decided on a course of action.[35] They would decide if it was a one-time offence or not, if the parents or caregivers were able "to punish the child judiciously for the offence", "if the future upbringing of the child was in good hands" and if the child was not yet too delinquent to be redeemed at home. If PJ thought it was the right thing to do, the association would advise the public prosecutor or magistrate to drop the prosecution and place the juvenile under its supervision. Its general committee would then seek out one of its members to become a patron. "If the child does not behave according to the orders of its patron prosecution could still be started." The association was cautious with re-education sentences because it meant that the government would take the child away from their family for many years. "So in most cases this measure has far-reaching consequences and before it is used it should have been clearly established that the child has an extremely depraved character and lives in an unwholesome environment."[36]

If the judge did decide to commit a child at the behest of the government, PJ could still fulfil an important task. The association would collect information about the child and its environment to advise the government about the trajectory deemed most suitable for each specific child. The options that were considered by PJ were sending the child to a state reformatory, placing him or her with a family that was deemed "suitable and willing" or sending the child to a "charitable institution that P. J. sees as fitting for that child."[37] The PJ civil servant talked informally to court officials, some of whom were members of the organization too, and went to court sessions of the *landgerecht* and *landraad*. During the sessions he would give the judge all the information he had about the child, and offer his advice.[38] Because the archives and records of the colonial courts were destroyed during and shortly after the Second World War it is impossible to find out how many cases PJ was actually involved in, and what the results of its research and advice were. But it seems likely that its research provided the judges with much needed information and might have prevented some of the mistakes that will be discussed in the next section.

Mistakes in juvenile verdicts

Judges were often aware of the fallacies involved in their own administration of the law. Snouck Hurgronje described judicial officials who doubted their own ability to properly judge court cases in the Indies. These judges feared that their verdicts, "while wrought according to the best knowledge and in accordance with the law", lacked a reliable underpinning.[39] The challenges of the colonial court system were a source of frustration and anxiety for many of them. In the course of the twentieth century lawyers often came to the Indies with lofty expectations and the intention "to do good". Under the influence of the Leiden University professor Cornelis Van Vollenhoven (1874–1933), a specialist in customary law [*adatrecht*] and colonial law, the idea that lawyers could promote the welfare of the inhabitants of the colony became common-place.[40] Van Vollenhoven was a staunch supporter and promoter of the "ethical colonial policy", the Dutch version of the "white man's bur-den", which was intended to bring the colony under firmer rule and to uplift and educate its population until they were able to administer their own independent country.[41] To be clear, even the most "progres-sive" commentators saw this as a process that would take an indefinite amount of time and effort, and independence was always seen in the light of a strong and ongoing relationship with the Netherlands.

The ethical policy was no doubt to some extent a product of noble ideas and most supporters felt it their duty to improve life in the colonies. But their concerns were also driven by the imperatives of inter-national politics and the wish to remain firmly in power. The early liberal, social and Christian founders of the ethical policy believed in an "Association Principle"; the colonial population could and should be taught "Western" values and ideas which would make it possible to create a modern, democratic colonial state led by Indonesians – but remaining under Dutch rule. During the First World War the neutral Dutch promised more political influence for indigenous inhabitants but their establishment of the advisory body named the *Volksraad* (1918) was a disappointment to most in the nationalist movement. Increas-ing Indonesian nationalism and stronger criticism of colonial rule gave conservative colonial administrators the ammunition they needed to denounce the positive influences of the ethical policy and its Association Principle. Indigenous culture increasingly came to be seen as something essentially different from the West that should be preserved and pro-tected. In this vision, "Eastern" society would always need "the West" to lead and protect it. "The Ethical Policy was increasingly seen in terms of a permanent welfare task, saving Indonesians because they could not – and perhaps would never be able to – save themselves."[42]

Van Vollenhoven promoted the idea that lawyers had the duty and ability to promote "order and civilization" in the colony. Many of his students were infected with this zeal and saw their judicial career in the Indies as something that would not only benefit their own fortunes but also the people they would be administering. "A more beautiful work-ing environment than that of the chairman of the *landraad* is difficult to imagine," stated Boekhoudt in 1916.[43] But for quite a few judges the unfamiliar, complicated – and often impenetrable – reality of colo-nial society was a shock. Some managed to overcome this and made an honest effort to learn the local language, build strong networks and relations with indigenous officials and clerks and thoroughly administer the law.[44] But not everyone was able to adapt, excel and find creative solutions for the colonial conundrum; there were a lot of dropouts and complaints. One judge told Snouck Hurgronje that his nerves had suffered heavily under the pressure of a responsibility he felt unable to carry.[45]

Judges were sometimes willing to admit their mistakes to their superiors and tried to correct them. An example of this is the case of nine-year-old Jahmad, a cattle herder from Papoengan (Blitar, Java). Jahmad was brought before the *landgerecht* of Kanigoro on 27 March 1926 because he had admitted to taking two pieces of sugarcane from the field of the local sugar plantation. He explained that he was thirsty after working on the *sawa* (fields) of his father. The boy was caught by *djogabajo* Soekarto, the local member of the village board responsible for policing, and was summoned to come before the court. Soekarto declared during the court session that he had told the parents of the boy to accompany him to court, so they could immediately pay a fine if they had to. "But the father did not want to have anything to do with his son. He did not want to accompany him, and in case his son was fined he did not want to pay the fine," declared Soekarto.[46] It is unclear whether Soekarto had also explained to the father the consequences of his refusal to come to court with his son.

Because of Soekarto's story, the judge, Mr. F.L. Cayaux, decided to send Jahmad to the reformatory as a government pupil, something he would have usually avoided. "It is my habit to let juvenile sugarcane thieves pay a fine, with the intention that the father or guardian, who pays this fine, gives his son or pupil a good spanking at home," he wrote on 15 May 1926 to the recently appointed Governor General De Graeff. But if Jahmad or someone else could or would not pay the fine, then the boy would automatically be sent to prison. This was against all the principles and rules of the re-education law and this led Cayaux to think that the only proper solution was to send the boy to a reformatory as a government pupil, "especially", in this case "because the father [...] seemed to be a bad parent and educator".[47] Cayaux felt he had made a mistake, however, after he received a request from Jahmad's father, Kasanredjo. Kasanredjo wrote to Cayaux that he had been ill and bound to his bed, and had not come to the court because he did not understand why this was necessary.[48] Cayaux suggested to the Governor General that his mistake should be corrected and the boy should be returned to his father.[49]

The office of the Supreme Court, responsible for reviewing the verdicts of the lower courts, decided differently, however. According to Attorney

General Nauta there were no special reasons to change the verdict in this case and Jahmad was kept under the tutelage of the government. Nauta reasoned that a re-education sentence was an "administrative measure", which did not qualify for clemency requests.[50] The Governor General agreed and his office sent a message with a rejection of their request to Jahmad's parents and Judge Cayaux in June 1926.[51] This might have been hard to swallow for the judge. Sending a nine-year-old boy, without prior problems and with a caring father, to a reformatory for seven years, for stealing two pieces of sugarcane, was a punishment that stood out of all proportion to his actions.

In the case of Peri, mentioned in the first part of this chapter, Judge De Kruyff also admitted that he had sent the boy to a reformatory based on incomplete and incorrect information. Again a letter from a parent made the judge change his mind; indigenous parents who wrote clemency requests to judges were apparently taken seriously. Jason Loembantobing, Peri's father, had also missed his son's court session and only heard a few days later that he had been put under the care of the government to be reformed. He wrote an elegant clemency request to the Governor General to protest the verdict. Loembantobing was a well educated Christian merchant, living in Taroetoeng in the Batak area of Sumatra, and he wrote that he felt ashamed of his son. Loembantobing had given Peri 30 guilders to travel to Pematang Siantar and visit the city, and he had thought this amount would be sufficient. The boy had apparently spent more money than he could afford and tried to solve the problem by stealing. Loembantobing felt that Peri had committed his crime under the influence of bad friends and explained why he felt justified in asking for mercy: "I send this petition to ask for clemency, since he has committed this crime in his stupidity and innocence. He has never stolen or committed a crime before. Moreover, I am willing and able to raise the child," stated Loembantobing.[52] Judge De Kruyff believed the explanation offered by Peri's father and requested the Governor General to change the reform sentence and give the child back to his parents. For De Kruyff the background of Peri's family was the most important factor in the case, more important than the boy's crime: "The parents of the little boy are wealthy enough to give him an education and are very upset that their child will be taken away from them."[53]

The letter from Loembantobing and the advice from De Kruyff were first sent to the Governor of Sumatra's East coast, who agreed with De Kruyff and also advised the attorney general to acknowledge Loembantobing's request and give the boy back to his parents.[54] Attorney General Nauta in the faraway capital of Batavia, however, just looked to see if the verdicts were made according to the proper pro-cedures and rules of the law and again rejected the appeal for clemency on the basis of judicial arguments. Four months later Peri was put under the care of PJ Medan and placed either with a family or in the small childcare facility of the association until he was 18 years old.[55] It is with the help of these cases that we can see how the judicial realities of the colony – bad communication between judge and juvenile defendant, the absence of parents during the court case, insufficient background information and so on – clashed with the formalities of the legal system and its upper-level enforcers like the attorney general and the Governor General.

Nauta acknowledged that mistakes had been made, but felt supported by the rule of law to uphold the verdict. Instead of criticizing the sys-tem he blamed Judge De Kruyff: "It is regretful that the judge has taken this extreme measure without being properly informed about the back-ground, parents and family of the child," wrote Nauta in his advice to the Governor General.[56] We know now that this criticism was not com-pletely fair, because most judges were limited in their ability to access background information about the defendants in their courts. Parents were often not informed or were misinformed about the upcoming trial of their children, and could thus not provide essential information either. This situation is indicative of the limited insight that the colonial state had into the society over which it ruled.

Even for parents who did know about the prosecution of their child there were other reasons to stay away from the court session. The courts were usually only established in the regional capitals and this meant that people from the small villages had to travel far to attend trials. Distances might have been too great to cover in the short time between notification and the actual court session. Or parents might have been unable to miss a day of work, for financial or practical reasons. Moe van Emmerik of the agricultural colony, Witte Kruis (White Cross), described the hassle and discomfort of the colonial justice system for ordinary people in 1924. She told how a boy who had stolen a chest full of clothes from another family in the colony had been caught and sent to the local police headman (assistant wedono). The elderly owner of the clothes and his son were summoned five times by the police in Getassan to come to them to give information; the court in Semarang also requested their attendance four times. Not only was it a long walk to either place, but they also lost nine workdays each. Moe van Emmerik calculated that the father and his son each missed 7.20 guilders in income. On top of this, the authorities kept the chest of clothes for months, because it served as evidence of the theft. Moe van Emmerik declared that it was easily understandable why the Javanese avoided any involvement with the police and court system if they could.[57]

Judges mistakenly sent juveniles to reformatories who could have been safely sent home with a fine and a reprimand from their parents. Another frequent mistake was to send juvenile offenders who were officially too old for a re-education sentence to the reformatory. Juvenile reform was only prescribed for children under 16 years old, but the age of a defendant was often unknown and hard to establish. While European children were registered with the local authorities at birth, for the other ethnicities no civil registry existed. Children often did not know their own year of birth or age, and when parents and proper background information were absent as well this became hard to establish for the police and the judge. The law did not prescribe who should establish the age of the juvenile defendants and how this should be done. In daily practice it was the police, who came in touch with juvenile offenders first, who made an estimate of their age and recorded this in the summons. The judge often accepted their judgement without questioning.[58]

A 1924 article in a colonial judicial magazine stated that almost everyone failed to establish the proper age of indigenous and Chinese juveniles. "In general we can state that Europeans, including medical doctors, think that indigenous people are significantly younger than they really are," wrote M. Tuiten, who was the director of the state reformatory in Semarang in the 1920s.[59] He concluded that indigenous doctors almost always established the age of the boys in the reformatory to be two or three years older than the estimation of European doctors and laypersons like judges. Tuiten believed that Europeans had no good insight into the age of indigenous and Chinese youngsters because they were from a different "race".[60] The consequence of these mistakes was that some juveniles who ended up in the reform system were technically too old to be in there, and this caused significant problems.

In indigenous society, stated Tuiten – who did not make an effort to note that indigenous society consisted of many different cultures and ethnicities – juveniles became adults much earlier than in Europe; they usually married when they were 16 or 17. Indonesians who were thought to be younger than they actually were ended up in a reformatory and were treated as children, when they had already been living adult lives in their own environment. "Consequentially, there is often unrest among the older pupils; indifference, mental depression, or recalcitrance; sometimes a tendency to satisfy sexual urges in an unnatural manner and especially attempts to gain freedom by their own authority [escapes]," concluded Tuiten.[61] In the state reformatories they tried to readjust the assigned ages of pupils through a thorough physical examination carried out by the director and the institution's physician, both of whom had a lot of experience with indigenous juveniles. They almost always increased the age of their pupils by two or three years, in comparison with the ages the police and judges had estimated. This eventually benefited the pupils since they would be released sooner; the maximum age of discharge was 21 until 1925 and 18 after that. But this adjustment did not solve the problem of pupils who came to the reformatory when they were already too old. For this, Tuiten proposed that the courts consult an indigenous physician in cases where juveniles were thought to be approximately 16 years old, but this was never formally enacted.[62]

Images of parenthood in the communication between parents and the colonial justice system

Sarpani from Kampong Mlajo in Semarang was illiterate but he did manage to send a clemency request to the Governor General in faraway Batavia in 1917. Another man, Darmo, also signed the letter, although he could not read and write either. It is unknown who wrote their letter, but from other clemency requests it becomes clear that the majority of the letters of illiterate parents were written by a public writer, notary, lawyer or local court official.[63] The majority of the letter writers had not been present during the trial of the child in question, and writing or commissioning the writing of a letter was probably their only way to tell their version of what happened. The letter of Sarpani and Darmo was a plea for mercy in formal and humble Javanese, meant to get back their sons. Darmo was the father of eight-year-old Sarban, and Sarpani had two boys, Basinan (seven years old) and Soedjono (six years old). The boys had been caught in the act by the Semarang police when they tried to steal bricks, and were brought before the court of Semarang, despite their young age. The court decided on 15 December 1917, just a day after their offence, to send them to a reformatory. The court documents that may explain why the judge decided on such a serious course of action are missing, but the parents of the boys did not accept the verdict.[64] Darmo and Sarpani promised that they would look after their boys really well and keep a close eye on them; they begged the authorities to send the boys home so that they could give them a proper punishment themselves.[65]

Before the opening of the state reformatory in Semarang (*Landsopvoed-ingsgesticht* LOG Semarang) in March 1918 it was not uncommon for the Governor General to send government pupils back to their own parental home for "re-education". This was a temporary measure that was allowed by law as long as the colony did not have a proper and official reformatory, and because private families were often hard to find. But Darmo, Sarpani and their sons were out of luck. The director of the Justice Department responded to their request with the argument that the recently opened reformatory in Semarang was a real reform institution – as described in the law – and that the old temporary measures were therefore no longer valid. He argued that all juvenile delinquents with a reform sentence could automatically be sent to LOG Semarang and that the Governor General no longer had the authority to decide the place where a juvenile should be re-educated; the judges now decided this.[66] The Governor General and his advisors accepted this idea, and supported the rejection of the clemency request by Darmo and Sarpani.

The two fathers had written their requests in January 1918 – two months prior to the opening of LOG Semarang – but it took the government nine months to reply. The letter had been lying around in the court office in Semarang, waiting to be forwarded to the Justice Department in Batavia. When it finally arrived there, the civil servant responsible for dealing with juvenile reform cases was away on an inspection journey of the different private reformatories, as the director of the department explained later.[67] The director of the Justice Department then set a precedent with his argument that the Governor General could no longer decide the place of residence of government pupils. Later rejections were often based on this reasoning or on the argument that a re-education verdict was not a punishment but an administrative measure that did not qualify for a pardon. Whatever argument was used, and regardless of known mistakes and misinformation during the trial, the reality was that none of the parental clemency letters that were sent to the authorities between 1918 and 1940 were successful.[68]

The written clemency requests offer a fascinating view of colonial society. In particular, they show us something of the image of themselves parents chose to present to the colonial authorities to convince them to give back their child. While the letters do not paint a representative picture of the true feelings and behaviour of parents, they do give an idea of how parents thought they could convince the government of their good parenting – and sometimes of the innocence of their children as well. The father of Peri, for example, wrote that he had the money and ability to raise his son. He also showed that he had a true bond with his son by saying that he and his wife were extremely upset that the boy was gone from their home. Lastly he proved that he knew right from wrong by saying that he felt "ashamed" and "embarrassed" about his son's behaviour and his prosecution. The Europeans involved in the re-education system tended to view a feeling of shame as one of the "higher" emotions. Educational officials were preoccupied with instilling the ability to feel regret, guilt and shame into their pupils. Peri's judge was sensitive to his father's arguments; his wealthy background as a Christian merchant and his sadness about the loss of his son were mentioned in particular as reasons to let the boy go back home.[69]

The arguments that parents used to try and get back their children played subtly with the expectations and values of the colonial rulers. Parents spoke a "language of power", using the official and desired stories of colonialism, to try and convince the authorities to support their case; their letters show many similarities in the use of language and arguments. Jenneke Christiaens, a Belgian researcher, came to similar conclusions with regard to Belgian parents who tried to get their sons out of the youth prison in Ghent in the nineteenth and early twentieth century. They wrote letters to the director of the prison facility to ask for clemency for their offspring. Many of their arguments are similar to the ones used by Indonesian parents, but the Belgian parents often discuss their own failure and previous inability to educate their children, while this is hardly hinted at in colonial clemency requests. In colonial letters the innocence or ignorance of both parents and the child is often a central argument. This might be explained by the difference in the crimes of juveniles in the Indies and in Belgium. Christiaens discusses letters about children who were considered "unimprovable" and were placed in the strictest section of a juvenile prison. The government pupils in the Indies were often re-educated for much lighter offences.[70]

Almost all the parents in the Indies wrote that they would keep a closer eye on their children and keep them on a shorter leash from now on.[71] Just like Darmo and Sarpani, other parents also promised to give their child a fitting punishment at home. In many clemency requests are promises about a good education and a better upbringing, as in the letters about Samil bin Ganal from Borneo. The father in this case, Ganal bin Sihai, and the mother, Atjoet binti Tjoeloek, wrote three letters to ask for the release of their 12-year-old son between July and December 1926.[72] "I promise I will properly care for the boy and will educate him by sending him to the government school in Moeara Baroe, to make him a better man," wrote Ganal.[73]

Ethical ideas of improvement are also found in the letter from the Javanese Hadji Sapei, a farmer in desa Nagrak in West-Priangan. He promised to take good care of his son Djoemsari "so he will grow up to be a useful member of society".[74] This was obviously exactly what the colonial elite aimed at with the re-education of juvenile offenders. Both Ganal and Hadji Sapei wrote their own letters and seem to have been familiar with the ethical-liberal ideals of improvement and uplift. Maybe they even believed in these notions; they were able to read and write and had possibly benefited from colonial schooling themselves in that they were able to raise their own position in their family or community.

Besides promises about proper chastisement and education of their children, parents also tried to get their offspring absolved by writing about mitigating circumstances. They carefully questioned the judge's decision and tried to offer another perspective on the behaviour of their child. Ganal wrote about his son Samil, who had hit an older boy on the head, that Samil had no idea what he had done and did not understand the difference between right and wrong. "Moreover, [Samil] would never hurt someone of his own age on purpose, and especially not a person who is older." He pleaded with the Governor General to forgive the deeds of his son and argued that it was just a fight between children. He also asked understanding for the suffering of himself and his wife as parents. Samil was their only child and he had never been separated from them.[75] All levels of the colonial administration read Ganal's letters, from the judge to the resident, the attorney general and the office of the Governor General, but they failed to impress. Everyone involved rejected the first two letters, of July and August 1927, but seven months later the resident of South and East Borneo changed his mind. He stressed that the boy had never been involved with the court before and that this could be a reason to send the boy home.[76] This was rejected, as usual, by those in the higher echelons.

Not all parents wrote in "the language of power"; some wrote in their own language. The mother and stepfather of 15-year-old Richart Eisar Pinontoan from Tateloe, Celebes, believed they were not to blame for the theft their son had committed in late 1929. It had happened outside of their home and was outside of their range of influence, they wrote. They wanted the boy back home because they needed him to work in the house and on the land. No promises about a good education here, but purely economic arguments.[77] The judge who had sentenced the boy was not impressed; the content of the letter only confirmed his verdict. He wrote that he would only take a child away from the parents after careful deliberation, but that the boy had such a bad life at home that it was the only proper action. "Because of this neglect other disreputable characters take their chance to let [Richart] do their dirty work," declared the judge. Only a strict re-education could save the boy from life as a criminal and turn him into the desired "useful member of society", or so the judge believed.[78]

In all indigenous clemency requests judicial arguments for an early release or reconsideration of the verdict were missing. Apparently indigenous parents were not informed about the possibilities of challenging the validity of the trial. They did not complain about the court procedures, their own absence during the trial, or incomplete background research. The few cases in which parents used some kind of judicial arguments all concerned Indo-European children with a European father. Ex-soldier Petelle wrote in 1923 to the Governor General to request the release of his son Johann from the state reformatory in Semarang. He dared to complain about the quality of the institution because his son was refusing to write in Dutch and only communicated in Malay since he entered the reformatory. He also argued that many adults had received pardons in honour of the government jubilee of Queen Wilhelmina and why could this not be applied to his son?[79] He received the same answer as most other letter writers: clemency was not a possibility for juvenile government pupils.

How colonial officials felt about the personal letters from parents is hard to find out. Because some judges were willing to reconsider their verdict on the basis of these letters, it is probably safe to say that they took them seriously. Others might have found them sentimental, unreliable or irrelevant. A judge in Manado, Sulawesi, was positively enthusiastic about a clemency request he received in January 1930. While he stated that he disapproved of the way the parents treated their son (the aforementioned Richart Eisar Pinontoan, who had stolen something and was abused by his stepfather) and he was not planning to grant the request, the judge was pleased with the fact that the parents had made an effort to stand up for their child. "The request itself I was happy to receive because this is the first protest from parents whose child has been put under the tutelage of the government. So far I have sent more than ten children from Minahasa to Java," wrote the judge.[80] He apparently saw the clemency letter as a sign that parents cared for or were concerned about their children, despite the functional language that was used in the request (the parents wanted their son back so that he could help them with the work in and around the house).[81]

Conclusion

Applauding and encouraging the participation of indigenous individuals in the colonial justice system fitted with ideas of the "ethical" civilizing mission, which many government workers still believed they were carrying out. Indigenous individuals and groups who became more outspoken were seen as proof that assimilation, emancipation and maybe even self-government were possible. As long as "the Natives" were not voicing or attempting outright attacks on the colonial rulers, state officials could see their protest letters and clemency requests as a sign of progress and civilization, especially when it was easy to dismiss those requests without further consequences.

The authorities refused to acknowledge the lawful basis of clemency requests and parents stood virtually powerless once their children were sentenced to re-education. They could write letters and those were read, commented upon and eventually forwarded to the office of the Governor General, but in every case the writers of clemency requests received a letter or telegram from the government with a rejection of their request. The protests against juvenile re-education that the state government had worried about in 1917 and 1918 never broke out. There are no stories, documents or newspaper articles that indicate any serious upheaval surrounding the colonial reform system. Individual parents and family members could oppose what happened to their child, but the indigenous political parties and the general population seemed to accept its existence, its purpose and the way that it functioned.

Notes

1. Clemency request of Jason Loembantobing from Taroetoeng to the Governor General, Pematang Siantar, 1 mei 1926. AS, ANRI., Ag 29870–1926.
2. "Invisible" because their activities and opinions are usually difficult to research because of a lack of sources and records dealing with "subaltern" groups.
3. See for example Elsbeth Locher-Scholten, *Ethiek in Fragmenten. Vijf studies over koloniaal denken en doen van Nederlanders in de Indonesische archipel, 1877–1942* (Utrecht: HES Publishers, 1981).
4. Thanks to the participants of the "Colonial Fears" workshop in Leiden, November 2009, who pointed this out to me.
5. Owen White, *Children of the French Empire: Miscegenation and Colonial Society in French West Africa 1895–1960* (Oxford: Clarendon Press, 1999), pp. 2–3.

6. Summons recorded by the Adjunct Djaksa of the landraad Pematang Siantar, no. 98, p. 24, April 1926. AS, ANRI. Ag 29870–1926.
7. Letter from *Landrechter* J. De Kruyff to the Governor General, Pematang Siantar, 5 May 1926. AS, ANRI. Ag 29870–1926.
8. The *Landrechter* in Malang, Mr. C.T. Bertling, stated that he tried to discern if a child enjoyed proper guidance from parents or guardians, and if the transgression of the child came from a "truly criminal psyche" or was merely situational behaviour. See "Pro Juventute en rechter", p. 52, in S.H.H. Nahuys and J.C. Hoekstra (eds), *Vijftien Jaar Pro-Juventute Werk in Nederlandsch-Indië* (Leiden: Koninklijke Boekhandel en Drukkerijen G. Kolff, 1932).
9. See the many yearly reports and detailed case studies of the PJ Associations in the Indies for the background stories of juvenile suspects and neglected children. For examples of the reports written by PJ workers to send to the Justice Department, see, NA, MvK, V. inv.no. 2588 and inv.no. 2361.
10. For more on PJ in the Netherlands see Dr. Jan-Paul Verkaik, *Voor de Jeugd van Tegenwoordig. Kinderbescherming en jeugdhulpverlening door Pro Juventute in Amsterdam, 1896–1994* (Utrecht: Uitgeverij SWP, 1996).
11. "Pro Juventute. Lezing door Mr. F.M.G. van Walsem op Maandag 5 Februari te Batavia gehouden", printed in *Indisch Tijdschrift van het Regt, 1918, no. 108*, pp. 17–20.
12. *Oprichtingsvoordracht van Mr. H. J. Boswijk* in "Verslag der Werkzaamheden van de Vereeniging 'Pro Juventute' te Medan over het jaar 1918" (Varekamp & Co. Medan, 1919), pp. 24–25. Jaarverslag "Vereeniging Pro Juventute" te Medan, 1918–1938, microfilm collection, MM14T-100230. KIT, Amsterdam.
13. See, for example, Nahuys and Hoekstra (eds), *Vijftien Jaar Pro-Juventute Werk in Nederlandsch-Indië*, and the different yearly reports of PJ available in the Netherlands in the Royal Tropical Institute Amsterdam (KIT) and in Indonesia in the National Library in Jakarta (PNRI).
14. For a short and clear overview of the Indies justice system see Albert Dekker en Hanneke van Katwijk, *Recht en Rechtspraak in Nederlands-Indië* (Leiden: KITLV uitgeverij, 1993).
15. About the clothing of judges, see A.W.H. Massier, *Van "Recht" naar "Hukum". Indonesische juristen en hun taal, 1915–2000* (Proefschrift Universiteit Leiden, 2003), p. 96, footnote 181.
16. This is a description of how juveniles arrived at the reformatory once they had been sentenced by the judge, so they probably looked the same during their trial. Taken from *Verslag omtrent het beheer en den toestand van de Landsopvoedingsgestichten te Semarang, Malang, Ngawi, en Tangerang. Gedurende de dienstjaren 1926 en 1927. Samengesteld bij de afdeling Tucht-, Opvoedings- en Armwezen (Departement van Justitie)* (Strafgevangenis te Pekalongan, 1928), p. 3.
17. Massier, *Van "Recht" naar "Hukum"*, p. 89.
18. Chairman of the Volksraad J.W.Meijer Ranneft to the Governor General, Batavia, 3 September 1931, Volksraad no. 2450. AS, ANRI. Bgs 16-02-1932 245/a.
19. Attorney General to the Governor General, Batavia-Centrum, 21 januari 1932, no. 307. AS, ANRI. Bgs 16-02-1932 245/a, AS, ANRI.
20. Massier, *Van "Recht" naar "Hukum"*, pp. 84–85, also footnotes 108–112.

21. Boekhoudt, 1916, 341 also cited by Massier, *Van "Recht" naar "Hukum"*, pp. 91–92.
22. E. Gobée en C. Adriaanse (ed.), *Ambtelijke adviezen van C. Snouck Hurgronje 1889–1936. Eerste deel.* ('s Gravenhage: Nijhoff, 1957), p. 496.
23. The first indigenous judge was Moehamad Hamid, who became chairman of the *landraad* in Kraksaän, Eastern Java on 16 januari 1925. According to Massier, *Van "Recht" naar "Hukum"*, p. 78, noot 66. For the background of Dutch judges see C. Fasseur, *De Indologen. Ambtenaren voor de Oost, 1825–1950* (Amsterdam: Bert Bakker, 1993), p. 436. There were no female judges in either the Indies and the Netherlands until after the Second World War. Women did work in administrative government functions in the Indies; for more about this see Fasseur, *De Indologen*, p. 386.
24. Fasseur, *De Indologen*, pp. 246–247.
25. Massier, *Van "Recht" naar "Hukum"*, p. 68. Massier describes a literary fragment about the translation procedures in court from Augusta de Wit's famous novel *De Godin die Wacht*, in footnote 9, pp. 68–69.
26. Massier, *Van "Recht" naar "Hukum"*, pp. 79–80.
27. E. Gobée en C. Adriaanse (red.), *Ambtelijke adviezen van C. Snouck Hurgronje 1889–1936. Eerste deel* ('s Gravenhage: Nijhoff, 1957), p. 497.
28. Article by Rutgers, 1911, in Massier, *Van "Recht" naar "Hukum"*, 83.
29. *Verslag omtrent het beheer en den toestand van het Landsopvoedingsgesticht te Semarang gedurende het dienstjaar 1919* (Weltevreden: N.V. Boekh. Visser & Co., 1920), p. 8.
30. *Verslag Semarang 1919*, pp. 8–9.
31. Ibid., p. 7.
32. Massier, *Van "Recht" naar "Hukum"*, p. 92, footnote 166.
33. See for example the statements of Boswijk, chairman of PJ Medan, in *Oprichtingsvoordracht van Mr. H. J. Boswijk* in "Verslag der Werkzaamheden van de Vereeniging 'Pro Juventute' te Medan over het jaar 1918" (Varekamp&Co. Medan, 1919), p. 22. KIT, microfilm collection, MM14T-100230.
34. *Verslag PJ Soerabaja, 1927*, p. 3. KIT, microfilm collection, MM14T-100230.
35. *Verslag Pro Juventute Medan, January–June 1920*, NA, MvK, V. inv. no. 2222.
36. *Oprichtingsvoordracht van Mr. H. J. Boswijk* in "Verslag der Werkzaamheden van de Vereeniging 'Pro Juventute' te Medan over het jaar 1918" (Varekamp&Co. Medan, 1919), pp. 22–23. KIT, microfilm collection, MM14T-100230.
37. *Oprichtingsvoordracht van Mr. H. J. Boswijk*, pp. 22–23.
38. *Verslag Pro Juventute Medan, January–June 1920*, NA, MvK, V. inv. no. 2222.
39. Gobee en Adriaanse, *Ambtelijke adviezen van C. Snouck Hurgronje, Deel I*, p. 497.
40. Van Vollenhoven's ethical idealism was not restricted to the Dutch colonies; he also believed the Dutch had to conduct a broader international ethical politics. He wrote in 1910 that the Netherlands had a calling to promote worldwide peace by establishing an international peacecorps. See Henk te Velde, *Gemeenschapszin en Plichtsbesef. Liberalisme en Nationalisme in Nederland 1870–1918* (Proefschrift, Groningen, 1992), p. 233.
41. In 1899 an article by Lawyer C. Th. van Deventer had brought to popular attention the idea that the Dutch had a "debt of honor" to the colony that had brought them so much revenue. The need for "ethical" colonial rule was

announced by the Dutch Queen in 1901 and won support from all political parties, although they each developed their own ideas about what its implementation would look like. For a fuller discussion of the many aspects of the ethical policy, see Elsbeth Locher-Scholten, *Ethiek in Fragmenten*.

42. R.B. Cribb, *The Late Colonial State in Indonesia: Political and Economic Foundations of the Netherlands Indies, 1880–1942* (Leiden: KITLV Press, 1994), p. 8
43. Massier, *Van "Recht" naar "Hukum"*, p. 92.
44. Based on the articles of Boekhoudt (1916) and Sibenius Trip (1905), Massier concludes that these judges had a "calm, thorough approach and the capacity to understand indigenous social life, respect for the other person and a dislike of rushed work". Both judges also tried to learn the local languages better. See *Van "Recht" naar "Hukum"*, p. 92.
45. Gobee en Adriaanse, *Ambtelijke adviezen van C. Snouck Hurgronje, Deel I*, p. 497.
46. *Afschrift van de rol van de Landrechter, mr. F.L.Cayaux, zitting 27 maart 1926 te Kanigoro* and *Korte aanteekening van de terechtzitting*, in Ag 19552–1926. ANRI, AS.
47. *Blitar, 15 mei 1926, Landrechter Cayaux aan de GG*, in Ag 19552–1926. ANRI, AS.
48. *OngedateerdeBrief van Kasanredjo aan de Gouverneur-Generaal*, in Ag 19552–1926. ANRI, AS. Kasanredjo could probably not read and write because he signed the letter with a cross at his name. Thanks to my friend Yudi Bachri for helping with the translation.
49. *Blitar, 15 mei 1926, Landrechter Cayaux aan de GG*, in Ag 19552–1926. ANRI, AS.
50. *Weltevreden 27 mei 1926, Consideratieen en advies van den Procureur-Generaal Nauta*, in Ag 19552–1926. ANRI, AS.
51. *BT 10 juni 1926 no 7*, in Ag 19552–1926. ANRI, AS.
52. *Jason Loembantobing aan de Gouverneur-Generaal, via tussenkomst van het landgerecht te PematangSiantar, Pematang Siantar, 1 Mei 1926*, Ag 29870–1926. ANRI, AS.
53. *Landrechter J.* De Kruyff to the Governor General, Pematang Siantar, 5 May 1926, Ag 29870–1926. ANRI, AS.
54. *Gouverneur der Oostkust van Sumatra aan de Procureur-Generaal te Weltevreden, Medan, 21 mei 1926*, Ag 29870–1926. ANRI, AS.
55. W.S. de Haas (Director of the Disciplinary and Education system of the Department of Justice) to the Algemene Secretarie, Weltevreden 15 October 1926, Ag 29870–1926. ANRI, AS.
56. Attorney General Nauta to the Governor General, Weltevreden 5 June 1926, Ag 29870–1926. ANRI, AS.
57. Moe van Emmerik, *Witte Kruis Blad, April 1924*, p. 3.
58. M. Tuiten, "Over leeftijd en leeftijdsvaststelling van Regeeringspupillen", *Indisch Tijdschrift van het Regt*, 121 (1924), pp. 274–276.
59. Ibid., p. 276.
60. Ibid., p. 276.
61. Ibid., p. 280.
62. Ibid., pp. 277–278.
63. The letter of Darmo and Sarpani is the earliest clemency request that is available in the archives of the Algemene Secretarie. In other cases it is often clear

who wrote the clemency request for parents. Matseman, Doegal and Dirdja
from Kandangan, Borneo, for example, asked the chairman of the local *landraad* to write their letter for them. Meester Raden Mas Gondowinoto was
one of the first indigenous judges in the colony. He declared that Matseman,
Doegal and Dirdja were brought to him by the *pembekal* (member of the village government) Matali and that he had clearly explained the content of
the letter to them, after which they put their thumbprints on the letter. This
is explained in various documents from Ag 21008–1926. ANRI, AS.

64. Darmo and Sarpani to Governor General, Semarang 19-01-1918, in BT 23-
10-1918, no 2. ANRI, AS.
65. Ibid.
66. Director of Justice to Governor General, Batavia 28-09-1918, in BT 23-10-
1918, no 2. ANRI, AS.
67. Ibid.
68. I was able to find approximately 65 of these letters in the archives of the
Algemene Secretarie; there might have been more that never made it from
the local authorities to the Governor General, or were lost and went unreg-
istered for other reasons. Sincere gratitude to the Indonesian Encompass
students who studied in Leiden between 2006 and 2009 and helped me with
the translation of these letters.
69. See the various letters in Ag 29870–1926. ANRI, AS.
70. Jenneke Christiaens, *De Geboorte van de Jeugddelinquent: België, 1830–1930*
(Brussels: Vubpress, 1999), pp. 248–253.
71. See for example the letter of Matseman, Doegal and Dirdja for their cousin
Toepa, in Ag 21008–1926. ANRI, AS.
72. Ag 30080–1926 and Ag 20771–1927, both dealing with the case of Samil bin
Ganal. ANRI, AS.
73. Clemency request from Ganal and Atjoet to the Governor General, Amoentai
31 December 1926, Ag 20771–1927. ANRI, AS. This request was also written by someone else and signed with thumbprints, of both the father and
mother of Samil bin Ganal. According to Yudi Bachri, who helped to translate the documents, the letters were very well written in a style that is close
to current-day Bahasa Indonesia. The writer was probably well educated in a
modern school/university.
74. See Ag 8945–1928. ANRI, AS.
75. Clemency request from Ganal and Atjoet tot the Governor General,
Amoentai 31 December 1926, Ag 20771–1927. ANRI, AS.
76. Letter from the Resident of Borneo to the Attorney General and Governor
General, written by his secretary H. de Heanen,Bandjermasin 23 April 1927,
in Ag 20771–1927. ANRI, AS.
77. *Verzoekschrift van A. Sibij en A. Kamagi aan de GG van Nederlands-Indië,Tateloe,
4 januari 1930*, in Bt 18 Maart 1930 no. 10. ANRI, AS.
78. *Van de fd. Magistraat aan de Gouverneur-Generaal, Manado, 25 januari 1230*, in
Bt 18 Maart 1930 no. 10. ANRI, AS.
79. *Brief van J.C.D. Pettelle aan Mr. D. Fock, Gouverneur-Generaal van Nederlands-
Indie. Bandoeng, 17 september 1923*, in Ag 39013/1923. ANRI, AS.
80. In Bt 18 Maart 1930 no. 10. ANRI, AS.
81. *Verzoekschrift van A. Sibij en A. Kamagi aan de GG van Nederlands-Indië.Tateloe,
4 januari 1930*, Bt 18 Maart 1930 no. 10. ANRI, AS.

Part II

Juvenile Delinquency and Transnational Migration

4
It Takes a Village: Budapest Jewry and the Problem of Juvenile Delinquency

Howard Lupovitch

Writing in 1851, Abraham Hochmut, the architect of Jewish educational reform in nineteenth-century Hungary, offered the following instructions to teachers in the soon-to-be created network of Hungarian state-sponsored Jewish schools:

> Discipline in school is like discipline in the army: it is the dominating spirit on which success depends. As is known to every leader, and to every team in the midst of a military operation, this spirit cannot be replaced, and without it victory can be snatched away so, too, a school can be derailed by the same lack of regulation and control. It must be a permanent, uniform element from the lowest to the highest class, and must be implemented with rigour so that the impact of education is not paralyzed by the misconduct of a few bad apples.[1]

These instructions, harsh by twenty-first century pedagogical standards, are more easily understood and appreciated when one considers that Hochmut's aim was not to give teachers licence to treat schoolchildren like soldiers, but rather to incorporate problem children – orphans, indigent and, above all, delinquent children – into the Jewish community school system. As such, Hochmut's instructions pointed to a central tension that confronted, and at the same time confounded, Jewish educators and communal leaders in their search for an optimal school system – how to make Jewish education accessible to all Jewish children in the community, regardless of social caste, religious outlook and public demeanour, while providing a quality of education high enough to attract and meet the needs of the most capable students; or, to put it another way: how to educate delinquent children without allowing their less than ideal behaviour to undermine the education of the rest of the children. For educators like Hochmut, who regarded Jewish education as the best guarantor of Jewish continuity and survival, this tension between accessibility and quality was, and remains, a central preoccupation.

Yet this commitment to include wayward children in the communal education system was not without a measure of ambivalence. The desire to provide high-quality education to all Jewish boys made it difficult to ignore the fact that the presence of delinquent children undermined the educational process and thus compromised the quality of communal education. This, in turn, pointed to the possible advantages of educating wayward children and orphans separately, thereby allowing less- or un-problematic children to learn more quickly and effectively, that is, without the disruptions of poorly behaved students. While the Jewish community generally did not employ this strategy explicitly, communities that had sufficient resources and members with children often operated parallel networks of elementary and middle schools in which at least one elementary and middle school required tuition fees while the other admitted children free of charge. Though the latter were maintained principally and officially to provide education to the poor and orphaned, in practice communal leaders encouraged the parents of juvenile delinquents to send their children to the free schools.[2]

Hochmut, of course, did not fault these children. On the contrary, he attributed their disruptive demeanour to the fact that they had been denied a proper upbringing by circumstances or by providence. For this reason, he regarded the education of these children, above all, as not simply a means of imparting knowledge but rather a form of surrogate parenting that might be the only way to instil in them a proper sense of morals and values, and to guarantee that they would grow up to be productive members of the Jewish community and of society as a whole. This comprehensive notion of communal education, far exceeding the aims of the traditional Jewish curriculum, would be one of the cornerstones of Hochmut's programme of educational reform, and would be emulated by subsequent efforts to improve the quality of Jewish education and thereby ameliorate the lives of delinquents, Jewish orphans and the children of the Jewish poor.

As such, Hochmut's approach to delinquency reflected a dual worldview that was shaped by his particular origins and the social and religious milieu in which he came of age as an intellectual. Born in Moravia, educated in Prague and then appointed as a school teacher and administrator in Miskolc (Hungary) and then Pest, Hochmut lived at the crossroads of the more traditional Jewish intellectual world of east central Europe and the more progressive intellectual world of Vienna and other parts of German central Europe. As a student of leading Prague rabbis such as Solomon Judah Rapoport, Hochmut was steeped in the rabbinic legal and moral principles that characterized the Yeshiva world of eastern Europe. As a graduate of a leading Prague university, he was also well versed in contemporary theories of education and psychology, particularly those of Johann Herbart. Hochmut's aims and tactics in the realm of education reform, including the problem of dealing with delinquents, apposed and combined rabbinic notions of rehabilitation through education with Herbart's notion that delinquent behaviour was acquired rather than inherent and could be changed through a proper education.[3]

Along the same lines, his outlook reflected the broader prevailing view in nineteenth-century Pest and, after 1873, Budapest; a view that combined comfortably traditional Jewish notions of rehabilitation through education with nineteenth-century notions of moral rehabilitation. Budapest, too, situated at the crossroads of eastern and western Europe, was an amalgam of older, traditional attitudes transplanted and imported from Moravia combined with novel ideas from the more cosmopolitan world of Prague. It was a city whose cultural and intellectual world increasingly resembled that of Vienna, Berlin and even Paris during the nineteenth century.[4] Not surprisingly, Hochmut's working definition, like that of Jewish communal leaders in Budapest generally, combined the traditional Jewish notion of delinquency as religious laxity and irreverence with novel notions of delinquency as connected to criminal and immoral behaviour stemming from a non-productive lifestyle.

During the half-century following the publication of Hochmut's treatise, Hungarian Jewry, spearheaded by the towering Jewish community of Pest, experimented with and implemented multiple courses of action to find this balance between quality and accessibility. These courses of action not only emanated from a particular segment within the Jewish community, but each reflected a particular combination of the old and the new. As such, the various Jewish responses to the challenge of rehabilitating delinquent children and incorporating them into the Jewish community represent an amalgam of amalgams – a variety of different combinations of tradition and innovation.

Three Jewish strategies, in particular, are noteworthy in this regard: those of the mainstream Jewish community, the Orthodox minority community and the Jewish Women's Association. Though the three organizations' particular notions of juvenile delinquency differed from one another, all three possessed a notion of juvenile delinquency that combined older, pre-existing notions of communal responsibility, child-rearing and pedagogy with novel solutions to the decadent behaviour of Jewish youth. The mainstream Jewish community, dominated by a moderately progressive Neolog movement, strove in all matters to harmonize the best elements of traditional Judaism with novel conceptions of social reform by harmonizing them to complement the other – and hoped to fashion its response to child delinquency accordingly. This meant, above all, rehabilitating delinquents by effectively combining the edifying ideas of traditional Judaism and the interrelatedness of education, morality and productivity that was finding an ever wider audience during the nineteenth century among central European statesmen and social reformers – thereby transforming delinquents into productive members of both Jewish and Hungarian society.[5]

By contrast, the Orthodox community, starting from the presumption that morality and religious observance necessarily went hand in hand, often regarded such novel ideas of the Enlightenment not as a solution to, but rather as the source of juvenile delinquency. They believed that, left to its own devices, Jewish tradition and the traditional Jewish community had capably managed all aspects of Jewish life, and that juvenile delinquency was simply another problem that Jews should continue to address in the same way as they had other problems for centuries; they also attributed juvenile delinquency and other Jewish communal problems to the intrusion of modernity and change. As such, the Orthodox community believed that sequestering Jewish delinquents from the decadence, corruption and temptations of mainstream society would most effectively and expeditiously transform disruptive young people into morally upright, observant Jews.[6]

The Pest Jewish Women's Association, a voluntary society for women affiliated with the main Jewish community, was founded in the 1860s and grew into one of the largest Jewish women's associations in Europe by the turn of the twentieth century, followed a third strategy that was a variation on the mainstream Jewish progressive strategy.[7] While agreeing with the main Neolog community that a combination of traditional and novel ideas might form a useful basis for transforming delinquents into contributing members of the Jewish community, the women of the Association believed that the efforts of male-dominated institutions approached the problem of delinquent children as though the latter were adults. Instead, the Women's Association believed that, more than anything else, the source of juvenile delinquency was a lack of nurturing and good parenting, and that providing these to delinquent children was not merely the best but the only promising course of action.

Despite the differences between the three strategies, it should be noted that a common thread between them was an emphasis on education. All three groups regarded a proper education – as each understood it – to be the most effective means of rehabilitating these children and indispensable in accomplishing this aim. The centrality of education at once simplified and complicated each group's tactics: simplified, on the one hand, because the solution to the problem was concentrated in a single institution, and complicated, on the other, because this meant that dealing with the problem of delinquency was inextricably linked to the complexities of communal education: funding, locating and training qualified teachers, and obtaining space and rabbinic endorsement.

Moreover, collective efforts to improve communal education were, in no small part, a novel aspect of Jewish life during the nineteenth century. In most pre-modern Jewish communities, and particularly in pre-modern Ashkenazic communities, the generally low standard of communal education precluded any concern about compromising the level of education by integrating miscreants. In general, affluent children did not attend Jewish communal schools, but were home-schooled by private tutors; needless to say, they received an education that far surpassed the education provided in communal schools. That students of communal schools generally came from less fortunate families, whose expectations tended to be quite low, further lessened the concern with the quality of communal education.[8]

This situation changed dramatically during the nineteenth century, as the education of the children of the Jewish elite became a model for communal education. One of the chief aims of Jewish education reform, in Hungary and across much of central and western Europe, from the late eighteenth century onward was to reproduce on a communal scale the superior education that had hitherto been provided to the children of the rich. As this aim came to fruition, the standards and expectations of communal education rose steadily, thus magnifying the concern that wayward children would undermine the quality of communal education. In addition came the challenge of procuring the additional funds necessary to provide a higher quality education; that is, the added cost of providing a dual education, hiring and training better teachers, and erecting and maintaining buildings that were more amenable to learning. Not to mention that all of these improvements had to conform both to the strictures of Judaism and the emerging bourgeois aims of progress and civic improvement.

Jewish precedents

In no small part, the working definition of juvenile delinquency employed by Jewish communities of all stripes, no less than the obligation of managing delinquent children, derived from centuries-old biblical and rabbinic notions of this phenomenon. The injunctions regulating the status of delinquent children date all the way back to biblical scripture. From the outset, delinquency was defined differently with respect to male and female children. Regarding the former, a delinquent son was defined as disobedient, disrespectful and non-observant of Jewish laws. Deuteronomy 21:19–21 instructed parents who were incapable of handling a "stubborn and rebellious son" to rectify the situation by bringing the child to the elders of the city for judgement, which, in this instance, meant death by stoning.

By contrast, the delinquent behaviour of a daughter was defined primarily in terms of sexual impropriety. Deuteronomy 22:20–21 authorized communal leaders to take draconian measures in response to such behaviour:

> But if this thing be true, that the tokens of virginity were not found in the damsel; then they shall bring out the damsel to the door of her father's house, and the men of her city shall stone her with stones that she die; because she hath wrought a wanton deed in Israel, to play the harlot in her father's house; so shalt thou put away the evil from the midst of thee.

Though her crime was defined differently from that of a delinquent boy, both shared the same fate – death by stoning.

Post-biblical Jewish tradition quickly distanced itself from such harsh measures. While not directly challenging the basic biblical instruction, it narrowed the definition of a wayward child and then moved away from the death penalty mandated in Deuteronomy, in the direction of rehabilitation. Accordingly, rabbinic interpreters, inferring additional nuance from the particular language of the Bible, restricted the definition of a wayward child to sons (excluding daughters) and to post-pubescent children, since "minor children are not yet bound by the commandments". The rabbis also indicated that simply stealing food or drink from one's parents did not constitute wayward behaviour; to merit this, it would have to be proved that a son stole the food or drink and then consumed it elsewhere.

Moreover, since the Bible defined a wayward child as a glutton and drunkard, the rabbis of the *Mishnah* stipulated that excessive consumption of any food other than meat and any drink other than wine did not constitute wayward behaviour. Later, the rabbis of the Talmud further stipulated that a child is not liable "unless he eats raw meat and drinks undiluted wine". Moreover, excessive consumption of poultry was also excluded from punishment. In addition they also precluded one parent, father or mother, from claiming the child to be wayward without the agreement of the other, and forbade either parent who was physically or mentally challenged (*Gidem* or *Ilem*), or seeing or hearing impaired from claiming the child to be wayward. Having thus complicated the process of damning a child as wayward, the rabbis also eased the punishment for first offenders, from capital to corporal punishment – only repeat offenders were subject to the death penalty. In general, the rabbis concluded that "there never has been a 'stubborn and rebellious son,' and never will be", and this remained the case into the nineteenth century. In fact, some rabbis underlined the putative absence of such cases by redefining the whole category of wayward children as a pedagogic tool rather than a legal category: "Why then was the law written? . . . . That you may study it and receive reward."[9]

To be sure, not all rabbinic thinkers regarded this downgrading of delinquency as a positive thing. Commenting on this passage from the Talmud, the sixteenth-century Rabbi Samuel Eliezer Edels (also known by his rabbinic acronym Maharsha) lamented:

> In our times, we pay no attention to gluttonous and defiant sons, and everybody covers up the sins of his children; even where they might be liable to flogging or to capital punishment under the law, they are not even reprimanded. Many such children are leading purposeless lives and learn nothing – and we know that Jerusalem was destroyed because children loafed around and did not study.[10]

Ultimately, however, such sentiments were more the exception than the rule.

In a similar way, the rabbis redefined the penalty for a sexually promiscuous girl, albeit more gradually – perhaps not surprisingly given the sexual nature of the transgression in this instance. The Talmud still maintained the capital nature of her crime: "If witnesses appeared against her in the house of her father-in-law [testifying] that she had played the harlot in her father's house she is stoned at the door of her father's house, as if to say, 'See the plant that you have reared.' "[11] Eventually, though, the punishment for this transgression was commuted by the rabbis from death to shaming. The Sifri, an early Midrashic commentary on the Bible, interpreted the stigma of *Nevela be-Yisrael* as the perpetrator having "shamed not only herself but all maidens in Israel".[12]

The result of this was that rabbinic tradition, uncomfortable with the harsh penalty delineated in Deuteronomy, went to great lengths to preclude a child from being condemned as rebellious or stubborn. Not satisfied with the biblical injunction that the community stone wayward children to death, the rabbinic interpreters quickly set aside this harsh solution, opting for rehabilitation instead of execution. In practice, this meant impressing the proper Jewish moral and religious way of life upon wayward children. Jewish communal leaders were loath to ostracize a child except under more extreme conditions; rather, they preferred to rehabilitate and, in so doing, to reintegrate the child into the normative tracks of communal life. In some cases, this meant apprenticing a Jewish boy or teenager to train under the tutelage of a master who would double as a mentor.

More often than not, in the pre-modern Jewish community, the task and responsibility of rehabilitation was assigned to the Jewish community school. Such a strategy presumed that the wayward child lacked a proper education, or perhaps a proper home life that would reinforce the lessons and values he or she learned in school. Either way, the overriding assumption was that a proper education was the most straightforward and effective solution to delinquency.

Delinquents and orphans

The day-to-day reality of Jewish communal life further complicated the task of Jewish communal leaders in Budapest in dealing with delinquent children. Often, there was considerable overlap between delinquent children and orphaned children; thus the general attitude toward delinquents merged with the Jewish view of orphans. The latter were defined by Jewish tradition as among the most deserving of support and compassion. Throughout the Hebrew Bible, and particularly in the teachings of the Biblical prophets, orphans were listed together with strangers, widows and the indigent as groups not only deserving of charity and assistance, but those for whom assistance was a divinely ordained commandment.

Rabbinic tradition was no less strident in its insistence that Jews – as individuals and as a community – assist orphans tirelessly. Three rulings by the medieval Jewish jurist Meir of Rothenberg underline this point. Underscoring the incessant concern for aiding orphans, Rabbi Meir stated: "The rabbis did not decree anything disadvantageous to the interests of orphans."[13] Yet Jewish tradition went beyond simply authorizing assistance for orphans, placing care for them on a par with the all-important responsibility of raising children. In response to a query as to whether or not parents had the same obligation to an orphan whom they had adopted as to their own biological children, Meir of Rothenberg equated the two responsibilities: "A person who brings up an orphan in his house is in the same position as the orphan's father."[14] Finally, Rothenberg extended the responsibility of providing proper parenting for orphans beyond individual Jewish households to the Jewish community as a whole: "The choice for the proper guardian for [an orphan] does not lie only with his parents' siblings but with the elders of the community who are the fathers of all orphans."[15]

Rulings like these, echoed countless times elsewhere in the legal and ethical corpus of rabbinic tradition, would eventually become a cornerstone of the Jewish community's eleemosynary activities. This was especially evident in the Statutes of Moravian Jewry (*Takanot Meheren*), local and regional regulations published originally in the seventeenth century which contained an extensive array of communal statutes that regulated virtually every aspect of Jewish communal life. Given the fact that most rabbis and lay leaders in nineteenth-century Hungary were the children, grandchildren or great-grandchildren of Jewish immigrants from Moravia, this collection often provided the basis for communal administration in Hungary. Among other things, this collection of statutes consolidated the obligation to integrate orphans into the communal school network:

And with regard to orphans who have neither father nor mother, the trustees of charity (*gaba-ey zedakah*) are required to oversee that no orphan be excluded from school until after the age of thirteen. The community is required either to pay for every orphan's education if the orphan in question is indigent, for they are like the parents of the orphan; or to send the orphan to live with relatives – just so the orphan is not excluded from school until after the age of thirteen, for the study of Torah is the most important thing of all (*Talmud Torah ke-neged kulam*). In those communities where a guardian is appointed for an orphan, the guardian shall manage the orphan in the aforementioned manner, and make certain that the orphan is not excluded from school until after the age of thirteen.[16]

As with the case of delinquent children, moreover, the traditional Jewish attitude toward orphans varied between boys and girls. Orphan boys were regarded as potential delinquents because they were regarded as lacking proper direction and heading potentially toward a life as a derelict or criminal. Orphan girls were seen as difficult to marry off, and thus doomed to turn to crimes like prostitution or theft as the only way to earn an adequate living. As a result, the Jewish community's concern for, and solution to, the problem of delinquent children was largely an internal Jewish affair that was handled in combination with the obligation to assist orphaned children.

Civic improvement and productivity

From the late eighteenth century onward, the problem of delinquent Jewish children was amplified as the strengths and especially the weaknesses of Jewish education emerged as a key element in the larger debate regarding *Judenverbesserung*. This term, coined by Christian Wilhelm von Dohm in his seminal 1781 treatise *Über die bürgerliche Verbesserung der Juden,* was invoked not infrequently in public debates over the most effective ways to transform Jews into productive subjects or citizens. Such debates often focused on the social barriers between Jews and non-Jews, and on the putative Jewish penchant for commerce and money-lending as the major impediment barring the Jews from becoming more economically productive. In this regard, the rehabilitation of delinquent Jewish children was part of a broader effort by the state to rehabilitate non-productive members of society. Habsburg Emperor Joseph II, for example, regarded Dohm's notion of *Judenverbesserung* as the most effective means of transforming Jews into productive subjects.[17]

At the heart of these debates was the powerful assumption that Jewish particularism and non-productivity was reinforced in every generation by an antiquated education system that imbued Jewish youth with a warped sense of civic duty and a narrow sense of economic possibility. As a result, the Jewish community's treatment of delinquent children and orphans came under the broader, more intense scrutiny of Jewish communal education as a whole. Increasingly during the eighteenth century, the amelioration of Jewish education came to be regarded, by Jews and non-Jews alike, as the most expedient and expeditious way to transform and enlighten Jews. In this milieu, the presence of delinquent

Jewish children was often cited as evidence of the decrepit state of traditional Jewish life and the Jewish community's inability to change the situation.

At the heart of this attitude was a dual assumption. First, it was assumed that the decline and deterioration of traditional Jewish life stemmed in no small part from the narrow, antiquated condition of Jewish education and, in particular, from what was considered by many the most decrepit of traditional Jewish institutions: the *Heder*, or Jewish primary school. Second, there was a prevailing notion that any and all efforts toward *Judenverbesserung* had to begin with the transformation of Jewish education. In this way, the rehabilitation of wayward children was woven into the fabric of virtually every initiative to reform and improve Jewish education at this time. As proponents of *Judenverbesserung* such as Dohm placed the responsibility for transforming the Jews onto the state and onto the Jews themselves, Jewish communal leaders regarded with growing urgency the task of rehabilitating delinquent children. No longer was the rehabilitation of delinquent children solely a matter of fulfilling a religious obligation – which itself was never taken lightly, but it was now also considered a means to obtain full acceptance into mainstream society and, no less important, civic equality and full citizenship.

This sense of urgency intensified as the public debate over Jewish emancipation heated up during the nineteenth century, particularly in the German states but also in the Habsburg monarchy. Often, debate over Jewish emancipation revolved around whether or not a particular Jewish population could be easily assimilated into mainstream society and, if so, how? Even the most ardent supporters of Jewish emancipation insisted that Jews transform themselves, either as a prerequisite to emancipation or as the result of emancipation.

Either way, the presence of delinquent children, ever more conspicuous as the behaviour of Jews was scrutinized more and more closely, raised the ominous possibility that Jewishness and an immoral disposition were somehow linked. In Hungary, Baron Joseph Eötvös, the ideological architect of Hungarian Jewish emancipation and one of the most outspoken champions of the emancipation of Hungarian Jews, could not help noting a connection between some Jews, at least, and a life of crime.[18] In *The Village Notary*, Eötvös' landmark novel about the corruption of Hungarian society, Eötvös portrayed a Jewish antagonist, Jancsi the Glazier, who conspires with the Baroness Rety to destroy the title character, an innocent and largely powerless low-level bureaucrat – the notary of a small village. Eventually, the Jew and his partner in crime are exposed, arrested and condemned to rot in prison. In a remarkably progressive twist, Eötvös forgives the Jew while condemning the noblewoman.[19]

Yet Eötvös' exoneration of Jancsi the Glazier does not diminish the extent to which Hungarian society, and even Hungarian liberal society, associated Jews with criminal behaviour, even when such behaviour was foisted upon them by circumstances. Even though he exonerates the Jewish criminal and attributes corrupt behaviour by Jews to centuries of ill-treatment and exclusion, Eötvös nonetheless saw a lingering affinity among Jews for a life of corruption and crime. Hungarian Jews, immersed in an intense campaign for full citizenship, regarded such an association as a potentially serious impediment. This placed even greater weight on rehabilitating delinquent children through communal education as quickly as possible.

Though every Jewish community had delinquent children, this problem was far more serious in Pest than anywhere else in Hungary.[20] In terms of sheer numbers, Pest Jewry was many times larger than any other Jewish community in Hungary, indeed larger than all but a few Jewish communities in Europe. Nagyvárad (today Oradea, Romania), the second largest Jewish community in Hungary, peaked at around 18,000 Jews at the end of the nineteenth century. Pest Jewry exceeded that figure during the 1850s, and eventually increased to more than ten times that size; the vast majority of the just over 200,000 Jews who lived in Budapest by 1910 lived in Pest rather than Buda or Óbuda. A much larger Jewish community meant a much greater number of delinquent children. Most of the less affluent Pest Jews lived in Terézváros [Theresa District]; not surprisingly, this part of the city had the most instances of delinquency. The sheer size of the Jewish community in Pest, moreover, deprived its members of a useful means that smaller communities had of dealing with delinquents. Smaller communities, where Jews (to paraphrase Mack Walker) "knew each other and needed each other" and were generally within no more than two or three "degrees of separation" from each other, functioned like extended families.[21] This aided parents of delinquents in their efforts to keep track of and control their troublesome offspring, and deprived delinquent children of anonymity, an important enabling element of delinquent behaviour. The size and accompanying anonymity of Pest Jewry allowed delinquent children to elude with less difficulty the authoritative arm of parents, relatives and other familiar adults.

The administrative growing pains of the city of Pest further enabled and facilitated delinquent behaviour. Until the second half of the nineteenth century, the local government in Pest struggled to keep pace with the rapid physical and demographic expansion of the city.[22] Until the end of the eighteenth century, the city of Pest did not extend very far beyond the walls of the inner city [*belváros*] and the city government was fashioned and staffed accordingly. The rapid growth of the outer city (*kulváros*), five of six districts that ringed the inner city, and the rapid growth of the population therein, created a city whose size and population were far beyond the administrative capacity of the city fathers and their bureaucratic entourage. This meant that crime control was limited and law and order difficult to maintain, much like a frontier- or boomtown. Indeed, much like other boomtowns, the districts of the outer city were saturated during the nineteenth century by Jewish and other settlers who had come to Pest driven by an entrepreneurial spirit and a sense of adventure. Furthermore, the minimal means which did exist to maintain law and order in Pest were periodically strained and challenged by natural disasters such as the great flood of 1838 and outbreaks of cholera in 1831, 1849 and 1855; and by political upheaval, in particular, the revolution of 1848 and the ensuing War for Hungarian Independence.[23]

Moreover, the Jewish communities of Pest – like other Hungarian Jewish communities – lacked one option that was available to communities elsewhere, particularly in the Russian Empire. There, the enactment of the Conscription Law of 1827 required, among other things, each Jewish communal council to select an annual quota of Jewish boys for service in the Tsar's army. In many Jewish communities, this quota was first filled with delinquent Jewish boys (*meshovavim*); only when this source was exhausted were others subject to conscription. Alongside the harshness of this decree and the rift it opened between Jewish communal leaders and the Jewish rank and file, it provided a convenient and uncomplicated solution to the problem of Jewish delinquency – conscription.[24]

In Hungary, too, Jews were conscripted into the Habsburg Imperial Army and the Hungarian *Honvéd* from the 1850s on. Yet this did not solve the problem of delinquency as it had in Russia, for one simple reason: service in the Habsburg army or Hungarian *Honvéd* never instilled the sense of fear and dread which service in the Tsar's army did. On the contrary, service in the Habsburg and Hungarian military, though not the preferred choice of every Jew, was regarded by many as a means of social advancement and acceptance. Neither was there any pressure on Jewish communities to fill quotas. As a result, in Hungary, it was not necessary to use Jewish delinquents as a means of filling a conscription quota and thereby sparing other Jews the onus of military service.[25]

Living in circumstances that promoted anonymity and social drift, and under the scrutiny of those deciding whether or not Jews were worthy of citizenship, the Jews of Pest had the daunting task of managing the problem of juvenile delinquency. It is unclear how many Jewish children in Pest were delinquent. In the absence of reliable statistical evidence, one must rely on anecdotal evidence to be able even to speculate about how serious the problem was. Based on the minute books of the Pest Jewish Community, the annual number of reported cases of Jewish juvenile delinquency varied widely, from as many as several hundred cases in 1848 and 1849 (years of revolution and war) and during the 1880s (when there was an influx of Jewish immigrants from Galicia and the Pale of Settlement, and immigrants from Hungary's more impoverished northeastern counties) to as few as several dozen during the 1850s and 1860s. Contemporary observers and officials who were opposed to extending civic equality and social acceptance to Jews, moreover, often exaggerated the problem of juvenile delinquency to fortify their position in the debate over Jewish emancipation.[26]

Even more important perhaps was the fact that even contemporary officials and observers – Jewish and non-Jewish – who claimed to be impartial in describing and assessing the pervasiveness of delinquency among Jewish children tended to conflate delinquent children with other "problematic" children, namely, orphans and the poor. These officials rarely singled out delinquency as a problem in and of itself, but rather lumped it together with the problem of raising orphans in lieu of parents and ameliorating the meagre conditions of poor children. Initially, efforts in this direction were mostly individual acts of benevolence. In 1823, for example, an affluent Pest Jew, L.M. Rosenfeld, endowed a communal fund that annually provided "proper instruction and trousers made of real cloth" to ten underprivileged students, thereby "encouraging diligence, self-respect, and proper performance". The rapid growth of Pest Jewry, though, rendered such individual acts of beneficence, however generous, grossly inadequate.[27]

From the 1850s on, the situation in Pest started to stabilize, beginning with the imposition of Habsburg neo-absolutism, whose efforts to head off Magyar nationalism by Germanizing Pest incidentally resulted in the expansion of Pest's city government and the development of a more orderly city. The departure of the Habsburgs after 1860 and the ensuing Magyarization policies further expanded and developed the city of Pest, such that, by the time Pest was amalgamated with Buda and Obuda into Budapest in 1873, the boomtown character of an earlier generation was replaced by a better ordered and more developed European metropolis like Vienna. Not surprisingly, the most concerted efforts by Pest Jewry – and, after 1873, by Budapest Jewry – to address the problem of delinquency through education reform began during the 1850s, first and foremost with the reforms of Abraham Hochmut.

During the 1840s, Hochmut had "cut his teeth and earned his wings" as a reformer of Jewish education in Miskolc, a mid-sized Jewish community 150 kilometres northeast of Pest, where he was employed by the Jewish community as superintendent of Jewish schools for all of Borsod County. In this capacity, he oversaw the implementation of the Brody Education Fund, a substantial gift that funded, among other things, the creation in Miskolc of a new dual-curriculum school, a teacher's training institute and a free school for Jewish orphans.[28] He would use this experience as a blueprint for his next, much larger project: designing an education programme with which to implement the National Education Fund Act of 1851. This fund was the result of Emperor Franz Joseph commuting a massive fine which he had imposed on Hungarian Jews for siding with the Hungarians against the Dynasty in 1848 into the fund that would create a network of state-sponsored Jewish schools in Hungary. State funding, coupled with the support of local community members meant that children could attend these schools virtually free of charge, thus allowing Hochmut to integrate delinquent children along with orphans and poor children into these new schools.

Waiving tuition fees, though making the schools fully accessible and inclusive, did not solve the problem of students without proper parents disrupting and impeding the educational process in these schools. When an orphan acted disrespectfully the teacher could not enlist the cooperation of parents in disciplining the child. The community provided orphans with shelter and education, but the task of raising these children and instilling in them a proper set of morals and decorum fell on their teachers. In response, Hochmut used the fund to expand the teacher training institute in Miskolc and to establish several others, whose curriculum included specific training to provide parental guidance for children without parents or who had received little or no parental guidance at home.

More importantly, perhaps, Hochmut advocated the idea that these schools, in addition to providing a first-rate Jewish and general education, should offer students the possibility of learning an occupation or trade. For orphans, the indigent and delinquents, in particular, this provided a means to move beyond the difficult and often limiting situation in which they lived. Graduates of the schools who completed this train-ing would be apprenticed to a local Jewish artisan or merchant, and thereby learn on site the practical side of a productive occupation. In order to ensure that enough sponsors would be available, the Jewish community offered various incentives: reduction of communal dues, added benefits of communal memberships and religious honours in the synagogue or cemetery.

Finally, Hochmut introduced a crucial new dimension to Jewish communal education: education for Jewish girls as well as boys. The *Mädchenschule* that he established became a permanent feature of Jewish communal education, in Pest and elsewhere in Hungary. As was the case with delinquent Jewish boys, these schools provided a new way to rehabilitate delinquent Jewish girls. Hitherto, the most frequent way to help these girls was by situating them in a stable Jewish household as a domestic servant. In this way, it was assumed or at least hoped that the moral environment of the workplace would rub off, thereby lead-ing these girls down a better path. Ideally, communal leaders imagined that working for an upright Jewish family might help an erstwhile delin-quent marry someone from an upright family, and perhaps even provide some badly needed upward mobility.[29]

Variations on a theme

Ultimately, the effectiveness of these schools in rehabilitating delin-quent boys and girls is difficult, if not impossible, to gauge. There are few reliable statistics regarding juvenile delinquency in Budapest, and even fewer regarding Pest Jewry. For its part, the Jewish community of Pest periodically proclaimed the decidedly positive impact of the schools on many facets of Jewish life, including the rehabilitation of juvenile delinquents.[30] More telling perhaps was the fact that the use of education as a cure for delinquency set the tone for two other Jewish communal organizations, which, with some variation, used Hochmut's strategy and the curriculum of the Pest *Normalschule*, on a smaller level: the Pest *Hevra Shas* (also known as the *Talmudverein* or *Talmudegylet*) and the Pest Jewish Women's Association [*Pest zsido nőegylet,* hereinafter PZsN].

The Hevra Shas was from the outset an autonomous association that operated independently of the Jewish Community council. Like other voluntary associations in Pest, it collected its own membership dues, endowments and voluntary donations. In 1852, the statutes of the Hevra Shas were approved by the Hungarian Minister of Religion. At the same time, the *Hevra Shas* was consistently overshadowed by two larger Jewish voluntary associations: the *Chevra Kadisha*, founded in 1788, which paid out more than 70,000 forints in annual benefits in 1870 at a time when no other Jewish association in Pest paid more than 5,000 forints; and the *Zion Verein*, founded in 1851, which allocated virtually endless interest-free loans to aid the needs of the sick.

Founded in 1842 by Ede Fleischmann and Gusztáv Taub, the organization aimed to "support Biblical and Talmudic discourse and assure that all deceased members have someone saying *Kaddish*...." To this end, the organization maintained a prayer-house and a house of study (*bet midrash/tanintézet*), and later a library. By 1929, it had more than 3,000 members and an annual budget of more than 30,000 pengő, of which more than half went to charitable donations, to supporting indigent Talmudic scholars and building a library with more than 2,000 volumes. The organization also supported and engaged the instructional services of two Talmudic scholars, one of whom gave a lesson in Talmud every morning and evening, while the other delivered a discourse on the Bible in the evening and on the weekly *Haftorah* before Saturday morning services.[31]

In no small sense, the Hevra Shas is best understood in terms of the ways its leaders engaged with the challenges of Jewish communal life in an urban setting during the second half of the nineteenth century. During the 1840s and 1850s, the *Hevra Shas* provided a haven for a small traditionalist enclave amid the rapid expansion of the dominant Neolog movement and the growing inclusion of Jews in a broadening array of leisure activities such as coffeehouses and casinos. During the 1860s, the Hevra Shas was co-opted by the Orthodox leadership as part of a strategy to establish a foothold in Budapest, a variation on what Glenn Dynner has termed the "men of silk" strategy.[32] Reminiscent of the wealthy laity whom Hasidic leaders won over to establish themselves in Warsaw, Orthodox leaders in Budapest co-opted the support of wealthy donors in their city by encouraging them to support the Hevra Shas. As the Hevra Shas emerged as the cornerstone of an increasingly prominent Orthodox community trying to establish a foothold in Budapest, it came eventually to be situated at the fault line between competing Orthodox elites. For these elites, control of the Hevra Shas became a central point of contention between two factions vying for control over the Budapest Orthodox community, each with a distinct view of the non-Orthodox world that informed its attitude toward the Hevra Shas as a means of regulating Jewish activity.

Thirdly, by the 1880s, as Budapest Orthodoxy began to grow into the largest concentration of Orthodox Jews in Europe, the Hevra Shas placed increasing emphasis on developing its own philanthropic programmes, which allowed a less well-educated constituency to participate in its activities including non-scholarly affluent laity.[33] More than anything else, the expanding role of affluent Orthodox women as donors and fundraisers pointed to this overall expansion. Like its counterparts in Warsaw and other parts of eastern Europe, amid this growing emphasis on philanthropic support the Hevra Shas expanded its efforts toward rehabilitating children regarded as delinquent, particularly by providing opportunities for religious learning and participation in communal religious rituals. Their aim was to maximize the time that these children spent with religiously observant Jews, thereby minimizing their exposure to the corrosive effects of non-Orthodox Jews and non-Jewish society.

In a larger sense, the development of the Pest Hevra Shas points to the multifarious role of urbanization in the formation and growth of Jewish communities in large cities like Budapest. On the one hand, the anonymity and cultural diversity of a city like Budapest challenged the integrity of a Jewish community by offering its members compelling non-traditional alternatives that were generally not present – or, at least, far less pronounced – in smaller towns. Such alternatives were especially enticing to younger and more marginally connected members of the Jewish community, leading at times to disaffection and drift. On the other hand, the large concentration of religiously observant Jews in a relatively small physical space buttressed traditional Jewish organizations like the Hevra Shas.

The impact and importance of the Hevra Shas is best understood in terms of its providing a traditional framework for the leisure time of traditional and Orthodox Jews.[34] In so doing, it provided a source of communal coherence that had been eroded by the transition from pre-modern traditionalism to the Orthodoxy of the nineteenth century, and the ensuing intra-communal conflicts between the Orthodox and non-Orthodox elements of the Jewish community. In this way, the Hevra Shas extended communal efforts toward curbing juvenile delinquency into the ranks of Budapest's small but growing Orthodox community. Founded originally to provide a setting for Orthodox men to study rabbinic texts during their leisure time, the Hevra Shas expanded its scope of activities from the 1880s on, as its membership grew in size from a few hundred in 1868 to more than 5,000 by 1900, and in diversity to include women. As such the Hevra Shas expanded its array of charitable activities. This included the establishment of a school, initially for indigent children whose parents could not pay tuition fees.

By 1895, the school recruited delinquent boys as well, with the same goal as the community schools: rehabilitation. In this case, though, rehabilitation meant not simply weaning the boys away from a delinquent lifestyle, but also abandoning depravity for an Orthodox way of life. In this regard, the Hevra Shas' school apparently defined delinquency not only as moral depravity, but also as much more of a religious laxity or indifference. The students in this school were not only provided with a traditional education, but also immersed into the world of Budapest Orthodoxy. Based on a handful of anecdotal accounts, it seems that the problem of delinquency provided a common cause that prevented Budapest Orthodoxy from entirely severing its ties with the rest of Budapest Jewry.

By the turn of the twentieth century, the Hevra Shas expanded its range of activities in a way that broadened its ability to aid delinquent children. This broadening reflected the subtle but unmistakable influence of the nineteenth-century notion of productivity on the otherwise traditional Hevra Shas. More specifically, following a significant infusion of capital through a major endowment in 1907, the Hevra Shas began arranging for some of the underprivileged under its tutelage to be apprenticed with Jewish master craftsman so as to learn a trade.

To be sure, by the turn of the twentieth century, this endeavour did not seem as radical or progressive as it had a century earlier. In a period of industrialization and mechanization, the world of the master craftsman, Jewish or otherwise, had an old-worldly and socially conservative feel. Thus, this addition to the rehabilitation programme of the Hevra Shas was consistent with its overall socially conservative outlook. More broadly, it mirrored the broader dichotomy which the leaders of the Hevra Shas drew between non-Jewish society, with which they were willing to interact out of necessity, and non-Orthodox Jewish society, which they regarded as taboo.

Most importantly perhaps, the apprenticeship programme did not diminish the time that the students of the Hevra Shas spent studying religious texts, but was an extra-curricular programme. This, perhaps more than anything else, made it possible for the leadership of the organization to sanction it. In any case, the combination of Torah study with artisanal training did represent the combination of old and new Jewish tactics toward rehabilitating delinquent Jewish youth.

This combination of the old and the new was even more visible in the programme of the PZsN. Founded in 1866, the PZsN had 900 members by 1874 and more than 2,500 by the end of the century. The membership and, in particular, the officer corps of the PZsN consisted almost exclusively of women from propertied Jewish families. Its annual budget exceeded 340,000 gulden by 1910. The prominence of these women would provide invaluable resources and connections to accomplish the new organization's diverse goals.

From its inception, the character of the PZsN reflected the interplay between traditional Jewish life and non-Jewish society. Typical of Jewish women's organizations, the PZsN originated as an extension of the Jewish men's voluntary associations (*Hevrot*) and Christian women's societies, notably the Pest Women's Charitable Society (*Pesti Jótékony Nőegylet*), which had been founded half a century earlier.[35]

In general, the need to locate a suitable, updated role for women in the Jewish communities of the nineteenth century remained a central aim of these organizations, one that continued to draw on its dual origins and press the membership to search for a balance between traditional Jewish and modern women's organizations. As elsewhere the leadership structure and overall aim of the PZsN was to hasten Jewish acculturation while preserving a commitment to Judaism and Jewish communal life. The PZsN was originally formed at the behest of Pest Jewry's male-dominated leadership and assigned a limited mandate of "tackling social problems caused by widespread poverty, particularly the plight of young single women in the city". The PZsN almost immediately exceeded this limited task by transforming itself within two decades into one of the most important providers of social services in Budapest, for Jews and non-Jews alike. By the 1880s, the successes of the PZsN had attracted the attention of the city fathers, who enlisted its members to spearhead their initial attempts at aiding and managing the growing number of poor children and orphans. Here there was a certain irony: excluded from government and public life, and confined to private endeavours like charity, the women of the PZsN expanded and developed their private realm into an increasingly integral part of Jewish communal life and eventually municipal government.[36]

Among the many successes of the PZsN, the Jewish orphanage was one of the most important with respect to communal education and delinquency. Completed in May 1867, it was filled to capacity within a month. The leaders of the PZsN devoted considerable effort and creativity to ensuring that the orphanage was funded more than adequately.[37] The annual budget initially allocated only 300 forints to the orphanage, and, in difficult economic years, barely 200. To shore up financial support, in 1876 they organized a masquerade ball whose proceeds raised more than 4,000 forints, including 600 forints from the Ministry of Religion and Cults and 100 forints from the royal family. This additional funding allowed the leaders of the PZsN to expand the orphanage from a mere physical refuge for parentless children to a place in which to educate these children and raise them as proper Jews and Magyars; and to extend care not only to orphans but to wayward girls as well. To this end, in 1875 the orphanage division of the PZsN laid out a six-part plan that included arranging for Sabbath and holiday services at the orphanage, afternoon tea accompanied by edifying lectures for the children, better lighting for the orphanage to enhance evening programmes and socializing, and a 200 forint annual stipend for any resident who got engaged to be married.

The women who ran the orphanage, unbeholden to city or Jewish communal educational conventions, experimented with novel methods of education that fused different theories of child-rearing and pedagogy. In the orphanage, the school year was designed according to the rhythm of Jewish and Magyar holidays. At the close of the school year in the late spring, the vacation began with carefree games and a well deserved period of recreation. By the mid-1870s, the Pest women's society began to address the growing concern about increasing levels of religious laxity and moral depravity. They organized an annual Chanukah party at the orphanage that soon became a major communal event. In addition, the women's society organized cultural and social events at local synagogues.[38] In tandem, the efforts of the main Jewish community, the Women's Association and the Hevra Shas reflect how widespread the concern for delinquency was within Budapest Jewry, and also the pervasiveness of the notion that education was the surest antidote to delinquency in Budapest, and in other large Jewish communities situated in large urban centres.

More broadly, the tapestry of tactics employed by these communal organizations reflected the extent to which the response of a Jewish community like Budapest – itself a tapestry of mentalities – was an amalgam of older ideas still prevalent in the traditional Jewish world of eastern Europe and newer ideas emanating from points further to the west. In nineteenth-century Budapest juvenile delinquency presented a particular set of challenges in an age when the behaviour of Jewish youth had implications beyond the internal management of the Jewish community. This new situation demanded multiple novel solutions, tactics and aims. Appropriately, this challenge was met by multiple Jewish organizations, each with its own concerns and strategies.

More importantly perhaps, the array of Jewish responses to delinquency was an indication of the extent to which, for Jews in Budapest, new ideas and methods for dealing with communal problems did not displace older, established ideas, but rather complemented them. Older Jewish responses to delinquency were not set aside during the nineteenth century, but were retained as a useful point of departure and a usable framework with which to fashion something viable and applicable to modern circumstances. The combination of the old and the new within the Jewish response to delinquency in nineteenth-century Budapest revealed not only something about Jewish communal strategies but also the fact that the broader world of nineteenth-century Europe was made up of a tapestry of possibilities, requiring a tapestry of solutions, each building on pre-existing successes.

Notes

1. Hochmut, *Die Jüdische Schule In Ungarn: Wie Sie Ist Und Wie Sie Sein Soll* (Pest, 1851), pp. 54–55.
2. On the centrality of Jewish education in Jewish communal life, see Jacob Katz, *Tradition and Crisis: Jewish Society at the End of the Middle Ages* (Syracuse: Syracuse University Press, 2000), pp. 183ff; Mordechai Eliav, *Ha-Hinukh ha-Yehudi be-Germaniya bimei ha-Haskalah* [Jewish Education in Germany in the Period of Enlightenment and Emancipation] (Jerusalem: Jewish Agency Publications, 1960); "The very world rests on the breath of a child in the schoolhouse" (Babylonian Talmud: Shabbat, 119b).
3. For biographical information on Abraham Hochmut, see Mór Klein "Abraham Hochmut", Magyar Zsidó Szemle, XI (1894); for a recent reappraisal of Prague as a crossroads of European Jewry and Ashkenazic culture, see Maoz Kahana, "Mi-Prag le-Pressburg: Ketiva Halachatit be-'Olam Mishtane me-ha-Noda'", *Biyehuda el ha-Hatam Sofer, 1730–1839* (Doctoral Dissertation, Hebrew University, 2010), pp. 73ff; On Rapoport, see Chaim Landerer, "R' Shlomo Yehuda Rapoport (Shir), Champion of Jewish Unity in the Modern Era", *Hakirah*, 8 (2009), pp. 109–114; on Herbart, see B.B. Wolman, "The Historical Role of Johann Friedrich Herbart", in Wolman (ed.), *Historical Roots of Contemporary Psychology* (New York: Harper & Row, 1968), pp. 29–46.
4. Pest was the most economically developed and culturally vibrant of the three towns that were amalgamated to form Budapest in 1873. Andras Gerő and Janos Poor (eds), *Budapest: A History from Its Beginnings to 1998* (Boulder: East European Monographs, 1998) especially pp. 95–110.
5. On the Jewish Community of Pest see Michael K. Silber, "Budapest", in Gershon David Hundert (ed.), *YIVO Encyclopedia of Jews in Eastern Europe*, Volume I (New Haven: Yale University Press, 2008), pp. 262ff; Howard Lupovitch, "Beyond the Walls: The Beginnings of Pest Jewry", *Austrian History Yearbook*, 36 (2005), especially pp. 42–50.

6. On Budapest's Orthodox community see Aron Fürst, "Budapest", in *'Arim ve-Imahot be-Yisrael: Mivzat Kodesh le-Kehilot Yisrael she-Nechervu Bidey 'arizim u-teme'im be-Milhemet 'Olam ha-Aharona* Part II (Jerusalem: Mossad Ha-Rav Kook, 1948), pp. 164ff.
7. Katalin Gerő, *A Szeretet Munkásai, A Pesti Izraelita Nőegylet Története, 1866–1937* (Budapest, 1938).
8. Eliav, *Jewish Education*, pp. 37–39.
9. Babylonian Talmud, *Sanhedrin* 71b.
10. Samuel Eliezer Edels (Maharsha), *Chiddushei Halachot ve-Agadot* on Shabbat 119:b and sanhedrin 71:a.
11. Babylonoan Talmud *Ketubot 45:b*.
12. *Sifri* on Deuteronomy 21:20.
13. Meir of Rothenberg on Hoshen Mishpat #506, quoted in Irving A. Agus, *Rabbi Meir of Rothenburg, His Life and His Works as Sources for the Religious, Legal, and Social History of the Jews of Germany in the Thirteenth Century* (New York: Ktav Publishing, 1947), p. 463.
14. Ibid., Hoshen Mishpat #665, quoted in Agus, p. 604.
15. Ibid., Hoshen Mishpat 705m quoted in Agus, p. 627.
16. *Takanot Medinat Mehren*, p. 7. On the Moravian origins of Hungarian Jewry see Michael K. Silber, "The Historical Experience of German Jewry and Its Impact on Haskalah and Reform in Hungary", in Jacob Katz (ed.), *Toward Modernity: The European Jewish Model* (New Brunswick, NJ: Transaction Books, 1987), pp. 108ff; László Varga, "Zsidó bevándorlás Magyarországon" [Jewish Immigration into Hungary] *Századok* 126:1 (1992), especially pp. 61–67.
17. On Dohm, see Horst Möller, "Über die bürgerliche Verbesserung der Juden": Christian Wilhelm Dohm und seine Gegner", in Marianne Awerbuch (ed.), *Bild und Selbstbild der Juden Berlins zwischen Aufklärung und Romantik; Beiträge zu einer Tagung* (Berlin: Colloquium, 1992), pp. 60–62; Robert Liberles, "The Historical Context of Dohm's Treatise on the Jews," in *Das deutsche Judentum und der Liberalismus: Dokumentation eines internationalen Seminars* (Sankt Augustin: COMDOK-Verlagsabteilung, 1986), pp. 44–51. For a partial English translation of Dohm's treatise, see Paul Mendes-Flohr and Yehuda Reinharz (eds), *Jew in the Modern World: A Documentary History* (3rd edition, Oxford and New York: Oxford University Press, 2011), pp. 27–33.
18. On this dimension of the debate over Jewish emancipation in Hungary, see Guy Miron, "Between 'Center' and 'East': The Special Way of Jewish Emancipation in Hungary", *Jewish Studies at the Central European University* 4 (2004–2005), pp. 113–114.
19. Baron József Eötvös, *The Village Notary: A Romance of Hungarian Life*, trans. Otto Wenckstern (New York, 1850).
20. Michael Silber, "Budapest", pp. 267–268.
21. Mack Walker, *German Home Towns: Community, State, and General Estate, 1648–1871* (Ithaca: Cornell University Press, 1998), p. 33.
22. See my discussion in Lupovitch, "Beyond the Walls: The Beginnings of Pest Jewry", *Austrian History Yearbook* 36 (2005), pp. 45–46.
23. Ibid., pp. 50–51; Silber "Budapest", p. 265.
24. Michael Stanislawski, *Tsar Nicholas I and the Jews: The transformation of Jewish society in Russia, 1825–1855* (Philadelphia: Jewish Publication Society of

America, 1983), pp. 39ff. Cf. here the use of conscription as a potential solution to juvenile delinquency during the First World War in Germany in the chapter in this volume by Sarah Bornhorst.

25. Gábor Bona, "Az 1848–49-es honvédsereg zsidó születésü tisztjei" [Jewish Officers in the Army in 1848–49] *Múlt és Jövö* 1 (1998), pp. 59–61.
26. See, for example, *Protokol der Pest Juden Gemeinde* #17 (1847); #111 (1855); #21 (1873).
27. Ibid., #34 (1823).
28. For a detailed account of Hochmut and the Brody Fund, see Howard Lupovitch, *Jews at the Crossroads: Tradition and Accommodation during the Golden Age of the Hungarian Nobility* (Budapest: CEU Press, 2007), pp. 176ff.
29. Hochmut, "Die Jüdische Schule", p. 181.
30. See, for example, *Protokol der Pest Juden Gemeinde* #25 (1846); #122 (1856); #26 (1873).
31. "Budapesti Talmud Egylet", in Péter Újvari (ed.), *Magyar zsidó lexikon*, (Budapest, 1929), p. 158.
32. Glenn Dynner, "The Hasidic Conquest of Small-town Central Poland, 1754–1818", *Polin: Studies in Polish Jewry* 17 (2004), pp. 53ff.
33. Estimates of the size of the Budapest Orthodox community range from 30,000 to 50,000. To my mind, the most accurate calculation is that of Kinga Frojimovics, summarized in Frojimovics, *Szétszakadt Történelem: Zsidó vallási irányatok Magyarországon, 1868–1950* (Budapest: Balassi Kiadó, 2006), pp. 126–127.
34. "Traditional" and "Orthodox" refer to two distinct though overlapping categories of religious observant Jews. Michael Silber aptly distinguished between the two by defining traditional as unselfconscious observance and Orthodoxy as a more self-conscious choice to observe. Silber, "Ultra-Orthodoxy: the Invention of a Tradition", in Jack Wertheimer (ed.), *The Uses of Tradition*, pp. 21–22.
35. Árpad Tóth, "Asszonyok a városi szegénység ellen: a pesti Jótekony Nöegylet korai története" (1817–1833) [Ladies against urban poverty: the early history of the Pest Women's Charitable Society], in Gyáni Gábor and Séllei Nóra (eds), *Nök a modernizálódó társadalomban* [Women in a modernizing Society] (Debrecen: Csokonai Kiado, 2005), pp. 147–162.
36. Katalin Gerő, *Szeretet Munkásai*, p. 86.
37. In 1886, for example, only 199 forints were allocated. See *"Pest Zsidó Nöegylet"*, in *Magyar Zsidó Szemle* XIV (1887), p. 391.
38. Katalin Gerő, *Szeretet Munkásai*, pp. 229–230.

5
Latina/o Youths Gangs in Spain in Global Perspective

Miroslava Chávez-García

On 28 October 2003, 15-year-old Ronny Tapias was gunned down in the late afternoon outside his school in Barcelona, Spain. News of his death sent shockwaves throughout the Catalonian city and beyond. Alarmed about the growing skirmishes involving youths in the region, the press dubbed it a gang-related killing. The public, in turn, became incensed about the crime, attributing it to the recent waves of Latin American immigrants to Barcelona specifically and Spain generally. Ronny Tapias, you see, was not a native-born Catalonian or Spanish youth, but rather a "Latino" youth of Colombian origin.[1] Reportedly, the Ñetas, a gang in Barcelona with ties to Latin America and the US, killed him because they believed he was a member of *los Latin Kings*, a rival Latino and Latina (or Latina/o) gang originating in the US, specifically in Chicago and, later, New York City. Tapias was not a member of either group, however. His murder, the police reported, was a case of mistaken identity.[2]

Despite Tapias's tragic death, the press, politicians and the public used the incident to incite a moral panic over the troubling and growing presence of what were (and are) known as "Latino" immigrants and "Latino" youth gangs in Barcelona and across Spain. Though the majority of Spanish-speaking Latin American and Caribbean peoples did not (and still do not) identify as "Latinos" prior to their arrival in Spain, it is through a process of what Carles Feixa, an expert on Latina/o youth gangs in Barcelona, calls "triangulation" that this occurs. That is, through the process of migration and through the youths' interactions with Catalan, Spanish and other Latin American youths in public spaces – in the parks and schools – Spanish-speaking youths from Latin America and the Caribbean adopt an identity as Latinas/os that serves to differentiate them from native, Catalan and Spanish youth. Latina/o youths' phenotype, language, style and tastes in music also work to mark them as non-natives – as Latinas/os, according to Feixa. The media, in turn, uses the label to reinforce their status as outsiders and as ignorant, impoverished and criminally minded members of society. In the process, the media maligns their character, culture and larger purpose in the country.[3]

In the instance of Tapias's murder, the media used the incident among Latina/o youths to marginalize further already socially, economically and politically disenfranchised immigrant communities and to criminalize them, a process that began in the 1980s, when Latinas/os migrated in significant numbers to southern Europe in search of employment opportunities.[4] It was only in recent years, in the early 2000s, with state policies promoting family reunification, that the migration of young Latin Americans to southern European countries increased significantly.[5] While in the case of Tapias's murder the majority of Spaniards called for swift, punitive measures against perceived Latina/o gang members and their allies, only a few called for investigations into understanding the nature of immigration from Latin America, the gender, racial, ethnic and class profile of immigrants, youths and gangs and their place in Spanish society.

Indeed, to quell the growing crisis and restore civic order as well as the public image of Barcelona, the prevention unit of the city's town council – *Ayuntamiento de Barcelona* – sought the services of academics and community activists who could provide insight into the circumstances surrounding Tapias's murder, Latina/o youth culture and Latina/o youth gangs.[6] Among the leading scholars they contacted was Carles Feixa, an anthropologist at the Universidad de Lleida in Catalonia, who had researched and published extensively on youth cultures in the region as well as in Spain and Mexico. Intrigued by the growing presence of these youths and what they represented in Catalonia and beyond, Feixa, in turn, assembled a group of academics, students and community activists at the local, national and international level to take part in a summit where they could devise a research agenda focusing on Latina/o youth gangs and Latina/o youth culture – as well as Latina/o culture and peoples in general – in the urban centres, particularly in Barcelona.

Through the use of extensive oral histories, focus groups and participant observation, they launched a project inquiring into the nature of urban youth culture in public spaces, an issue that had become hotly contested at the regional and national levels. That research, in turn, prompted growing attention to the study of Latina/o youths throughout Spain and, to some extent, in other regions of Europe. The work brought greater understanding to the larger processes of gang formation and its manifestation in Europe and helped to ease tensions over the increasing Latina/o immigrant population. It also helped to unravel the role of transnationalism and globalization in the formation of global, migrant communities and youth cultures.[7] Not surprisingly, European researchers were (and continue to be) responsible for carrying out the majority of investigations focusing on Latina/o youths in Spain and elsewhere in Europe, while US scholars generally ignore Latina/o youths abroad and the parallels between these young people and Latina/o youths in the US. While a few academics have begun to explore the experiences of Latina/o youths across the globe as well as the processes of migration, globalization and marginalization and the impact on identity, belonging and citizenship, few scholars in the US have yet articulated the ways in which Latina/o youths across the globe in places such as Italy and Spain share similar experiences. Rather, much of the US-based work on Latina/o youths and Latina/o youth gangs remains squarely within national-political borders. Indeed, a transnational or comparative approach toward Latina/o youths is still lacking.[8]

To come to a better understanding of Latina/o youths and Latina/o youth gangs or *bandas* in Spain, in particular, and to begin to comprehend how their experiences compare to those of their counterparts in the US, this chapter explores the early research on Latina/o youths and Latina/o youth gangs as well as their intersection with migration, marginalization and globalization in Spain. It demonstrates that, while a handful of scholars, such as Carles Feixa, Margaret Gibson and Silvia Carrasco, have expanded the scope and depth of our knowledge considerably, much more research needs to be done to answer many new questions emerging from the research, particularly dealing with the youths' perspectives and voices, which are too often obscured in academic research and in everyday life. A few younger scholars, including Anne Rios-Rojas and Jennifer Lucko, have begun to address a host of unresolved issues such as citizenship, identity and belonging as well as the role of educational tracking in the forging of Latina/o identities, though much more needs to be done if we are to listen to the voices of Latina/o youths on their own terms and to develop appropriate mechanisms for social integration that take into account and allow room for cultural and racial differences. Only then will the young people thrive in their new environments and find productive ways to contribute to their communities and the larger society.

Studying Latina/o youth gangs in Spain

This research on Latina/o youth gangs in Barcelona builds upon recent studies by the "Eurogang" network of scholars who examine the impact of migration, ethnicity and gender on youths in an increasingly global economy.[9] My own work demonstrates that the rise of delinquency or perceived delinquency among Latina/o youths in Spain did not develop as it did in the US, as a result of early twentieth-century "modernization" and the problems resulting from industrialization, urbanization and immigration in ethnic neighbourhoods and, later in the mid-twentieth, post-Second World War period, as the processes of deindustrialization, suburbanization and expansion of the urban underclass led to few opportunities for those in urban areas and especially communities of colour. Rather, late twentieth-century changes in the global economy, gender roles and relations, and migration patterns, as well as the rise of violence from the US-led "drug wars", increasingly proto-nationalist states and global youth culture – fuelled by new media and technologies – have contributed to the marginalization, criminalization and racialization of immigrant, Latina/o youths. These processes emerged most visibly in the 1990s and 2000s, when globalization and changing social, economic, political and cultural dynamics in Latin America, the Caribbean, the US and Europe led increasing numbers of Latina women, many of them single mothers, to migrate across the Atlantic in search of a livelihood for themselves and the families they left behind with loved ones. Rather than risk the increasingly militarized zone and tightening immigration policies of the US, as generations had done before them, migrants from the Americas have turned their attention to Europe, particularly with its lure of contract work in unskilled fields, including child care, elderly care and agriculture. After 2000, as a result of family reunification policies in Spain, Latinas sent for children they had not seen in years, expecting to create a fulfilled home life. The reality was the contrary, however, particularly when the migrant youths, many of them dark-skinned, impoverished, lacking two-parent households, were racialized in a European context. Alienated in their new environment and estranged from their parents, they sought peers who shared a similar youth culture and understanding of the challenges of living in a foreign land where they were (and are) misunderstood at best and shunned at worst.

This chapter also contributes to the history of children and childhood by exploring how Latina/o youths in Spain are viewed not as children or minors who need special attention. Rather, they are often treated in the media and the law like their adult immigrant counterparts. Like the growing number of undocumented and unaccompanied minors crossing the US-Mexico border with the aim of reuniting with mothers and fathers who have gone before them, Latina/o youths in Spain are forced to take on "adult" roles and responsibilities when they migrate abroad to reunite with family. As recent migrants, lacking deeply rooted family and social networks as well as cultural resources, as compared to young Mexican immigrants to the US who can more easily adapt to the Latino-influenced "American" society, Latina/o youths in Europe are often thrust into a society in which they must negotiate institutions and individuals largely on their own. While cultural and community-based organizations (*casals* and *casals de juventuds*) are growing in working-class, immigrant, ethnic neighbourhoods, they are too few and far between to accommodate the needs of Latina/o youths who must negotiate a new language, culture and educational expectations.[10] Mexican immigrant youths, in contrast, whose family members have migrated for generations to the US and once called the present-day southwest "home", have access to extended family networks, cultural resources and self-help community centres that assist them in their transition to the new society. Moreover, Mexican immigrants and second generation Mexican Americans make up significant sectors of the population, particularly in major cities such as Los Angeles, Chicago and San Antonio. In many if not most communities in Mexico, travelling to the US is a rite of passage and cultural expectation for young men and, increasingly, young women.

Scholars have only recently paid serious attention to Latina/o youths in Europe and the development of these Latina/o youth cultures and street gangs, or *bandas*, in Spain. This was largely a result of the public and media pressure on the authorities to "do something" about Latina/o youth gangs following Ronny Tapias's murder in 2003, mentioned earlier. For nearly a decade prior, researchers had examined patterns of migration, globalization and marginalization within the context of Latin America and Europe, with much of the work focusing on the regions of and flows from South America and the Caribbean to Spain, yet few had or have explored the experiences of the youths who have only recently arrived.[11] In Spain, Tapias's death and the calls for a thorough investigation led several scholars to turn their attention to researching the gangs involved in Tapias's death, particularly the most visible group, los Latin Kings, an organization with ties to the Latin Kings in the US and Ecuador.[12] Unlike US hard-core street gangs or *pandillas*, which up until recently defined themselves by territory and illicit activities, *bandas* are not defined by geography but do involve some level of criminal activity. Experts and the local authorities in Barcelona generally do not agree, however, on los Latin Kings' status as a "gang". The group's incorporation in 2006 as a "cultural organization" in Barcelona further called into question their gang status. Yet, alongside the "Reyes and Reinas Latinos" (Latino Kings and Queens) of Barcelona, a street-oriented branch of los Latin Kings continues to exist, reinforcing the belief among many that they are, indeed, a gang.[13]

As we saw at the beginning, among the principal researchers to become involved in studying Latina/o youth gangs and youths in general in Spain was Carles Feixa. As a leading scholar on youth cultures in Catalonia, Spain and Mexico, the press – television, radio and print media – sought his expertise on youth culture, hoping that he could explain more clearly the recent phenomenon of Latina/o youth gangs in Spain in the early 2000s.[14] Following Feixa's appearance on a widely viewed Catalonian television show, *La Nit al Dia* (From Night to Day), geared to Catalonian-speaking audiences, he received a lot of attention. Feixa, along with local officials, including Lluis Paradell, a *moço de escuadra* (state policeman) with the Barcelona police department and key player in connecting with and befriending Latina/o youths in the region, fielded questions about Latina/o youth gangs, specifically los Latin Kings. The public was much more interested in learning about los Latin Kings, rather than los Ñetas, explained Feixa, because of the former's hyper-visibility in the public arena and their greater number. Los Ñetas, in turn, a more modest group with roots in Puerto Rico and New York, maintained a low profile. "Since then other groups have emerged but the Latin Kings have always captured the spotlight," Feixa stated.[15]

Ironically, Feixa confessed in an interview that, at the time of the television appearance, he knew little about los Latin Kings in Barcelona. Despite his limited knowledge, the episode was a hit with audiences, for Catalonians desired to learn more about these young people, who up until that point had remained largely unknown and in the shadows of Catalonian and Spanish society. The television show, in turn, piqued Feixa's curiosity and motivated him to delve into the study of los Latin Kings, for their presence seemed to him *"una cosa extraña"* (a strange phenomenon). While he knew about the varieties of youth gangs in Spain and Mexico and the increased migration from Latin America and the Caribbean to Spain, he said he knew little about the presence of street-oriented youth gangs modelled on Latina/o gangs in the US, the *pandillas*. *Bandas*, in contrast, as noted earlier, are less structured, non-institutionalized groups of young people. Through the process of migration, he stated, Latina/o youth gangs, such as los Latin Kings, have emerged in places such as Barcelona and Madrid, Spain and Genova, Italy. To what extent Latina/o gangs were directly exported from the US or some other country to Spain or organized in Spain by young people adopting images from the US-dominated media and popular culture, is uncertain, however. Scholars have only recently begun to explore their emergence in cities throughout Europe and their link to earlier, nineteenth- and twentieth-century notions of delinquency as they emerged in the West and spread across the globe.

Today, the term "Latino gangs" (or *"bandas Latinas"*) has become naturalized in Barcelona and Spain with reference to gangs in general. Despite the long-term presence of other racial/ethnic gangs in Barcelona and Spain, today only Latinas/os are linked directly to *bandas*. Originally, the term *"bandas"* emerged in the 1970s and 1980s to describe suburban street youths, primarily gypsies and the sons and daughters of recent migrants from the south of Spain, involved in petty crime or in trafficking heroin. In the 1980s and 1990s, the term "urban tribes" supplanted "gangs" to describe loosely organized groups of street-oriented youths in Spain. It was not until the emergence of significant numbers of Latina/o youths in the early 2000s that the term *"bandas Latinas"* resurfaced to describe groups of young Latinos gathering in public spaces, apparently up to no good. Unsupervised, uneducated and unemployed, they represent the antithesis of a modernized society with modern family values and structures rooted in late nineteenth- and early twentieth-century middle-class Western notions of propriety and decorum. As such they come to embody delinquency, or *delincuencia*, a visible threat to the stability of the Catalonian and Spanish state. "Paradoxically," Feixa stated, "Moroccan minors, who often appear to be 'typical' gang members, are rarely described [in a similar way]."[16] In short, among their peers, Latina/o youths have been racialized and criminalized as delinquent youths, or *delincuentes*, most notably in the Spanish media.

Tracking the marginalization of Latina/o youths and Latina/o youth gangs in Spain

The racialization and criminalization of Latina/o youth gangs in the late twentieth century is not surprising, given that most Latina/o immigrants and their children in Barcelona and in Spain more broadly, the majority foreign-born, live in the shadows of society. Strict immigration rules and regulations as well as public attitudes toward non-European

Union immigrants make it nearly impossible for Latina/o families to live on a par with native-born Spaniards or other western Europeans living in Spain. Such immigration laws first emerged in the mid-1980s, with the attempt to control and stimulate labour migration from across the globe to meet the demand for workers in Spain following the strengthening of its economy after many years of stagnation under the Franco regime and the joining of the European Union (EU). While the first law, the 1985 Organic Law on the Rights and Liberties of Foreigners, guaranteed the rights of foreign residents and immigrants' integration into Spanish society, it made distinctions between desirable and undesirable migrants, that is, between EU immigrants and non-EU immigrants respectively. The former were guaranteed all the rights of free movement, residence and work in Spain, while those outside the EU required visas. Those who planned to stay longer than 90 days also required permits, which guaranteed them rights of assembly, public education and unionization, as long as they did not infringe on the national interests or "rights and liberties of Spaniards". The laws also outlined the terms for deportations and made it so that lacking a proper residence or work permit, engaging in anti-government activities or being convicted of a felony, among other activities, guaranteed expulsion. In short, Latina/o immigrants and their counterparts from other non-EU countries faced many restrictions that their EU counterparts did not.[17]

To deal with the perceived increase of illegal immigrants and to "protect" other EU countries from the spread of undesirable migrants, Spain passed a law in 1991 regularizing undocumented workers, guaranteeing them legal status for one year. Yet, that same year, another measure was passed restricting the entrance of immigrants from Peru and the Dominican Republic as well as the Maghreb countries, requiring them to have visas, when they had been previously exempt. At the same time, increased immigration restrictions and labour shortages particularly in domestic service – as a result of changing gender roles in the Spanish home and women's entry into the labour force in significant numbers – resulted in the passage of annual quotas for foreign workers in domestic service, agriculture and unskilled construction work, among other job categories. The new quotas, in turn, reshaped labour migration patterns, leading to the feminization of the migrant labour force, particularly from Latin American and Caribbean countries including the Dominican Republic, Colombia, Ecuador and Peru.[18] Despite the strict laws, Spain was forced to recognize the presence of a large undocumented population and passed a law – the third of its kind – in 1996 providing for the legalization of undocumented workers, those whose work permits had lapsed and who had been unable to renew them. A significant departure in recent years, it allowed permanent residence status and work permits for those who could prove they had legal status for at least six years, successfully renewing their permits with no lapses, along the lines of the US' Immigration Reform and Control Act (IRCA) of 1986, more commonly known as "amnesty". Despite the effort to bring a segment of the society from out of the shadows, the law was unevenly applied at the local and regional level.[19]

Latina/o immigrants witnessed perhaps the most progressive move in immigration policies in 2000, though the gains were short-lived. In April of that year, the Organic law was revised once again, enhancing immigrants' rights and the process of legalization, and broadening access to social services. It also extended the right to public education to all immigrant children, regardless of legal status. Immigrants, too, were given the right to access the national health care system, public housing and social security provisions. Not all segments of the Spanish population welcomed the measures. In fact, an upsurge in opposition emerged and within four months, combined with a change in the governing political party, the new government repealed nearly all the provisions and enacted a harsh set of new measures dealing with undocumented and documented migrants. In effect, the new law denied illegal immigrants the rights of assembly, collective bargaining, strikes and joining labour unions and allowed police to hold undocumented immigrants for up to 45 days in detention centres and to deport them within 72 hours. It also eliminated most rights of undocumented immigrants to access social services except health care, compulsory public education and legal assistance for asylum proceedings and in many ways linked immigration violations with criminal violations. Legal immigrants also felt the brunt of this law, for it limited family reunification to immediate family members and restricted legal and public aid. It also placed many conditions on permanent residency requirements, including five years of continuous legal work contracts and work permits. For those undocumented in Spain, legalization through the quota system was cut off. Only newly arrived workers with contracts in hand were eligible to legalize their status.[20]

The strict laws forced Latinas/os – as well as other non-EU immigrants, primarily Africans and eastern Europeans – to live in largely segregated communities as a result of limited access to work permits, decent wages and residency rights. In 2004, a report estimated that there were likely "up to 1 million undocumented residents in Spain".[21] Many of those were (and are) Latina/o immigrants living in Barcelona and Madrid and, like many undocumented Latinas/os in the US, they find employment in low-paying domestic service work, agriculture, tourism, construction or the underground economy. And, like their counterparts in the US, they, too, are disproportionately incarcerated as a result of racial profiling and strict residency laws and are likely to receive much harsher sentences than their Catalonian counterparts. As unskilled, poor and often dark-skinned foreigners from rural areas of the Caribbean and Latin America, Latinas/os find they are wanted for their labour, but unwelcomed as members of society, forcing them to live on the margins of society. As Kitty Calavita argues, despite the public and legal discourse of inclusion of immigrants in Spain, the reality is exclusion, racism and marginalization in many aspects of daily life, including work, housing, health care and education.[22]

Legislation aimed at Latinas/os has not yet surfaced in Spain or in Barcelona, according to Carlos Feixa. State legislators have, however, as noted earlier, passed exclusionary and coercive laws affecting all foreigners whose country of origin does not belong to the EU. Moreover, in Madrid, where (according to Catalonians) the laws are more restrictive against immigrants than in Barcelona, los Latin Kings are classified as an "illicit association", alongside well known terrorist groups such as ETA and Al Qaeda.[23] Even in Catalonia, a region that prides itself on the "inclusion" of foreigners, including *bandas*, the authorities have taken measures to toughen their stance against gangs. In 2006, for instance, a law was passed making any crime, committed by a known gang member, an aggravated offense. More recently, with the economic crisis in Spain, Feixa expects that lawmakers will increase the penalties against suspected gang members and immigrants committing crimes. "The new centrist-right leaning government in Catalonia", Feixa acknowledged, "is pushing a 'zero tolerance' policy against *bandas*, unraveling the inroads to integration made with such groups in the past".[24]

Ironically, as Feixa, Kitty Calavita and other scholars argue, immigrants are crucial to the Spanish economy and society. "The birthrate in Spain is low, with less than 1.2 children per couple," Calavita reports, indicating that the society is not replacing itself. By the year 2050, "they will have the oldest population in the world". Immigrants' natural reproduction is, however, easing the depopulation of the country. Immigrants also play an important role in the nation for their ability to pay into the pension system, which is currently "billions in debt". "Today, immigrants are credited with adding a surplus to the social security system in Spain," Calavita writes.[25]

Despite the limited opportunities in Spain, Latin Americans are often forced to leave their economically distressed countries of origin, some of those places ravaged by war and violence and others by political corruption, to find ways to maintain their families. With the increasingly strict immigrations laws of the US, particularly those introduced in the 1990s and those following 11 September 2001, making it nearly impossible for those without family members to migrate to *el norte* (the north, the US), Latinas/os have been forced to migrate to European countries, including Spain and Italy, to work as contract labourers and often as undocumented workers. After a number of years, many of these migrants bring their children to their new home country, expecting educational opportunities and, eventually, social mobility. Yet, soon after they arrive they find that their children must negotiate a host of new social, cultural, economic and political environments, bringing a level of uncertainty and unease in their transition.[26]

Working with los Latin Kings and los Ñetas in Barcelona

In the early 2000s, when Ronny Tapias's death occurred, many Catalonians remained unaware of or indifferent to the underlying conditions shaping the changing demographics and cultural landscape of the region that had given rise to Latina/o youth gangs. In contrast, the Barcelona City Council, specifically Josep Lahosa, from the city prevention services unit, was interested in understanding the Latina/o youth gangs, their nature, influences and roles in society. Lahosa, like the press, turned to Feixa to lead an academic and community-based inquiry into the nature of Latina/o youth gangs and Latina/o youth culture more broadly. Lahosa was particularly interested in having Feixa provide alternatives to the media reports, for the city official doubted the largely inflammatory press coverage and wanted to quell public outcry. "Complaints arrived from fathers and mothers of Spanish and Catalonian youths who had joined the Latin Kings, of the fights in the *barrios* (neighbourhoods), problems in the schools," Feixa noted. Yet when the local authorities, social educators and police sought answers to the questions posed by parents, they had few sources of information. The internet contained little on los Latin Kings in Catalonia and Spain, only links to the US FBI, to Chicago and to New York. All they had to go on, Feixa noted, were the legends and myths about los Latin Kings in Barcelona.[27]

With the assistance of scholars in Barcelona, Feixa set out to build a research team of national and international and scholars to delve more deeply into Latina/o youth gangs and Latina/o youth culture more broadly. Among those recruited was Marcia Esparza, a sociologist from the John Jay School of Criminal Justice at the City University of New York. Esparza, in turn, provided access to publications and contact with Luis Barrios, the Anglican priest and psychologist who had worked with the US-based Latin Kings in New York and with David Brotherton, a sociologist from the John Jay School of Criminal Justice at the City University New York and co-author with Barrios of *The Almighty Latin King and Queen Nation*, a study of the evolution of the Latin King and Queen Nation in New York.[28] In Feixa's discussions with the US-based scholars, "[w]e began to see that there were some possible links" across the globe, he noted.[29]

In addition to reading everything he could find pertaining to los Latin Kings, Feixa and his team focused on carrying out ethnographic research to learn about Latina/o youth culture and gang culture in particular. Yet, the most difficult aspect of the research was, Feixa admitted, securing access to los Latin Kings. Initially, Feixa learned from the city council that youth gangs met regularly at a local *casal de juventud*, a city-funded youth centre. The director of the *casal*, Feixa noted, was open to his presence at the youth centre but had no idea of the themes he pursued. Feixa's presence and attempts to speak to the youths brought the young people unwanted attention, for as soon as the staff learned that they were members of a *banda*, they alerted the police. Feixa had to work to prevent the police from expelling the Latina/o youths from the *casal*, which was an area of city youth services in the hands of the *Esquerra Republicana*, the left-wing, pro-independence branch of the Catalonian Independence party. According to Feixa, the Republicans argued that city youth centres were "not spaces for delinquents". In contrast, the political party in charge of city security, the Socialists, responded to their presence by saying, "leave them a bit more space, let's see what happens". The city council, in turn, also supported the notion of befriending los Latin Kings, saying: "Before expelling them, let's see what they're like, let's not prejudge them." Fortunately, the director of the *casal* also opened the doors to them.

A month later, Feixa sent los Latin Kings a letter, requesting an interview and offering to collaborate with them in mediating city institutions. To gain the young people's confidence, Feixa included another letter of support from and signed by the team of researchers in the US, Luis Barrios, David Brotherton and Marcia Esparza, who had connected with and befriended the New York-based Latin Kings and Queens. Even though Feixa had yet to meet Barrios, Brotherton and Esparza, he hoped the written communication would facilitate a dialogue with los Latin Kings. The letters seemed however to have little effect in establishing a line of communication with los Latin Kings until they found themselves surrounded by police looking to eject them from and arrest them at the *casal*.

One Sunday, during which an *"universal"* or assembly of Latin Kings was held at the *casal*, there was also a massive police raid apparently aimed at the *casal* and los Latin Kings. The director took the opportunity to remind the youths of Feixa's letters, to which they had yet to respond. Seeing few alternatives, "Manaba", a young male leader of los Latin Kings, called Feixa from the *casal* with palpable anxiety, asking for his assistance. After the phone call, Manaba apparently calmed down after Feixa managed to convince the police not to detain anyone, though they did record their identities in police records (*"ficharon a todos"*, Feixa noted). "I didn't promise him anything," Feixa stated, "only the possibility of speaking on their behalf." Manaba saw few options, Feixa concluded; either the young men would land in jail or in the hands of the researchers. They were not completely convinced of the researchers' intentions, but they opted to take their chances.[30]

With the support of the city council, Feixa assembled a group of academics, community leaders, immigrant activists and young Latina/o researchers as well as members of *La Nación de los Reyes y Reinas Latinos* and *la Asociación Ñeta*, to carry out one-on-one interviews, focus groups and observations of Latina/o youths, Latina/o youth gangs and Latina/o youth culture in social settings and public spaces in and around Barcelona. In a collective effort, they interviewed dozens of Latina/o youths, non-Latina/o youths in middle and high school, and a variety of adults from all walks of life, including prevention educators, psychologists, parents, teachers and international academics. They found most of their interviewees through personal contacts, community-based organizations and word of mouth. Through that process, they amassed dozens of narratives and hundreds of pages of notes based on "floating" observations, which Feixa explained was not a "pure" ethnographic approach, but rather a process that allowed for the analysis of social boundaries of cultural groups. At the same time, they researched archival records including city reports and the role of the media – newspapers and television news shows – in its portrayal of Latina/o youths generally and in its coverage of the trial in the case of Ronny Tapias's death, the youth gunned down in 2003. Coincidentally, that trial was underway while they carried out the research, doubtless giving their work a greater sense of urgency.[31]

From the research, Feixa's team found no simple answers to the questions about the character and nature of Latina/o *bandas* in Spain. Rather, the team determined that ambiguity characterized the presence of Latina/o gangs in a transnational context, specifically in Spain. That is, it remained unclear if the youth groups were exports from the Americas to Europe, if they were grassroots organizations developed in Spain by Latin American youths influenced by popular images of US gangs and gang culture, or if they were a result of a combination of influences from abroad and at home. Among the few things the team did determine was that the term "*banda*" or "*pandilla*" reflected negatively on all Latina/o youth, regardless of the professed nature of membership in a youth group. Whether Feixa's team realized it or not, through its study on *jovenes* Latinas/os and los Latin Kings, the team also worked to label or identify the youths associated with the study as "gang" members or affiliates, a risk that is undertaken when such research is carried out.[32] Yet, Feixa argued, it was important to focus on the presence of groups that identified as gangs in order to call attention to the existence of real challenges and barriers to social integration for immigrant youths in Spain. If society failed to pay attention to the exclusion of these youths, he concluded, it became easy to ignore it and assume it did not exist.

Despite the limitations of some of the research, the team did determine that *bandas* were often linked to particular nation states or nationalities and operated as sources of identity, belonging and citizenship. Youth gangs in Spain, they found, were more closely allied to the North American gangs than to the Latin American tradition of *pandillas* or *naciones*. *Pandillas* are urban in character, have territorial power and are located in specific zones. The territory of a *pandilla* is sacred, primarily because the majority of the members are born into these organizations. As the researchers described them, the gang members should be seen neither as victims nor heroes in society. North American gangs, in contrast, traditionally base their membership on nationality, territory and masculinity, while today they are increasingly understood as being more highly developed and complex mechanisms that do not solely function or base their power on territory alone. The Latin Kings in New York, for instance, at one point viewed as an apolitical organization, have a political purpose and are considered a social movement (with a more elaborate structure). Today, some believe the US-based Latin Kings have transnational franchises with multiple global connections.[33]

Feixa's team of scholars also determined that Latina/o youth gangs, as peer groups, are critical sources of identity, belonging and citizenship for young Latina/o immigrants, who are often relegated to the economic, social, cultural and political margins of Spanish society. When they arrive in Europe, the youths often wonder: "Who am I?" and "Where is home and where do I belong?" Implicitly, they question: "What claims can I make on the nation-state and what, in turn, are my obligations to it?" At the same time that Latina/o youths grappled (and continue to grapple) with questions of identity, belonging and citizenship in their adopted country, the researchers found that through the experiences of migration, integration and exclusion, in which youth subcultures collided and came together as hybrid cultures across transnational and cyber spaces, new pan-Latina/o identities and youth cultures emerged. Though unstable as a result of immigration policies and practices, Latina/o youth cultures and youth gangs in Spain are constantly evolving and in motion.[34]

In addition to organizations such as los Latin Kings, Feixa's team found that some other Latina/o youth gangs structure their group on the tradition of transnationalism. Such gangs participate in youth subcultures known as "urban tribes" or *tribus urbanas* who are known to pick and borrow from transnational youth cultures. They are often in conflict and sometimes they work creatively. The researchers also found that some *bandas* are associated with the "virtual" tradition. These are *bandas* that occupy new spaces – cyberspace – to create communities based on mutual understandings and issues relevant to the group. These groups reach across the globe, have nomad identities and inhabit what Feixa calls "post-industrial sites" of belonging.[35]

Listening to Latina/o youth gangs speak out

The ethnographic research carried out on Latina/o youths has not only provided insight into the nature of Latina/o youth gangs but also an opportunity for the "voices" of the young people themselves to emerge. These voices, in turn, came together to give witness to the common experiences of migration, belonging and identity. Most of these youths voiced a strong connection to their home country, where they spent much of their childhood under the care or tutelage of an extended family member, while their mothers (or fathers or both parents) worked and lived in Spain. They experienced adolescence in what the researchers recognized as a "transnational family", in the care of grandparents or other relatives in their native country, while their biological parents resided elsewhere.[36] For the youths, the simple act of leaving behind this network of family and friends as well as the familiar sights and sounds of childhood – local spaces, public arenas, parks and nature as well as local musical styles, schooling and language – was described as traumatic and made worse when they landed in a large urban city and reunited with parents, increasingly their single mothers, whom they hardly knew. Forced to adjust to a new environment and a new mode of living, increasingly hidden away, not in the public spaces they frequented in their countries of origin, they expressed feeling an emptiness and an overwhelming sense of *destierro* (displacement) that shaped their longing for home over "there" and stability in their new home "here".[37]

Most youths also experienced a series of familial hardships once they arrived at their new destination. Among the first things they learned was that their parents had a distorted image of their own children, given the distance and time that had lapsed since they had last lived together. For the parents, time had stood still, while the children had grown quickly in the time of their parents' absence. The alienation between parent and child or children resulted quickly in strained relations, leading to tensions and battles. The youths also found that they no longer had consistent sources of money, as they had experienced in their home countries, where their parents regularly sent money to a grandmother or other relative to pay for their education, nutritious meals and diversions that would otherwise have been beyond their reach. The relatively low cost of living in their home countries meant that the remittances from abroad allowed them to live a comfortable life.[38] In contrast, the high cost of living in their new environment, in Spain, coupled with their parents' relatively low-paid employment, severely limited their economic choices, forcing them to go without. The youths soon realized that all they had with them were the belongings they brought them from home. Taken together, the shock of a new environment, lack of familiar faces and places, the sense of disconnection they felt from their parents, apparent impoverishment and marginalization in the larger society led to feelings of isolation and loneliness for many of them.[39]

Latina/o youths also expressed notable tensions with Catalonian youths over a range of issues. They noted that, being undocumented or unable to secure residency permits or work permits that would enable them to obtain residency, they were mistreated. Like their undocumented parents and adult peers, youths were disparaged openly for their outsider status. Latina/o youths also differed in their attitudes toward gender and sexuality. When asked to discuss differences between themselves and Catalonian youth, Latina/o youths said little about economic differences or class oppression but focused on attitudes toward gender roles and sexual mores. Catalonian girls, the Latina/o youths observed, were "liberal" with their dress and lifestyles, as compared to their young Latina counterparts. Españolas (or, *pavas*) too, who, the Spanish-speaking youths remarked, were often seen in company of Dominican males, who are generally regarded as highly suspect with their seemingly charged masculinity. European girls, they say, prefer Dominican youths for their "cool" hip-hop style and hyper-masculinity, as compared to their Catalonian counterparts. In many ways, the researchers found, the Latina/o youths uphold the idea of a virile, sexually dominant male, while disparaging sexually "loose" females, such as those they encountered in the Barcelona region.[40]

Latina/o youths' sense of identity is not necessarily rooted in a social and political consciousness in relation to the larger society, Feixa's team of researchers found. Nor is it linked to larger notions of what it means to be a Latina/o or to be part of a larger Latina/o community. Rather, Latina/o youth rely on an array of symbols and markers of identity to distinguish themselves in the public and in the larger society. They use language, their native Spanish, with its own unique tones and inflections, rather than learning the native Catalan. In fact, they find that they can manage without learning Catalan, even in the public school system, which mandates instruction in the language. There, as a last resort, youths are able to communicate with their teachers in Spanish. Many Latina/o youths also use their appearance, their dark skin and use of hip-hop cultural styles, specifically the rapper style, "*el ir de rapero*", including the baggy pants, hats, hairstyles and colour-coded wear, to distinguish themselves. While the hip-hop style has gone global in the last ten to 15 years, the Spanish continue to see it as being of foreign origin. The Latina/o youths use their musical tastes, too, dance music, specifically reggaeton, which they claim they carry "in their blood", to further identify themselves. Among the main activities that mark them as Latina/o youths, the researchers found, are *rapear* (rapping), playing basketball, tagging, playing soccer and hanging out.[41]

For Latina/o youth gangs, crime or criminal activity is not a defining feature of their identity. In fact, Feixa and a team of researchers – known as the Yougang project – are currently investigating the connection between youth gangs and criminal activities. It is true that Latino youths (as well as their adult counterparts) are overrepresented in jails and prisons, a condition of their hyper-criminalization. And, it is true that the majority of crimes they commit involve bodily injuries carried out in groups, but Feixa is hesitant to affirm that they carry out criminal acts to affirm their identity. "Rather, it is an involuntary result of their marginal status in the social and employment sector."[42]

Like the young Puerto Ricans Phillipe Bourgois studied in Spanish Harlem in New York, Latina/o youths, including Latina/o youth gangs, in Barcelona are in "search of respect".[43] The youths, however, often confuse respect with "recognition" and "equality" in society. The feelings of isolation and the stereotypes they face lead many of them down the path of gang formation and affiliation. Yet, not all youths who professed to have joined gangs were involved equally. Feixa and his team of researchers found variety among those who claimed gang member status. Nevertheless, membership in the youth groups or gangs provides them with protection and an affirmation of their identity vis-à-vis native Catalonian and other non-Latina/o youths.[44]

As the researchers found, a clear divide exists between the youths' countries of origin and their new homes, yet even "the ocean divide [did] not prevent the collapsing of both places and spaces– through memories and personal and collective contacts".[45] This collapsing of spaces has been facilitated through social networking and social media sites and tools, including instant messaging and, increasingly likely today, Skype, a video-audio connection enabling easy access to communication across the globe. Indeed, Latina/o neighbourhoods in Barcelona are filled with internet cafes where locals can communicate easily with family and friends across the Atlantic Ocean. The sense of "here" and "there", Feixa and the researchers have found, contributed to the forging of a "Latina/o identity". Indeed, that identity was formed through a dual process, that is, through the confluence of pre-existing national identities and through their interaction with new identities – Spanish-speaking youths from other Latin American and Caribbean countries as well as native Catalonians – in their new social environment, primarily in school and public spaces. Their identity is not primordial, Feixa and his team found, but is reproduced upon arrival and is formed in relation with other immigrants and adults, many of whom reject them. They come to an understanding of their own identity through shared experiences with those "*de aqui*" (from here, or the native-born) and those "*de alla*" (from there, those in their native country).[46]

Apparently, most adults, with the exception of the Latina/o youths' mothers, had little sympathy or empathy with the Spanish-speaking young people. In the interviews with Catalonian professors, educators and social workers, in which they spoke at length about the youths' experiences, including the solitude of arrival, the passage into the

Catalonian educational system, labour pool and *ambitos de relación* (places of leisure), many of the adults characterized Latina/o youngsters as problems. They pointed to the conflicts they experienced in the household with their families, low educational attainment and trouble in the streets with other youths and authorities as evidence of their inability to adjust to the society. Many Catalonians relinquished responsibility for their integration into society by simply noting, "they are not ours".[47]

The mothers of Latina/o youths, in contrast, laid blame on the larger structural experience of migration and integration as the primary causes of their estrangement in Spanish society. For the youths, they explained, the transformation of the family structure in the new environment, that is, the transition from having an extended family to perhaps having very few members of the family in the household, was traumatic. Moreover, mothers noted that they had little time to spend with or supervise their children because of their long hours at work, leaving them with a sense of a loss of control over their children's schooling and future in general. Doubtless, many of the generational issues they faced with their children were common to native-born Catalonian families but Latina mothers had to deal with older, often estranged youths, not with the young children or even toddlers they left behind in their countries of origin. As Nina Sorenson and Luis Guarnizo have found in their research on Colombian female migrants in Spain, "The women pay for their children's education, hoping to break the chain of poverty. In the process, these women risk their relationships with their children and their maternal love."[48] Indeed, both the mother and child have quite different expectations when they meet or see each other following an extended period of separation. Many mothers expected their children to study and ascend the socioeconomic ladder but the shock of the new place and new customs, such as having more freedom in the European city, and not being able to keep close watch over their schooling, has led some of the women to return their children to their country of origin (sometimes temporarily). Other women, who keep their children in Spain, turn for assistance to Latin American associations, who are generally supportive.[49]

Educators and professionals who work with Latina/o youths generally agreed that the change in family life was traumatic, particularly when they arrived in Spain and realized their mothers were not living a "high" lifestyle, despite the remittances sent home. Instead, the young people learned that their mothers occupied lowly positions as domestics and had few economic means, which, in turn, meant that they too had limited future options. Going abroad, the educators observed, led them to lose the most important aspects of their childhood: the lifestyle of their home country and their family and friends as well as their grand-mothers, in particular, who often raised them when their mothers were not around. The educators and professionals also noted that schooling and employment were among the most difficult issues for the Latina/o youths. The language barrier in school and their relatively low level of schooling in their countries of origin contributed to their challenges. They do poorly, the educators noted, even though they have high ambitions, which sets them up to fail.[50] Moreover, the teachers noted, the Spanish-speaking youths tended to stay with youths from their country of origin, though Ecuadorians intermingled with Colombians as did Argentinians with Chileans. Doubtless, the practice of Catalonian youths' shunning of their Latina/o counterparts contributed as well to the segregation of youth along ethnic and cultural lines. The Latina/o youths' proclivity to spend time in outdoor public spaces, as they often did in their countries of origin, also caused unease and contributed to their "othering" or outsider status. *"Hacen mucha vida en la calle"* (they spend a lot of their time in the streets), the teachers reported, and *"son mas callejeros [que nosotros]"*, that is, they spend more time in the streets than we, "Catalonians", do.[51]

Latin American associations, in contrast, are more sympathetic toward the Latina/o youths than the educators and professionals and fight on their behalf. The association representatives denounced the legal differences in the way migrant and native-born Catalonian youths (*autoctonos*) are treated and complained that the state allowed immigrant youths to come to Spain but provided few resources to help them in their transition to the new society. The representatives noted that Latina/o youths have few places of leisure where they can simply hang out and face discrimination in general because of their foreign origins. A Catalonian youth, they argued, can commit an anti-social or delinquent act and nothing is said, while, in contrast, when Latina/o youths carry out similar acts, they face the full brunt of the law and the authorities.[52]

Conclusion

While Latin American community organizations provide Latina/o youths with general support, it is the young people who must navigate a sea of competing interest groups, including Catalonian educators, professionals and youths as well as the Spanish media, public, legal authorities and even their own parents, among others, when seeking to define themselves in relation to the larger society and to shake the image of the "juvenile delinquent". It is a monumental task for them to understand – let alone negotiate – the expectations of a new social and cultural environment while remaining true to their own sense of what it means to be a Latina/o youth in a transnational context.

Only recently have we begun to understand what it means to them to belong, to identify as Latina or Latino in Barcelona and Spain more generally, and to claim citizenship – and not delinquency – in an increasingly globalized society. Today, a handful of well established and emerging scholars are making great strides in building our knowledge of Latina/o youths and Latina/o youth gangs in Spain and dispelling the myths behind their presence, culture and criminal tendencies. Margaret Gibson and Silvia Carrasco, for instance, well-known scholars in the US and Spain respectively, have collaborated on a comparative study analysing the experiences of Latina/o youths in the school systems of Barcelona and California. They find that despite the "welcoming" nature of the educational system for immigrants, the reality is that the young people face an unwelcoming environment and significant contradictions – both strengths and shortcomings – in the Spanish and US educational systems that ultimately fail the youths and the larger society.[53] Similarly, Jennifer Lucko, a young scholar, examines Latina/o (specifically Ecuadorian) youths' experience with schooling in Madrid and finds that academic tracking into low-achieving classrooms shapes the students' "emergent ethnic identity" in specific ways, while Anne Rios-Rojas, another young scholar, explores the ways in which Latina/o youths negotiate the multiple and, at times, contradictory messages about belonging and citizenship. Rios-Rojas finds that youths must negotiate "discourses that at times locate them as delinquents and terrorists and, at other times, as victims who require saving – but always as outsiders".[54]

Feixa and his team of researchers, including Luca Palmas, author of *Latino Atlantic* and the forthcoming *Public Enemies: The Fabrication of Gangs in Contemporary Europe*, suggest that we continue with collaborative investigations to examine the ways in which Latina/o youths claim public space as well as the nature of Latina/o youth gangs and delinquency, the structure and purpose of these organizations and the ways in which young people – immigrant or not – are attracted to them.[55] We must investigate, they urge, the role of migration and, we might add, marginalization and globalization in the formation of national and transnational gangs and of juvenile delinquency. They also suggest probing intervention strategies so as to move away from solely reactive and repressive approaches to troublesome youths and to work with migrant families in providing outreach, resources and education. And, ultimately, we must carry out these labours with their cultural needs and specificities at the forefront. Rather than obliging them to conform to some sense of what Catalonians or Spaniards expect of them, they should be allowed to carve out their path to citizenship and belonging on their own terms.[56]

As I have suggested, we cannot continue to use old approaches – studying the role of "modernization" and its effects on youths regardless of the specific cultural, social and historical contexts. Scholars need to pay attention to emerging transnational migratory flows, the role of sending and receiving countries and the role of new media and technologies in fostering and maintaining social and cultural links among youths abroad, at home and across the globe. Along with archival materials, we need to employ critical ethnography, oral interviews and popular culture analysis as well as traditional views of the economy, polity and society to look at the interplay between youths and the state as well as youths and the family and how they shape understandings and practices of juvenile delinquency. Only by doing so can we come to a closer understanding of the complicated dynamics shaping Latina/o youth cultures and Latina/o youth gangs in Barcelona, in Spain and across the globe.

Notes

1. I use the term "Latino" and "Latina" (or "Latina/o") to refer to male and female individuals of Latin American ancestry. I include foreign- and Spanish-born Latina/os in this category as well, though the overwhelming majority are first-generation immigrants. Not all identify as Latinas or Latinos; however, I use the term to link them with their Spanish-speaking counterparts in the US, with whom they share affinities. The largest groups in Spain are Colombians, Peruvians, Ecuadorians and Dominicans respectively. In Barcelona, Ecuadorians constitute the majority (23%) of Latinas/os in that city.

2. For more scholarly interpretations of Tapias's death, see, for instance, C. Feixa, L. Porzio, C. Recio and N. Canelles, "Jovenes y 'Bandas' Latinas en Barcelona: Fantasmas, Presencias, Espectros", in J.M. Valenzuela Arce, A.N. Domínguez and R.R. Cruz (eds), *Las Maras: Identidades Juveniles al Límite* (Casa Juan Pablos: El Colegio de la Frontera Norte, 2007), pp. 209–242. Leaders of the Latin Kings in the US dispute these claims. For instance, they challenge the notion that Latin Kings and Ñetas are enemies. Rather, they state, they work in partnership in the US. For the "official" point of view of the Latin Kings, see K. Mission, *The Official Globalization of the Almighty*

Latin King and Queen Nation (2008). Most recently, Carles Feixa stated that he now believes Tapias's death was the result of a struggle between Tapias and another youth over a female companion. Feixa is now in contact with one of the youths who was imprisoned as an "accomplice" in Tapias's murder. Interview, Carles Feixa, Barcelona, Spain, 9 July 2012, in author's possession. For UC Davis IRB approval, see Protocol # 306764–1, "Latina/o Youth Gangs in Global Perspective: An Interview with Dr. Carles Feixa".

3. For more on "Latina/o" identity, see C. Feixa, L. Porzio and C. Recio, *Jovenes Latina/os en Barcelona: Espacio Publico y Cultura Urbana* (Latina/os in Barcelona: Public Space and Urban Culture, 2005), especially Chapter 4. My information on "triangulation" for this essay comes from an interview with Feixa (Interview, Carles Feixa, Barcelona, Spain, 5 July 2012) and from my personal communication with legal scholars and members of the GERdis (Grup d'Estudis I Recerca sobre Drets I Inclusio Social) at the University of Barcelona, Carme Panchon and Isaac Ravetllat Balleste, 5 July 2012. For attitudes toward "foreigners", as reported in the international press, see, for instance, A. Ham, "Nervous Spaniards Count Cost of Growing Intake of Migrants", *The Age* (Melbourne, Australia), 11 March 2006, p. 24. "In Spain, you never had to worry about armed people coming into your homes," Fernando, a Madrid office worker, told *The Age*. "Now things are different and it's because of the immigrants."

4. For more on migration from Latin America to Spain, see, for instance, A. Bermudez, "The Transnational Political Practices of Colombians in Spain and the United Kingdom: Politics 'Here' and 'There' ", *Ethnic and Racial Studies*, 33, 1 (January 2010), pp. 75–91; N.N. Sorensen and L.E. Guarnizo, "La Vida de la Familia Transnacional a Través del Atlántico: la Experiencia de la Población Colombiana y Dominicana Migrantes", *Puntos de Vista: Cuadernos del Observatorio de las Migraciones y la Convivencia Intercultural de la Ciudad de Madrid*, 9 (2007), pp. 7–28; Sorensen, "Narratives of Longing, Belonging, and Caring in the Dominican Diaspora", in J. Besson and K.F. Olwig (eds), *Caribbean Narratives of Belonging* (London: MacMillan, 2004), pp. 222–242; Sorenson, "New Landscapes of Migration? Transnational Migration between Latin America, the US and Europe", in B.F. Frederiksen and N. Sorensen (eds), *Beyond Home and Exile: Making Sense of Lives on the Move* (Roskilde: Roskilde University, 2002), pp. 97–126; and, A. Pellegrino, *Migration from Latin America to Europe: Trends and Policy Challenges* (International Organization for Migration, 2004).

5. Regularization or legalization programs aimed at bringing many Latina/os from out of the shadows of society also contributed to the visible expansion of the Latina/o population in Spain. Pellegrino, "Migration from Latin America to Europe", p. 21.

6. The specific name of the unit is Prevention Services of the City Council of Barcelona, the Institute of Childhood Studies (Serveis de Prevencio del Ajuntament de Barelona al Consorci Institut d'Infancia y Mon Urba, CIIMU).

7. For Feixa's team of researchers, see Feixa, Porzio, Recio, *Jovenes Latina/os en Barcelona*. For Feixa's response to the emergence of these youths, see Interview, Carles Feixa, 15 April 2012.

8. For work on or about Latina/o youths in Spain, see, for example, Feixa, et al., *Jovenes Latina/os en Barcelona*; Feixa, Porzio, Recio and Canelles, "Jovenes

y 'Bandas' Latinas en Barcelona"; C. Feixa, N. Canelles, L. Porzio, C. Recio and L. Giliberti, "Latin Kings in Barcelona", in F.V. Gemert, D. Peterson and I. Lien (eds), *Street Gangs, Migration, and Ethnicity* (New York: Willan Publishing, 2008), pp. 63–78; A. Rios-Rojas, "Beyond Delinquent Citizenships: Immigrant Youth's (Re)Visions of Citizenship and Belonging in a Globalized World", *Harvard Educational Review*, 81, 1 (2011), pp. 64–94; J. Lucko, "Tracking Identity: Academic Performance and Ethnic Identity among Ecuadorian Immigrant Teenagers in Madrid", *Anthropology & Education Quarterly*, 42, 3 (2011), pp. 213–229. A few scholars have, however, studied Latina/o youths in comparative contexts, (US–Spain). See, for example, M. Gibson and S. Carrasco, "The Education of Immigrant Youth: Some Lessons from the US and Spain", *Theory into Practice*, 48 (2009), pp. 249–257.

9. The "Eurogang" network formed in the late 1990s in response to the need to organize an agenda for studying, researching and publishing findings about the role and relationship among migration, ethnicity and gangs. For two fairly recent books, see F.V. Gemert, D. Peterson and I. Lien (eds), *Street Gangs, Migration, and Ethnicity* (Portland, Oregon: Willan, 2008). This collection focuses on France, Moscow, Mexicans in the US, Latinos in Spain and Pakistanis in Norway. See also S.H. Decker and F.M. Weerman (eds), *European Street Gangs and Troublesome Youth Groups* (Lanham, MD: AltaMira Press, 2007).

10. For instance, Fundacio Marianao in Sant Boi de Llobregat, Casal del Infants in El Raval in Barcelona and Fundacio Ateneu Sant Roc in Badalona all work with immigrants and youths of various origins.

11. For scholars examining patterns of migration, globalization and marginalization of Latin Americans within the European context, see studies cited above. For a history of the Eurogang Program or network, see M.W. Klein, "Introduction", in *European Street Gangs and Troublesome Youth Groups* (Lanham, MD: AltaMira Press, 2005), pp. 1–10. The Eurogang Program's definition of gangs is: "A street gang is any durable, street-oriented youth group whose involvement in illegal activity is part of its group identity." Klein, "Introduction", pp. 4–5.

12. On negative views held by academics about Latina/o youths in Spain, see, for instance, M. Lopez Corral, "Barcelona y Madrid: Dos realidades distintas ante el fenómeno de las bandas Latinas", *Revista CIDOB d'Afers Internacionals*, 81 (2008), pp. 191–206.

13. "*Bandas*" is used throughout this study, rather than "*pandillas*", to refer to youth street gangs. According to Carles Feixa and his colleagues, *bandas* are groups of individuals, not necessarily all youths, which are structured around criminal activity with little symbolic elaboration or ties to a particular locale, while *pandillas* are groups of youths centred around a particular local territory and structured around leisure and illicit activities. The latter characterize the street gangs usually found in the US. See, Feixa, Porzio and Recio, *Jovenes Latina/os en Barcelona*, p. 90. Information on the existence of a cultural group as well as a street-oriented youth group comes from Interview, Carles Feixa, Barcelona, Spain, 5 July 2012.

14. Feixa explained the process through which he became involved in studying Latina/o youth gangs in the interview and through follow-up correspondence, dated 4 May 2012. For more of Feixa's work on youth cultures, see

C. Feixa and L. Porzio, "Jipis, Pijos, Fiesteros: Studies on Youth Cultures in Spain 1960–2004", *Young*, 13, 1 (2005), pp. 89–113; C. Feixa, "Tribus Urbanas and Chavos Banda: Being a Punk in Catalonia and Mexico", in C. Feixa and P. Nilan (eds), *Global Youth? Hybrid Identities, Plural Worlds* (New York: Routledge, 2006), pp. 149–166; C. Feixa, C. Costa and J. Pallarés, "From Okupas to Makineros: Citizenship and Youth Cultures in Spain", in A. Furlong and I. Guidikova (eds), *Transitions of Youth Citizenship in Europe: Culture, Subculture and Identity* (Strasbourg: Council of Europe Pub., 2001), pp. 289–304 ; C. Feixa, *De Jovenes, Bandas, y Tribus: Antropologia de la Juventud* (Spain: Editorial Ariel, 1998).
15. Interview, Carles Feixa, Email Correspondence, 8 May 2012.
16. Interview, Carles Feixa, Barcelona, Spain, 5 July 2012.
17. See, K. Calavita, *Immigrants at the Margins: Law, Race, and Exclusion in Southern Europe* (Boston: Cambridge University Press, 2005), especially Chapter 2.
18. In fact, before the 1990s, immigrants to Catalonia and Spain were primarily males – 72% and 67% respectively. Today, the reverse is true. For more on the feminization of labour migration see, for instance, A. Escriva, "The Position and Status of Migrant Women in Spain", in F. Anthias and G. Lazaridis (eds), *Gender and Migration in Southern Europe: Women on the Move* (Oxford: Berg Publishers, 2000), pp. 199–225; N. Ribas-Mateos, "Female Birds of Passage: Leaving and Settling in Spain", in *Gender and Migration in Southern Europe*, pp. 173–197; and, Pellegrino, "Migration from Latin America to Europe", pp. 30–39.
19. Calavita, *Immigrants at the Margins*, Chapter 2.
20. Calavita, *Immigrants at the Margins*. For more on residency permits, see also Pellegrino, "Migration from Latin America to Europe", pp. 27–31. For more on IRCA, see, for instance, D. Gutierrez, *Walls and Mirrors: Mexican Americans, Mexican Immigrants, and the Politics of Ethnicity* (Berkeley: University of California Press, 1995).
21. Pellegrino, "Migration from Latin America to Europe", p. 23.
22. For more on the rhetoric of immigrant inclusion and the reality of exclusion in Italy and Spain, see Calavita, *Immigrants at the Margins*.
23. According to Feixa, unlike los Latin Kings of Barcelona, those in Madrid are known to have committed serious crimes and are a different organization altogether. Interview, Carles Feixa, Barcelona, Spain, 9 July 2012.
24. Interview, Carles Feixa, Barcelona, Spain, 5 July 2012.
25. Calavita, *Immigrants on the Margins*, Chapter 1.
26. I would like to thank Luis Guarnizo for his personal communication on the difficulties of adjustment for Latina/o youths in Spain. For the society's general exclusion of immigrants, see Calavita, *Immigrants on the Margins*.
27. Interview, Carles Feixa, Email Correspondence, 15 April 2012.
28. D. Brotherton and L. Barrios, *The Almighty Latin King and Queen Nation* (New York: Columbia University Press, 2004).
29. Interview, Carles Feixa, Email Correspondence, 15 April 2012.
30. Feixa stated: "Él lo vio como la última posibilidad: de perdidos, al río; no nos fiamos, pero vamos a ver qué pasa." Interview, Carles Feixa, Email Correspondence, 15 April 2012.
31. Many of these findings are found in Feixa, Porzio and Recio, *Jovenes Latina/os en Barcelona*. For more on the methodology of the research, see Ibid.,

pp. 1–38. See, also Feixa, Canelles, Porzio, Recio and Giliberti, "Latin Kings in Barcelona".
32. For more on the "risks" of doing research with "gangs", see, J. Aldridge, J. Medina and R. Ralphs, "Dangers and Problems of Doing 'Gang' Research in the U.K.", in *Street Gangs, Migration, and Ethnicity*, pp.31–46.
33. Feixa et al., *Jovenes Latina/os en Barcelona*, pp. 1–38.
34. Feixa et al., *Jovenes Latina/os en Barcelona*, especially Chapter 2 ("Jovenes 'latinos' en Barcelona: relatos de vida") and Chapter 3 ("Jovenes 'latino' en Barcelona identidades culturales").
35. Feixa et al., *Jovenes Latina/os en Barcelona*, chapters 2 and 3.
36. This is similar to what Pierrette Hondagnue-Sotelo refers to as "transnational motherhood" in the US-Mexico context, in which women are forced to leave their children behind while they secure employment and a stable home. See, P. Hondagnue-Sotelo (ed.), *Gender and US Immigration: Contemporary Trends* (Berkeley: University of California Press, 2003).
37. Feixa et al., *Jovenes Latina/os en Barcelona*, chapters 2 and 3.
38. The overwhelming majority – more than 90% – of Latin American migrants send remittances to their countries of origin. Pellegrino, "Migration from Latin America to Europe", p. 46.
39. Feixa et al., *Jovenes Latina/os en Barcelona*, chapters 2 and 3.
40. Ibid.
41. Ibid., Chapter 3.
42. Interview, Carles Feixa, Barcelona, Spain, 5 July 2012.
43. P. Bourgois, *In Search of Respect: Selling Crack in El Barrio* (Boston: Cambridge University Press, 2002).
44. Feixa et al., *Jovenes Latina/os en Barcelona*, p. 105.
45. Ibid., chapters 2 and 3.
46. Ibid.
47. Ibid., Chapter 4 ("Jovenes 'latinos' en Barcelona: la vision de los adultos").
48. Sorensen and Guarnizo, "La Vida de la Familia Transnacional a Través del Atlántico", p. 19.
49. Feixa et al., *Jovenes Latina/os en Barcelona*, Chapter 4.
50. Ibid., p. 81.
51. Ibid., p. 86.
52. Ibid., Chapter 4.
53. Gibson and Carrasco, "The Education of Immigrant Youth".
54. Lucko, "Tracking Identity", and Rios-Rojas, "Beyond Delinquent Citizenships". Quote cited on Ibid., p. 64.
55. For Luca Palmas's work, see *Dentro le gang* [*Inside the Gang*] (Ombre Corte, 2009); *Atlantico Latino* [*Latino Atlantic*] (Carocci, 2010); and *Enemigos Públicos: La fabricación de las bandas en la España contemporánea* [*Public Enemies: The Fabrication of Gangs in Contemporary Europe*] forthcoming, 2014.
56. I would like to thank C. Feixa, A. Rios-Rojas, L.E. Guarnizo, L. Palmas and the editor of this volume for their assistance with this essay.

Part III

Juvenile Delinquency and War: Early Twentieth-Century Perspectives

6

Bad Boys? Juvenile Delinquency during the First World War in Wilhelmine Germany

Sarah Bornhorst

In the city of Ulm in the southwest of the German Empire on 12 March 1917 two boys, aged 16 and 17 years old, went into a house and broke into the basement of a local widow. They stole 20 bottles of sparkling wine, 150 eggs and a bucket full of soft soap. At that time, the impact of the First World War had reached its climax on the German "home front". Though food had been rationed since 1914, by 1917 the situation had deteriorated to the point that in the district of Blaubeuren, people were allotted a ration of 30 eggs for a whole year.[1] The winter of 1916–1917 had brought massive supply shortfalls. The only available food for large parts of the population gave that winter its infamous name: Swede winter. Swedes were considered as food for animals in times of peace. Many people suffered from hunger and the rationing of everyday items had deeply affected almost the entire population (with the exception of the upper class). As the father of one of the boys said to his son: "There, you can see how people are still living in the third year of the war, you should take it from them." And actually, his son did on several occasions.[2]

This brief example reveals many aspects which are relevant to the topic of this chapter. Juvenile delinquency during the First World War, as it is represented in the records of the county court of Ulm, mostly took the form of property or poverty crime, and the young delinquents were mostly boys. Nor, in general, were these delinquents viewed as the black sheep of the family. Rather, they ensured the functioning of the family as a social system under conditions of war.[3] Their crimes may be described as "self-sufficient criminality" to compensate for the shortcomings of everyday life during wartime.

But for society as a whole, delinquent behaviour as a breach of norms was considered particularly dangerous because the nation was seen as already threatened from without by the war. The judges, who had to pronounce sentence on juvenile delinquents, were – in their own minds – on duty at the home front.[4] Youth criminality was an important topic for jurists and social reformers before the outbreak of war. Modern developments such as urbanization and industrialization were seen as a threat to young people, because these developments seemed to destroy proven institutions of social control such as the family or rural village society. Traditional moral concepts seemed to be vanishing and losing their supporting function. The outbreak of war was seen as a turning point by bourgeois observers with the potential to bring a stop to these developments, but soon the war came to be perceived rather as a catalyst for delinquent behaviour. Consequently, it is not surprising that wartime saw the development of new instruments in juvenile criminal policy. Many reform efforts were not successful before the war because of ongoing discussions in national parliaments, at international congresses and among local social reformers. The First World War acted as a motor accelerating and driving forward the reform of the juvenile criminal law. For example, there was a long ongoing debate about a new youth court law in Germany. Despite the possibility of establishing it before the war, it only came into force in 1923, after the first turbulent years of the Weimar Republic.[5]

This chapter will examine the subject of juvenile delinquency in First World-War Germany from a micro-historical perspective by focusing on one particular district – Ulm in the southwest of the country. The main questions it seeks to investigate are: what forms of delinquency did judges have to deal with, and how did they handle such delinquent behaviour?

The chapter is divided into six parts. Firstly, the county court district of Ulm which serves as the case study for this chapter will be analysed. Secondly, it will explore what was meant when speaking of "juvenile delinquents" (*jugendliche Verbrecher*) in the period under examination. Following this, an overview of the forms of contemporary criminality will be presented and, finally, popular discourses on "juvenile delinquency" at the time (especially under conditions of war) will be explored in the context of the legal judgements given. Furthermore, the chapter questions the idea of "war" acting as a catalyst for the resocialization of juvenile delinquents through conscription into the armed forces by reviewing a new instrument of juvenile delinquency politics introduced in First World-War Germany: the "conditioned amnesty".[6]

The county court district of Ulm

The county court district of Ulm belonged to the kingdom of Württemberg and consisted of eight local court districts. In terms of economic and industrial development and population structure, Württemberg was typical of Germany of this period.[7] In the course of the Second Industrial Revolution Germany caught up with more economically established countries, rivalling the British Empire in terms of industrial output as Britain lost its dominant position as an industrial powerhouse.[8] In a wider perspective, while the economic development of Germany and of course Württemberg had its own specificities, it showed strong parallels with economic patterns in the rest of western Europe.

The county court district represented a broad spectrum of social reality in Wilhelmine Germany, including urban as well as rural contexts. Studying an area like this enables us to extend the scholarly view of juvenile delinquency in imperial Germany, whose focus has previously lain mostly on post- or pre-war Prussia. Especially when studying the development of criminality, and, even more so, the reaction to criminality or the development of criminal politics, there are major differences between Prussia and other parts of Germany. For example, the police force was professionalized to a much greater extent in Prussia than in Württemberg at the beginning of the twentieth century.[9]

At that time, Ulm was the major city in the district of Württemberg, which in 1910 numbered over 56,000 inhabitants. Ulm hosted a garrison with over 7,000 men before the war. During the war, this number increased to 21,000. The district also contained a number of somewhat smaller cities with industries, which later became important for warfare, such as WMF (the *Württembergische Metallwarenfabrik* or Württemberg metal products factory) in Geislingen and the engine-building industry in Göppingen and Ulm. There was also a well established cement industry in Blaubeuren, which was hit hard by the breakdown of the building industry after the outbreak of war. As such, the types of industry represented varied significantly across the region of Württemberg, which, in turn, meant that the impact of the war on the region was similarly varied.[10]

Most of the county court district was rural and consisted chiefly of villages, where most of the population made a living from farming. However, in contrast to other rural areas in Germany, more people came into touch with industry. This is because in the industrial centres, many of those employed still lived in villages – this type of home-to-work commuting was quite specific for Württemberg at that time.[11]

Under the conditions of war, the economic situation of large parts of the population in Germany deteriorated gradually. In southern parts, the situation was not as bad as, for example, in Berlin or the Ruhr Valley, which held special positions. The relatively better situation of southern regions can be illustrated by the following: during the war, people known as "hamsterers" travelled from the town to the countryside to buy food directly from farmers without food stamps. A local newspaper in Ulm articulated its fear of holidaymakers from northern parts of Germany who might go to Württemberg as "hamsterers" and buy up their food.[12]

In Ulm, the mayor of the city tried to mitigate the supply difficulties by giving land to members of the local population so that they could cultivate vegetables.[13] However, this did not prove an adequate solution to the problem, with many people also suffering from pauperism in this area.

The situation of juveniles in the county court district changed in a number of specific ways during the war. Firstly, the routine at school changed. At the start of the war, when the German army enjoyed a number of significant victories, lessons were cancelled for victory celebrations. Then, when there was nothing more to celebrate, pupils were deployed for collections of money and basic materials like copper to help toward the war effort.[14] These changes to the school routine disturbed everyday life for the pupils. Because there was a shortage of coal for heating the buildings it was frequently too cold for lessons in winter.[15] Thus, the pupils, who also suffered from a coal shortage at home, could not warm themselves at school any longer. And because the school baths had to close the hygiene situation also became worse.[16] In addition, pupils from the city were recruited to help with the work of farming in the countryside. The Ministry of Education in Württemberg itself tried to systemize this recruitment process.[17] Clearly, in the eyes of the government, everyone at the home front was important – even children and juveniles. And so their delinquent behaviour could not be ignored.

Juvenile delinquents

When talking about juvenile delinquency in the First World War, it is important to note that the term "juvenile delinquents" corresponds to children from 12 years of age to teenagers of 17 according to the contemporary German criminal law.

Although the legal procedure regarding this group of young people was defined in the penal code by three articles, §55–§57, there was no specific juvenile criminal law.[18] They were treated like adults, although the extent of possible sentences was limited in comparison to those for adult delinquents. Because the law was focused on the offences committed, there seemed to be no need to alter the law especially for juveniles. The German Criminal Code of 1871 was based on an understanding of law from the beginning of the nineteenth century. In the way it dealt with delinquent juveniles it was very similar to the regulations of the French *Code Pénal* of 1810.[19] In other words, the penal code of 1871 was already "old-fashioned" before it came into force.

In addition, the German Code of Criminal Procedure from 1879 specified that juveniles under 16 years of age needed a criminal defence lawyer for their trial before the criminal court who could make use of the special conditions which the law prescribed for juveniles.[20] The act also stated that the criminal divisions of district courts would be responsible for crimes committed by juveniles which, in most cases, excluded the possibility of sentencing by jury courts. Misdemeanours fell within the responsibility of local courts.

These legal regulations created the framework for the jurisdictional procedure for juvenile delinquents prior to the establishment of the Juvenile Court Act (*Jugendgerichtsgesetz*) in 1923. However, this does not mean that there were no efforts to reform this old-fashioned legal system.

At the end of the nineteenth century and the beginning of the twentieth, defining different types of criminality, tracing their origins and working out how to fight them were key topics for politicians and scientists across Europe and in North America. One reason for this was the general perception that the crime rate among juvenile offenders was increasing.[21] The participants at international penal congresses also showed an increasing interest in delinquent juveniles.[22] A very influential progressive thinker was the German jurist Franz von Liszt. He was one of the most important actors in international criminal law reform and co-founder of the IKV (the *Internationale Kriminalistische Vereinigung* or International Criminological Union). Among the national sections of the IKV, the German section was one of the largest and so German jurists played an important role in the developing reform movement.[23] One of the main concerns of the IKV was how the judicial system should deal with juveniles. The First World War worked to stymie this international congress reform movement. The congresses stopped during the war, bringing the movement to a halt and the climax of international reform efforts was effectively over.[24] But this does not mean that the development of new instruments for fighting juvenile delinquency stopped as well. The international congresses provided a focus for national efforts and a forum for discussion, but the legislative work was to be done by national governments, whose reform efforts began after the end of the First World War. We will see this in relation to the conditioned amnesty, which is also linked to the idea of "war as an educator".

But long before the outbreak of war, the first criminal court especially for juvenile delinquents was established in 1899: the Cook County Juvenile Court, better known as the Chicago Juvenile Court.[25] This court was only for defendants below the age of 16 and from 1905 onwards for male defendants under 17 and female defendants under 18. However, that was not the only innovation in Chicago. For young adults, who were too old for the juvenile court but too young for a normal court, the Chicago Boys' Court was established in 1914.[26] It was "the first and only socialized criminal court in America equipped with full power to try and sentence young men between seventeen and twenty-one".[27] These developments in the US were an important driving force behind international reforming efforts. The first German juvenile court was established in Frankfurt am Main in 1908.[28]

The parallel formation of movements for the reform of the criminal law for juveniles in several (western) states was based on other shared experiences; above all, industrialization and urbanization as well as a fear of their consequences. For one consequence seemed to be a rising juvenile crime rate which generated this form of "moral panic" as well as a search for solutions. The prevailing legal framework during the nineteenth century was a system of law which was focused on the criminal act. Under the growing influence of the new science of criminology, criminal law reformers promoted the idea of a change to a legal framework which was supposed to be focused on the offender. This was based on the theory of the Italian psychiatrist and coroner Cesare Lombroso. He thought of criminals as "born criminals" who were – in his conception – atavistic types of human beings. His ideas became influential around Europe and North America during the last two decades of the nineteenth and the beginning of the twentieth century, although his ideas were not adopted everywhere wholesale. His ideas inspired criminologists and lawyers to think about the criminals themselves and no longer just about the crimes they committed. In contemporary Germany, for example, Lombroso's theories gave criminologists the impulse to enter into controversial debates about the nature of criminals. While rejecting his thesis formally, they revised it according to their own concepts.[29] Nobody – except the psychiatrist

Hans Kurella – accepted the atavistic aspects of Lombroso's theory, but German criminologists did believe that there were "born criminals".[30]

This was an important change of view toward crime and criminality. Before coming to focus on the criminal, the emphasis had always been, for example, in cases of theft on the stolen objects. The question judges had to answer was "what?" – not "who?" or "why?".[31] With this change of emphasis, the different "types" of actual and potential criminals became the focus of attention. Under these circumstances, juvenile criminals were increasingly understood by the science of criminology as *juvenile* criminals.

There is another important parallel between Germany and other European and North American countries: the focus on boys as the stereotypical "juvenile criminal". As became clear at the conference from which this volume arose, boys were seen as "problematic" or "deviant" in several cultural systems in the Far East, Europe and America. One manifest consequence of this view is the Chicago Boys' Court. We will come back to this point later when focusing on the explanations for delinquent behaviour, but it is important for understanding the reform movement too. In late nineteenth-century Canada, for example, juveniles arrested by the police were mostly white, poor, urban boys with a low level of education. They were called "street Arabs".[32] In Germany, these boys were called "*Halbstarke*" ("yobs").[33] And in France they were called "apaches".[34] Each country has its own word for this stereotype. A plausible explanation for focusing on boys and ignoring the girls (they seemed to be much more at risk of falling morally than of turning criminal) is the influence of global concepts of masculinity and femininity. From this point of view, men are active; women are passive, men work and live outside the household, women within. Thus, it seems to be consistent to concentrate on boys or men as potential criminals; since when and why should "passive" girls or women inside the household commit crimes which are dangerous to society?

Forms of juvenile delinquency during the war

During the years of the First World War, court records indicate that rates of criminality among young people increased substantially across imperial Germany in general, and in the county court district of Ulm, in particular.[35] The number of indictments increased between 1907 and 1913, but then declined suddenly in 1914, the first year of the war. This most likely happened because many local policemen had been called to the army.[36] As a result, the minister of the interior ordered them back from the front in 1915.[37] This move led to an increase in the number of indictments. Although the register for the year 1917 is missing, it can be deduced from other available statistics that the number of indictments continued to rise in 1917. The rising crime rate is mainly based on growing levels of property crime, which can be illustrated with the following chart (Figure 6.1):

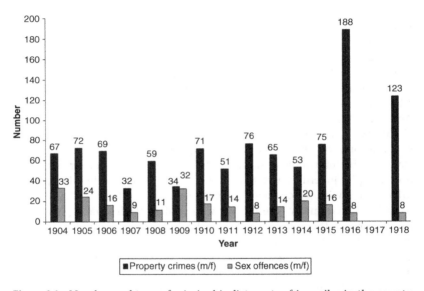

Figure 6.1   Number and type of criminal indictments of juveniles in the county court district of Ulm, 1904–1918

Of course, there were also other types of crime which came before the county court. The comparison between the rates of sex offences and property crimes committed, shown in the chart above, clearly reveals the dominant role of property crimes. Sex offences were one of the three most significant categories of crimes after property offences. One reason for the dominant role of property crimes was the hard economic situation. The story of the two boys from Ulm who broke into the widow's basement which we mentioned at the beginning of this chapter illustrates this point well.

But there is another important reason for the rising rate of property crime. In general, people's tolerance for dealing with conflicts among social groups declined during the war. This can also be illustrated by the case of a boy who lived with his parents in a house which belonged to the railway company in Ulm. Only railway employees and their families lived there, so they were not just neighbours but also colleagues. In 1916 this 14-year-old boy had stolen meat from a neighbour's garret.[38] Under "normal circumstances" the parents might have given their neighbour money for this and it would have been settled. But it was the third year of war and nothing could substitute meat. Thus, the real value of the piece of meat was much higher than its actual price of three Reichsmark. It was not possible to buy anything freely as most goods were rationed and people needed food stamps to receive anything. This means that there was no space for any form of informal conflict resolution, ensuring that the case inevitably found its way to the court.

These causes were intertwined. With the rising crime rate popular sensibility to criminality increased as well. And with the growing shortage of food and necessities the willingness to solve these problems informally declined. In addition, during the war there was a general tendency to prioritize one's own needs, which resulted in juveniles securing their own needs and the needs of their family at the cost of other people.

The convictions of lower courts, like the local court in Kirchheim unter Teck, show an even higher rate of criminality caused by rationing. The judges had to deal with a great number of juveniles who had stolen fruit or other agricultural products.[39] The prosecution was based on a new penalty decree from 1917 from the military leadership of Württemberg, which banned anyone from taking fruit from the fields. The juveniles were mostly fabric workers and technical apprentices from local factories. They were simply trying to increase their ration of food.

As mentioned when explaining the reform movement, there was a noticeable difference between the numbers of boys and girls on trial at the county court: the majority of juvenile delinquents on trial during the period under examination were boys. Only 12% were girls and 88% boys. That meant that 797 boys and 105 girls were prosecuted by local authorities in the years between 1904 and 1918. Reasons for this included the fact that the popular stereotype of the young criminal, which directed the focus of criminal prosecution, was male as well as the fact that girls were actually involved in fewer incidents.[40]

Crime rates which fell initially before rising significantly were not a phenomenon unique to imperial Germany. Rather, they could be found in other European nations at war as well.[41] But we can also observe a degree of variation. In Italy, for example, the conviction rates of juveniles fell – which does not mean that there was no fear of juvenile delinquency during war.[42] Statistical information does not necessarily conform to popular perceptions of a situation.

The state of affairs on the home front generated new forms of criminality which, for this reason, may be called "war criminality". "War criminality" may be defined as crimes which not just increase during times of war, but which can only be committed under the special circumstances of war. During the First World War, this entailed new objects of theft as well as the development of new criminal laws and new groups of victims. New objects were the food ration cards and army postal parcels. The theft of these parcels was (from the viewpoint of an offender) very worthwhile, because relatives from the home front sent food, cigarettes, soap and other such items to their fathers and sons at the front. They tried to send them valuable items to make their situation easier. Thus postal workers had the rare opportunity to compensate for wartime rationing. A 17-year-old boy from Geislingen, for example, had stolen items from different parcels between March and July 1917. He found food, soap, cigarettes and even lighters.[43]

In another case, a group of boys and girls had produced fake rationing cards for their families so they could get more potatoes than allowed. In this case the judges accepted, which they did not do very often, that there was real economic distress. It is interesting that in this specific incident there were more girls than boys involved.[44] The general logic applied here was that while boys stole luxury foods for their own needs, the criminal activities of girls focused on supplying the needs of their families. A new group of victims of crime to emerge were prisoners of war. This aspect will be discussed in the next part of the chapter.

Explanations for delinquent behaviour in times of war

These were some of the offences and offenders which the judges of the county court in Ulm had to cope with. To understand the circumstances under which they made their judgements, it is necessary to look back to the nineteenth century. As early as the 1880s, the topics of "youth" and "delinquency" had each separately become the focus of attention. One reason for this was the influence, from the 1880s onwards, of the so-called "discovery of youth", which led to important changes in the way young people and young criminals were perceived. The way of life of "bourgeois youth" was idealized in a manner similar to the ideal of the "bourgeois family" and other forms of youth culture were compared to this ideal. In the developing debate authors identified an increasing waywardness among teenagers. This discourse reached its climax under the circumstances of war, but it did not begin here. During the war, important new aspects entered the discourse which took place in the professional journals of pedagogues, lawyers and youth welfare practitioners, in local newspapers, and which also found its way into the legal regulations of the military leadership of Württemberg on the home front.[45] This discourse was pretty consistent with most of the participants holding the same view. On the one hand, young people were ascribed an important role during war: as a resource for the army, as providing a helping hand on the home front and as the future of the nation. On the other hand, they seemed to be enormously endangered by circumstances which originated in the war. Commentators remarked upon a rising crime rate among young people, for which they identified three causes. First, a growing lack of parental authority caused by the war, second, the changing economic situation during wartime and third, the general impact of war on the juvenile psyche. The lack of authority was seen to stem from the fact that mainly the fathers, but also the teachers and other male authority figures were serving at the front. The changing economic situation, on the other hand, led to new opportunities to earn money in the war industries. Teenagers had the chance to quickly climb to important positions. This was considered dangerous by the authorities, as they were confronted with previously unknown seductions and became accustomed to a new standard of living. In contrast, only very occasionally was poverty identified as a cause for criminality (which is quite surprising when we think of the rising poverty levels during war). And some commentators felt that young boys wanted to play soldiers and therefore stole warfare equipment.[46]

As crime rates soared in several countries, these explanations were not limited to imperial Germany. The assumption that rising crime rates were linked to a lack of parental authority was widespread in Britain as well.[47] Stereotypical descriptions of boys becoming delinquent because of their fathers serving at the front could be found in English and French newspapers as well as in German publications.[48]

From the standpoint of contemporary bourgeois observers the typical juvenile criminal was an urban proletarian who worked in a factory which was essential for the war effort. That is why he earned too much money, which he wasted hedonistically on smoking. His father was at the front and his mother lacked the strength and authority to control his behaviour. As a result, he became morally wayward and finally criminal to satisfy his prodigal needs. To put it succinctly, in the opinion of bourgeois observers, youth criminality during the First World War was a "boy problem".

But did the judgements – and the judges who gave the verdicts – of the court of Ulm reflect this discourse? Did the judges hold similar views or did they take account of the new pressures and temptations of wartime highlighted by scholars at the time such as a lack of paternal authority and the unprecedented economic situation? The Minister of Justice in Württemberg, Schmidlin, had certainly demanded a stronger orientation toward the juvenile offenders themselves as early as 1911.[49] He was clearly affected by new criminological ideas such as the concept of "mental inferiority" and tried to integrate these concepts as far as possible (without a complete reform of criminal justice, which was of course outside of his influence) in the criminal procedure against juveniles.

To answer these questions, we have to look at the 136 written judgements against juveniles which exist for the county court of Ulm. In 30 of them the judges did not try to explain at all why the young people committed a crime. They were not obligated to do this; they simply had to punish the delinquent for the crime committed, and under the laws of the time, they did not have to analyse its causes. In this period, however, criminal justice in Germany was being transformed under the influence of the so-called "modern school" of criminal law, from a legal framework which focused on the act to one which focused on the offender, as was shown before. The Minister of Justice in Württemberg, who was the senior authority in legal matters, enacted several laws which point in this direction. This might well have led to a greater focus on the origins of criminality.

But only in 13 of the judgements did the judges refer to explanations of criminality which seemed to be caused by the situation at the home front.[50] They also reverted to other explanations. Nearly all of these judgements dealt with property crimes, with only one involving a sex offence. With respect to these property-related crimes, which were a particular feature of wartime conditions, as we saw earlier, the judges acknowledged the war as a cause of crime. These judgements, with only one exception, concerned boys who had been accused of committing an offence. If the judges referred to the situation at the home front, they used explanations that were in line with the discourse described above. The most important explanation they mentioned was a lack of paternal authority, which the judges referred to in seven of the 13 judgements. In five cases they explained the criminal act with reference to the economic situation (but only in three of these cases was economic distress cited as a reason) and in one case they thought that boys stole military equipment because they were excited about the war.

The influential stereotype of the war-torn home being responsible for juvenile delinquency also found its way into the judicial practice of the judges:

> His father is at the front, so the mother has to take care of the seven children, of which the defendant is the second eldest. As she has to leave home for work during the day, the children are left to their own devices and the defendant hangs around on the streets, as the school-day is reduced by half. Doing this, he made friends with the 16-year old plumber's apprentice Karl J., who has a tendency towards stealing, avoids education with his foreman and who has already stolen money from one of his teachers when he was still going to school at the orphanage in Ochsenhausen. This boy certainly did not have a good influence on the defendant; he also took part in the act of the defendant.[51]

This explanation mentions several factors which could, from the bourgeois observer's standpoint, lead a teenager to become delinquent: a lack of paternal authority, bad company and hanging around on the streets. The description could easily have been taken from a pedagogical journal, but it is in reality taken from a legal judgement.

One interpretation of criminality during times of war, which might have been suspected by judges on duty at the home front, is missing in their judgements, namely criminality and juvenile delinquency as a "foreign" or "anti-German" behaviour. Their explanations and estimations are very focused on the particular circumstances of the crime scene. On the other hand, in some cases, the judges ascribed to indicted boys a "mean attitude" – and here there is a connection to the war, but only, in one case, in an international sense. Here, a boy had stolen money from a prisoner of war. In cases where juveniles had stolen things from soldiers (for example, from army postal parcels), the judges pronounced them to possess a "mean attitude" and took this into account when handing down a more rigorous punishment. Theft from a prisoner of war constituted a specific kind of "anti-German" behaviour for the judges, because, as they pointed out, this would "damage the respect for our nation".[52]

Other explanations for juvenile delinquency apart from the situation at the home front can be found in the judgements. It is possible to divide them into different groups, reflecting the various concepts of contemporary criminology.[53] First, we find sociological explanations which focused on external reasons for young people's descent into criminality.

Such sociological explanations might involve such cases as judges who thought someone turned criminal because a father serving at the front led to a loss of authority in the household or someone stole an object because of economic hardship. In a few cases judges used biological explanations, claiming that boys had committed a crime due to "juvenile high spirits", for example.[54] But there were biologistic explanations too which drew on new concepts within contemporary criminal biology, such as the language used by judges who found a girl to be "pathologically degenerated".[55] In other cases, the judges operated with the stereotype of a "habitual offender", which was quite a common concept in contemporary criminology.[56] In addition, however, to these explicit criminal-biological explanations, judges used essentializing labels which vacillated between new criminological concepts and older, moral explanations of criminality. This was the case when the explanation given for an offence was the pursuit of "hedonism" (with very negative connotations) or "work shyness".[57] Here we find a mixture of new concepts and traditional explanations. Indeed, it seems as if the judges adapted new criminological concepts for their everyday work. In this way they developed often quite vulgar adaptations of scientific criminological explanations for their everyday needs.

Which explanations of juvenile delinquency led judges to label boys and girls as "deviant persons"? If only sociological explanations were present in a judgement, the offender was not normally stigmatized as "abnormal" or "deviant". Rather, this was the case when biologistic or essentializing explanations played a role, too. Some three quarters of juvenile delinquents were not stigmatized by judges in this way. The main reason for this is that the judges still administered justice with a focus on the act itself and were only just beginning to take the actor into account as well. A lot of judges were also serving at the front, so the workload of those who had remained at home had grown substantially. This was not a situation which was conducive to an expansion of the judges' work, which is what greater research into the causes of crimes would have meant. In this way the judgements of the county court in this period showed a tribunal in transition.

Reaction: The conditioned amnesty

When looking at the punishment of juvenile delinquents during the war, there is an interesting connection between criminality and the idea of "war as educator". The notion that the war could in any way serve as a solution for the problem of delinquency would seem quite paradoxical, if we were to mention the fear about the situation at the home front and its impact on juvenile delinquency. The connection became relevant in conjunction with the so-called "conditioned amnesty".

If a juvenile was found guilty at the court, there was no other possibility than letting him or her serve the sentence. Most of the sentences were short-term imprisonment, because the juveniles were mostly convicted for petty crime. This seemed to be a problem from the perspective of "modern school" jurists, because there was no possibility of influencing juveniles positively, to resocialize them when they had to stay, for example, only two weeks in prison. Moreover, a prison seemed to be an "academy of vice" as one of the most famous criminologists of that era, Gustav Aschaffenburg, put it.[58] This problem, it was intended, should be solved with the introduction of the conditioned amnesty. This measure was introduced in several states of the German empire from the 1890s onwards: in the kingdom of Württemberg in 1896, for example, only one year after Prussia, the trailblazer of changes in criminal policy, introduced it.[59] Other countries used similar instruments as well. In the UK, for example, the Summary Jurisdiction Act was passed in 1879. It allowed the suspension of a sentence for juvenile delinquents when their parents were able to pay bail.[60] For criminal law reformers in Germany, the conditioned amnesty was not the ideal instrument, but it was all that could be achieved for the moment.

In Württemberg, the conditioned amnesty was modified during the period from 1896 to 1907. In 1911, the Ministry of Justice published a comprehensive decree which replaced the older regulations.[61] The south-west German kingdom was lagging behind the rest of Germany with its reform efforts, a fact that the Minister of Justice was not amused about.[62] The conditioned amnesty was an option to grant parole, in particular to young delinquents. The judges must declare in their judgement whether they would recommend the mentioned juvenile for conditioned amnesty. If this was the case, the Minister of Justice (in the name of the king) decided whether or not to grant them parole. And normally the minister would follow the recommendations of his judges. But, as the name indicates, when granting parole as conditioned amnesty, the young person was not released into civic life without conditions. In order for the desired educative effects of parole to be achieved, it was only granted under the condition that the youth would behave especially well during the parole period. Not every young delinquent was able to achieve this and the decision as to who could be successful rested with the lawyers who first consulted relevant information from the juvenile probation unit.

The period of probation was usually two or three years, which is quite a long time for a juvenile to be under observation who was only sentenced to go to prison for three weeks. But nevertheless, critics complained about the ineffectiveness of the conditioned amnesty because, they argued, the juvenile delinquents would not "feel" the punishment and because of this would not care about it.[63] To refute this criticism, the rules regarding the conditioned amnesty were concretized in 1916. The Minister of Justice suggested that "even under the special circumstances of the current time" the conditioned amnesty promised success, which simply means that from his point of view it was a fitting instrument in time of war.[64] From now on, there was not only the requirement of good behaviour from the juvenile involved, but also concrete prohibitions and rules such as a ban on visiting public houses and the requirement to leave any job which seemed to be unsuitable for a young person.[65]

If we look at how often the conditioned amnesty was granted over time as a proportion of overall sentences handed down, it rose from the lowest rate of 14% in 1905 to a climax in pre-war times in 1911 of 61 and 68% in 1916.[66] This means that using the conditioned amnesty as an instrument of criminal policy toward juvenile offenders did not lose its importance in wartime, as one might think. The Minister of Justice was a staunch supporter of the conditioned amnesty. He prophesied that especially in wartime the conditions attached to the conditioned amnesty would gain in importance for re-educating delinquents, as we have seen above.[67]

The idea of "war as educator" became a remarkable factor in determining the conditions that could be imposed by the judges as part of the conditioned amnesty. As one can see in the judgements, the conditioned amnesty was sometimes recommended under the condition that the delinquent would join the army and therefore go to the front. Such judgements reveal the hope that young male delinquents, who might not be disciplined under "normal" conditions, would be transformed into dutiful, law-abiding citizens when sent to fight at the front. The juvenile probation unit in Ulm, for example, expressed this hope as follows:

> In peaceful life, it was too cramped for them. Under the influence of military discipline in the hazardous battle for such an important thing, they composed themselves and proved their manhood.[68]

The strict military regime of an army at the front and the experience of taking part in a "great national battle" would, it was hoped, serve as a magic bullet against the delinquent behaviour of wayward boys. After the outbreak of war a juvenile militia was established in several parts of Germany. The idea was to give young boys a pre-military education and to limit bad influences, especially those of the Socialist party on proletarian youth.[69] In the county court district, there were 114 juvenile militias. At the end of 1915 they had some 2,728 members. However, there was a dividing line. In the mainly industrial area of Göppingen, there were just five juvenile militias with only 180 members.[70] The young industrial workers who should have been the main target group could not be reached. One reason for this was the time when the lessons were held: in the evening and on Sundays, when workers had their only opportunity to relax and recover their strength. As a result, there was no possibility to put into practice the prophylactic effect of military education to prevent boys from becoming wayward and criminal.

What remained was to send delinquent boys to the front. Military discipline was accepted as a tried and tested method of juvenile education; the army seemed to be an important site of socialization for male citizens. Moreover, the army seemed to be a refuge from what were perceived by many as harmful modernist developments, among which was included the rising crime rate among juveniles.[71] And politically, it was hoped, the army would avert the influence of leftist movements and parties.

Doing service at the front could, from this perspective, have a positive, resocializing influence on delinquent male youths. Kurt Wittig, a teacher at the juvenile department of the prison in Bautzen in Saxony, and one of the youth welfare practitioners, expressed this hope: "War has a healing effect and shows many juveniles the way back to life!"[72] However, it should be pointed out that this option served as a last resort for handling delinquent boys. In 1916 the juvenile probation unit forced only six boys to join the army.[73]

In some cases, juvenile delinquents adopted similar arguments to those just described in order to gain the conditioned amnesty instead of serving a prison sentence, however short. Even if the court did not recommend the conditioned amnesty, the delinquent could apply for it. Furthermore, weight could be lent to this application by expressing a wish to serve at the front. This argumentation was not necessarily successful, but, in some cases, the Minister of Justice granted the amnesty.[74] There was even one case when the young delinquent was still in prison because the court had voted against the conditioned amnesty but the minister upheld the boy's application. At the end of June 1918, the 17-year-old boy who was convicted of theft exchanged the prison garb for the uniform of the German army.[75] When the war was going badly for Germany everybody was needed to help prevent defeat.

In other cases, the judges recommended the conditioned amnesty if the convicted boy declared himself ready to join the army.[76] Their belief in the resocializing effect of serving at the front is even more visible in the conviction proceedings against a boy who was found guilty of theft. The judges would not support a conditioned amnesty because of the seriousness of the crime. The boy had broken into a house and a shop and had stolen a great number of valuables such as a wallet containing 30 Reichsmark. However, they pointed out that they would not try to prevent the granting of amnesty for any delinquent ready to join the army voluntarily.[77]

The paradox of this was that from the perspective of many people working with youths, the war could be seen in two ways. At the home front it was considered a curse as it brought about such a massive change in social and economic life and resulted indirectly in a rise in deviant behaviour; at the front itself it was seen as a blessing by opening up a new possibility for disciplining the very same youths. Bourgeois observers could not or would not see that serving at the front in this brutal war might rather lead to the opposite of the hoped-for effect. The brutality of warfare could easily knock the youths off course, so that living a normal life after the war would no longer be possible.[78]

Conclusion

During the First World War, the number of crimes committed by teenagers rose; in particular poverty-related crimes. This was accompanied by a discourse about the rising waywardness and criminality of youth, especially male youth. This discourse was alarmist, which is very typical for a changing society. The fear of criminals and criminality can be seen as a yardstick for change and the acceptance of change in a society. And the developments during the First World War brought massive changes to Wilhelmine society. The end of the war meant the end of the current political system. Changing societies try to secure endangered values by identifying and labelling persons who deviate from these values as "delinquent". In Wilhelmine Germany, these persons were, in the main, male, urban, proletarian youths who seemed to be in danger of becoming wayward, criminal or socialist. Similar discourses can also be observed in present-day Germany. These discourses deal, in particular, with young migrants. Such "criminal young (male) foreigners" are considered a threat to a society in change.

In this view, the neglected, young male proletarian of the First World War is the young multiple offender with a migration background of today.[79]

Notes

1. See a report from 8 May 1917, HStAS, M 77/1, Bü 476.
2. Conviction of the Criminal Division of the County Court Ulm from 3 and 4 May 1917, against M. Jakob et al., StAL E 350a, Bü 950. ("[...] da kann man sehen, wie die Leute im dritten Kriegsjahr noch leben, denen gehöre es genommen".)
3. See Ute Daniel, "Der Krieg der Frauen 1914–1918: Zur Innenansicht des Ersten Weltkrieges in Deutschland", in Gerhard Hirschfeld, Gerd Krumeich and Irina Renz (eds), *Keiner fühlt sich hier mehr als Mensch...: Erlebnis und Wirkung des Ersten Weltkrieges* (Essen: Klartext, 1993), p. 141.
4. See Franz Riß, "Wir Richter und der Krieg", *DRZ*, 6 (1914), p. 722.
5. See Thomas Crofts, *The Criminal Responsibility of Children and Young Persons: A Comparison of English and German Law* (Aldershot: Ashgate, 2002), pp. 108–110.
6. This chapter is based on my PhD thesis, see Sarah Bornhorst, *Selbstversorger: Jugendkriminalität während des 1. Weltkriegs im Landgerichtsbezirk Ulm* (Konstanz: UVK, 2010).
7. See Manfred Scheck, *Zwischen Weltkrieg und Revolution: Zur Geschichte der Arbeiterbewegung in Württemberg* (Köln: Böhlau, 1981), p. 11.
8. See Karl Ditt, *Zweite Industrialisierung und Konsum: Energieversorgung, Haushaltstechnik und Massenkultur am Beispiel nordenglischer und westfälischer Städte 1880–1939* (Paderborn: Schöningh, 2011), p. 759.
9. See Bornhorst, *Selbstversorger*, pp. 99–103.
10. See ibid., pp. 63–67.
11. See Wolfgang von Hippel, "Wirtschafts- und Sozialgeschichte 1800 bis 1918", in Hansmartin Schwarzmaier (ed.), *Handbuch der baden-württembergischen Geschichte. Dritter Band: Vom Ende des Alten Reiches bis zum Ende der Monarchien* (Stuttgart: Klett-Cotta, 1992), pp. 639–640.
12. See the local newspaper *Ulmer Tagblatt*, 13 July 1916.
13. See Kristin Dannenberg, "Kommunale Selbstverwaltung in der Weimarer Republik. Daseinsvorsorge und Zukunftsplanung im Spiegel der Ulmer Gemeinderatsprotokolle", *Ulm und Oberschwaben*, 52 (2001), pp. 98–99.
14. See Bornhorst, *Selbstversorger*, pp. 75–79.
15. See the local newspaper *Ulmer Tagblatt*, 10 February 1917.
16. See Christoph Sachße and Florian Tennstedt, *Geschichte der Armenfürsorge in Deutschland. Volume 2: Fürsorge und Wohlfahrtspflege 1871–1929* (Stuttgart: Kohlhammer, 1988), p. 49.
17. See the relevant act of disposal in the gazette of the Royal Ministry of Church and School Württemberg: "Erlass des Kgl. Württembergischen Ministeriums des Kirchen- und Schulwesens vom 12.3.1917 betreffend die Mitwirkung der Schuljugend bei landwirtschaftlichen Arbeiten", *Amtsblatt des Kgl. Württembergischen Ministeriums des Kirchen- und Schulwesens* (1917), pp. 17–19.

18. See the Criminal Code for the German Empire, e.g. Reinhard Frank, ed., *Das Strafgesetzbuch für das Deutsche Reich nebst dem Einführungsgesetze* (Tübingen: Mohr, 1915), §§55–57. See also Crofts, *Criminal Responsibility*, 104.
19. See Sarah Fishman, *The Battle for Children: World War II, Youth Crime and Juvenile Justice in Twentieth-Century France* (London: Harvard University Press, 2002), pp. 13–16.
20. See Code of Criminal Procedure for the German Empire, e.g. Ewald Löwe, *Die Strafprozeßordnung für das Deutsche Reich nebst dem Gerichtsverfassungsgesetz und den das Strafverfahren betreffenden Bestimmungen der übrigen Reichsgesetze* (Berlin: J. Guttentag, 1913), §§140 sec. 1, pp. 340.
21. See Sylvia Kesper-Biermann and Petra Overath, "Internationalisierungsprozesse in der Geschichte von Strafrechtswissenschaft und Kriminalpolitik (1870–1930): Deutschland im internationalen Kontext", in Sylvia Kesper-Biermann and Petra Overath (eds), *Die Internationalisierung von Strafrechtswissenschaft und Kriminalpolitik (1870–1930): Deutschland im Vergleich* (Berlin: Berliner Wissenschafts-Verlag, 2007), p. 3.
22. See Chris Leonards, "Border Crossing: Care and the 'Criminal Child' in Nineteenth Century European Penal Congresses", in Pamela Cox and Heather Shore (eds), *Becoming Delinquent: British and European Youth, 1650–1950* (Aldershot: Ashgate Publishing, 2002), p. 108.
23. See Richard F. Wetzell, "Criminal Law Reform in Imperial Germany" (PhD diss., Stanford University, 1991), p. 166.
24. See Sylvia Kesper-Biermann, "Die Internationale Kriminalistische Vereinigung. Zum Verhältnis von Wissenschaftsbeziehungen und Politik im Strafrecht 1889–1932", in Kesper-Biermann and Overath (eds), *Internationalisierung*, pp. 97–98.
25. See David S. Tanenhaus, "The Evolution of Juvenile Courts in the Early Twentieth Century: Beyond the Myth of Immaculate Construction", in Margaret K. Rosenheim and Franklin E. Zimring and David S. Tanenhaus (eds), *A Century of Juvenile Justice* (Chicago: University of Chicago Press, 2002), p. 42.
26. See Michael Willrich, *City of Courts: Socializing Justice in Progressive Era Chicago* (Cambridge: Cambridge University Press, 2003), pp. 209–210.
27. Ibid., p. 210.
28. See Detlev J.K. Peukert, *Grenzen der Sozialdisziplinierung: Aufstieg und Krise der deutschen Jugendfürsorge 1878 bis 1932* (Köln: Böhlau, 1986), p. 87.
29. See Mariacarla Gadebusch Bondio, "From the 'Atavistic' to the 'Inferior' Criminal Type: The Impact of the Lombrosian Theory of the Born Criminal on German Psychiatry", in Peter Becker and Richard Wetzell (eds), *Criminals and Their Scientists: The History of Criminology in International Perspective* (Cambridge: Cambridge University Press, 2006), p. 184.
30. See Richard Wetzell, *Inventing the Criminal: A History of German criminology, 1880–1945* (Chapel Hill: University of North Carolina Press, 2000), p. 53, 59.
31. See Rebecca Habermas, "Eigentum vor Gericht. Die Entstehung des modernen Rechtsstaates aus dem Diebstahl?", *WerkstattGeschichte*, 42 (2006), pp. 37–38.
32. See D. Owen Carrigan, *Juvenile Delinquency in Canada: A History* (Ontario: Irwin Publishing, 1998), p. 81.

33. The term *"Halbstarker"* for deviant boys was established among social reformers by the pastor Clemens Schultz (Hamburg), see Clemens Schultz, *Die Halbstarken,* Leipzig 1912. Originally it described male working-class juveniles in opposition to bourgeois juveniles.

34. See C. Bettina Schmidt, *Jugendkriminalität und Gesellschaftskrisen: Umbrüche, Denkmodelle und Lösungsstrategien im Frankreich der Dritten Republik (1900– 1914)* (Stuttgart: Franz Steiner, 2005), pp. 95–117.

35. All figures are taken from the register of criminal proceedings at the County Court Ulm, see Kgl. Landgericht Ulm, *Strafprozesslisten 1904–16 and 1918,* StAL E 350a, Vol. 104–16 and Vol. 118. The register for 1917 is missing.

36. For Düsseldorf in Western Germany see Herbert Reinke, "'…hat sich ein politischer und wirtschaftlicher Polizeistaat entwickelt': Polizei und Großstadt im Rheinland vom Vorabend des Ersten Weltkrieges bis zum Beginn der Zwanziger Jahre", in Alf Lüdtke (ed.), *'Sicherheit' und 'Wohlfahrt': Polizei, Gesellschaft und Herrschaft im 19.und 20.Jahrhundert* (Frankfurt am Main: Suhrkamp, 1992), p. 230.

37. See Walter Wannewetsch, *Das Württembergische Landjägerkorps und die reichseinheitliche Gendarmerie in Württemberg mit einer Rückschau auf die Anfänge der Landespolizei* (Stuttgart: Gewerkschaft der Polizei, 1986), p. 66.

38. See Conviction of the Criminal Division of the County Court Ulm, 13 June 1918, against Anton L. and Ferdinand Sch., StAL E 350a, Bü 1087.

39. See the register of criminal proceedings at the Local Court of Kirchheim, Kgl. Amtsgericht Kirchheim, *Strafprozessliste 1918,* StAL F 276 II, Bü 78.

40. Female juvenile delinquents were underrepresented, for example, in Italy, too. See Mary S. Gibson, "The Criminalization of Youth in Late Nineteenth- and Early Twentieth-Century Italy", in Louis A. Knafla (ed.), *Crime, Punishment, and Reform in Europe* (Westport: Praeger, 2003), p. 126.

41. See Emsley, *Crime, Police, and Penal Policy,* pp. 233–234.

42. See Gibson, "Criminalization of Youth", pp. 125–126.

43. See Conviction of the Criminal Division of the County Court Ulm, 20 August 1917, against Florian N., StAL E 350a, Bü 998.

44. See Conviction of the Criminal Division of the County Court Ulm, 4 April 1918, against Albert K. et al., StAL E 350a, Bü 491.

45. See for example the prohibition for juveniles on visiting a pub from the military leadership of Württemberg: "Verordnung des Stellvertretenden Generalkommandos des XIII. Armeekorps vom 8.2.1916", in *Staatsanzeiger für Württemberg* 34 (11 February 1916).

46. See Bornhorst, *Selbstversorger,* pp. 279–283.

47. See Philip Rawlings, *Crime and Power: A History of Criminal Justice 1688–1998* (London: Longman, 1999), p. 128.

48. See Emsley, *Crime, Police, and Penal Policy,* p. 233.

49. See the relevant directive of the Royal Ministry of Justice: "Verfügung des Kgl. Württembergischen Justizministeriums vom 24.1.1911 betreffend das Strafverfahren gegen Jugendliche", *Amtsblatt des Kgl. Württembergischen Justizministeriums* 1911, p. 12.

50. See the Convictions of the Criminal Division of the County Court Ulm against Michael Sch., Bü 2; Marie K., Bü 194; Wilhelm Karl K., Bü 202; Anton W., Bü 865; Johannes Sch. e. a., Bü 871; Julius B., Bü 878; Karl T. and Gustav K., Bü 892; Georg B. et al., Bü 903; Wilhelm Johannes Daniel W.,

Bü 929; Wilhelm H., Bü 966; Anton L. and Ferdinand Sch., Bü 1087; Ewald
O., Bü 2106; Karoline T., Bü 2583, all StAL E 350a.

51. Conviction of the Criminal Division of the County Court Ulm, 20 September
1915, against Anton W., StAL E 350a, Bü 865:

([S]ein Vater ist im Felde, so daß die Mutter die alleinige Aufsicht über
ihre sieben Kinder, von denen der Angekl. das zweitälteste ist, zu führen
hat. Da sie tagsüber auswärts in Arbeit ist, sind die Kinder sich selbst über-
lassen u. der Angekl. treibt sich viel auf der Straße herum, da die Schulzeit
um die Hälfte verringert ist. Dabei kam er auch in Kameradschaft mit dem
16 J. alten Flaschnerlehrling Karl J., welcher Neigung zum Stehlen hat,
der Zucht u. Arbeit bei seinem Meister gerne aus dem Wege geht u. schon
als noch schulpflichtiger Zögling im Waisenhaus Ochsenhausen einem
seiner Lehrer Geld entwendete. Dieser J. übte sicherlich keinen guten Einfluß auf den Angeklagten aus; er war auch bei der in Frage kommenden
Tat desselben beteiligt.)

52. See Conviction of the Criminal Division of the County Court Ulm, 15 March
1917, against Christian H., StAL E 350a, Bü 938. (*"niedere Gesinnung", "[...]
stellt die Achtung vor unserem Volk bloß"*).
53. See detailed Bornhorst, *Selbstversorger*, pp. 272–278.
54. See for example Conviction of the Criminal Division of the County Court
Ulm, 10 October 1915, against Alfred R. et al., StAL E 350a, Bü 2194.
(*"jugendlicher Leichtsinn"*).
55. See Conviction of the Criminal Division of the County Court Ulm, 17 August
1917, against Marie W. et al., StAL E 350a, Bü 779. (*"krankhaft entartet"*).
56. See for example Conviction of the Criminal Division of the County Court
Ulm, 29 January 1917, against Matthäus E., StAL E 350a, Bü 917.
57. See for example Conviction of the Criminal Division of the County Court
Ulm, 4 April 1918, against Leonard R., StAL E 350a, Bü 1075.
58. Gustav Aschaffenburg, *Das Verbrechen und seine Bekämpfung: Einleitung in
die Kriminalpsychologie für Mediziner, Juristen und Soziologen; ein Beitrag zur
Reform der Strafgesetzgebung* (Heidelberg: Winter, 1906), p. 242 (*"Hochschule
des Lasters"*).
59. See Dietrich Oberwittler, *Von der Strafe zur Erziehung? Jugendkriminalpolitik in
England und Deutschland (1850–1920)* (Frankfurt am Main: Campus, 2000),
p. 298.
60. Ibid., p. 280.
61. See the act of disposal of the Royal Ministry of Justice: "Verfügung des Kgl.
Württembergischen Justizministeriums vom 29.4.1911 betreffend die bedingte Begnadigung", *Amtsblatt des Kgl. Württembergischen Justizministeriums*
1911, pp. 241–250.
62. See the compilation of the German parliament: "Anlage 2, Übersicht
I. Bewilligung des bedingten Strafaufschubs bis zum 31. Dezember 1906",
in: Zusammenstellung der statistischen Ermittelungen über die Anwendung
des bedingten Strafaufschubs bis Ende 1906, Reichstagsdrucksache Nr. 234,
Drucksachen des Reichstags. XII. Legislaturperiode, I. Session. III, 1907.
63. See a passage from a letter from the Central Leadership for Charity in
Württemberg (*"Zentralleitung für Wohltätigkeit"*) to the Royal Ministry of the
Interior, November 1915, HStAS E 151/09, Bü 156.

64. See a passage from a letter from the Royal Ministry of Justice to the Royal Ministry of Interior about the education of youth during war, HStAS E 151/09, Bü 156.
65. See the act of disposal of the Royal Ministry of Justice: "Verfügung des Kgl. Württembergischen Justizministeriums vom 31.3.1916 betreffend die bedingte Begnadigung", *Amtsblatt des Kgl. Württembergischen Justizministeriums* (1916), p. 27.
66. These values were calculated from records of the County Court Ulm, see Kgl. Landgericht Ulm, *Strafprozesslisten 1904–16 and 1918*, StAL E 350a, Vol. 104–116 and Vol. 118.
67. See a letter from the Royal Ministry of Justice to the Royal Ministry of the Interior about the education of youth during war, HStAS E 151/09, Bü 156.
68. Annual Report of the Juvenile Probation Unit Ulm 1915, 10, StAL E 191, Bü 5568. ("Im friedlichen bürgerlichen Leben war's ihnen zu eng gewesen. Unter dem Einfluß der militärischen Zucht, im gefährlichen Kampf, in dem es um ein so Großes ging, haben sie sich gefaßt und ihren Mann gestellt.")
69. See Klaus Saul, "Jugend im Schatten des Krieges: Vormilitärische Ausbildung, kriegswirtschaftlicher Einsatz, Schulalltag in Deutschland 1914–1918", *MGM* 2 (1983), p. 93.
70. See the list of juvenile militias, after 1 December 1915, attachment to a letter of the Working Committee of the Youth Militia Württemberg ("*Arbeitsausschusses der Württembergischen Jugendwehr*") to the Royal Ministry of the Church and School System, 17 February 1916, HStAS, M 77/1, Bü 556.
71. See Ute Frevert, *Die kasernierte Nation: Militärdienst und Zivilgesellschaft in Deutschland* (München: C. H. Beck, 2001), pp. 133, 273–274, p. 258.
72. Kurt Wittig, "Der Einfluss des Krieges auf das jugendliche Verbrechertum", *Zeitschrift für Kinderforschung* 20 (1915), p. 439 ("Der Krieg wirkt heilend und ebnet vielen Jugendlichen den Weg ins Leben!")
73. See Annual Report of the Juvenile Probation Unit Ulm 1916, 12, StAL E 191, Bü 5568.
74. See for example the directive of the Royal Ministry of Justice about the conditioned amnesty of Theodor Z., 10 July 1918, StAL E 350a, Bü 1092.
75. See the directive of the Royal Ministry of Justice: "Erlass des Kgl. Württembergischen Justizministeriums an die Kgl. Landesgefängnisverwaltung in Rottenburg vom 28.6.1918 bezüglich des bedingten Strafaufschubs für Bernhard R. (Abschrift für die Kgl. Staatsanwaltschaft in Ulm)" and a letter from the prison: "Schreiben des Kgl. Landesgefängnisses in Rottenburg an die Kgl. Staatsanwaltschaft Ulm vom 1.7.1918", both documents StAL E 350a, Bü 1075.
76. See Conviction of the Criminal Division of the County Court Ulm, 3 and 4 May 1917, against Jakob M. et al., StAL E 350a, Bü 950.
77. See Conviction of the Criminal Division of the County Court Ulm, 16 May 1918, against Karl H., StAL E 350a, Bü 1089.
78. See Hans Mommsen, "Militär und zivile Militarisierung in Deutschland 1914 bis 1938", in *Militär und Gesellschaft im 19. und 20. Jahrhundert,* ed. Ute Frevert (Stuttgart: Klett-Cotta, 1997), pp. 270–271. Mommsen calls it a "destruction of civil society" in post-war Germany. It was a topic for contemporary authors, too. See for example Erich Maria Remarque, *Der Weg zurück* (Berlin: Propyläen, 1931).

79. See Hajo Funke, "Vom Landesvater zum Polarisierer. Eine Nachlese der Landtagswahlergebnisse in Hessen 2008", in Micha Brumlik (ed.), *Ab nach Sibirien? Wie gefährlich ist unsere Jugend* (Weinheim: Beltz, 2008), pp. 29–31. As an example of the presentation of this subject in the mass media see Jan Schütz, "Kriminelle Ausländer: Diese mutige Richterin redet Klartext", *BILD*, 23 January 2010, accessed 20 July 2012, http://www.bild.de/news/vermischtes/richterin/redet-klartext-ueber-kriminelle-auslaender-5879218.bild.html.

List of abbreviations used in endnotes:

Bü	Büschel (Cluster)
DRZ	Deutsche Richter-Zeitung (German Judge-Journal)
HStAS	Hauptstaatsarchiv Stuttgart (Main Public Record Office Stuttgart)
Kgl.	Königlich (royal)
MGM	Militärgeschichtliche Mitteilungen (Military History Notifications)
StAL	Staatsarchiv Ludwigsburg (Public Record Office Ludwigsburg)

7
Empire's Little Helpers: Juvenile Delinquents and the State in East Asia, 1880–1945

Barak Kushner

This chapter explores the historical image and issue of Japanese juvenile delinquency as it specifically relates to pre-1945 East Asia. In the West, such behaviour was often easily labelled under the rubric of "juvenile delinquency" but as we will see, such a simple classification does not allow for the sort of historical investigation that is required when looking at the issue of empire and youth in East Asia. Unfortunately, while acknowledging this heuristic problem, we have precious little other vocabulary in our lexicon to describe the situation. Thus, I will retain the term "juvenile delinquency" but offer specific commentary on new ways of linking delinquency with politics and Japanese imperialism in China and Korea, concerning the symbols and rhetoric of pre-war and wartime Japanese youths on the Chinese mainland. Such an examination should hopefully bring to the forefront some of the pitfalls in too liberally appropriating the same terms across geography and history. The history of juvenile delinquency has often been written from a purely national perspective, or criminological orientation, with less in the way of comparative or transnational studies.[1] In other areas such scholarship attempts to reveal a pattern of Westernization, where non-Western nations learn from the West. Particularly lacking are studies which explore the construction and understanding of juvenile delinquency in the cultural sphere of East Asia and, equally important, how this delinquency was woven into the fabric of empire. The very query "What is 'juvenile delinquency'?" starts us off down a tricky path due to the very disparate nature of how what many see as a peculiarly Western idea was understood or conceived outside of western Europe and the US, at least from the late nineteenth century onward. How was the notion of juvenile delinquency extended to and applied in different areas of the British and German empires, for example? How did these adaptations differ from those in the Japanese empire? The Japanese approached the issue in a different manner in the modern era, after the Meiji Restoration in 1868, because its own society had been unstable for so long during the shift from Tokugawa rule. Delinquency was not only seen as a response to modernity – it had existed before as a response to millenarian discomfort with changes in mid-nineteenth century society and of course during earlier eras as well. Japanese understandings of juvenile criminality and anti-social behaviour among its own population did not, therefore, merely replicate Western values and norms.

It is telling that for the last 25 years or so, Western scholarship has primarily focused on high politics and the military in its analysis of the spread of Japanese imperialism on the Chinese continent. Historian Albert Feuerwerker suggested that we should not try too hard to produce a precise definition of imperialism because the term tended to be burdened with "ideology that deadened wit". Nonetheless, he offered a broad definition when he suggested that we could conceive of imperialism to mean "the employment of force or the threat of force by a stronger nation to control or influence, and to extract privileges from, a weaker nation".[2] Historian Tak Matsusaka cemented such reasoning in his remarks on the topic of the Japanese pushing into Manchuria before it became a formal puppet empire. "Japan's subjugation of Northeast China," he reasons, "began in 1905 with the acquisition of a railway concession in the southern part of the territory...."[3] While these analyses are obviously well argued, what they miss is an important precursor to formal state imperialism. For that we need to look at the lower echelons of society, those individuals who did not engage with state policy but were rather motivated by a different set of factors such as cultures of grassroots violence, or a desire for fame and fortune, on a much smaller scale and in less formalized fashion than under a state banner. What needs to be remembered is that the events of 1895, which saw Japan's first formal colonial acquisition – Taiwan, followed by its slow absorption of Korea over the next decade – led to further encroachment into the north China area known as Manchuria. The Japanese saw these lands as areas for providing buffer security against a Russian threat, as outposts for economic expansion, and as sectors to absorb what was feared to be an exploding Japanese overpopulation. At the time, much of the world, including the West, often believed that Japan's goals were no different from their own and that Japanese imperial inroads and colonial administration were a boon rather than a burden, for these not yet "modernized" parts of the Far East.

This chapter will focus on moments in history that demonstrate how the Japanese conceived of juvenile delinquency in order to provide a new window on imperialism outside of the formal framework of the state – one not necessarily aligned with capitalist concerns, nor politics, nor the military in the strict sense of the word. This set of examples revolves around the idea that social interest in juvenile crime was intimately linked to the expansion of Japanese imperialism. The aim is to sketch out the historical narrative, the context in which these national conversations about youths and youth crime in general interacted with the state and empire. To that end, the chapter is broken up into two broad sections. The first conceives of juveniles as key nodes of imperial growth, where interest in youths focused, on the one hand, on identifying the causes of youth crime that were seen to have a deleterious effect on the structure of the nation as a whole, but, at the same time, defined similar behaviour as enabling and contributing to the extension of empire. These seemingly paradoxical definitions extended broadly in Japan throughout the Meiji era and up to the end of the Second World War. The second moment I concentrate on is the actual transformation of the delinquent into the young imperial stalwart, be he a soldier or soldier of fortune, a process which saw young men move from the role of passive observers to one of active involvement in, and contribution to, Japan's imperial expansion.

These two moments tie into a larger supposition that delinquents in Japan can be conceived of as "empire's little helpers": domestically, as the agents of political violence outside of the mainstream which aided the rise of the state during the new Meiji government's infancy, and internationally, as the arm of Japanese political strength abroad albeit divorced from the law and order of the state. In the later nineteenth century, delinquents frequently functioned as the arm of the empire in terms of pushing national boundaries wider. It is not clear that these youths belonged to what was labelled the lower classes. Many had received a decent education, though a fair number could also be considered recidivist. Extreme examples also demonstrate that some were from the middle classes, motivated by national ideology that they perhaps never fully understood. Class was by no means the sole identifying feature.[4] Later, they also served as soldiers on the front line fighting against foreign encroachment. In this regard, they stand as very different subjects in their relationship to the state and authority from our standard conception of delinquents as those on the fringes of society in

opposition to existing structures of power. These are not the same categories we often associate with the notion of delinquency in the West.
We should consider them delinquents, though, because their actions
contravened the law and they were young, though their exact age and
the precise nature of the law remain debatable, as we shall see. In Japan
such delinquency sometimes took the form of imperial adventuring,
frequently labelled as *tairiku ryônin*, "mainland adventures" or *Shina
ryônin*, "China adventurers", from the 1880s onward as official dynas-
tic rule waned in both the Qing dynasty and the Yi dynasty in Korea.
More importantly, the compelling idea in Japan of helping to lead Asia
out of its quagmire at the turn of the century and then "overcoming
modernity", both oft quoted ideals in pan-Asianist Japanese literature,
mirror the nation's own attempts to build an empire and then consolidate it during the 1931–1945 war, with its own utopian aims in the
Greater East Asia Co-prosperity sphere. These ideals held that the world
had come to a turning point during the Second World War and that it
was time for a re-evaluation of modernity and "Japan's role in taking it
to the next stage".[5] Regardless of empire or its ultimate aims, the key
to remember is that *rônin* (adventuring), generally speaking, was not an
older man's game.

Given the somewhat diffident nature of East Asian history concerning
juvenile delinquency, it behoves us to first grapple with terminology.
A cornucopia of terms have made their way back and forth between
China and Japan to refer to those under adult age who committed
crimes or acted outside of contemporary norms, and who were hence
labelled as "juvenile delinquents" in the English language. The main
word denoting youth in Japanese would generally be *seinen*, while
shônen might be reserved for those more of elementary school age and a
separate term existed for girls – *shôjo*. These terms are slippery enough in
English but in East Asian languages they are often used interchangeably,
which, at the same time, carried with it specific historical baggage and
ideology not inherent to the Western terms.

From the outset, the terms relating to juvenile delinquency muddy
our understanding of whom and what we are talking about within East
Asian history. Juvenile delinquents came in many shapes and sizes.
Sometimes he/she was merely a youth who transgressed social norms
and behaviours. These included truancy, disrespect for social conventions in public, underage sex, but also political threats, extortion and
imperial bullying of those considered inferior to the Japanese race. Other
times these actions extended to outright crimes such as larceny, rape or
even murder. All of these categories got pushed into the tight linguistic

container of "juvenile delinquency", whose perpetrators formed an emerging class not yet belonging to the category of fully adult imperial Japanese subjects. It is important to note that the definition in Japan was broader. Generally speaking, for East Asia, such terminology concerned those who ranged in age from seven to 25 (and maybe even at times up to age 30), which is somewhat more expansive perhaps than legal codes would accept in other regions. This does not mean we should conceive of the entire corpus of East Asia as a single juvenile delinquent monolith, but that the social meaning of "youth" or "juvenile", and "delinquent", mixed in confusing ways, given their epistemological origins in the Japanese language and borrowing from Chinese concepts and tradition. Moreover, because Japan was moving through its tumultuous transition from the Meiji (1868–1912) to Taisho (1912–1926) to Showa (1926–1989) eras, behaviour that was strongly nationalistic or jingoistic (which could, under different circumstances, be described as "delinquent") was frequently labelled otherwise.

For the sake of developing a more historically oriented understanding of the terminology, we should move away from these terms, as they tend to originate from a Western understanding of juvenile delinquency and cover over the linkages between young hoodlums and Japanese imperialism in East Asia. The problems with our current categories are thrown into sharper relief when we look at other non-Western regions, such as Africa. Early twentieth-century boys who lazed about or were held to have a "glib tongue" were viewed as delinquents.[6] In Japan, while this may have also been the case, the "delinquency" I am describing has more to do with Japan's younger generation serving as the "sharp end of the stick" for imperial advancement. In that regard, these youths would not necessarily have always been viewed negatively in Japan, whereas non-Japanese would have perhaps seen them as contravening social norms in other locations in East Asia. "Juvenile delinquency" immediately constrains our understanding of the situation because it assumes normative values within one national context that did not necessarily translate elsewhere.

During the late nineteenth and early twentieth centuries, Japan and China were rife with youth crime.[7] Society was not placid and stable as the venerable myth of a harmonious Confucian or Tokugawa society suggests. Young criminals often belonged to the *liumang* class in China (non-permanent with no visible means of employment) or the *hinin* or *kabukimono* sectors in Japan. These lawbreakers were also known as *akutô* or *warumono* in the Japanese language, which might translate best as "bad guys".[8] Early modern East Asian societies were formerly much more aggressive and violence on the streets was not uncommon. This type of crime was not just directed internally but externally as well. The first British diplomat to be posted to Japan, Sir Rutherford Adcock, noticed the extreme umbrage young Japanese took at the foreign presence in the 1860s, with rocks being thrown and swords drawn generally unpleasant quotidian experiences. Danger was constant and almost intolerable.[9] Between 1862 and 1864 there were approximately 70 assassinations of foreigners and elites in Japan and not a few of them were carried out by the angry young men who were debating how to revolutionize Japan in the face of adversity. Many of these young and lawless ruffians, known as *sôshi*, came to epitomize Japan's push to change its political and social order, and some also linked up with nefarious gangs who exerted a certain political influence during subsequent eras. These young political revolutionaries, who transgressed, threatened and, at times, beat political opponents were not the only delinquents in Japan. They were at times vulgar but could also prove deeply effective as popular mobilizers due to their political songs that frequently championed Japan's imperial goals in East Asia.[10] One of these songs extolled Japan as "the England of East Asia, this is the duty our country has accepted".[11] Such was the fervour that at one time during the early days of the Sino-Japanese war in 1894 one singer, Soeda Azembô, found himself attacked by a mob when he deigned to suggest that the Japanese should not underestimate the Qing Empire, even though they appeared weaker. Even after the crowd dispersed, he still feared enough for his safety to be walked home with a police escort.[12]

There are deeper sub-layers to the concept of the juvenile delinquent in Japan that tie into the idea of empire. As historian Zhao Jun elucidates, "mainland adventurers" played a significant role in Japan's political and military machinations in China. Many of these youths were young men from lower ranking former samurai families from the Fukuoka region in Kyushu, Western Japan. These boys/young men had been shunted aside by the drastic changes the Meiji Restoration had wrought. They glamorized their role as "bushido warriors", supposedly battling to help China fight against the West but they were also without work or "proper means of daily income", and thus easily definable as juvenile delinquents in our current understanding of the term.[13] Obviously, not all were "men of purpose", as they often deemed themselves, and the "mainland adventurers" were often delinquents. But a large enough contingent existed for us to consider the manner in which Japanese imperialism spread at the fringes of empire through the activities of youths bent on illegal behaviour. As historian Sheldon Garon, has noted, in Japan it was quite possible for liberal social attitudes to coexist with political fascism.[14] The Japanese, one could say, were zealots of modernity but often imposed this ideal on their neighbours through rough or violent ways – in other words, delinquent behaviour. This would certainly have been true of youths who were dedicated to Japanese political ideals of modernity and attempted to find kindred spirits on the Chinese mainland and in Korea. Cultural historian Mark Driscoll notes that pimps and prostitutes preceded the spread of official Japanese imperialism in China. Also important in this sense were "soldiers of fortune", the term he chooses to define *sôshi* or young hoodlums.[15] What is more, by the late 1910s, Driscoll asserts, trafficking of women had become crucial for Japanese business in northeast China and "Japanese prostitutes were recognized as indispensible for the spread of related consumer products: beer, sake, Japanese food, makeup, and Japanese clothes."[16] Historian Jun Uchida echoes Driscoll's comments in her study of Korea. As she writes, "the earliest to blaze the trail were lower-class Japanese – a mixed bag of sojourners, petty merchants, laborers, carpenters, artisans, impoverished farmers, maids, prostitutes, and *rônin* [adventure-seekers]".[17] Thus delinquency, according to these two historians, acted as a harbinger of Japan's imperial expansion.

It was not always the case, however, that these young supporters of empire were as delinquent as assumed. Certainly the appellation was slippery and flexible, depending on society's response. We need to ask how much of a role these youths played in the expansion of what historians used to refer to as Japan's informal empire.[18] Scholars have normally sketched out the development of the state and the establishment of political networks as an extension of the new Meiji government but rarely in these previous historical analyses have those who arrived before the state been seriously considered. Instead, they have been conceived of as the discarded and youthful riffraff of modern society. There is certainly ample room for rethinking our notions of how the Japanese empire elongated its reach. There is a tendency to talk about the early Japanese state, with Saigô Takamori's push toward subjugating Korea and Ôkuma Shigenobu's plans for increasing Japanese influence in and eventual absorption of Taiwan, as a sort of domestically driven story.[19] By contrast, in the words of historian Erik Esselstrom, who has examined the ways in which the Japanese Ministry of Foreign Affairs conducted its police force abroad, and of Andre Schmid, who analyses how historians have written traditional Japanese history, we need to look beyond national borders and think more cogently about writing history that is inherently transnational.[20]

These notions of empire and the image of Korea and China as lands of great opportunity for both legitimate and exotic, illegitimate business expanded, in part, as a function of the Japanese media industry's proliferation of this image. In particular, such an image strengthened the Japanese populace's conviction of the need for Japan to assist its languishing Asian brethren. Obviously, the media did not promote thuggery as a pastime but the concept of the Chinese mainland as a geographical space where Japanese could move without too much regard for the law slowly gained attention in the late Meiji and early Taisho reigns. In 1914 the Japanese publisher Noma Seiji launched a successful youth magazine entitled *Shônen Club*, mostly aimed at schoolboys. In his words, "[m]ost of the existing juvenile magazines were little better than those of my youth written in an academic stilted style, too difficult even for ordinary adults to read...." Noma wanted to make a companion magazine for schoolboys. He believed that much of Japan's new educational system was adopted from the West and that they needed to put "Japanese national culture" back into education but in the form of home schooling.[21] Much of that imagery actively encouraged Japanese boys to find their adventure abroad, outside the boundaries of the nation. Already a dual image of youth in Japan existed – on the one hand, the political thug, and, on the other, the bookish schoolboy. In 1916, the illustrious journalist and political pundit, Tokutomi Sôho expressed further concern in a book entitled *Youth and the Future of Empire in the Taisho Era*. He argued that Japanese youth were the core of Japan's prospects for the future and needed to be educated accordingly. Tokutomi publicly asserted that juvenile delinquency was not only a personal failing but could lead to disaster on a national scale. He explained the situation thus: "Even a tattered ship with a broken rudder, torn sails and damaged engine can with the right wind and conditions limp into port." However, he argued, Japan could not afford to leave the education of its young people to chance since it needed proper leadership to keep the empire moving forward. For a country that is "just left to nature", he continued, "becomes a country that is unprepared for the future".

Unlike Noma's use of the term *shônen*, which often indicated "children", Tokutomi's use of *seinen*, "youth", often referred to juveniles in a slightly higher age bracket from 16 to 20. *Shônen* and *seinen* were often also used as labels to identify thugs on the streets, denoted with the Japanese prefix *furyô*, or "not good". Throughout the Meiji era and the early twentieth century in Japan such youths were also referred to as *sôshi*, though their ages were probably often in the upper teens and early twenties bracket. As Tokutomi explained in his late Meiji magazine *Friend of the Nation*, these hoodlums, *furyô seinen*, were the enemy of the real youth of Japan, the ones who would keep Japan from sliding back into its "feudal ways".[22]

The terms and examples presented here can be seen as markers, momentary representations that illuminate specific elements of official, civil and media debates that formed and shaped the public understanding of what juvenile delinquency was. This variety of definitions and interpretations also means that from the outset there was little in the way of a shared East Asian interpretation of juvenile delinquency but there may have been weaker shared historical tropes. These tropes are constantly fluid categories, as they are in most countries, and my hope in the limited scope of this chapter is merely to chart these and not necessarily to pin down any one definition that applied across the board. More importantly, these examples serve to reaffirm that juvenile delinquency was not just a post-war phenomenon in East Asia that grew in relation to increased contact with the West. As will become clear, these connections between the call for social renovation, either through helping Korea shed its traditional shackles or by promoting the Qing dynasty from an empire to a republic, or by Japanese society calling on youths to assist in the expansion of empire, all demonstrate strong linkages which show the importance of youth and their behaviour for the national psyche.

Japanese delinquents

The Meiji Restoration, a great phase of social tumult that began in the late 1860s, implemented a new political order and transgressed traditional social norms. This movement was led by young men, many of whom were already in their late twenties, but just as many more of whom were in their late teens and early twenties, which still placed them in this category of "youth" within an East Asian context. Once the restoration took hold, the whole thrust of Meiji Japan aimed to transform the nation and the next generation. A psychological sea change was underway. Youths were now imbued with a sort of national fever as they were deemed to be the ones to deliver Japan from its feudal bonds and to take the next generation toward a greater modernity. Over the next few decades a deep national interest surrounding youth, their role in society and their education arose. As historian Brian Platt notes,

The concern for the well-being of the children of Japan's new urban slums was mixed with fear of those children who succumbed to their unhealthy environment and sank into a life of deviance and crime. Journalists and reformists revealed to a middle-class public a dark subculture of youths on the streets of the big city, telling stories of young people who joined gangs and scavenged and stole to support themselves.[23]

David Ambaras, one of the key scholars in the English language in this field, notes that by 1895 Japan had acquired colonies and so required national subjects (*kokumin*) who could support these imperial aims. Victory over Russia in 1905 only served to increase this imperial fervour. Youths who went against this trend, boys begging in streets and girls pulled into the unlicensed sex trade, were thus seen by the population, the media and Meiji officials, as stains on the national body.[24] Early twentieth-century Japan, with its growing urbanization drawing the undereducated and unemployed from rural areas into the cities, saw an expansion in the floating population of slums where fathers drank and young boys pickpocketed; young women, often girls, sold sex or lasciviously slept with men who could offer them protection, a livelihood or amusement. Not until 1916 were children under 12 banned from being employed. As much as the Japanese authorities believed they were in need of correction, officials did not separate Japanese juveniles from the general prison population at first. In the 1890s, there were already between 20,000 and 28,000 minors in prison mixing with inmates of all other ages.[25] At the same time, historian Melanie Czarnecki reminds us that the definition of "bad girls" was still fairly broad at this time; sometimes it could refer to girls who simply held hands with boys![26] It is also important to realize that newspapers printed and often inflated such stories to gain readers because such salacious stories sold copy.[27]

What we also see at this time, as David Ambaras' research makes explicit, is that for many imperial Japanese youths

> seizing urban territory could be a prelude to the adventure of colonial conquest, while fighting with working class toughs offered training for dealing with recalcitrant Chinese or Koreans. But Japan's imperial enterprise had room for working class punks as well, and those who got into too much trouble at home could find a ready outlet in Korea or Manchuria.[28]

Figure 7.1   A hoodlum attacking a constable
Source: *Asahi Newspaper*, morning edition, Tokyo, 24 February 1903.[29]

Japanese police and authorities faced more than just mere juvenile delinquents at home; they were now facing a larger and more mobile population of imperial delinquents moving back and forth across porous international boundaries into lands whose ruling regimes were crumbling (Figure 7.1).

Note the form of dress, typical of the *sôshi* with rakish hat, *hakama* trousers, tall *geta* (wooden sandals) and instead of a staff, here a sword.

Not all Japanese youths necessarily transgressed norms; some actively supported them, just in slightly less than legal terms. From the turn of the century, Japanese "continental adventurists", those better known as *tairiku rônin*, came to see going to China as an expression of their imperial destiny as Japanese. Uchida Ryôhei (1874–1937) was one of the better known individuals and his case is, perhaps, indicative of this type of behaviour which may be labelled as juvenile delinquency with an imperial twist. Uchida was a protégé of Tôyama Mitsuru, a Meiji pan-Asianist who founded one of the earliest political pressure groups called the *Genyôsha*, or "Dark Ocean Society", named after the straits between Kyushu and China. Tôyama and his supporters were very critical of early Meiji plans and later spawned other similar political societies because they feared Japan was losing its national essence. While the society had a series of rather loosely defined goals, one publicly stated aim was that its members wanted to keep honor for Japan and "lead the rest of Asia out of slavery".[30] Uchida was only 20 in 1894 when he joined the *Genyôsha* to collaborate with reformist Korean groups to drive the Chinese out of the Korean peninsula.[31] The Korean group were known as the Tonghaks and were bent on reforming Korea from within. The Japanese "adventurers" did not share all the same values or goals with their Korean counterparts, but perceived an opportunity to overthrow the traditional Yi dynasty in Korea, which both sides viewed as corrupt and damaging to Korea's future interests.

The similarity between a newspaper drawing about "thugs" or *sôshi* in Japan and these *sôshi* in China is striking (Figure 7.2). On this cover from a Japanese book about beating the "fleeing Chinks" during the Sino-Japanese war, we see a Manchu soldier with his "pigtail" flopping in the wind when he runs away. A Japanese "continental adventurer" dressed in the very costume of a political thug in Japan, complete with very tall *geta* [wooden sandals], a somewhat rakish appearance and carrying a big stick.[32]

One reason this motley band of Japanese youths and mercenaries took part in the Tonghak rebellion was because they saw themselves as anti-traditionalists who wanted to help change Korea and Asia in general and save them from marauding colonialists. These young Japanese imperialists formed a smaller, elite group called the *Tenyûkyô*, and Uchida was part of this group. The famed historian of Japan E.H. Norman translated *Tenyûkyô* as the "Society of Heavenly Salvation for the Oppressed", although recently historian Oleg Benesch has provided a more succinct rendering as the "Order of Divine Chivalry", which may fit better with what the aims of the Japanese youths actually were. These young Japanese men travelled to the Korean peninsula and essentially terrorized Korean villagers they met along the way as they trekked from Pusan in the south of the Korean peninsula.[33] In February 1894 in the Jeolla (Cholla) province of Korea, a massive internal peasant uprising, known as the Tonghak rebellion, flared up once again as it had many times since its inception in the early 1860s. The Tonghak had grown substantially from the rural force it had been at this time, especially in the southwest. In the spring of 1894, the Tonghak, now significantly expanded, had two aims: to overthrow their own Queen Min's rule and to drive the Japanese out of Korea. It was essentially a movement that opposed the high taxes and corrupt officials introduced by Japan, but it caught the attention of nationalistically minded Japanese who ironically saw links to their own cause and a way of ending foreign intervention on the Korean peninsula that was supposedly at the root of many of these

Figure 7.2 A Manchu soldier fleeing from a Japanese "continental adventurer"
Source: *Songs about Crushing the Qing Soldiers*, Fūrinkan 1894, front cover.

domestic disturbances. However, the Tonghak were not pro-Japanese, like other Korean reformist groups. In fact, one of the Tonghaks' slogans was "Drive out the Japanese dwarfs!",[34] a seemingly intractable stance against the nascent empire, but this did not seem to prevent the

Tenyûkyô from pursuing an unlikely alliance with the Japanese. Historian Carter Eckert writes that most of the Japanese who were active in Korea, and who accounted for a large portion of the trade exchange, were from "lower and depressed elements of Japanese society" and thus some may also have felt empathy with those they presumed were as economically disadvantaged as themselves.[35]

While the Korean court and government strove to suppress the Tonghaks, jingoistic Japanese "delinquents" tried to join forces with them in a seeming gesture of camaraderie directed against foreign encroachment into East Asia. The *Tenyûkyô*'s offer was to help the Tonghak start up again after their initial defeat by the Qing and Korean government forces. Members tried to steal arms from the Japanese consulate in Pusan and dynamite from mines to give to the Tonghak as weapons.[36] Joined by a few more stalwarts from Japan, including Uchida, they were successful in stealing dynamite but the Japanese consulate uncovered the plot and sent the police to deal with the situation. By the time the dust settled, the Qing dynasty and the Japanese were fighting each other in Korea for colonial power. What is more, the *Tenyûkyô* had seemingly abandoned their initial task of linking up with the anti-Qing Tonghak and were now bent on supporting Japanese imperial aims. Ultimately, the Tonghak managed to establish a ceasefire with their enemies but by then China and Japan had sent in their own imperial armed forces to the peninsula to quell unrest and from July 1894 the two nations ended up fighting over Korea in the first Sino-Japanese war. The following year, in October 1895, a Japanese "mainland adventurer", Miura Gorô, orchestrated a gang of Japanese, two of whom were members of *Tenyûkyô* and part of a team that assassinated and burned the corpse of the Korean Queen Min.[37]

Juvenile delinquency is difficult to define not only with respect to age but also in terms of behaviour. It is wise, therefore, to move away from strict legal or age-bracket definitions and examine a range of social and cultural markers in order to clarify how juvenile delinquency was viewed and experienced in East Asia in the nineteenth and early twentieth centuries. Part of the reason why historians have so far declined to see these "continental adventurers" as delinquents is the tendency of English language scholarship to view their actions in terms of political conspiracy and imperial agency instead, which has masked the youth and independent-mindedness of the individuals involved. For example, one standard book on the topic writes that the "*Tenyûkyô*, a group of hand-picked *agent provocateurs* [were] sent into Korea as agitators".[38] The author gives preference to the *Tenyûkyô*'s actions as agents of the state, while in reality they were mostly a gang of hoodlum youths acting in concert with imperial but not necessarily state aims.

The problems involved in working out precisely how Japanese delinquency was viewed in Korea and China remain considerable because, as post-war scholarship illuminates, most of the literature on these fringe imperial delinquent groups stems from other right-wing groups' own histories of themselves or similar activities and they are consistently eager to inflate their own achievements.[39] In addition, several of the major works that were published were produced during the 1930s by right-wing publishers who eulogized these actions and made it seem as if the delinquents were traditional "knights errant", protecting the weak and helping the poor.[40] In 1930s Japan the military wielded ever more control over domestic politics and foreign policy, resulting in a more strongly censored media that at first failed to exert its independence and then quickly started goose-stepping behind imperial military officers. Within a few years, newspapers rarely carried any criticism of policy and lavishly heaped praise upon the military in strident and jingoistic terms. Formerly, the men responsible for the Meiji Restoration were known as *shishi*, translated in English as "men of high purpose", a parallel idea to those who believed they were protecting Asians from themselves and their own backwardness. Right-leaning, nationalist literature would not have used the more Chinese literary term, "knights errant" (*wuxia*), but certain passages did note that these "Enlightened Gentlemen", (*senkaku shishi*), as Japanese adventurers were labelled, had helped to encourage the circumstances which led ultimately to the establishment of Manchukuo.[41] Uchida Ryôhei certainly existed and was among the youngest of the nationalistic continental adventurers, which may have been the reason he later received so much media attention. In actuality, the *Tenyûkyô* was a small group of approximately 14 individuals.[42] Such incidents did not go unnoticed and were detailed in major Japanese newspapers, which notified the public that the *Tenyûkyô* was trying to smuggle dynamite into Korea to join up with the Tonghak rebellion. Eventually, the group's attempts to join forces with the Tonghak were thwarted and Uchida was attacked by Korean villagers to within an inch of his life and then arrested.[43] The Japanese ruffians mostly disbanded when they heard about the start of the Sino-Japanese war a few months after their initial forays. Following this incident and banking on his growing charisma, Uchida stayed on in the region and set up his own martial arts school. Undaunted by his initial failures, in 1901 he started his own right-wing group, *Kokuryûkai*, or the Amur River Society, and many of these men started collecting intelligence on Russia and China for the Japanese military, which was later employed in a haphazard fashion in the 1904–1905 Russo-Japanese War.[44] Even though they were essentially lawless ruffians, these Japanese delinquents couched their actions in glorious language. In one example, their dreams were encapsulated in a song called "the realm of the continental adventurer", which regaled their virtues, claiming "they would break the determination of the foreigners [blue-eyed and brown-haired], and the continental warriors would show them the sharpness of their blades to defend the realm".[45] There was, strangely, therefore, a sort of romantic notion on behalf of the Japanese delinquent that he was going to the continent to save Korea, and later China, from rapacious Western foreigners. Such beliefs also stemmed from a sense of burgeoning pan-Asianism but limitations of space prevent a fuller analysis of this dimension here.[46] These shared pan-Asian ideals and their prominence in the news continued as China moved from a dynasty to a modern republic in 1912. As Zhao Jun notes, the Japanese who were growing in number on the mainland were actually there to secure Japan's "national benefits" and these efforts included many adventurers whose activities Zhao labels as "civilian diplomacy".[47] The Japanese on their own islands were well aware of these actions because in October 1911 Tôyama Mitsuru, Uchida Ryôhei and others, including Miyazaki Tôten (who had earlier befriended Chinese reform leader Sun Yat Sen), held a "rônin meeting" at a huge public rally in Hibiya Park, Tokyo, to discuss Japan's attitude toward China's budding revolution.

Delinquents on the mainland seemed to mirror social problems back at home during the 1910s and 1920s. The conundrum of what to do with youths who did not follow the collective aims of the new Japan and empire began to draw social commentary in the growing Japanese media. A collection of readers' letters to a column devoted to social problems in the 1910s first appeared in the *Yomiuri Newspaper*. Readers with little access to fuller information on hygiene, sex, male–female relations and issues involving young people had many anxieties and the newspaper offered a new outlet for them to express their worries. A letter dated 9 April 1922 from a youth of 18 who had just failed his exams may be taken as typical. The youth attended a commercial higher school in Osaka but wrote that "delinquent girls" in his area, *furyôshôjo*, were a growing problem. He could not keep away from them as hard as he tried, he wrote, and as they knew he came from a family of means, "they use all their tricks of the trade to seduce me", he lamented to readers. The youth wrote that a few years ago this was not really an issue but now he was starting to fall in love and could no longer concentrate on his studies. "They have even brazenly shown me nude pictures of themselves," he penned.

> I am trying to steal myself away and avoid them but I don't seem to be able to. I resolved to leave home for a boarding house but my parents are worried that leaving home will not permit me to focus enough on my studies to pass the exams. What am I to do?[48]

he asked. The Japanese anguished about domestic delinquency but did not consider Japanese actions outside of its main islands, on the continent, to be delinquent but rather nationalistic and thus tended to construe such actions in a more positive light. It was, to be sure, an interesting dualistic mindset, driven, in part, by the importance they placed on the construction of empire.

Fallen girls were a particular issue for Japanese society, in particular *karayuki*, or Japanese prostitutes, who gained employment abroad because many in Japan believed that these girls undermined Japanese modernization efforts throughout the empire. In trying to limit the number of girls and women who travelled abroad the Japanese government was keenly aware of the image of *karayuki*. This was one reason why so many male Japanese labourers lived lonely lives of isolation in the US, especially California.[49] Guidebooks issued to Japanese women journeying as "picture brides" to the US instructed them not to discuss domestic issues with white Americans because this would cause embarrassment to the nation of Japan.[50] The fact that such a responsibility was placed on these young women also indicates the effort Japanese authorities went to in order to improve the image of the Japanese abroad. In the minds of the Japanese politicians during the late Meiji and Taisho eras the proliferation of Japanese prostitutes travelling abroad to ply their trade was a serious problem that they worried would be responsible for more stringent American anti-Asian immigration policies.[51]

As the issue of youth crime for young men and women grew, although rarely defined as an imperial issue, a trend toward a more narrow focus on how such deviance affected the image and development of the state emerged. As such, "children came into the purview of public discussion and state policy – not only as victims of the various social problems that plagued modern urban society, but as social problems in and of themselves".[52] By the 1920s, child welfare projects amounted to 60% of the Home Ministry's budget. Justifying this expansion in child-centred programmes and legislation, the Home Ministry's Social Bureau Chief declared in 1925 that "social weaknesses regarding children are the root of all social problems".[53]

Because Japan was an empire, with the acquisition of Taiwan and Korea, not to mention northern China and later the inclusion of Manchuria, by the 1920s the police were increasingly worried that undesirables from across the empire would be able to connect with one another. The authorities concluded that many juvenile delinquents were flooding in from the supposedly less civilized parts of Japan's imperial reach and coordinating anti-social efforts with young Japanese. In truth, their fears were not unfounded though the reasons often had to do with oppressive Japanese imperial management itself. Young Koreans who were opposed to Korea's inclusion in the Japanese empire formed the *Futeisha* (Company of Malcontents), a group that in part gave rise to this popular fear. It was not only Koreans coming to Japan but also Japanese who travelled to Korea and joined forces with unsavoury elements there that further compounded political anxiety.[54] Kaneko Fumiko, a Japanese anarchist from the early twentieth century, is a prime example of a politically delinquent young woman from this era. An underprivileged Japanese, she went to Korea at the tender age of nine and returned when she was 16. In Korea, she lived among the impoverished and oppressed, and upon returning to Japan eventually came into contact with Korean anarchist Pak Yeol.[55] She grew martial in her anti-imperial stance toward her mother country, especially after 1 March 1919, Korea's March for Independence Day, which saw 2,000 dead and 20,000 arrested, and resulted in Japan easing its colonial policies to maintain social order. In 1922 Kaneko joined the *Futeisha* anarchist group and she was arrested with Pak in September 1923, just after the Great Kanto earthquake. In the immediate aftermath of the earthquake Tokyo was in complete disorder, and 1,000 Koreans were attacked and murdered in the belief that they were poisoning wells and wreaking havoc.[56] During the Great Kanto earthquake, for all his previous support of the Korean Tonghak group, right-wing leader Uchida Ryôhei "later vehemently protested police attempts to criminalize the vigilantes as the sole perpetrators of Korean killings, and wrote: 'The whole city witnessed that police officers ran around shouting 'when you see a Korean behaving violently, you may beat him to death then and there.' "[57]

The Tokyo police supposedly placed Pak and Kaneko in "protective custody", though in reality charges were not brought until two years later. In court, at one point, a photograph was taken of the two with Kaneko sitting comfortably in the lap of Pak and, according to historian

Mikiso Hane, "the picture presented to the general public was that of a degenerate, nefarious woman".[58] Years later, in 1926, they were finally tried and convicted. Kaneko and Pak were both handed sentences of execution but the Showa emperor commuted them. Furious with her inability to become a martyr for the cause, Kaneko eventually committed suicide in prison as a political statement. Pak remained in prison until the end of the Second World War and returned to Korea, where he died decades later in the 1970s.[59]

Throughout the first decades of the twentieth century Japanese street toughs also entered the national and international picture. They were referred to as *yotamono, yota* or *furyô*. They congregated in parks, shrine grounds, movie theatres and cafes, drawing on images of Japanese outlaw heroes which further fed their appetite to try their criminal luck abroad. An article in the *Asahi* newspaper on 7 June 1928 reported that one gang was acquiring their ill-gotten gains by embezzling and mugging to pay for the journey to set up a new life for themselves as bandits in Manchuria. This was the Shibuya Horseshoe Gang.[60] Eighteen members who had together amassed 10,000 yen (a fortune then) were arrested when they were planning to abscond to the "free" colonial lands (Manchuria) where a Japanese could seemingly commit crime with impunity. The vice-ringleader, as the article stated, was a young waitress of just 20 who worked in a café in the less than virtuous *Dogenzaka* area of Shibuya. She would fleece customers by staging arguments or mug women and girls who were walking through a nearby park area.[61]

The Chinese response to Japanese delinquents

Japanese "delinquents" of many shapes and sizes served in China as the vanguard of Japanese imperialism but also helped to create an enduring myth in China about Japanese behaviour and goals on the continent. Chinese youth groups, in turn, formed in response to these incursions and perceived Japanese aggression – in many areas where it existed and perhaps in a few where it did not. In a similar manner to those of Japan, Chinese children therefore became central to plans for national change through foreign education and renovation. Here though this was not connected with a desire for empire but was in fact decidedly anti-imperial. This was true not only in the spiritual sense but in a very physical sense as well. The creation of the Pure Martial Athletic Association, *Jingwu tiyuhui*, is one example of many such young men's associations which eventually located in Shanghai and whose founder Huo Yuanjia become well known for beating Japanese "continental adventurers" in martial arts contests which pitted Chinese and Japanese techniques against each other.[62] Although accounts of Japanese involvement in Huo's death are still disputed, it remains a popular Chinese myth. This is similar to the myth that his students during the 1920s would fight Japanese ruffians, which served as a leitmotif for over half a century of martial arts films.[63] The image of a Japanese male "delinquent" roughing up patriotic young Chinese men is an enduring motif even in contemporary Chinese film, but a long-standing mainstay of popular culture in Chinese martial arts films since the 1970s, starting with Bruce Lee's first international blockbuster film, *Fist of Fury* (1972). The deep-seated historical links and connections to contemporary popular culture should remind us of the constructed nature of juvenile delinquency on several levels. While the Japanese viewed such behaviour as juvenile crime fed by opposition to their imperial rule, the Chinese praised it as heroic resistance and muscular nationalism. Once again, one society's delinquents are another's heroes.

As much as the previous century's Japanese delinquents proclaimed that they were on the continent to assist China, Chinese students studying in Japan from the early part of the twentieth century continually remarked, amid other gripes about, for example, the poor quality of Japanese food, that even children in the neighbourhoods where they lived, would taunt them. A form of Japanese delinquent behaviour toward exchange students developed – not dissimilar to rough Japanese behaviour on the continent. When asked why they abandoned their studies in Japan, many Chinese students commented that they could not endure the incessant taunts of Japanese children constantly hurling insults of "Chink! Chink!" at them wherever they walked.[64] In the early part of the century, many of the first Chinese students to study in Japan still maintained the imperial Qing hairstyle, sporting the queue, or ponytail of hair, and Chinese complaints that they were treated as second-class citizens were a constant reminder of the growing racial and cultural divide between Japan and China at the turn of the century, even among youths. Young Japanese could behave publicly with some impunity toward those they regarded as inferior inhabitants of East Asia.

Conclusion

There are strong links between Japanese juvenile delinquency and the rise of imperialism on the Asian continent that have not yet been explored by historians. In Japan, for example, Inoue Nissho was the mastermind behind a series of assassinations in which the former Finance Minister Inoue Junnosuke and the Director General of Mitsui, Dan Takuma, were killed in February and March 1932. The Inoue group had actually planned 20 assassinations but could only carry out a few. However, the key point is that in 1910, at the age of 24, Inoue had travelled to China and sought adventure, behaving like a "wild animal" in his own words. Historian Stephen Large illustrates how he lived: "These were years of heavy drinking, whoring, and living recklessly on the knife edge of danger, as if he deliberately courted death to escape from his continuing sense of existential despair."[65] Japanese delinquents seemingly trained in Korea and China for later careers as political thugs and domestic ruffians and further research is needed to more fully investigate this relationship and trajectory. In some ways the dissolution of Japan's empire after 1945 allowed for both Chinese and Japanese society to change drastically even if the process threatened overall cultural stability. Japan experienced a worrisome spate of crime in the immediate post-war years although the levels tapered off. However, it should be noted that in recent years the Japanese media has whipped up society once more into a frenzy concerning heinous juvenile crime. Social historian Nanba Kôji concludes that in Japan, during the Meiji generation, youths were expected to shoulder the burden of national renovation and change and were thought of as a group with their own history and culture. In post-war Japan this belief changed dramatically and youth has come primarily to be seen as just another age group. The Japanese media now employ the term *seinen* much less, replacing it with the less historically laden term *wakamono*.[66] Several early post-war authors insist that pre-war Japan actually had little concept of youth culture in general and that until young people were drafted into the armed forces they were considered children, in essence, with no real independent judgement. For boys, once drafted into the military, were suddenly adult. There was no middle ground. Social historian Minami Hiroshi argues that it was not until the 1950s that the category of teenager, as something in between, really appeared.[67]

In the end, we must ask where all this leaves us in relation to East Asia? Juvenile crime reflects state fears about itself and the future but is also influenced by political events and the media. The stretch from the nineteenth to the twentieth century in China and Japan reveals more disparity than parity in terms of historical narrative about juvenile delinquency. It is hoped that this chapter has provided a new perspective on the interconnections between empire and the ways in which states conceived of juvenile crime in this period as well as their policies and anxieties concerning its implications. In addition, for China the idea of resistance both during the Second World War and long after the war was over encouraged the creation of a certain type of juvenile delinquent who became the cultural representation of resistance against the Japanese *guizi*, or "devils", as the Japanese imperial military was colloquially referred to in the Chinese language.[68] Juvenile delinquency is hard to pin down precisely but by referencing its location within imperialism we can begin to understand the contours of its development and discover aspects of overlap with other regions of the world.

Notes

1. This chapter uses the terms "juvenile" and "youth" deliberately to point out the fluidity of their definitions in East Asia. This is explained throughout the essay.
2. Albert Feuerwerker, "Japanese Imperialism in China: A Commentary", in Peter Duus, Ramon Hawley Myers and Mark R. Peattie (eds), *The Japanese Informal Empire in China, 1895–1937* (Princeton: Princeton University Press, 1989), p. 432.
3. Yoshihisa Tak Matsusaka, *The Making of Japanese Manchuria, 1904–1932* (Cambridge, MA: Harvard University Asia Center, 2001), p. 1.
4. For more on class and children in Japanese history, see Mark Jones, *Children as Treasures: Childhood and the Middle Class in Early Twentieth Century Japan* (Cambridge, MA: Harvard University Asia Center, 2010).
5. Harry Harootunian, *Overcome by Modernity: History, Culture, and Community in Interwar Japan* (Princeton: Princeton University Press, 2000), p. 34; Richard F. Calichman, editor and translator, *Overcoming Modernity, Cultural Identity in Wartime Japan* (New York: Columbia University Press, 2008), pp. 1–41.
6. Laurent Fourchard, "Lagos and the Invention of Juvenile Delinquency in Nigeria, 1920–1960", *Journal of African History*, 47 (2006), p. 125.
7. David Howell, "Making Sense of Senseless Violence in Early Meiji Japan", in David L. Howell and James C. Baxter (eds), *History and Folklore Studies in Japan* (Kyoto: International Research Center for Japanese Studies, 2006), pp. 57–75.
8. David Howell, *Geographies of Identity in Nineteenth-century Japan* (Berkeley, CA: University of California Press, 2005), p. 98.
9. Eiko Maruko Siniawer, *Ruffians, Yakuza, Nationalists – The Violent Politics of Modern Japan, 1860–1960* (Ithaca: Cornell University Press, 2008), p. 15.
10. Michael Lewis (translated and annotated), *A Life Adrift: Soeda Azembô, Popular Song and Modern Mass Culture in Japan* (New York: Routledge, 2009), pp. 15–27 for a full explanation of *sôshi* popular songs.
11. Michael Lewis (translated and annotated), *A Life Adrift: Soeda Azembô, Popular Song and Modern Mass Culture in Japan* (New York: Routledge, 2009), p. 16.
12. Michael Lewis (translated and annotated), *A Life Adrift: Soeda Azembô, Popular Song and Modern Mass Culture in Japan* (New York: Routledge, 2009), p. 48.

13. Zhao Jun, "Kindai Nihon to Chûgoku no ichi setten", (Point of Contact Between Early Modern Japan and China) *Komazawa joshi daigaku*, kenkyû kiyô, dai ni go (1995), p. 62.

14. Sheldon Garon, "Rethinking Modernization and Modernity in Japanese History: A Focus on State-Society Relations", *Journal of Asian Studies*, 53, 2 (May 1994), p. 350.

15. Mark Driscoll, *Absolute Erotic, Absolute Grotesque: The Living, Dead, and Undead in Japan's Imperialism, 1895–1945* (Durham, NC: Duke University Press, 2010), p. 29.

16. Mark Driscoll, *Absolute Erotic, Absolute Grotesque: The Living, Dead, and Undead in Japan's Imperialism, 1895–1945* (Durham, NC: Duke University Press, 2010), p. 62.

17. Jun Uchida, *Brokers of Empire: Japanese Settler Colonialism in Korea, 1876–1945* (Harvard University Press, 2011), p. 37. See also Alain Delissen, "Denied and Beseiged: The Japanese Community of Korea, 1876–1945", in Robert Bickers and Christian Henriot (eds), *New Frontiers: Imperialism's New Communities in East Asia, 1842–1953* (Manchester: Manchester University Press, 2000), pp. 125–145. Delissen notes, however on p. 132, that this "half-adventurist, half-lout penny capitalist", collection of individuals later changed to a more respectable colonial population by 1905–1906. For the larger discussion of this interaction see E. Taylor Atkins, *Primitive Selves: Koreana in the Japanese Colonial Gaze, 1910–1945* (Berkeley, CA: University of California Press, 2010); and Mark Caprio, *Japanese Assimilation Policies in Colonial Korea, 1910–1945* (Seattle: University of Washington Press, 2009).

18. Peter Duus, Ramon Myers and Mark Peattie, eds., *The Japanese Informal Empire in China, 1895–1937* (Princeton: Princeton University Press, 1989). It is interesting to note that although the term "informal empire" was employed, most of the case studies in this epochal volume dealt with top-down forms of structure and not the delinquents and fringes of society that Driscoll, Uchida and others select as the progenitors of empire.

19. Robert Eskildsen, "Of Civilization and Savages: The Mimetic Imperialism of Japan's 1874 Expedition to Taiwan", *The American Historical Review*, 107, 2 (April 2002), pp. 396–397.

20. Erik Esselstrom, *Crossing Empire's Edge: Foreign Ministry Police and Japanese Expansionism in Northeast Asia* (Honolulu: University of Hawaii Press, 2009), p. 5; and Andre Schmid, "Colonialism and the 'Korea Problem' in the Historiography of Modern Japan: A Review Article", *Journal of Asian Studies*, 59, 4 (November 2000), pp. 953–954.

21. Seiji Noma, *The Nine Magazines of Kodansha* (London: Methuen and Co., 1934), pp. 184–185.

22. Kimura Naoe, *Seinen no tanjô* (The Birth of Youth), Shinyôsha, 1998, p. 46.

23. Brian Platt, "Japanese Childhood, Modern Childhood: The Nation-State, the School, and 19th-Century Globalization", *Journal of Social History* (Summer 2005), p. 978.

24. David R. Ambaras, *Bad Youth: Juvenile Delinquency and the Politics of Everyday Life in Modern Japan* (Berkeley: University of California Press, 2006), p. 31.

25. Ibid., p. 46.

26. Melanie Czarnecki, "Bad Girls from Good Families: The Degenerate Meiji Schoolgirl", in Laura Miller and Jan Bardsley (eds), *Bad Girls of Japan* (New York: Palgrave Macmillan, 2005), p. 50.
27. Ibid., p. 60.
28. David R. Ambaras, *Bad Youth: Juvenile Delinquency and the Politics of Everyday Life in Modern Japan* (Berkeley: University of California Press, 2006), p. 146.
29. Compare this image with the one in Eiko Maruko Siniawer, *Ruffians, Yakuza, Nationalists – The Violent Politics of Modern Japan, 1860–1960* (Ithaca: Cornell University Press, 2008), p. 50.
30. Joel Joos, "The Genyôsha (1881) and Premodern Roots of Japanese Extremism", in Sven Saalar and Christopher W.A. Szpilman (eds), *Pan Asianism, Documentary History, volume 1: 1850–1920* (New York: Rowman and Littlefield, 2011), p. 63.
31. E. Herbert Norman, "The Genyosha: A Study in the Origins of Japanese Imperialism", *Pacific Affairs*, 17, 3 (September 1944), pp. 261–284.
32. Nishimori Takeki, *Shinpei taiji no uta* (*Songs about Crushing the Qing Soldiers*), Fūrinkan, 1894, front cover.
33. Eiko Maruko Siniawer, *Ruffians, Yakuza, Nationalists – The Violent Politics of Modern Japan, 1860–1960* (Ithaca: Cornell University Press, 2008), p. 55.
34. Bruce Cumings, *Korea's Place in the Sun: A Modern History* (New York: W.W. Norton, 1997), p. 115.
35. Carter Eckert, *Korea Old and New, a History* (Cambridge: Harvard University Press, 1990), p. 215.
36. Kang Chang-Il, "Tenyûkyô to Chôsen mondai: Chôsen rônin no tôgaku nômin sensô e taiô to kanren shite" (The Order of Divine Chivalry and the Korean Problem: Issues Relating to Continental Adventurers in Korea and Responding to the Peasant Tonghak war), *Shigaku zasshi*, 97, 8, p. 1330.
37. Andre Schmid, *Korea between Empires: 1895–1919* (New York: Columbia University Press, 2002), p. 28; Bruce Cumings, *Korea's Place in the Sun: A Modern History* (New York: W.W. Norton, 1997), p. 121.
38. Terry Crowdy, *The Enemy Within: A History of Spies, Spymasters and Espionage* (London: Osprey Publishing, 2006), p. 216.
39. For example see Kokuryûkai ed., *Tôa senkaku shishi kiden* (Recorded Tales of East Asia's Enlightened Men of Purpose), vol. 1 (reprint of 1935 original) Harashobô, 1966, pp. 173–257.
40. Uchida Ryōhei kenkyūkai, ed., *Kokushi: Uchida Ryōhei* (National Loyalist: Uchida Ryôhei), Tentensha, 2003, p. 55.
41. Kokuryûkai ed., *Tôa senkaku shishi kiden* (Recorded Tales of East Asia's Enlightened Men of Purpose), vol. 2 (reprint of 1935 original) Harashobô, 1966, p. 1 in the introduction.
42. Uchida Ryōhei kenkyūkai, ed., *Kokushi: Uchida Ryōhei* (National Loyalist: Uchida Ryôhei), Tentensha, 2003, p. 57.
43. Ibid., p. 63. See Oleg Benesch, "Bushido: the Creation of a Martial Ethic in Late Meiji Japan", PhD in Asian Studies (University of British Columbia, 2011), pp. 99–102.
44. Jason Karlin, notes the growth of sôshi to imperial adventurers in "The Gender of Nationalism: Competing Masculinities in Meiji Japan", *Journal of Japanese Studies*, 28, 1 (Winter 2002), p. 61. See also Sven Saalar, "The Kokuryûkai, 1901–1920", in Sven Saalar and Christopher W.A. Szpilman

(eds), *Pan Asianism, Documentary History, volume 1: 1850–1920* (New York: Rowman and Littlefield, 2011), pp. 121–132.

45. Zhao Jun, "Kindai Nihon to Chûgoku no ichi setten" (Point of Contact between Early Modern Japan and China), *Komazawa joshi daigaku*, kenkyû kiyô, dai ni go, 1995, p. 65.

46. Peter Duus, *The Abacus and the Sword: The Japanese Penetration of Korea, 1895–1910* (Berkeley, CA: University of California Press, 1995), p. 202.

47. Zhao Jun, "Shingai kakumeiki ni okeru Nihon no tai Chûgoku minkan gaikô" (Japan's Cultural Diplomacy toward China during the Xinhai Revolution), *Chiba shôka daigaku kokufutaigaku kaisoku*, 41, 3 (2003–2012), p. 2.

48. Katarogu hausu, eds., *Taishô jidai no mi no ue sôdan* (Personal Advice columns during the Taishô Era) (Chikuma shobô, 2002), pp. 69–71.

49. Yuji Ichioka, "Amerika Nadeshiko: Japanese Immigrant Women in the United States, 1900–1924", *The Pacific Historical Review*, 49, 2 (May 1980), p. 343.

50. Yuji Ichioka, "Amerika Nadeshiko: Japanese Immigrant Women in the United States, 1900–1924", *The Pacific Historical Review*, 49, 2 (May 1980), p. 353. Erik Esselstrom, *Crossing Empire's Edge, Foreign Ministry Police and Japanese Expansionism in Northeast Asia* (Honolulu: University of Hawaii Press, 2009), p. 17, notes that young Japanese prostitutes were a considerable portion of Japanese settler communities in pre-nineteenth century NE Asia.

51. Bill Mihalopoulos, *Sex in Japan's Globalization, 1870–1930: Prostitutes, Emigration and Nation-Building* (London: Pickering and Chatto, 2011), p. 44.

52. Brian Platt, "Japanese Childhood, Modern Childhood: The Nation-State, the School, and 19th-Century Globalization", *Journal of Social History* (Summer 2005), p. 978.

53. As quoted in Brian Platt, "Japanese Childhood, Modern Childhood: The Nation-State, the School, and 19th-Century Globalization", *Journal of Social History* (Summer 2005), p. 979.

54. The connections between young political thugs travelling to the mainland for work of various sorts and later connecting with the Japanese military was not lost in the post-war as well. Kodama Yoshio was a notorious figure of this sort who was implicated in many post-war Japanese political/financial scandals. Chalmers Johnson, *Journal of Japanese Studies*, 12, 1 (Winter 1986), pp. 12–13. It was also rumoured that Kodama spoke good Korean from his lengthy trips there for various dubious reasons.

55. Many European families believed their children would be contaminated when their families lived abroad. See Ann Stoler, *Carnal Knowledge and Imperial Power: Race and the Intimate in Colonial Rule* (Berkeley: University of California Press, 2010) (new edition), p. 112.

56. Andrew Gordon, *A Modern History of Japan: From Tokugawa Times to the Present* (London: Oxford University Press, 2003), p. 154.

57. As quoted in Sonia Ryang, "The Great Kanto Earthquake and the Massacre of Koreans in 1923: Notes on Japan's Modern National Sovereignty", *Anthropological Quarterly*, 76, 4 (Fall 2003), pp. 733–734.

58. Kaneko Fumiko, *The Prison Memoirs of a Japanese Woman*, (translated by Jean Inglis) (London: M.E. Sharpe, 1991), p. xvii.

59. Helene Bowen Raddeker, *Treacherous Women of Imperial Japan: Patriarchal Fictions, Patricidal Fantasies* (London: Routledge, 1997), pp. 199–226.
60. David R. Ambaras, *Bad Youth: Juvenile Delinquency and the Politics of Everyday Life in Modern Japan* (Berkeley: University of California Press, 2006), pp. 143–144. *Asahi shimbun*, Tokyo edition, morning edition, 7 June 1928.
61. *Asahi shimbun*, Tokyo edition, morning edition, 7 June 1928.
62. Andrew Morris, *Marrow of the Nation: A History of Sport and Physical Culture in Republican China* (Berkeley: University of California Press, 2004), p. 187.
63. Fabio Lanza, in *Behind the Gate: Inventing Students in Beijing* (New York: Columbia University Press, 2010), pp. 54–55, depicts how the image of students at China's premier university (Beida or Beijing University) changed during this time from weaklings to more muscular and they shed their "feminine" dress to appear more Western and thus masculine.
64. Sanetô Keishô, *Chûgokujin nihon ryûgakushi* (Chinese exchange students in Japan), p. 38.
65. Stephen S. Large, "Nationalist Extremism in Early Shōwa Japan: Inoue Nisshō and the 'Blood-Pledge Corps Incident', 1932", *Modern Asian Studies*, 35, 3 (July 2001), p. 536.
66. Nanba Kôji, "Sengo yûsu sabukaruchâ ni tsuite: taiyôzoku kara miyukizoku e" (Post-war Youth Subcultures: From the Beach Crowd to the Urban Cool), *Kansai gakuin daigaku shakai gakubu kiyô*, dai 96kan (March 2004), p. 163.
67. Ibid., p. 164. Minami Hiroshi wrote this in November 1954 in the magazine *Chisei*.
68. I discuss the evolution of how Japanese were seen in various elements of Chinese society in Barak Kushner, "Unwarranted attention: the image of Japan in twentieth century Chinese humour", in Jessica Davis and Jocelyn Chey (eds), *Humour in Chinese Life and Culture: Resistance and Control in Modern Times* (Hong Kong: Hong Kong University Press, 2013), pp. 47–80.

Part IV
Cold War Contexts

8
A Soviet Moral Panic? Youth, Delinquency and the State, 1953–1961

Gleb Tsipursky[1]

The keynote speech at the 11th Moscow city Komsomol[2] conference in 1954 took the unusual step of condemning "unworthy, amoral, and occasionally even criminal behavior among a certain portion of the youth".[3] Exploding in frequency at conferences, in resolutions and in newspapers in subsequent years, such sentiments reflected the initiation of a broad campaign by the Party-state[4] which targeted young people perceived as spending their free time in inappropriate ways. The Soviet Union shares its experience of rising concerns about youth transgressing sociocultural norms with post-Second World War developments in "western" capitalist democratic countries.[5] In the latter, expert commentary on and newspaper stories about youth misbehaviour inspired widespread popular worries, which in turn propelled an exaggerated and coercive government backlash against alleged young people perceived as juvenile delinquents. Scholars termed this phenomenon a "moral panic".[6] This chapter explores the Soviet anti-deviance campaign of the mid-1950s, asking: what motivated the post-Stalin leadership to launch the anti-deviance campaign? How did the authorities implement it? What does the new initiative reveal about the nature of the Soviet system in the 1950s and 1960s? Can we term this campaign a "moral panic" in the western sense of the term? What can it tell us about how different societies react to perceived deviance?

The period after Stalin's death in 1953, referred to as the Thaw, witnessed the new Soviet administration, led from 1955 by N.S. Khrushchev, initiate a re-energized effort to construct a socialist version of modernity. By "socialist modernity" is meant a society, culture and way of life widely perceived as progressive and advanced, as informed by Marxism-Leninism and as actively constructed by human efforts.[7] Like the western model of modernity, the socialist version implicitly promised that people could build a perfect society based on reason and rationality.[8] From the very beginning, however, the Soviet project endeavoured to construct an alternative to the dominant western paradigm of a capitalist and individualistic modernity by forging a different path to the future – a socialist and collective modernity. While the early Soviet years involved a series of radical social, political, cultural and economic transformations in the USSR, by the mid-1930s the Stalinist Kremlin decided that it had reached the appropriate stage of development and shifted its focus to protecting its achievements.[9] The need to build a broadly appealing socialist modernity took on a renewed prominence during the Thaw, as the new leadership under Khrushchev revived the drive to transition from socialism to the utopia of Communism, which the Stalin leadership had let lapse after deciding that it had already achieved the necessary level.[10] The Soviet efforts at constructing a socialist version of modernity represented the foremost among a multitude of political and ideological projects designed to forge a path to the future at variance with the western model, a phenomenon scholars have termed "multiple modernities". Perceiving the Soviet Union as promoting one instance of such an alternative modernity provides significant analytical benefit by helping us to move beyond the Eurocentric emphasis of traditional modernization theory that assumes the eventual convergence of all societies on a western model of modernity.[11]

As an integral part of the Thaw-era renewal, the new leadership instituted a fundamental transition from Stalinist authoritarian rule to a novel populist governing style, meant both to appeal to popular desires and engage the citizenry in the governing of the country. The Kremlin considered these two elements central both to attaining Communist utopia and to helping consolidate the domestic front in the context of the Cold War.[12] An essential aspect of this drive involved the attempt to create young model citizens, "New Soviet People" – faithful to socialism and the Party, cultured and moral, collectivist and patriotic. Furthermore, after the losses of the Second World War, individuals under 25 years old constituted just under half of the population in 1959, making their integration into society central not only to the achievement of an ideal Communist future, but also to the needs of the present.[13]

Despite the importance of the subject, Soviet youth studies only began to attract the attention of Anglophone historical scholarship during perestroika, acquiring real significance only in the last few years when several ground-breaking publications have appeared that have begun to define this emergent subfield.[14] While these works provide an essential foundation for my study, I also engage with debates within "western" youth scholarship to locate this chapter in a broader context.[15] Though showing parallels to the emphasis on social instruction[16] and political disciplining[17] of the New Economic Policy (NEP) in the early and mid-1920s, the Thaw-era initiative denoted a break with the post-war Stalinist status quo. My work contributes to a recent re-evaluation of the Thaw as a time not only of liberalizing reforms, but also of the introduction of more powerful coercive elements, as identified by Oleg Kharkhordin.[18] The present chapter shows that, at least in regard to young people's free time, the Party-state's social controls penetrated deeper into everyday life than in the post-war Stalin years, but authority figures possessed substantially weaker punitive potential. Relying on a range of Soviet primary sources – archival documents,[19] youth newspapers,[20] instruction booklets and memoirs – this chapter investigates the Party-state's initiative against perceived youth delinquency from its beginnings in the early post-Stalin years to the seminal 22nd Communist Party Congress in mid-October 1961.[21] It argues that the campaign against "deviant" youth behaviour sprang from the renewed ideological drive and the populist tenets of the new Thaw-era governing style, with its implementation reflecting these roots. These conclusions, illustrating that both the motivation for the Party's anti-deviance initiative and its realization differed in certain significant ways from those in "western" countries, complicate the application of the "moral panic" model, popular in "western" scholarship on juvenile delinquency, to the Soviet context.

Moral panics in post-1945 US, Britain and West Germany

The US first experienced the "youth problem" of the post-war years, with novel, autonomous styles of youth behaviour[22] emerging in the mid-to-late 1940s. The press and youth "experts" criticized young people for engaging in violent behaviour, "deviant" sexuality, "excessive" consumerism and "degenerate" popular culture, such as listening to jazz and later rock'n'roll, and dancing the twist and other novel dances.[23] Analogous developments occurred in Europe in the early 1950s, as the British Teddy Boys and then the Mods and Rockers, the German *Halbstarken* and many others paralleled earlier American "deviants".[24] Ideologues, cultural critics, youth experts and law enforcement figures labelled these young people "juvenile delinquents" and condemned them as undermining the traditional "moral community", and even

potentially threatening the Cold War struggle.[25] Informed by such sentiments, the media fanned the flames of public confusion over the novel
youth cultural practices of the late 1940s and 1950s, constructing a perception of such behaviour as inherently deviant and criminal through
the sensationalizing of episodic violence, despite little real evidence of
growing youth crime.[26] Impelled by alarmist media articles, societies
across western Europe and America pressured the state to deal with
deviant young people.[27]

Disregarding the lack of reliable statistics on crime and the minor
threat of actual physical violence posed by these youths, the governments in these countries invested substantial resources in implementing
a series of coercive measures against alleged juvenile delinquents. The
West German parliament instituted youth protection laws in the early
1950s which enabled the police to detain youths at any time and take
them back to their parents.[28] The extensive measures taken against
Mods and Rockers in Britain allowed police to abuse their coercive
powers, and turned court proceedings into didactic "kangaroo trials".[29]
In the US, local governments utilized the police force to monitor newly
implemented puritanical behaviour codes.[30] In her contribution to this
volume, Nina Mackert likewise describes the rising concerns in the
US over juvenile delinquency, and in particular brings out the role and
impact of parents in the discourse on how to solve this perceived social
problem.[31] Based on a close investigation of the imposition of social
controls on the Mods and Rockers, Stanley Cohen promulgated a theory
explaining the exaggerated societal response to perceived deviance. He
argued that this reaction, a "moral panic", results when ideologues and
so-called experts label a group of individuals, typically young males, as
a threat to social values, morals and interests. The mass media presents
these "folk devils" in a stylized, sensationalized fashion, placing them in
the category of the "Other". This labelling results in the use of extraordi-
nary, exaggerated coercion against the "folk devils" by the government,
under the weight of public pressure – which indicates that in reality
the panic springs from broader concerns within society.[32] The concept of moral panic soon began to find widespread application among
sociologists, anthropologists and historians in varied chronological and
geographical contexts, forming the basis for much of the subsequent
research on societal response to "deviants".[33]

The Thaw-era campaign against youth misbehaviour

The worries expressed by the Soviet Party-state, to a great extent,
paralleled those prevalent in western societies, but divided into two

distinct categories: first, violent behaviour by young working-class males and second, "deviant" cultural consumption by middle-class youth. Concern with the former has a long history in the Soviet Union, dating back to imperial Russia. "Hooliganism", a term imported from England in the late nineteenth century, came to refer to a whole set of behaviours associated with mostly working-class and almost exclusively male individuals which were censured as inappropriate, immoral and uncultured by the authorities.[34] The prototypical hooligan fought frequently, both against other hooligans and innocent bystanders, drank alcohol excessively, mugged people, broke into shops, stole from his workplace, harassed women, swore and chain-smoked; generally, he "disturbed the public order". Despite borrowing significant aspects of their attitude toward hooliganism from "western" settings during the imperial Russian period, the 1917 revolution marked a significant break, with the Soviet authorities forging a new path toward the future, with their treatment of those labelled delinquent forming an important part of this. Persecuted harshly in the imperial Russian era, those labelled hooligans experienced better treatment in the 1920s. Soviet criminologists in that period blamed social conditions for youth misbehaviour, and promoted rehabilitation over coercive means of dealing with juvenile delinquency, resulting in one of the most progressive and tolerant approaches to this issue in the world. However, the situation changed once again at the end of the 1920s and early 1930s when Stalin seized power. At that point, official discourse claimed that everyone was responsible for his or her own actions, and those committing acts defined as hooliganism received very harsh punishments.[35] Despite official repression, hooliganism continued into the post-war decades.

In contrast to traditional hooliganism among young working-class men, a novel type of youth "deviance" appeared in the USSR after 1945, consisting of cliques of upper and middle-class males, and some females, inspired by western European and especially American popular youth culture. Disparagingly homogenized with the label of "*stiliagi*"[36] (or the "style-obsessed") by the Party-controlled press, these youths listened to jazz and later rock'n'roll, tried to emulate the twist and boogie-woogie, used anglicized slang and drank cocktails in restaurants.[37] Moreover, they engaged in the black market via *fartsa*, an idiomatic term referring to illegal trade in "western" consumer goods.[38] Their diverse cultural practices, based on disjointed, semi-imagined impressions derived from the accounts of war veterans and from trophy films, often only distantly resembled the reality of "western" fashion: for example, outfits might include "jackets with very wide shoulders, narrow black pants, shoes with thick soles" and "Tarzan-style haircuts".[39] Although mostly limited to the children of top officials, the so-called "golden youth", in the post-war Stalin years, fascination with "western" culture quickly spread among young educated urbanites following Stalin's death, and especially the 1957 VI International Youth Festival in Moscow.[40]

The post-war Stalin years, 1945 to 1953, witnessed few public concerns with either hooligans or *stiliagi*, likely due to the Kremlin's emphasis on reconstructing the economic and political infrastructure after the war.[41] Thus at the 11th Komsomol Congress of 1949, P.A. Mikhailov, the First Secretary of the Komsomol, failed to mention hooliganism or *stiliagi* as a problem.[42] The few articles in youth newspapers that mentioned hooliganism tended to do so mostly in passing.[43] The public response of the post-war Stalinist state to the emergence of *stiliagi* proved even more sluggish.[44]

However, a substantial shift appears to have taken place in the first years of the Thaw, from 1953 onward. During the 12th Komsomol Congress in March 1954, the Komsomol's First Secretary, A.N. Shelepin, referred to both hooligans and *stiliagi* as a problem.[45] Soon afterwards, in June 1954, the Komsomol Central Committee (KCC) passed a decree against hooliganism, which called for a "decisive struggle with this evil".[46] Later that year, the KCC enacted a corresponding resolution on drunkenness, which cited the problem of young people committing "antisocial acts on the basis of drunkenness".[47] Regional Komsomol conferences were receptive to the signals from above. At the 1954 Moscow city Komsomol conference, the keynote speech highlighted hooliganism among school students and drunken "immoral behavior" by those in college, and criticized Moscow Komsomol organizations for ignoring the issue.[48] The conference, in a major break with past practice, even gave the floor to a Komsomol representative from the police, who roundly criticized the Komsomol city and several district committees for not working hard enough to achieve "model public order".[49] A public airing of criticism of mid-level Komsomol officials, forced through by lower-level Komsomol activists, was an unprecedented step and indicates both the seriousness of the issue and the new spirit of the Thaw.

In 1955, the issue of anti-social behaviour occupied even more of the KCC's time and energy, with four relevant items on its agenda, most significantly the closed letter of August 1955. Addressed from the KCC to all Komsomol organizations, and explicitly not intended for discussion in the press, the letter stated, "Instances of hooliganism, theft, and disgraceful conduct are not rare. They are a substantial evil"; it urged that much greater efforts be taken to combat such "vices". The bulk of the letter targeted hooliganism and drunkenness, though young people who "lead a partying lifestyle" – a euphemism for *stiliagi* – constituted a secondary target.[50] This missive, printed in 600,000 copies and sent to each Komsomol organization regardless of its size, represented an unprecedented event, as this was the first time that the Komsomol had ever made use of a mass closed letter.[51] This event highlighted the monumental significance of the new anti-deviance initiative. The KCC, in a break from regular practice, even asked for permission from the Party Central Committee (PCC) to send the missive: in the request justifying the letter Shelepin unequivocally noted that the actions taken previously "are not giving the necessary results".[52] The PCC, in a note to the KCC, approved this step.[53]

Notably, the coinciding of the intensification of this campaign with Khrushchev's assumption of full power suggests that he served as a leading, if not the crucial, proponent of the anti-deviance initiative in the two years of collective leadership immediately following Stalin's death.[54] Furthermore, the August letter itself reflected a strongly populist approach – frequently associated with Khrushchev – in going around existing hierarchical governing channels, and appealing to primary Komsomol organizations and Komsomol members themselves to take charge of this issue. The implicit criticism of the bureaucracy revealed itself explicitly when the KCC sent a commission into the Rostov region to check on the implementation of the closed letter, and discovered very little had been done. The KCC decreed in June 1956 that the Rostov region Komsomol committee had "behaved irresponsibly" with regard to the KCC's directives.[55] Moreover, in another populist move, the KCC mailed a closed letter to all Komsomol cells in the Rostov region, stating that in Rostov "many hooligans, drunks, and debauchers have an easy life", and reprimanding the regional Komsomol.[56] In the years leading up to 1961, the KCC pronounced even more resolutions against alleged deviance, maintaining the pressure on regional branches of the Komsomol.[57]

One may validly ask whether the Party's concern with hooliganism resulted from an escalation in actual hooliganism, or at least from internal statistical data indicating such growth. In western Europe and America, for example, heightened attention from supposed youth experts, the press and law enforcement to crimes associated with youth, such as underage drinking, caused statistics on such crimes to climb swiftly, and resulted in growing worries among adults.[58] However, an internal report by the Procuracy to the PCC indicates a steady decrease in the number of people under 25 put on trial in Soviet Russia from 1948 to the beginning of the anti-hooliganism initiatives in 1954. In fact, there was a 40% fall in the number of youths on trial in 1954, despite the expansion of the population over the intervening period.[59] Notably, the data shows the minimal impact of the summer 1953 amnesty on youth crime, perhaps because the youths who were released had little time to become hardened criminals in jail.[60] Though *stiliagi* did increase after 1953,[61] their numbers and public impact did not escalate substantially until the 1957 Youth Festival, helping to explain the low priority assigned to them in the anti-deviance policies of 1954–1955.

If there is little evidence of a rapidly rising crime rate in Soviet Russia, what explains the campaign? The 1955 letter itself presents the motivation as inherently ideological, linking the current "concluding stage of the construction of socialism and gradual transition to Communism" to the need for a "decisive struggle" with the problems of "hooliganism, drunkenness, and licentiousness".[62] The resolution of the Seventh KCC plenum of 1957, which denigrated the inadequate implementation of the campaign against alleged deviance, notes that its criticism did not result from any sudden discoveries of major failures in the Komsomol's "upbringing [*vospitanie*] work". Instead, it expounds on the need to struggle with misbehaviour "with all our might, because it is especially intolerable right now, when the country is coming closer and closer to Communism every day".[63] In a March 1957 speech at a conference of the Moscow city committee, Shelepin developed this point further. He stated that, overall, young people were well behaved, and that while acts of violent delinquency did take place, "they occurred earlier, too. Many of the Komsomol activists present also brawled." Moreover, expressing concerns about the impact of the upcoming International Youth Festival, Shelepin called for "Komsomol organizations to lead the struggle against blindly kowtowing to all that is western".[64] The escalating rhetoric against *stiliagi* likely reflected the Party's growing concern about "westernized" young people disengaging from the construction of Communism, and the concomitant loss incurred on the ideological front of the Cold War. Overall, this chapter postulates that such rapid shifts in discourse and policy after Stalin's death, despite an actual decrease in youth arrests before the campaign began, highlight the important changes taking place at the top, and the re-energized initiative of the new leadership to build a socialist version of modernity as the crucial factors driving the anti-deviance policy. In marked contrast to the motivations behind initiatives against juvenile delinquency taken in capitalist democratic countries, which were and often are inherently backward-looking and reactive in trying to maintain an idealized "moral community", the campaign of the Thaw-era Soviet administration was proactive and future-oriented in striving to reach the eschatological goal of a Communist utopia.

Implementing the campaign

Analogously to "western" states, if for somewhat different reasons, the USSR deployed its law enforcement institutions to deal with young "deviants". The KCC's closed letter, though not mentioned by the state-controlled media, was widely discussed with representatives of the police and judiciary.[65] Police and court employees engaged in extensive deterrent work against supposedly delinquent behaviour. In Belgorodsk, for example, they gave extensive lectures to young people at events entitled "Maintain the honor of the city."[66] Police officers held one-on-one discussions in the station house, as described in an article about an officer telling a misbehaving youth that those who seek an "easy life" take "bourgeois scoundrels as an example", and that the "easy life" always "ends hard".[67] The police and courts used more forceful measures as well, embodied in a new 1956 law that allowed sentences of up to 15 days in prison for vaguely defined "petty hooliganism".[68] Advocating stronger anti-hooliganism initiatives, youth newspapers ran articles such as one censuring the police in Aleksin for a situation in which some hooligans detained by the police for trying to break into a female school dormitory and chasing a dorm monitor with a knife managed to return in a few days and beat up the monitor.[69] In 1960–1961, because of an explosion in the black market for "western" goods after the Festival, the government passed stringent laws against speculation.[70] These laws targeted both large-scale black-market traders and minor *fartsa* dealers.[71]

Soviet publications presented numerous descriptions of this struggle. For example, a booklet describes how the police uncovered a clique of youths who bought goods and currency from foreign tourists for resale in the Soviet Union, and put them on trial. The gang, led by "Big Kolya", arrested with $300, had members such as "Tolik the Nose", whose grasp of English enabled him to "meet foreigners and make various deals".[72] These publications strove to both warn speculators and instruct local authorities on the need to pay attention to *fartsa*. Internal documents such as a report by the KGB to the PCC on implementing the 1960–1961 anti-speculation policies drew an even starker picture. The report indicated that the market for foreign goods in the Soviet Union reached an apogee in 1959–1960 due to the country's opening to foreign visitors. Particularly alarming for the Party leadership, the

KGB stressed the role of "imperialist spy networks" in foreign goods speculation, citing the case of Dmitrii Izhdolbin from Leningrad State University. He bought jazz records and abstract paintings from foreigners, who, the KGB wrote, "worked him over ideologically, and eventually co-opted him" into spying.[73] Nevertheless, the campaign against hooligans and *stiliagi* failed to utilize the state's coercive powers to their full extent, due to the post-Stalin administration's shutting down of many of the late Stalin-era coercive institutions of vertical, top-down surveillance and policing.[74] This move represented a constituent component of Khrushchev's ideologically motivated attempt to shift social control functions from the state to the citizenry as a way of moving toward the goal of societal self-management in the anticipated Communist utopia.

A cardinal aspect of this transition involved the government's escalating reliance on press criticism of those it termed delinquent.[75] The KCC in a 1954 decree demanded that "Komsomol newspapers brand with shame specific careers of evil".[76] Instruction booklets called on the press to "help [the masses] correctly understand and judge – what evil and harm crime causes to the whole of society".[77] The accounts from Komsomol branch organizations on implementing the 1955 closed letter frequently included references to the multitude of satirical newspapers targeting hooligans and *stiliagi*. The Rostov Komsomol, for example, indicated that its local newspapers had begun to pay greater attention to harshly censuring "unworthy" behaviour.[78] Stories in national-level Komsomol newspapers bashing hooligans and stiliagi exemplify the rhetoric against supposed juvenile delinquents, with these articles serving as a model for regional youth newspapers.[79] A *Komsomol'skaia Pravda* (KP) article in January 1955 describing how in Michurinsk there were neighbourhood gangs that included Komsomol members focused on an incident where a school student who was a Komsomol member killed another student in a knife fight. The journalist ascribed blame for the situation to the city Komsomol committee's tolerant attitude toward and indecisive struggle with hooliganism.[80] Such stories endeavoured to both reprimand official organizations and mobilize youth opinion against hooligans. Other articles meant to shine a bright light of shame on misbehaving youths, for example a 1959 article entitled "Rockefeller from Noril'sk" describing the typical misdeeds of a *stiliaga*. The journalist harshly criticized the protagonist for legally changing his name to Andre Johnson Rockefeller, wearing "narrow pants with zippers", extorting money from his mother and harassing women.[81] Though scholars disagree over the extent to which the Party controlled the press during the Thaw, archival documents imply that youth newspapers followed official policy on the issue of youth misbehaviour.[82]

The wide reliance on shaming techniques links directly to the Thaw-era administration's belief in the power of collective judgment in the struggle to achieve Communism. At the 1957 Moscow conference, Shelepin cited a Chinese folk saying which states that if 1,000 people point to a thief, he will die: this, according to Shelepin, "is about the great power of the collective. If the whole army of the capital's Komsomol will say a decisive 'No' to drunks, hooligans, and debauchers, then there will be none."[83] The newspaper articles, becoming ubiquitous only after Stalin's death, set the goal of helping construct a self-surveying, authoritative collective, whose disparaging, shaming voice constitutes the only punishment necessary for correcting misbehaviour in the Communist utopia. Arguably, the press depictions of hooligans and *stiliagi* may have also helped the government by enabling it to illustrate a model of inappropriate conduct, elucidating the criteria of behaviour for ideal Communists.[84] In stark contrast to capitalist countries, where the press played the key role in pushing the state to coercive measures by exaggerating deviance, the impetus for the discussion of such questions in Soviet papers came from the post-Stalin leadership, with the intention of increasing public support for their policies and accelerating the transition to a Communist future.

Mobilizing public opinion against hooligans and *stiliagi* constituted a necessary basis for another of the Party's measures designed to combat such behaviour and mobilize young Komsomol members in the cause of Communism.[85] At the 13th Komsomol Congress in 1958, Khrushchev stated: "The decisive role [in rooting out hooliganism] belongs to the forces of society!"[86] The campaign launched by the 1955 closed letter resulted in the quick organization of Komsomol patrols under the auspices of local Komsomol committees across the country. The patrols, consisting of groups of ideologically committed young volunteers under the oversight of local Komsomol committees, strove to monitor and police the everyday activities of youth in their free time, and represented a substantial innovation when compared with the late Stalin years.[87] The Saratov regional Komsomol committee reported that 1,600 youths participated in public patrols in 1956.[88] Komsomol patrols occasionally launched massive raids against young "deviants", with the assistance of the police and Komsomol members who did not join patrols. For example, the Rostov region Komsomol organized 13 massive raids, with 10,000 participants overall, which arrested 900 individuals. The city committee created an elite patrol, supposedly consisting of the most courageous and disciplined Komsomol activists, that fought against "transgressors against the public order" such as *stiliagi* and debauchers.[89]

These Komsomol groups deployed surveillance, public criticism and violence against hooligans and *stiliagi*. A good example of the first two practices is provided by a list of instructions issued by the Moscow city Komsomol for preparing for the 1957 Festival. It directed patrols to raid all the districts of the city and inform the place of work or study of each violator of public order, to keep a close eye on convicts and school dropouts and publishers of satirical newspapers.[90] A 1958 article in KP reports how the Cheliabinsk Komsomol identified a *stiliaga*, Mai Belousov, and strove to convert him by calling him into the Komsomol base and holding long conversations with him – according to KP, successfully.[91] These groups directly fought supposed deviants as well. Another KP account relates how a patrol detained Iurii Iaroslavtsev in the middle of breaking chairs at a club, took him to the police and wrote to his workplace, "Tuimazaneftestroi", requiring the worker collective there to censure him.[92] Publishing such data in papers both highlighted the efforts of the patrols and served to name and shame the hooligan and his place of work. At a Moscow city Komsomol conference in 1957, the Komsomol secretary of the Likhachev automobile factory described how they once detained a drunken worker who, in an act of protest, "took off all his clothes three times"; in addition, he stated, "[we] help guys get a better haircut, with the help of scissors, of course", a euphemism for cutting off the "western" haircuts of *stiliagi*.[93] A former patrol member's memoirs include references to numerous fights with drunken hooligans. He also relates his dislike for *stiliagi*, who "to our high ideals juxtaposed narrow pants and loud ties" and recalls a number of fights with them as well.[94] By 1958, the Party judged the Komsomol's "social activation" experiment as successful enough to be extended to the whole of the populace. The PCC declared the need to create *druzhiny*, or people's patrol groups composed of both youths and adults, for every type of industry and institution, to achieve the "mass involvement of the working population and social organizations in defending the public order in the country".[95] By 1962, 3 million people, over 2% of the population, belonged to these groups, which enabled the police to decrease its staff in many places.[96]

The Thaw-era Party intended the patrols to impose horizontal social controls and expunge perceived deviance, thus removing the roadblocks toward the ideal Communist future. Simultaneously, the volunteer groups manifested the populist ruling style of the new administration. Composed of ordinary citizens, the patrols took on policing functions executed previously by state organs, and thus proved constitutive of the transition to societal self-management. Furthermore, the Komsomol patrols saved the state considerable effort and material resources by having young people police themselves. This approach denoted not only a shift from the late Stalin years, but also represented a pronounced counterpoint to the measures of the governments of "western" countries, in large part explained by the renewed ideological drive and populist approach of the post-Stalin authorities.[97]

Finally, the post-Stalin leadership, in a new initiative marking a break with governmental policy not only in the US, Britain and West Germany but also in the late Stalin era, called for the massive provision of state-sponsored youth leisure as a means of dealing with hooligans and *stiliagi*.[98] In the post-war Stalin years, the concept of using organized leisure activities to deal with "deviance" existed in theory, but made only rare appearances in internal discourse on this issue, usually only on the regional level, and was practically non-existent in federal-level policy discussions.[99] The Komsomol authorities tended instead to ascribe instances of even the most violent crime to insufficient political training and education. For example, when Leonid Gorenkov, born in 1936, a Komsomol secretary at the Nizkoborskaia school in Vitebsk, killed the fourth-grader Aleksandr Kishkin in December 1952, the regional Komsomol organization found that "This fact resulted from unsatisfactory political enlightenment and teaching in the school."[100]

In contrast, the 1955 KCC letter explicitly linked the lack of appropriate leisure activities to escalating youth misbehaviour and demanded that local Komsomol organizations organize more events for their members.[101] Shelepin's Moscow conference speech in 1957 highlighted the change from earlier methods of dealing with delinquents, stating that "only administrative measures are insufficient to liquidate all these phenomena. For this, we need [to undertake] the organization of youth leisure with true Komsomol energy."[102] One of the principal forms of such leisure, amateur arts (*khudozhestvennaia samodeiatel'nost'*), consisted of collectives of youth engaging in amateur music-making of all sorts.[103] In carrying out the directives of the closed letter, the Primorsk region not only mobilized coercive resources, but also founded 74 new collectives of amateur arts. In just one district within the region, Chernigovsk, 400 youths participated.[104] The government's decision to hold the International Youth Festival in Moscow worked to develop amateur arts as well. In the Krasnopresnenskii district, the authorities organized a district-wide competition of youth amateur arts, with the best collectives having the possibility of performing at the Festival.

The Krasnopresnenskii competition drew 1,035 performers from 88 collectives and inspired the creation of 37 new groups.[105] Participation continued to grow. If a total of 1,500 youths engaged in amateur arts in the Krasnopresnenskii district during 1957, in 1959 these collectives encompassed more than 3,000 youths of the district, who put on over 300 concerts for about 200,000 people.[106] Directly demonstrating how amateur arts served the purpose of making model Communists by providing alternative acceptable outlets for youth energy, a participant at a 1962 Moscow conference of club workers described how his club took 25 adolescents who "broke windows, pick-pocketed" from a police precinct and got them involved in the wind orchestra and dance collective.[107] The government also intended for amateur arts to inculcate the values of collectivism as well as appropriately Soviet tastes in both the participants and the audience, by playing Russian folk music and Soviet compositions instead of "western" music. In a case in point, Shelepin insisted in 1954 on the necessity of providing appropriate repertoires for amateur arts, for example, plays that "lucidly demonstrate the life and struggles of the Soviet people and its youth".[108] Amateur art collectives were meant to inculcate directly Communist ideology via the content of certain ideologically themed songs and skits, found not only in the repertoire of regular collectives, but also of cultural agitation brigades (*agitkul'tbrigady*). These groups of artistic youths went into working-class neighbourhoods and distant villages under-served by local cultural institutions. Such brigades explicitly targeted behaviour labelled deviant, as in a 1960 concert entitled "Seeing something outrageous, do not pass by."[109] Thus, the audiences at such concerts not only lacked the opportunity to engage in "deviance", but also, at the same time, received exposure to propaganda against such behaviour. Perhaps most crucial for the administration was its aim for amateur arts to advance the building of Communism by escalating social activation among performers and shifting extant state obligations to provide entertainment to the citizenry.

In addition to constructing Communism – at least as perceived by the authorities – the various measures taken against hooligans and *stiliagi* contributed to strengthening state power, as well as supporting Khrushchev's reformist course. By publicly highlighting alleged juvenile delinquency so soon after Stalin's death, the post-Stalin leadership may well have intended to cast blame on Stalin for such misbehaviour, and absolve themselves by underlining that hooligans and *stiliagi* constituted a pre-existing condition – therefore stabilizing the Thaw-era government. The widespread discussion on youth misbehaviour in

1954–1956 probably helped Khrushchev make the case for the necessity of discarding some aspects of the Stalinist line and instituting reforms at the Twentieth Party Congress in 1956. Taking some of the financial and organizational burdens of policing the populace and supplying musical concerts away from the state enabled it to devote more resources to other components of Khrushchev's reform programme. Providing youth with interesting leisure options served to satisfy the desires of at least some youths for entertainment and thus legitimated the government in their eyes – a fundamental aspect of Khrushchev's populist approach.

Nonetheless, some evidence hints at problems with realizing the Party's plans. Certain amateur art collectives received reprimands for taking "the wrong path of emulating" the style of "western jazz".[110] Occasionally, members of patrols acted in ways resembling those of hooligans, and newspapers condemned "angry, primitive people who due to a misunderstanding ended up in a people's patrol".[111] The extensive discussion of deviance had unexpected consequences, as hinted at by Goriunov, one of the participants at a Bureau KCC meeting devoted to editing the draft of the 1955 closed letter. He stated that "we should not fall into a real panic", implying that discussions of the letter inspired the voicing of widespread concerns among Komsomol officials.[112] At a 1956 Moscow city Komsomol conference, Vavilov, the secretary of a factory Komsomol cell, declared: "It is scary to walk in the streets of Moscow. Thefts and murders have become a massive phenomenon."[113] The speech by a secretary of the Moscow Party committee, Marchenko, at the conference directly contradicted this claim, stating that "comrade Vavilov, of course, exaggerated; the situation in Moscow is not that bad". This likely represented an attempt to try to stem concerns and protect the Moscow city committee's reputation.[114]

Conclusion

In the post-war decades, the social systems of both the Soviet Union and countries such as West Germany, the US and Britain expressed concerns over the perception of escalating juvenile delinquency. All shared the desire and undertook substantial measures to remove those "deviants" identified as disruptive of the social order, most commonly due to their violent conduct, "inappropriate" cultural tastes and excessive sexuality. Nonetheless, significant disparities existed as well. In capitalist democratic states, so-called youth experts and newspapers determined who would be labelled deviant with their concerns tending to revolve around the threat to "timeless" family values and an imagined traditional "moral community". In the Soviet Union, by contrast, as this chapter has striven to show, the catalyst for the wide-ranging anti-delinquency initiative of the post-Stalin years came instead from the new Thaw-era administration, which revived the struggle to build a socialist version of modernity, motivated by a future-oriented, eschatological goal of reaching a Communist utopia. The implementation of policies targeting those labelled deviant across the Soviet, European and American contexts shared a common involvement of the police apparatus – highlighting the similarity of tools available to modern bureaucratic states – yet differed in other regards.

Perhaps most crucially for the "moral panic" model, developments in Soviet Russia differed drastically from the traditional dynamics in "western" countries, where sensationalized press stories played the crucial role in stirring up public opinion and thereby bringing about coercive measures by the government against those labelled as juvenile delinquents. In contrast, the Soviet authorities oversaw the activities of the public media. As a result, journalists had little opportunity to induce top-level officials into a large-scale campaign against deviance. Thus, the driving force for the new campaign against juvenile delinquency came from the post-Stalin policymakers, not from the press or youth "experts", as in the US.

In fact, newspapers functioned primarily as a tool in implementing federal policy rather than as autonomous agents. The press acted to impose the power of the collective via shaming techniques, and, in mobilizing public opinion, encouraged the social activation of Komsomol patrols. These innovative groups constituted a powerful symbol of Khrushchev's attempt to transition toward social self-management, as well as his populist style in circumventing the existing hierarchy and state apparatus and appealing to the populace, all aimed at reviving the forging of a socialist modernity. Correspondingly, the provision of engaging leisure activities was intended to satisfy popular desires in a way conducive to achieving Communism, via the strengthening of social activation and striving to make sure that both performers and the audience appreciated official Soviet music instead of "western" rhythms. All of these measures resulted in horizontal social controls penetrating more deeply into everyday youth leisure activities than in the post-war Stalin years, though punishments such as naming and shaming in newspaper articles hardly compared to the severity of a labour camp sentence. Furthermore, the new initiative helped legitimate the Thaw-era state and pave the way for de-Stalinizing reforms. Overall, the efforts of the new leadership sought to bring about a situation in which youths would conduct themselves like ideal Communist citizens not only during work and study, but 24 hours a day – and by behaving like model Communists, become the future that they struggled toward.

More broadly, the research on which this chapter is based suggests the need to reassess the usefulness of "western" models when discussing non-"western" contexts. It posits that a "moral panic" in the sense described by Cohen cannot occur in a system where the government had such a powerful role in overseeing the sources of information via its management of the public media. In the USSR, it was not the media and "experts" stirring public opinion that pushed state organs to lash out against supposed juvenile delinquency; instead, top-level policy makers directed the media and "experts" in a concerted policy effort targeted against "delinquents" in an effort to create a modern socialist society conducive to building Communism and winning the Cold War. The dominant role of the state in this process reveals substantial differences between what scholars portrayed as the function of discourse on juvenile delinquency in "western" contexts. Overall, the chapter has sought to problematize the widespread supposition among scholars who study "western" settings that their theories and models are fully applicable to all societies.[115] Joining the recent wave of postcolonial scholarship that aims to "provincialize Europe",[116] the conclusions presented here point to the need to analyse the wide range of diverse non-"western" contexts in order to glean a more complete appreciation of how human societies function and the varied paths they take to reach what they perceive as their own version of modernity, confirming the validity of the "multiple modernities" framework.

Moreover, this chapter suggests the need to develop new theories and models based on the experience of non-"western" settings in order to enrich the analytical arsenal of all scholars. By highlighting the central role of political leaders and the state apparatus as well as the ideological motivation of reaching an idealized future, the case study of the Soviet campaign against hooligans and *stiliagi* in the mid-1950s suggests one way in which this might be done.[117] The Soviet leadership's decision to initiate an ideologically motivated anti-deviance campaign as part of a renewed drive for Communist construction indicates the need to broaden the traditional model of "moral panic" to include a new subcategory of "leadership-induced moral panic". This new concept would serve as an heuristic tool, allowing us to analyse cases where the government controls the media and can instigate moral panics to serve its own purposes.

Notes

1. I would like to acknowledge colleagues who helped shape this essay, as well as the broader project on which it is based, provisionally entitled "Patrolling Socialism and Post-Socialism: Volunteer Policing in Russia, 1945–2012". They include Donald J. Raleigh, Juliane Fürst, Anne Gorsuch, John Johnson, Paul Hagenloh, David L. Hoffmann, Catriona Kelly, Oleg Kharkhordin, Sharon Kowalsky, Brian LaPierre, Louise McReynolds, Hillary Pilkington, William Risch and Sergei Zhuk. My special gratitude to Heather Ellis, Lily Chang and the other participants of the "Juvenile Delinquency in the 19th and 20th Centuries: East-West Comparisons" conference from which this volume emerged. A grant from The Ohio State University's Mershon Center, a Mellon/ACLS dissertation completion fellowship and a Fulbright-Hays research abroad fellowship supported invaluable primary source research in Russia, where the staff at the Komsomol archive in Moscow, in particular G.M. Tokareva, proved very helpful.
2. The Komsomol, the Soviet mass organization for those aged 14–28 dedicated to socializing youth, grew rapidly in the 1950s, with half of all those eligible becoming members by 1958: participation was essential for attending college or joining the Communist Party. See A. Kassof, *The Soviet Youth Program: Regimentation and Rebellion* (Cambridge: Harvard University Press, 1965), pp. 14–18.
3. Tsentral'nyi arkhiv obshchestvenno-politicheskoi istorii Moskvy (TsAOPIM), f. 635 (Moscow city Komsomol), op. 13, d. 267, l. 44.
4. In the USSR, the Communist Party controlled the government apparatus, economic enterprises, cultural organs and social organizations such as the Komsomol and trade unions. Thus, the whole complex of Soviet institutions is frequently termed the Party-state. The Party leadership guided all Soviet policy and decision-making, with the PCC's decrees paramount at all levels. The Komsomol implemented the Party's youth policy.
5. I do not capitalize "western" and leave this term in quotation marks as I want to avoid homogenizing a widely varied set of historical experiences and make problematic claims to an inherent separation between "western" and "eastern". By "western" I refer to western Europe, the US and Canada. I am informed here by M.W. Lewis and K.E. Wigen, *The Myth of Continents: A Critique of Metageography* (Berkeley: University of California Press, 1997); E. Said, *Orientalism* (New York: Vintage Books, 1979); E. Said, *Culture and Imperialism* (New York: Vintage Books, 1993).
6. For the classical study of moral panics, see S. Cohen, *Folk Devils & Moral Panics: The Creation of the Mods and Rockers* (New York: Basil Blackwell, 1987).
7. On socialist modernity, see D.L. Hoffmann, *Stalinist Values: The Cultural Norms of Soviet Modernity, 1917–41* (Ithaca: Cornell University Press, 2003), pp. 1–14; S. Kotkin, *Magnetic Mountain: Stalinism as a Civilization* (Berkeley: University of California Press, 1995), pp. 355–366.
8. On "western" modernity, see Z. Bauman, *Modernity and Ambivalence* (Ithaca: Cornell University Press, 1991), pp. 5, 263; A. Giddens, *The Consequences of Modernity* (Stanford: Stanford University Press, 1990), p. 1.

9. For the Stalinist shift in the mid-1930s, see D.L. Hoffmann, "Was There a 'Great Retreat' from Soviet Socialism? Stalinist Culture Reconsidered", *Kritika*, 5, 4 (Fall 2004), pp. 651–674.
10. For one among many examples of top-level Thaw-era Soviet statements promoting ideological revivalism, see *Voprosy ideologicheskoi raboty* (Moscow: Gospolitizdat, 1961), pp. 144–158.
11. On the concept of multiple modernities, see D. Sachsenmaier, "Multiple Modernities – The Concept and Its Potential", in D. Sachsenmaier, S.N. Eisenstadt and J. Riedel (eds), *Reflections on Multiple Modernities: European, Chinese, and Other Interpretations* (Boston: Brill, 2001), pp. 42–67; S.N. Eisenstadt, "Multiple Modernities", in S.N. Eisenstadt (ed.), *Multiple Modernities* (New Brunswick: Transaction Publishers, 2002), pp. 1–30; and E. Ben-Rafael and Y. Sternberg, "Analyzing Our Time: A Sociological Problématique", in E. Ben-Rafael and Y. Sternberg (eds), *Identity, Culture, and Globalization* (Boston: Brill, 2001), pp. 3–17. For an application of the idea of multiple modernities to the Soviet Union, see D.L. Hoffmann, *Cultivating the Masses: Modern State Practices and Soviet Socialism, 1914–1939* (Ithaca: Cornell University Press, 2011), p. 3.
12. On the ideological motivations of the Khrushchev leadership, see M. Ilic, "Introduction", in M. Ilic and J. Smith (eds), *Soviet State and Society under Nikita Khrushchev* (New York: Routledge, 2009), pp. 1–8; W. Taubman, *Khrushchev: The Man and His Era* (New York: W.W. Norton, 2003), pp. 236–299; G. Breslauer, "Khrushchev Reconsidered", in S.F. Cohen, A. Rabinowitch and R. Sharlet (eds), *The Soviet Union since Stalin* (Bloomington: Indiana University Press, 1980), pp. 50–70. Especially on the Cold War under Khrushchev, see A. Fursenko and T. Naftali, *Khrushchev's Cold War: The Insider Story of an American Adversary* (New York: W.W. Norton, 2006); V. Zubok, *A Failed Empire: The Soviet Union in the Cold War from Stalin to Gorbachev* (Chapel Hill: University of North Carolina Press, 2007), pp. 123–191.
13. Out of 117,534,315 people in the RSFSR, 54,796,718 were under 25 years old in 1959. See Tsentral'noe Statisticheskoe Upravlenie, *Itogi vsesoiuznoi perepisi naseleniia 1959 goda, RSFSR* (Moscow, 1963).
14. For recent publications, see J. Fürst, *Stalin's Last Generation: Soviet Youth and the Emergence of Mature Socialism, 1945–56* (Oxford: Oxford University Press, 2010); A.E. Gorsuch, *Youth in Revolutionary Russia: Enthusiasts, Bohemians, Delinquents* (Bloomington: Indiana University Press, 2000); I. Halfin, *From Darkness to Light: Class, Consciousness, and Salvation in Revolutionary Russia* (Pittsburgh: University of Pittsburgh Press, 2000); C. Kelly, *Children's World: Growing Up in Russia, 1890–1991* (New Haven: Yale University Press, 2007); L.V. Silina, *Nastroeniia sovetskogo studenchestva, 1945–1964* (Moscow: Russkii mir, 2004).
15. For example, A. Bennett and K. Kahn-Harris eds, *After Subculture: Critical Studies in Contemporary Youth Culture* (New York: Palgrave Macmillan, 2004); William S. Bush, *Who Gets a Childhood? Race and Juvenile Justice in Twentieth-Century Texas* (Athens: The University of Georgia Press, 2010); *Lost Kids: Vulnerable Children and Youth in Twentieth-Century Canada and the United States*, eds. Mona Gleason, Tamara Myers, Leslie Paris and Veronica Strong-Boag (Vancouver: UBC Press, 2010); Christopher R. Manfredi,

The Supreme Court and Juvenile Justice (Lawrence: University of Kansas Press, 1998); J. Gilbert, *A Cycle of Outrage: America's Reaction to the Juvenile Delinquent in the 1950s* (New York: Oxford University Press, 1986); S. Mintz, *Huck's Raft: A History of American Childhood* (Cambridge: Harvard University Press, 2004); J. Springhall, *Coming of Age: Adolescence in Britain, 1860–1960* (Dublin: Gill and Macmillian Ltd., 1986); J.R. Gillis, *Youth and History: Tradition and Change in European Age Relations, 1770-Present* (New York: Academic Press Inc., 1981); U.G. Poiger, *Jazz, Rock, and Rebels: Cold War Politics and American Culture in a Divided Germany* (Berkeley: University of California Press, 2000).

16. Konecny, *Builders and Deserters*, pp. 232–234.
17. Disagreement existed between various groups within the administration in the mid-1920s over the best course of action in dealing with "deviant" youth; while some wanted to offer engaging leisure, most demanded an escalation of political propaganda, with the latter fully triumphant by 1928: Gorsuch, *Youth*, pp. 116–138.
18. O. Kharkhordin, *The Collective and the Individual in Russia: A Study of Practices* (Berkeley: University of California Press, 1999), pp. 279–302. For other scholarship on authoritarianism under Khrushchev, see M. Dobson, *Khrushchev's Cold Summer: Gulag Returnees, Crime, and the Fate of Reform after Stalin* (Ithaca: Cornell University Press, 2009); R. Hornsby, *Citizens against the State: Political Dissent and Repression in Khrushchev's USSR* (New York: Cambridge University Press, forthcoming); S. Fitzpatrick, "Social Parasites: How Tramps, Idle Youth, and Busy Entrepreneurs Impeded the Soviet March to Communism", *Cahiers du monde russe et soviétique*, 47, 1–2 (2006), pp. 377–408; B. LaPierre, "Private Matters or Public Crimes: The Emergence of Domestic Hooliganism in the Soviet Union, 1939–1966", in L.H. Siegelbaum (ed.), *Borders of Socialism: Private Spheres of Soviet Russia* (New York: Palgrave Macmillan, 2006), pp. 191–207; J. Fürst, "The Arrival of Spring? Changes and Continuities in Soviet Youth Culture and Policy between Stalin and Khrushchev", in P. Jones (ed.), *The Dilemmas of Destalinization: Negotiating Cultural and Social Change in the Khruschchev Era* (London: Routledge, 2006), pp. 135–153; G. Tsipursky, "Coercion and Consumption: The Khrushchev Leadership's Ruling Style in the Campaign against 'Westernized' Youth, 1954–1964", in W.J. Risch and K. Transchel (eds), *The Socialist Beat in the Soviet Bloc* (Lanham: Lexington Books, forthcoming in 2014).
19. From the Rossiiskii gosudarstvennyi arkhiv noveishei istorii (RGANI); Rossiiskii gosudarstvennyi arkhiv sotisial'no-politicheskoi istorii (RGASPI); Tsentral'nyi arkhiv goroda Moskvy (TsAGM); TsAOPIM.
20. My study draws on 1,074 relevant stories gathered from KP, the national organ of the Komsomol, and *Moskovskii Komsomolets* (MK), the Moscow city Komsomol organ.
21. The Congress resulted in increasingly coercive measures toward "deviants"; see Fitzpatrick, "Social Parasites", and Lipson, "Hosts and Pests: The Fight Against Parasites", in R. Cornell (ed.), *The Soviet Political System: A Book of Readings* (Englewood Cliffs: Prentice-Hall, Inc., 1970), pp. 323–333.
22. I do not use the term "subculture" due to this concept's indelible association with homogeneous, tightly bounded groups that practice class-based

resistance: A. Bennett and K. Kahn-Harris, "Introduction", in A. Bennett and K. Kahn-Harris (eds), *After Subculture: Critical Studies in Contemporary Youth Culture* (New York: Palgrave Macmillan, 2004), pp. 1–18. However, the models of "lifestyles" or "neo-tribes" presented by advocates of this post-subcultural approach have been effectively undermined as lacking adequate appreciation of local contexts: see an introduction to a special journal edition, H. Pilkington and R. Johnson, "Peripheral Youth: Relations of Identity and Power in Global/Local Context", *European Journal of Cultural Studies*, 6, 3 (2003), pp. 259–283.

23. Gilbert, *Cycle of Outrage*, pp. 11–23; M. Brake, *Comparative Youth Culture: The Sociology of Youth Cultures and Youth Subcultures in America, Britain, and Canada* (New York: Routledge, 1985), pp. 85–87; Mintz, *Huck's Raft*, pp. 310–334.
24. See Cohen, *Folk Devils*, pp. 71–91; Springhall, *Coming of Age*, pp. 224–235; Poiger, *Jazz, Rock, and Rebels*, pp. 31–70.
25. For the powerful effect of labelling, see the historiography on the "labeling theory", which posits that "deviants" become "deviant" when those with power successfully attach this label to them: S. Pfohl, *Images of Deviance and Social Control: A Sociological History* (New York: McGraw-Hill, Inc., 1994), pp. 345–398, and S.H. Traub and C.B. Little (eds), *Theories of Deviance* (Itasca: F.E. Peacock Publishers, Inc., 1985), pp. 277–332. For a work that widely utilizes the labelling theory approach in the Soviet context, see B. LaPierre, *Defining, Policing, and Punishing Hooliganism in Khrushchev's Russia* (PhD diss., University of Chicago, 2006).
26. Mintz, *Huck's Raft*, pp. 282–305; Gilbert, *Cycle of Outrage*, pp. 14–28; Gillis, *Youth and History*, pp. 185–210.
27. Polls suggest that Americans saw delinquency as more worrisome than nuclear weapons tests, school segregation or political corruption in the mid-to-late 1950s: Gilbert, *Cycle of Outrage*, p. 63.
28. Poiger, *Jazz, Rock, and Rebels*, pp. 31–70. For later conflicts between the German state and youth, see M. Fenemore, *Sex, Thugs and Rock'n'Roll: Teenage Rebels in Cold-War East Germany* (New York: Berghahn Books, 2007).
29. Cohen, *Folk Devils*, pp. 71–91.
30. See Brake, *Comparative Youth Culture*, p. 99, and Gilbert, *Cycle of Outrage*, pp. 52–59, 142–143.
31. Nina Mackert, "Danger and Progress: White Middle-Class Juvenile Delinquency and Motherly Anxiety in the Post-War United States".
32. Cohen, *Folk Devils*, pp. 1–59, 149–172.
33. For the use of "moral panics" elsewhere, see E. Goode and N. Ben-Yehuda, *Moral Panics: The Social Construction of Deviance* (Cambridge: Blackwell Publishers, 1994) and K. Thompson, *Moral Panics* (New York: Routledge, 1998).
34. J. Neuberger, *Hooliganism: Crime, Culture and Power in St. Petersburg, 1900–1914* (Berkeley: University of California Press, 1993), pp. 1–24, 158–215.
35. A. Gorsuch, " 'Smashing Chairs at the Local Club': Discipline, Disorder, and Soviet Youth", in C. Kuhr-Korolev (ed.), *Sowjetjugend 1917–1941: Generation Zwischen Revolution und Resignation* (Essen: Klartext, 2001), pp. 247–261; G.T. Rittersporn, "Between Revolution and Daily Routine: Youth and Violence in the Soviet Union in the Interwar Period", in Kuhr-Korolev (ed.),

Sowjetjugend 1917–1941, pp. 63–82; P. Hagenloh, *Stalin's Police: Public Order and Mass Repression in the USSR, 1926–1941* (Washington: Woodrow Wilson Center Press and the Johns Hopkins University Press, 2009).

36. Popularized by an (in)famous article by D. Beliaev in the satirical newspaper *Krokodil*, 10 March 1949, *"Stiliaga"*. According to one former *stiliaga*, "Western"-oriented youth considered the term "insulting", instead calling each other *chuvaki*: A. Troitskii, *Back in the USSR: The True Story of Rock in Russia* (Winchester: Faber and Faber, 1988), p. 13. Still, this chapter uses the term *stiliaga* as it eventually became widely accepted among such youth.

37. See studies of "Westernized" Soviet youth: M. Edele, "Strange Young Men in Stalin's Moscow: The Birth and Life of the Stiliagi, 1945–1953", *Jahrbücher für Geschichte Osteuropas*, 50, 1 (2002), pp. 37–61; K. Roth-Ey, "Mass Media and the Remaking of Soviet Culture, 1950s–1960s", (PhD diss., Princeton University, 2003), pp. 46–98; J. Fürst, "The Importance of Being Stylish: Youth, Culture and Identity in Late Stalinism", in J. Fürst (ed.), *Late Stalinist Russia: Society between Reconstruction and Reinvention* (New York: Routledge, 2006), pp. 209–230; S. Zhuk, *Rock and Roll in the Rocket City: The West, Identity, and Ideology in Soviet Dniepropetrovsk, 1960–1985* (Baltimore: Johns Hopkins University Press, 2010); W.J. Risch, *The Ukrainian West: Culture and the Fate of Empire in Soviet Lviv* (Cambridge: Harvard University Press, 2011), pp. 179–250; A. Yurchak, *Everything Was Forever, Until It Was No More: The Last Soviet Generation* (Princeton: Princeton University Press, 2006), pp. 158–206; G. Tsipursky, "Living 'America' in the Soviet Union: The Cultural Practices of 'Westernized' Soviet Youth, 1945–1964", in E. Stolberg (ed.), *The Soviet Union and the United States: Rivals of the Twentieth Century* (New York: Peter Lang, 2013), pp. 139–164.

38. E.R. Iarskaia-Smirnova and P.V. Romanov, "Fartsa: Podpol'e sovetskogo obshchestva potrebleniia", *Neprikosnovennyi zapas: Debaty o politike i kul'ture*, 5,43 (2005), http://magazines.russ.ru/nz/ (Accessed 31 December 2009).

39. See memoirs by V.P. Aksenov, *V poiskakh grustnogo bebi: kngia ob Amerike* (New York: Liberty Publishing House, 1987), p. 15, and V.I. Slavkin, *Pamiatnik neizvestnomu stiliage* (Moscow: " 'Artist.Rezhiser. Teatr,' " 1996), 5; A.S. Kozlov, *"Kozel na sakse": i tak vsiu zhizn'* (Moscow: Vagrius, 1998).

40. This remarkable event marked a key turning point in opening the USSR to "Western" influence: see P. Koivunen, "Overcoming Cold War Boundaries at the World Youth Festivals", in S. Autio-Sarasmo and K. Miklossy (eds), *Reassessing Cold War Europe* (New York: Routledge, 2011), pp. 175–192.

41. For the post-war Stalin state failing to express much public concern on hooligans or *stiliagi*, see Fürst, *Stalin's Last Generation*, pp. 167–249. For the Stalinist state's broader post-war concerns, see E. Zubkova, *Russia After the War: Hopes, Illusions, and Disappointments, 1945–1957* (Armonk: M.E. Sharpe, 1998), pp. 1–51.

42. P. A. Mikhailov, *Otchetnyi doklad na XI s"ezde komsomola o rabote TsK VLKSM* (Moscow: "Molodaia gvardiia", 1949), p. 32.

43. For a rare example, see MK, 7 February 1953, "Clean up the Skating Rink [*Navesti poriadok na katke*]".

44. For more on the minimal persecution of *stiliagi* under Stalin, see Fürst, *Stalin's Last Generation*, pp. 200–249.

45. RGANI, f. 5, op. 30, d. 80, ll. 18, 111–112.
46. RGASPI, f. M-1, op. 3, d. 831, l. 9. For more on hooliganism under Khrushchev, see LaPierre, *Defining, Policing,* and V.A. Kozlov, *Mass Uprisings in the USSR: Protest and Rebellion in the Post-Stalin Years,* trans. E.M. MacKinnon (Armonk: M.E. Sharpe, 2002).
47. RGASPI, f. M-1, op. 3, d. 841, l. 81.
48. TsAOPIM, f. 635, op. 13, d. 267, ll. 29–45.
49. TsAOPIM, f. 635, op. 13, d. 267, ll. 276–279.
50. RGASPI, f. M-1, op. 3, d. 878, ll. 76–78.
51. Noted in Fürst, "Arrival of Spring?"
52. RGANI, f. 5, op. 30, d. 128, l. 83.
53. RGASPI, f. M-1, op. 3, d. 878, ll. 79–80.
54. For Khrushchev's path to sole rule, see Taubman, pp. 236–269.
55. RGASPI, f. M-1, op. 3, d. 904, l. 28.
56. RGASPI, f. M-1, op. 3, d. 904, ll. 32–35.
57. For 1958, on alcoholism: RGASPI, f. M-1, op. 3, d. 966, l. 13. In 1959 and 1960 on struggle against "disturbance of the peace": RGASPI, f. M-1, op. 3, d.1020, l. 19 and d. 1024, l. 2. In 1961, against hooliganism and alcoholism: RGASPI, f. M-1, op. 3, d. 1058, l. 14.
58. Mintz, *Huck's Raft,* pp. 300–303, and Gilbert, *Cycle of Outrage,* p. 66.
59. In 1948, 246,126 youth were put on trial; in 1950, 191,512; in 1952, 161,344; in 1953, 160,476; in 1954, 146,215: RGANI, f. 5, op. 30, d. 232, l. 11. For data that a decrease in crime for people under 17 began as early as 1945, see Fürst, *Stalin's Last Generation,* pp. 167–199.
60. For this amnesty, see M. Dobson, *Khrushchev's Cold Summer: Gulag Returnees, Crime, and the Fate of Reform after Stalin* (Ithaca: Cornell University Press, 2009), pp. 21–49. For more evidence that the amnesty did not lead to a long-term rise in hooliganism arrests, see LaPierre, *Defining, Policing,* pp. 31–109.
61. For this increase, see Fürst, *Stalin's Last Generation,* pp. 342–365.
62. RGASPI, f. M-1, op. 3, d. 878, l. 79.
63. RGASPI, f. M-1, op. 3, d. 930, l. 6.
64. TsAOPIM, f. 635, op. 13, d. 546, ll. 13–17, 44–45.
65. For example, see a report on implementing the letter in Vladivostok: RGASPI, f. M-1, op. 32, d. 802, l. 84.
66. RGASPI, f. M-1, op. 32, d. 813, l. 1.
67. KP, 3 November 1957, "Policeman Ivanov [*Militsioner Ivanov*]".
68. B. LaPierre, "Making Hooliganism on a Mass Scale: The Campaign against Petty Hooliganism in the Soviet Union, 1956–1964", *Cahiers du monde russe,* 47, 1–2 (2006), pp. 349–375.
69. KP, 9 January 1957, "Why Are the Police Inactive in Aleksine? [*Pochemu v Aleksine bezdeistvuet militsiia?*]".
70. See H.J. Berman, *Justice in the U.S.S.R.: An Interpretation of Soviet Law* (Cambridge: Harvard University Press, 1966), pp. 84–86.
71. Kara-Murza, *"Sovok" vspominaet,* p. 79.
72. A. Lavrov and O. Lavrova, *ChP – darmoed!* (Moscow: "Znanie", 1961), pp. 6–16. For similar depictions, see G.A. Levitskii, *Protiv nikh – milliony* (Leningrad: Lenizdat, 1963), p. 10, and P.V. Evdokimov, *Otvetstvennost' lits, vedushchikh paraziticheskii obraz zhizni* (Minsk, 1963), p. 9.

73. RGANI, f. 5, op. 30, d. 429, l. 27.
74. L.I. Shelley, *Policing Soviet Society: The Evolution of State Control* (New York: Routledge, 1996), pp. 44–45.
75. For an in-depth investigation of Thaw-era newspaper criticism, see G. Tsipursky, "Citizenship, Deviance, and Identity: Soviet Youth Newspapers as Agents of Social Control in the Thaw-Era Leisure Campaign", *Cahiers du monde russe* 49.4 (September–October 2008), pp. 1–22.
76. RGASPI, f. M-1, op. 3, d. 830, ll. 4–5.
77. A.N. Kosarevich, *Sovetskaia obshchestvennost' v bor'be s prestupnost'iu* (Moscow: Gosiurizdat, 1959), p. 19.
78. RGASPI, f. M-1, op. 32, d. 813, l. 9.
79. RGASPI, f. M-1, op. 32, d. 821, l. 97.
80. KP, 23 January 1955, "This cannot be walked past [*Eto proiti mimo nel'zia*]". For other articles on hooliganism, see KP, 29 May 1956; MK, 25 May 1957; MK, 19 December 1959.
81. KP, 11 July 1959, "Rockefeller iz Noril'ska". For articles making similar points, see KP, 1 July 1960; MK, 10 March 1957; MK, 5 February 1956.
82. For example, as part of the 1954 decree against alcoholism, the KP sent the KCC a long list of planned article publications dealing with this struggle: RGASPI, f. M-1, op.3, d. 841, ll. 83–84. T.C. Wolfe finds that journalists willingly participated in the drive to construct model Communists: see T.C. Wolfe, *Governing Soviet Journalism: The Press and the Socialist Person after Stalin* (Bloomington: Indiana University Press, 2005), pp. 33–70.
83. TsAOPIM, f. 635, op. 14, d. 240, ll. 44–45.
84. This point is informed by the functional theory of deviance, which considers deviance to be socially useful in clarifying the boundaries of acceptability: E. Durkheim, *The Rules of the Sociological Method*, ed. George E.G. Catlin (New York: The Free Press, 1965), pp. 47–75. For more on the functional theory approach to the anti-hooliganism campaign, see B. LaPierre, *Defining, Policing*, pp. 1–30.
85. See Kosarevich, *Sovetskaia obshchestvennost'*, p. 3.
86. N.S. Khrushchev, *Vospityvat' aktivnykh i soznatel'nykh stroitelei kommunistich-eskogo obshchestva (rech' na XIII s'ezde VLKSM 18 aprelia 1958 goda)* (Moscow: "Molodaia gvardiia", 1961), p. 38.
87. Ideologically based volunteering, at least, was the ideal: for some Komsomol members, it likely had more to do with strengthening their record on public participation, rather than demonstrating an ideological commitment to a Communist future. For more on the patrols, see Fürst, "The Importance of Being Stylish". Brigades of police assistance existed previously, but they served under the direct supervision of the police, not as autonomous youth groups under the Komsomol's oversight; furthermore, according to extant scholarship, by 1953 these brigades had mostly atrophied, and their activities focused on traffic regulation: see Berman, *Justice in the USSR*, pp. 285–288. Notably, these brigades also showed much increased activation after Stalin's death, with a summary report on implementing the letter indicating that the Moscow Komsomol directed over 10,000 members into the brigades, Leningrad – 4,000, Rostov – 3,000: RGASPI, f. M-1, op. 32, d. 811, l. 46.

88. RGASPI, f. M-1, op. 32, d. 813, l. 20. Though these statistics are likely inflated, they show the attention paid to the leisure policy by Komsomol committees.
89. RGASPI, f. M-1, op. 32, d. 813, l. 8.
90. TsAGM, f. 429, d. 538, l. 10–13.
91. KP, 9 December 1958, "The 'king' of *stiliagi* is going to work at the factory [*'Korol' stiliag idet na zavod*]".
92. KP, 13 September 1956. "Base of culture [*Shtab kul'tury*]".
93. TsAOPIM, f. 635, op. 13, d. 546, ll. 75–76.
94. V.E. Ronkin, *Na smenu dekabriam prikhodiat ianvari: vospominaniia byvshego brigadmil'tsa i podpol'shchika, a pozzhe – politzakliuchennogo i dissidenta* (Moscow: Obshchestvo "Memorial", Izd-vo "Zven'ia", 2003), pp. 71–74.
95. Party Central Committee (PCC), *Spravochnik partiionogo rabotnika. Vypusk III* (Moscow, 1961), pp. 577–579.
96. See the following summary report on struggling with "deviance": RGASPI, f. M-1, op. 32, d. 1101, ll. 35–36. Evidence suggests that most were youths, with, for example, out of 53,336 patrol members in Orenburg region, over 30,000 belonging to the Komsomol: RGASPI, f. M-1, op. 32, d. 1102, l. 145.
97. For an intriguing parallel in East Germany, the *Ordnungsgruppen*, see Poiger, *Jazz, Rock, and Rebels*, pp. 196–197.
98. Notably, the Khrushchev-era initiative also reflected the growth in free time, especially for youth: RGASPI, f. M-1, op. 3, d. 877, ll. 3–4. Also see J. Bushnell, "Urban Leisure Culture in Post-Stalin Russia: Stability as a Social Problem?", in T.L. Thompson and R. Sheldoneds (eds), *Soviet Society and Culture: Essays in Honor of Vera S. Dunham* (Boulder: Westview Press, 1988), pp. 58–86.
99. For example, in an internal summary report describing how various regions implemented a major Komsomol plenum resolution on cultural-mass (*kul'turno-massovaia*) work in 1950, out of many Soviet regions only one – the Karelo-Finskaia SSR – connected the poor organization of cultural-mass work to the existence of hooliganism: RGASPI, f. M-1, op. 32, d. 630, l. 83.
100. RGASPI, f. M-1, op. 32, d. 742, ll. 25–26.
101. RGASPI, f. M-1, op. 3, d. 878, l. 77.
102. TsAOPIM, f. 635, op. 14, d. 546, l. 47.
103. For archive-based studies of amateur arts, see S. Costanzo,"Reclaiming the Stage: Amateur Theater-Studio Audiences in the Late Soviet Era", *Slavic Review*, 57, 2 (1998), pp. 398–424; B. Ostromoukhova, "Le Dégel et les troupes amateur. Changements politiques et activités artistiques des étudiants, 1953–1970", *Cahiers du monde russe et soviétique*, 47, 1–2 (2006), pp. 303–325; A.G. Borzenkov, *Molodezh' i politika: Vozmozhnosti i predely studencheskoi samodeiatel'nosti na vostoke Rossii (1961–1991 gg.), Chast' 2* (Novosibirsk: Novosibirskii Gosudarstvennyi Universitet, 2002); Gleb Tsipursky, *Having Fun in the Thaw: Youth Initiative Clubs in the Post-Stalin Years*. In the series, *The Carl Beck Papers in Russian and East European Studies* (Pittsburgh: University of Pittsburgh Press, forthcoming); G. Tsipursky, "Celebration and Loyal Opposition: Youth and Soviet Elections, 1953–68", in R. Jessen and H. Richter (eds), *Voting for Hitler and Stalin: Elections under 20th Century Dictatorships* (Frankfurt and Chicago: Campus and University of Chicago Press, 2011), pp. 81–102.

104. RGASPI, f. M-1, op. 32, d. 802, ll. 84–89.
105. TsAGM, f. 1988, op. 1, d. 46, ll. 8–9.
106. TsAGM, f. 1988, op. 1, d. 52a, ll. 8–9, and TsAGM, f. 1988, op. 1, d. 72, ll. 9–10.
107. TsAGM, f. 718, op. 1, d. 262, l. 18.
108. Shelepin, *Otchetnyi doklad*, p. 46. The Soviet state also strove to shape other aspects of consumer tastes to prevent "Western" influence: S.E. Reid, "Cold War in the Kitchen: Gender and the De-Stalinization of Consumer Taste in the Soviet Union", *Slavic Review*, 61, 2 (2002), pp. 211–252. This had only intermittent success: S.E. Reid, "Who Will Beat Whom? Soviet Popular Reception of the American National Exhibition in Moscow, 1959", *Kritika*, 9, 4 (Fall 2008), pp. 855–904.
109. TsAGM, f. 1988, op. 1, d. 84, ll. 5–6.
110. TsAGM, f. 429, op. 1, d. 532, ll. 218–223.
111. KP, October 6, 1960, "Under the mask of a people's patrol member [*Pod maskoi druzhennika*]".
112. RGASPI, f, M-1, op. 3, d. 869, l. 42.
113. TsAOPIM, f. 635, op. 13, d. 484, ll. 204–205.
114. TsAOPIM, f. 635, op. 13, d. 484, l. 249.
115. A claim made by Cohen for "moral panic". See Cohen, *Folk Devils & Moral Panics*, p. 1.
116. On decentring western European theories and models, see D. Chakrabarty, *Provincializing Europe: Postcolonial Thought and Historical Difference* (Princeton: Princeton University Press, 2000), pp. 1–5.
117. Other contributors to this volume also highlight the state as playing a central role in the construction of ideas of juvenile delinquency. See, in particular, the chapters by Kate Bradley and Nazan Cicek.

9
Danger and Progress: White Middle-Class Juvenile Delinquency and Motherly Anxiety in the Post-War US

Nina Mackert

In September 1948, Agnes Maxwell-Peters wrote a letter to Fredric Wertham, a noted psychiatrist, in which she expressed her worries concerning the behaviour of her sons:

> We have two boys, 7 and 13, with unusually high intelligence and excellent ability in school and in sports [...]. They have a library of fine books of their own and read library books almost daily, yet in the presence of comic books they behave as if drugged and will not lift their eye or speak when spoken to. [...] My boys fight with each other in a manner that is unbelievable in a home where both parents are university graduates and perfectly mated. [...] We consider the situation to be as serious as an invasion of the enemy in war time, with as far reaching consequences as the atom bomb. If we cannot stop the wicked men who are poisoning our children's minds, what chance is there for mankind to survive longer than one generation, or half of one?[1]

When Mrs. Maxwell-Peters wrote this letter, a fear of rising rates of juvenile delinquency started to emerge in US society. Experts like Wertham linked the misbehaviour of youngsters to a range of social and psychological phenomena: the harmful influence of mass culture and the alleged breakdown of familial structures were among the most common explanations of juvenile delinquency. Many people believed that these factors constituted problematic characteristics of the US-American post-war society.[2] Maxwell-Peters' letter shows that the discourse of juvenile delinquency exceeded concerns about children alone; because children stood for the future of "mankind", she regarded their endangerment as a serious threat to the future of American society. Thus, Maxwell-Peters saw urgent need for action. As a mother, she felt compelled to take measures: "What we would like to know is, what can be done about it before it is too late? [...] [W]hat can two parents do? Is there some organization of parents devoted to saving the children of America before it is too late?" As her letter shows, the alleged threat to contemporary youth was translated into the feeling of parental responsibility.

The worries displayed by Maxwell-Peters were especially prevalent at a time when the democratic constitution and global hegemony of the US seemed to be imperilled by outside forces as well as from the inside. Historians examining US-American culture during the Cold War have emphasized that this was a period when crucial notions of "Western" modernity and democracy were shaped and challenged.[3] As this chapter will argue, the contemporary delinquency scare was one of the cultural contexts in which this process took place. In the course of the Second World War, experts began to warn their fellow citizens about a rising wave of juvenile crime and misbehaviour. The fear of juvenile delinquency was not entirely new. Already in the first half of the twentieth century, the behaviour of juveniles regularly preoccupied US-American society.[4] However, the mid-century delinquency scare proved to be especially intense. Shortly after the label "teenager" had entered the discourse on youth, the (problematic) behaviour of young people was heavily discussed, at the level of the federal government as well as in popular magazines, newspapers and movies. Crime statistics provided by the FBI and the Children's Bureau seemed to show an increase in young offenders. The fear of juvenile delinquency had a profound impact on post-war society, for example, by triggering decisive changes in the juvenile justice system and contributing to the development of new educational and therapeutic techniques.[5] Scholars of the post-war delinquency discourse have pointed out that juvenile delinquents were increasingly represented as male, non-white, "poor" inner-city kids.[6] However, contemporaries also warned that delinquency would not pass by the doors of "good" suburban homes and the 1950s saw a growing preoccupation with the causes and prevention of "middle-class delinquency".[7] On the one hand, these worries reflected the broader concern about juvenile misbehaviour. On the other, they must be understood in the context of Cold War discourse. Against the backdrop of notions of white, middle-class youth as an important cultural resource, the Cold War provided delinquency discourse with a framework in which especially the phenomenon of white, middle-class delinquency could be connected to the question of democratic progress and the development of a modern social order.

This chapter aims to add to the cultural history of Cold War America by showing how delinquency discourse contributed to the perception of an inner-American malaise that had to be tackled in order to secure the future of a modern, democratic society.[8] By concentrating on the construction of white, middle-class delinquency, it will present two main arguments. Firstly, this chapter will show that the concept of youth as a crucial social resource created a profound ambiguity at the heart of the American delinquency scare. On the one hand, juvenile delinquency emerged as a dangerous symptom of the alleged social decline of American society and was thus perceived as a serious threat to "Western" modernity. On the other hand, social critics figured certain forms of juvenile misbehaviour as promising signs of youthful individuality in a mass society. Democratic individualism, seen as a crucial characteristic of "Western" citizenship, proved to be an important vanishing point of delinquency discourse. Secondly, this chapter will stress the discursive effects of delinquency discourse on another group of people: by linking juvenile behaviour to parental conduct, the post-war delinquency scare involved a growing conviction among parents that they needed to ensure their children's "wholesome" upbringing to secure the democratic constitution of US-American society. The research for this chapter draws upon two important methodological assumptions. In the first place, it is necessary to acknowledge that discursive representations of delinquency and families are structured by differently arranged categories of race, class, gender and age. However, the interdependence and particularity of these formations is discursively "hidden" behind allegedly universal signifiers.[9] Parenthood, for instance, although it was understood to be "natural", was in no way applied equally to all American families. And even the markedly particular construction of white, middle-class delinquency served as an umbrella term that incorporated highly diverse and even contradictory understandings of delinquency. One can assume that what was marked as white middle-class delinquency varied between different regional and social settings. Nevertheless, this chapter focuses on the production of hegemonic notions of white, middle-class delinquency that allowed the problem to be presented as a coherent, universal phenomenon which could thus take on a more than regional meaning.

Secondly, this chapter traces the consequences of discursive narratives for the ways in which people perceived themselves and their social role. Several historians have, for example, shown how questions of child-rearing, family life and nation-building were closely connected.[10] Although these studies have impressively revealed the discursive structures that characterized American post-war society, they have tended to stop short of an analysis of how people reacted to and cast themselves in this discursive framework. This chapter seeks to extend this research by analysing delinquency discourse as a "mode of subjection", that is, in Foucault's words, as a "way in which the individual establishes his relation to the rule and recognizes himself as obliged to put it into practice".[11] In this chapter, the post-war delinquency scare will therefore be used as a lens through which to examine the discursive construction of parents and parenting practices, and the ways in which parents could act upon prevailing notions of their responsibility.

After a brief outline of the US-American post-war delinquency scare and the genealogical roots of youth as a social resource, the chapter focuses on the special configuration of Cold War delinquency discourse. The ambivalent construction of juvenile delinquency will be explored by an analysis of the ways in which (a) US delinquency discourse represented the problem as prevalent in Soviet Russia as well as in the US, and (b) commentators not only conceptualized delinquency differently for both countries, but also drew distinctions within the US. It will then go on to show how these differences served to inform parents about their important role in "proper" child-rearing and rendered especially nonwhite, lower-class parents as fundamentally incapable of fulfilling this task. Finally, parental letters to experts and educational magazines will serve as examples of parents' (primarily mothers') attempts to perform "good" parenthood.

The discursive construction of adolescence

In the Cold War delinquency scare, no less seemed at stake than the very future of US society. Senator Robert Hendrickson, former chairman of the Senate Subcommittee to Investigate Juvenile Delinquency, declared in 1955: "Not even the communist conspiracy could devise a more effective way to demoralize, disrupt, confuse and destroy our future citizens than apathy on the part of adult Americans to the scourge known as Juvenile Delinquency."[12] It is remarkable how delinquency came to be viewed as a problem that could even outweigh the perceived threat of Communism. The idea of youth as an endangered national resource and its connection with adults and especially parents had a long historical tradition. While notions of juveniles as constitutionally unstable had already been prevalent in the nineteenth century, this construction was naturalized by the establishment of psychobiological knowledge in turn-of-the-century US. During that time, adolescence emerged as a distinct period of psychic imbalance. G. Stanley Hall was one of the best known experts to contribute to the establishment of adolescence as a psychobiological concept around 1900. Following the recapitulation theory of zoologist Ernst Haeckel, Hall conceived of growing up as a process in which individuals actually relived all stages of human evolution.[13] In the time of adolescence, he argued, young people would recapitulate the stage of "primitive" human beings, and should act out, but eventually overcome their "animal-like" drives to become "civilized" men. By placing adolescents at a lower stage of the "great chain of being", Hall's theory not only explained the "erratic" behaviour of adolescents as profoundly "natural", it also came with important consequences. First of all, he allotted the civilizing potential of coming-into-being primarily to white males and thus reproduced the construction of white men as carriers of civilization. Second, this conception of juveniles as a constitutionally unstable social asset sent a warning to all those who were concerned with the handling of juveniles, especially to parents: "[E]very step of the upward way", Hall warned, "is strewn with wreckage of body, mind, and morals. There is not only arrest, but perversion, at every stage, and hoodlumism, juvenile crime, and secret vice seem not only increasing, but develop in earlier years in every civilized land."[14] Juveniles, according to his narrative, had to be carefully monitored and guided in order to fulfil their future roles. As can be seen in the next section, the concept of youth as an inherently unstable social resource survived recapitulation theory and strongly influenced the ambivalent construction of juvenile delinquency in the post-war US.

Cold War delinquency discourse and its ambivalences

US-American Cold War delinquency discourse built on existing ambivalent constructions of youth and the accompanying concentration on parents. Fifty years after Hall's magnum opus, the psychoanalyst Erik Erikson explained youthful flightiness with a therapeutic concept that can be understood as the cultural heritage of recapitulation theory. Erikson conceptualized the process of growing up as a series of "normative [...] crises" that every individual had to go through in order to mature into a mentally healthy and socially responsible adult.[15] In adolescence, juveniles would experience the crisis of "identity v. role confusion" as a pivotal conflict which they had to overcome in order to gain the ability to recognize and fulfil their role in society.[16] While adolescence was perceived as a crucial point at which the success or failure of the maturation process would become obvious, it was also considered as a stage when a lot of things could still go wrong. Hence this concept of growing up did not do parents any favours. To ensure their children's successful journey toward social responsibility and thus to provide for their future ability to perform the duties of citizenship, parents had to carefully guide every step in their children's maturation process. For civilization to survive, Erikson stated, parents needed to provide their child with a "conscience which will guide him without crushing him and which is firm and flexible enough to fit the vicissitudes of his historical era".[17] Thus parents should be able to follow their offspring through this "age of turmoil" – and in the Cold War, this worked as a description of adolescence as well as of the state of the global order.[18]

A striking example of the ambivalent construction of youth and the consequent roles of parents are the inherently different representations of juvenile delinquency in Cold War America and the way in which American experts delineated the behaviour of US youngsters in comparison to those in Soviet Russia. On the one hand, delinquency was depicted as a serious problem of all modern societies (Russia included!), that was assumed to grow out of familial disorganization or over-conformity. On the other hand, US-American white, middle-class juvenile delinquents were sharply distinguished from their Russian counterparts: they could be portrayed as carrying the promise of an individual's opposition to allegedly "unhealthy" social conditions and thus as expressions of democratic modernity.

Danger: Delinquency as a result of familial breakdown and conformity

To explain the omnipresence and danger of juvenile delinquency, US-Americans pointed to an allegedly huge delinquency problem in Soviet Russia. Robert Hinckley, for instance, vice president of the American Broadcasting Company, argued in a series of Senate hearings that the severity of the Russian delinquency problem supported his assertion that the modern mass media could not be a decisive factor in producing juvenile delinquency. "[Russia] has raised a crop of juvenile delinquents as large as, if not larger, than our own," he declared, and pointed to the fact that only a small percentage of Russian households owned a TV-receiver; furthermore, comics directed at juveniles did not exist there. However, Hinckley found other equally likely explanations for juvenile delinquency in working mothers, badly equipped schools, crowded slums and the Soviet condemnation of religion. Harrison Salisbury, who had been a *New York Times* correspondent in Moscow for six years, similarly explained delinquency in Soviet Russia as the result of a "persisting high level of family disintegration".[19] It is significant that these explanations of Russian delinquency were not stressed in Russian delinquency discourse, as Gleb Tsipursky shows in this volume. Instead, they were paradigmatic of the importance of families in the Cold War US and closely connected with a contemporary diagnosis of increasingly unstable American families. One of the most influential surveys on the causes of juvenile delinquency was the long-term study of Eleanor and Sheldon Glueck, both psychologists at Harvard. The result of their analysis of male delinquent and non-delinquent youngsters was published in 1950. It suggested that familial stability and discipline played a central role in preventing juvenile delinquency.[20] In the post-war US, the importance of a carefully guided childhood was translated into an emphasis on family stability and functionality that served to regulate families in manifold ways. It is important to note that dominant conceptions of family stability were structured by hegemonic notions of heterosexual, white, middle-class families. Although the Gluecks had only examined white families in their study, sociologists and psychologists increasingly figured especially African American families as "dysfunctional" and thus as "breeding grounds" for juvenile delinquency.[21]

The preoccupation with Soviet delinquency revolved around a second problem that was considered to be a decisive factor in producing juvenile delinquency in Soviet Russia as well as in the US. Maxwell-Peters' fear of "poisoned" juveniles invoked Cold War mind control discourse and the alleged suggestibility of young people was heavily discussed at a time when the danger of conformity seemed to affect American society as well.[22] *The New York Times* informed its readers in November 1957 that the discipline in Soviet schools would be overly rigid: "The strictness with which Soviet children are trained to conform to a predetermined social pattern [...] has its effects in other directions," stated the newspaper and listed "outbursts of hooliganism and other forms of juvenile delinquency" as likely results of this forced conformity.[23] This reference to the dangers of conformity served as a powerful warning to Americans.[24] Contemporary cultural critics had already been worrying about a loss of individualism in American mass culture for several years.[25] Employing psychological knowledge to talk about adolescent development, delinquency discourse now explained youthful misbehaviour not only in Soviet Russia, but in the US as well as an outcome of an "over-organized" society. "Is it any wonder", the anthropologist Weston LaBarre asked in 1959,

> that our young people without any models of grown-up, self-responsible adults to copy, fly about aimlessly like a flock of starlings, obeying the cues now of one bird, now of another? They yearn to discover an identity, but how is this possible when they have no individuals to guide them, only the homogenized, tyrannical group?[26]

The influential psychiatrist Robert Lindner likewise explained the misbehaviour of juveniles in an Eriksonian manner, as being caused by an alarming decline of individualism: "[T]hese are the days of pack-running," he stated, "of organization into great collectivities that bury, if they do not destroy, individuality. [...] [T]he fee [the young] pay for initiation is abandonment of self and immersion in the herd, with its consequent sacrifice of personality."[27]

Those who criticized American conformity saw a loss of individuality primarily in the white, middle-class suburbs. Anti-conformist critic William Whyte, for instance, quoted a common joke describing suburbia as "a Russia, only with money".[28] And an article in the *Parents' Magazine* reflected this trend by depicting suburban life as a competitive quest for – ironically – sameness: "Between 'measuring up', 'being accepted', 'gaining recognition', improving the house and grounds as extensions of a family's feeling of worth, improving the community to make it 'a better place for the children to live in' – suburbanites find themselves too busy to find themselves as individuals."[29] Indeed, there is much to suggest that suburban juvenile delinquency was explained in connection to conformism and mass consumption. This construction served implicitly to distinguish white, middle-class delinquents in suburbia from those based in rural areas, who were rarely talked about in this strand of delinquency discourse.

The fear of too much conformism was profoundly structured by hegemonic notions of a desirable masculine individuality that served to depict juvenile delinquency as primarily a male problem. The author Paul Goodman understood youthful behaviour as a foreseeable consequence of conformist emasculation in the "organized system". "Positively, the delinquent behavior seems to speak clearly enough," he wrote in his famous book *Growing Up Absurd*: "It asks for manly opportunities to work, make a little money, and have self-esteem; [...]; to have a community and a country to be loyal to; to claim attention and have a voice."[30] Goodman here explained youthful delinquency with reference to juveniles' seemingly natural strivings for meaning and acceptance. His diagnosis hints at a possible, positive connotation of juvenile rebelliousness that was established parallel to the condemnation of delinquency. Precisely in the conception of delinquency as anti-conformist breakout, hope was hidden. As can be seen in the next section of this chapter, delinquency discourse allowed for a concept of juvenile truculence as culturally desired rebellion, of "necessary" rebels as carriers of democratic rescue.[31] It was this discursive formation that made it possible to diagnose a similar type of anti-conformist delinquency in both Soviet Russia and the US, yet at the same time to depict only some of America's youth as capable of this type of democratic citizenship.

Progress: Culturally necessary rebels

"[T]he health of a democracy", the *New York Times* asserted in 1960, "unlike the stability of a totalitarian nation, depends on the existence of citizens who know how to say no as well as yes, and who fight back when they are wronged."[32] In the post-war US and especially in anti-conformist critiques, this democratic potential was especially ascribed to youth because of the distinct characteristics that were associated with adolescence – instability and turmoil, but also fresh-sightedness and energy. *LOOK*'s counselling columnist, Norman Vincent Peale, was anxiously asked in 1954 whether the high numbers of young people seeking his advice indicated that they were "disturbed". Peale answered that juveniles were indeed disturbed, "for they were born into a disturbed world". "But", he promised subsequently, "they have fresh, keen, open minds, and they want real answers to real problems. Young people today are really thinking."[33]

Anti-conformist discourse bemoaned the alleged closure of a social space of (temporary) outbreak that especially adolescents would need to reach maturity, as Erikson had emphasized. Because of this concept of youth as the "natural" embodiment of outbreak, adolescents emerged as a solution to the malaise of conformism. Youth, by definition, carried the meaning of an independent, albeit malleable character, striving for an individual identity. Moreover, as Peale had suggested, adolescents seemed to be not yet fully affected by the harmful influences of modern society. Young people were associated with a refreshing breeze and invigorating display of self-will that the US seemed to be in desperate need of to maintain their democratic flexibility and modern society. Hence, certain embodiments of juvenile delinquency could paradoxically be embraced as desirable signs of mature individuality in an over-organized society. "[R]ebellion", experts stated at the Midcentury White House Conference on Children and Youth, "is the attempt of a child or youth to maintain his integrity as a person, to defend his dignity as a unique personality when threatened, damaged, or denied that integrity and dignity by other persons."[34] This observation was, moreover, supported by psychoanalytical knowledge. Lindner, for example, celebrated a specific kind of youthful behaviour as "positive rebellion" and even as evidence of a mature drive to foster "fundamental human values" and progress.[35] Lindner's answer to the question "Must You Conform?", as one of his books was entitled, was a determined "No!": "[N]o because there is an alternate way of life available to us here and now. It is the way of positive rebellion, the path of creative protest, the road of productive revolt."[36]

As the alertness of delinquency discourse indicates, the range available for expressing "positive rebellion" was limited: "We need nonconformists", the *PTA Magazine* declared in 1964, "not wild, irresponsible, self-destructive nonconformists but judicious ones."[37] Ironically, the "judiciousness" of nonconformity was found in a person's capability to conform to US-American values. According to Lindner, positive rebellion precluded behaviour that did not go along with a democratic system. Therefore, he qualified positive rebellion as an expression of maturity that was not determined by the age of the rebel. Lindner presented this maturity rather as a psychosocial disposition, as the concurrent display of rational independence and social responsibility. His conception of positive rebellion can be read as a psychological version of "Western" concepts of the ideal modern citizenship as it had been developed in Enlightenment social contract theories.[38] The *voluntary* consent of citizens, that is the capability of allegedly autonomous thinking combined with the ability to reach a consensus, was a powerful ideal in the Cold War, when the relationship of "free" individuals to the state was a pressing problem – especially in the US.[39] Paradoxically, the means by which individuality was to be saved and fostered was found in securing the given social order. In the Cold War US, the idea of crisis-stricken, but self-discovering juveniles served as a cultural promise to bring in line disparate notions of individuality and self-fulfilment in a standardized consumer society. The juvenile rebel embodied a democratic character, revolting against mass society, but principally able and willing to concur with suburban living and white-collar work – and thus with the basic values of US modernity.[40]

Interestingly, young people employed this configuration in order to defend their behaviour, as letters to magazines show. A teenager wrote to *LOOK*, reacting to a story on the dangers of conformity: "[The story] helped my father understand better what I mean in my crusade for nonconformity. Whenever I mentioned it, he used to snort, 'Lawbreakers!' and other phrases. Now he sees my side."[41] By displaying moral uprightness, juveniles could sometimes even claim the role of educating their parents, as, for example, Peale indicated. In response to a teenager's complaint about his/her mother lying to the father, the counsellor wrote: "Start re-educating her ethically and spiritually. Children, strangely enough, must often undertake the responsibility of helping parents to remake themselves."[42] Although the capability for socially useful revolt was primarily ascribed to male youngsters, it could be claimed by female teenagers, too. Sixteen-year-old Diane Strutz, for example, asserted in a letter to the *PTA Magazine* that "intellectual straitjackets" would surely "not come in my size". However, she deemed it necessary to distance herself from a "beatnik type of nonconformity – wanting to be different purely for the sake of difference".[43] Here, Strutz referred to the limits of "positive" rebellion which will be examined in more detail in the following section.

Determining democratic potential: Differentiating juveniles and parents

As Strutz' letter indicated, the possibility of reclaiming the label of positive rebellion was limited. Juvenile defiance could only be reconfigured as desirable breakout from too many constraints when the young offender could be discursively framed as having an inherently "upright" character. Psychologists and psychiatrists had declared that the establishment of a democratic character was connected to healthy psychosocial conditions in childhood and adolescence. Thereby, it was connected to (a) an upbringing in a democratic society and (b) the moral and educational capabilities of the parents. Connecting the democratic potential of teenagers to the conditions of their upbringing allowed for distinguishing American from Russian teenagers, as well as for establishing a distinction between different groups of teenagers inside the US.

American delinquency experts had worried about conformity as one possible cause of juvenile misbehaviour, thereby constructing a link between US and Russian delinquency. However, they outlined the character of the alleged conformist threat differently for both countries.

While conformity in Russia was described as forcibly imposed, the threat for Americans seemed to be a rather psychological problem rooted in modern mass culture and could thus, as psychologists suggested, be overcome by rational, independent citizens. Hence, by distinguishing the "stability of a totalitarian nation" from the "health of democracy", as the above-mentioned article in the *New York Times* did, delinquency discourse highlighted a fundamental difference between adolescents' upbringing in the US and Russia. The criminologist Walter Reckless argued in front of the Senate Subcommittee in 1954:

> Due to the forces of emancipation and the loosening of family and organizational structures, the individual child or young person is now able to ascend like a balloon, rising outward and upward without stabilizing ballast. He can struggle for position, for self-expression, for power, for luxury items, for excitement, for love. He can now express his restlessness. [...] He can protest. Consequently, much of delinquency today represents the individual person breaking through moorings, attempting to aggrandize himself. This is annoying. This is serious. But it is also progress, as contrasted with the subjected, the awed, the subdued, the confined, the hemmed-in, the reserved, the conservative self of yesteryears[...].[44]

Although Reckless marked a repressive sociality as historically overcome, contemporaries could recognize a well-known characterization of subjected Soviet citizens in his remarks. Lindner put it more precisely and linked "negative rebellion" directly to the USSR because of their "Mass Man" character.[45] Included in the concept of "positive" rebels as socially integral personalities was the notion that only a democratic social order could provide young people with the basic capabilities of "productive revolt". Here, it is remarkable how ideas of democratic progress aligned with notions of juvenile delinquency: by contrasting American teenagers with Russian ones, US delinquency discourse constructed American youth as a potentially promising asset not only of the US but of "Western" democracy as a whole. Here, juvenile delinquency literally symbolized democratic individualism and thus a concept of democratic "progress" that was closely connected with the construction of "Western" modernity. Jim Stark in *Rebel Without a Cause* can be seen as a paradigmatic embodiment of such an individualistic delinquency. Given the representation of Jim's overly adjusted, narrow-minded parents, Jim's misconduct might well have been understood by contemporaries as rebellious, yet comprehensible and democratic behaviour.[46]

However, even in the US, not everybody was seen as able to perform such a democratic responsibility and juvenile delinquency could not generally be "redeemed" by referring to youth's democratic potential. In stressing the need for the social integrity of "positive" revolt, only those juveniles could be accredited as "positive" rebels who were accepted as citizens. This excluded all those young people and adults to whom this status as democratic subjects was denied. Young African Americans, for example, who participated in civil rights activism, were regularly arrested as juvenile delinquents and placed in detention facilities.[47] In the 1960s, when delinquency was increasingly explained by pointing to the living conditions in inner-city slums, black juvenile delinquency was far less often linked positively with the discourse of democratic potential than was the case with white, middle-class delinquency.[48]

The development of responsible citizens was, as we have seen, closely connected to parental conduct. In February 1952, *LOOK* reported on a study that ascribed different democratic potentials to different groups of American youngsters. The study divided them into two categories, each linked to a characterization of their familial and regional background:

> The typical democratic type is likely to be a high-school senior, living in a town or city in the Midwest or West. His family's income places them in the upper-middle or upper economic bracket. His mother has gone to college. [...]The composite authoritarian type – the teenager who is most inclined to reject basic freedoms and accept many communist and fascist principles – is more likely to be in the ninth grade and live in the rural South. His mother had little education, and his family is in the low-income bracket.[49]

Here, a desirable democratic character was explicitly assigned to youngsters from affluent, educated families. Moreover, via the categories of geographical location, education and class, this narrative implicitly constructed promising future citizens as white, since the American Midwest and West were marked as predominantly white. In particular, the reference to rural areas is a striking example of how ascriptions of democratic potential could vary between families located in different demographic settings. Lastly it is important to note that the study especially emphasized the mother's role in child-rearing, since her educational background was highlighted. The quoted passage suggests a contemporary understanding of democratic child-rearing as a predominantly white, middle-class quality. Conversely, educational incompetence was associated chiefly with lower-class, non-white parents: many delinquency experts believed that it was these mothers above all who needed parenting advice, and criticized them as "inaccessible" when it came to offerings of education and help.[50] As the following remarks will show, delinquency discourse allotted a central, so to speak civilizing duty to parents, and especially mothers, to become successful educators of their children and to constantly reflect on their pedagogical skills.

Parent education and therapy

Delinquency experts considered it a chief element of "proper" parenting that parents were capable of distinguishing between "good" and "bad" juvenile misbehaviour. "To recognize when the rebellion is promising and when it becomes destructive is essential if we are to help him toward his goal of independence", the *National Parent-Teacher* wrote and urged parents: "The wise parent must try to discern where [it] is appropriate [...]."[51] To be able to make this important distinction, parents were prompted to seek educational advice.

A growing market in educational advice books hastened to provide parents with child-rearing instructions and simultaneously fuelled the imperative of gaining such knowledge.[52] The distribution of educational knowledge can be seen in a Foucauldian sense as one of several governmental techniques designed to regulate American families insofar as it fostered an active role for parents in this never-ending process of learning.[53] Juvenile delinquency was a productive topic for education manuals and an abundance of educational guidebooks, articles and pamphlets informed parents on how to prevent their children's delinquency.[54] *Parents' Magazine*, for example, had a section entitled "Family Clinic" in which mothers reported on how they had solved typical problems with their offspring.[55] Counselling columns, often with renowned experts, mushroomed in popular magazines and functioned as a form of therapy for anxious parents, mostly mothers. In addition to their basic counselling function, magazines like *Parents' Magazine* and *National Parent-Teacher* published their articles as part of broader parent education programmes that provided "Parent Study Groups" with additional material and guiding questions for further discussion.[56]

However, experts continued to view these parents with some mistrust, since their emotional stability was doubted on a fundamental, psychological level. According to Erikson, adults also had to cope with personality crises; one of them he described as a crisis of "generativity

v. stagnation", a conflict that arose out of the challenge of "establishing and guiding the next generation".[57] In this stage, Erikson's followers argued that adults needed to develop a "parental sense [...] indicated most clearly by interest in producing and caring for children of one's own". However, they diagnosed that "many parents who bring their children to child-guidance clinics are found not to have reached this stage of personality development".[58] Erikson closed the circle of crisis-stricken human development by locating the reasons for parental failure in their childhood experiences.[59] As a consequence, it seemed necessary to have a closer look at parents' psyches. Around mid-century, the character of educational counselling and help – for example in child-guidance clinics – had changed. Instead of the "problem child", mothers and their childhood experiences became a central therapeutic access point.[60] These practices show that in the post-war US, concepts of "good" motherhood went beyond ideas of "republican motherhood" that had been crucial to US nation-building since the American Revolution. "Republican motherhood" was now supplemented by notions of "therapeutic motherhood" concerning child-rearing and mothers' permanent engagement with their own psyches and educational skills.[61] Being a mother was deemed as constitutively problematic as being a juvenile. Mothers were hailed as a central socializing agency, but simultaneously blamed and doubted. Just like juveniles, they too incorporated both hope and danger.

As Elaine Tyler May has shown, concepts of "normal" families served as an important vanishing point of US politics on the Cold War home front. "Good" motherhood, in particular, played a central role in this process, as it was during this period that a motherly "domesticity" was reframed as "an expression of one's citizenship".[62] The cultural implications of these notions thus cannot be underestimated: to delineate the boundaries of "good" motherhood meant to delineate who was regarded as a legitimate part of society. However, these boundaries were a contested terrain.[63] The following analysis of private letters by parents shows that delinquency discourse can be examined as one of the cultural sites in which these negotiations took place.

Acting motherhood: Knowledge and anxiety

How did parents help to shape this discursive regimen? Agnes Maxwell-Peters had asked Fredric Wertham "what [...] two parents [could] do?" Her letter is one of the many instances where parents – and mostly mothers – followed the discursive imperative to acquire knowledge on proper child-rearing. Numerous letters to Fredric Wertham and educational magazines show furthermore that mothers adjusted their educational techniques to this knowledge and inscribed themselves into the profound anxiety of motherhood. The letters can be read as sources that show how delinquency discourse provided a space for parents to feel and act upon and simultaneously reproduce notions of mothers as primarily responsible for child-rearing and hence for securing the future's most important resource.

In these letters, the responsibility of parents for the development of their offspring seemed to be accepted as a matter of course. By beginning with phrases such as "As a mother", or "Being a mother", the writers suggested that motherly anxiety was a "natural" part of motherhood – this finding carried a distinctly gendered assertion that was obviously enough to justify writing the letter.[64] Moreover, the letters offer evidence that possession of educational knowledge provided mothers with a special perspective on their children. "Many thanks for the wonderful article 'Healthy – and Irritating – Signs of Independence'", one Mrs. Charles Muehlhausen wrote to the *PTA Magazine* in March 1960, and rejoiced: "It gave me an entirely new outlook on my seven-year-old daughter."[65] Another example of the profound effect of psychobiological knowledge on motherly child-rearing is a letter from one Roberta Goldstein to the same magazine, in which she reported about her children: "All four have maintained their own individualities and are resisting the common contemporary schedule that leaves no time for the personality to grow normally without pressure and tensions."[66] Goldstein here employed psychological notions of "healthy" growth to conceive of herself as a "good" mother.

Delinquency discourse lent an edge of urgency to the letters of mothers. One Mrs. Bill Stockwell, for example, wrote to Wertham in November 1954 that his remarks on juvenile delinquency had "shocked" her "out of an indifferent attitude".[67] And one Dorothy Conroy, who had received Wertham's book from a neighbour, admitted: "It embarrasses me to realize how indifferent we've been. [...] I've laughed with other mothers over the 'cute, violent games', all the gun play etc. Heavens!"[68] The much needed distinction between "good" and "bad" childish stubbornness also led parents to seek expert diagnoses. The Gluecks received many letters from parents wanting them to check on their children, such as the letter of one Helen Schroetter: "I was reading in a Junior Scholastic magazine that you have made up an IQ test for five year olds to tell if they will be juvenile delinquents or not." Schroetter wrote that her son wanted "to do everything his own way because he thinks he is grown up". Although he was not always "bad", she needed him to be tested: "I'd like him to take this test so I'll know if his misbehaving is normal."[69]

Since maternity was considered to be an arduous task per se, mothers could paradoxically perform "good" motherhood by calling attention to their faults and imperfections. A good example of this is the letter of one Georgann Thomas, mother of three children, to Wertham. Thomas marked her household as middle-class by listing a wide range of magazines and newspapers her children would read daily and worried that children in "underprivileged communities" would not have access to such publications. However, she saw signs of delinquency in her own son and traced them back to the fact that her children had "many problems to overcome, including those of very imperfect parents".[70] Thomas' letter sheds light on the complex accentuations and conditions of the performance of "adequate" motherhood. On the one hand, she reproduced the focus on the important parental role in producing or preventing delinquency and confessed her inadequacy to the psychiatrist. On the other hand, precisely this confession enabled her to inscribe herself into dominant, therapeutic notions of motherhood. By writing the letter, Thomas demonstrated her ability to reflect on her motherly imperfections, thereby fulfilling a central demand of modern motherhood. Yet, it is important to stress again that the success of such performances was linked to the possibility of rendering her family as basically adequate. By characterizing her family as middle-class, Thomas, like Maxwell-Peters, implied that the fundamental conditions for "proper" child-rearing were present in her household.

As another letter shows, such performances of "(im)perfect" motherhood could include narratives of therapeutical catharsis. In 1958, one Dorothy Rubens Binsky wrote to *LOOK* and recounted the process of dealing with her misbehaving child:

> After four years with a social worker, I reached the point of desperation and went to the University Psychiatric Institute [...]. I was firmly convinced I was the perfect mother and the entire problem was my child. After the first session with the psychiatrist (myself the patient), I came face to face with the problem.... In many cases where there is a disturbed child, you can lay the origin of the trouble at the door of the devoted but emotionally unstable mother.[71]

By displaying a seemingly "natural" motherly anxiety and the will to face up to parental inadequacies, mothers could inscribe themselves into normative notions of therapeutic motherhood.

Interestingly, the performance of parenthood in these letters could sometimes involve contradicting and rejecting the knowledge of "outside" experts. This is well shown in a letter to a local newspaper which was sent to the Gluecks by a colleague. "I wonder just how much Prof. Sheldon Glueck and his wife, Eleanor, know about delinquent children? Have they any children?" a mother asked in this letter. For her, it would be "rather odd that some professor, criminologist, or what have you, should pronounce children delinquents". She distanced herself from "such creatures" like criminologists and thus from an abstract expertise and constructed parents as "natural authorities" on child-rearing: "I thank God that I have a husband to be proud of and a young boy who is being brought up to be a good American."[72] At a time, when Benjamin Spock's influential *Common Sense Book of Baby and Child Care* advised mothers to primarily trust their "natural impulses", the widespread dependence on expert advice could also be condemned.[73]

Moreover, mothers sometimes saw no practical relevance in educational guidelines. Agnes Maxwell-Peters had stated she would not be able to "govern" her children's "every waking hour". Much sharper was the letter of one Norma Hammond, who wrote to the *PTA Magazine*, complaining about the "movie ratings" of the journal:

> How naïve can one be? So Mr. and Mrs. Parent, when they see "Suggested for Mature Audiences" applied to a film, are supposed to determine whether this particular film is wholesome fare for their children. Okay, I've determined that it isn't wholesome fare for my children. What do I do now? Chain my sixteen-year-old to the bed post so that he won't go to the movies with his pals? Tell him he has freedom to choose what he wears, what he eats, his friends, his vocation, but not the movies he wants to see? [...] [M]odern parents can [not] police modern children every hour of the day...[74]

Here, Hammond invokes the contradictory invocations of educational discourse in Cold War America: the postulated, but obviously not feasible balancing act of democratic child-rearing that should secure the children's individuality but simultaneously keep them from the "character damaging" influences of, for instance, the mass media. Moreover, she explicitly referred to an understanding of modernity that included the freedom of choices and was sharply distinguished from permanent (parental) control. The prevailing mind control discourse and the symbolic importance of democratic individualism allowed parents to reject calls for a stricter control of their youngsters.

Against the backdrop of the arduousness of child-rearing and the impossibility of doing everything "right", it became also possible for parents to reject their alleged role in producing juvenile delinquency. While it was quite common in such letters to bemoan the blame that was loaded onto parents in the delinquency scare, a few letters can be found, interestingly written by fathers, which denied parental responsibility for delinquent behaviour, even though their own children were affected. One Herbert Lorenz, for instance, wrote to Wertham that two of his three adopted children had become "juvenile delinquents". While Lorenz felt "well qualified to express an opinion on this subject", he could shift the blame for his children's delinquency onto the greater influence of the mass media: "On reviewing everything that has passed, we both honestly feel that the filthy comics were one of the factors in spoiling their young minds and did much to make bad children out of them."[75] Cold War delinquency discourse provided parents with a discursive space in which they could accept or reject the question of parental guilt.

Conclusion

As this chapter has shown, the post-war delinquency discourse in the US can be analysed as a site of worries over democratic progress in a modern society. Via notions of "Western" modernity and psychosocial abilities, juvenile (mis)behaviour could be framed as either a danger to or a promising asset for US-American society. This discursive arrangement served to distinguish American or "Western" from Russian youngsters and to differentiate "positively rebelling" teenagers inside the US from those who were regarded as dangerous delinquents. In this way, delinquency discourse circumscribed the boundaries of democratic competence and civic ability and thus both shaped and was shaped by notions of "Western" modernity.

Furthermore, this chapter has shown that the direct linking of juvenile delinquency to parental conduct shifted a good deal of attention from youngsters to their parents. Notions of "adequate" families were highly exclusionary; and dominant narratives of parental conduct denied this label to parents who were seen as incapable of securing the social responsibility of future citizens. White middle-class parents were discursively installed as a bridge between society and its youngsters, an important bridge which had to bear the burden of being responsible for the future of the American nation. However, the ability of America's parents to do so was heavily discussed. In this way, delinquency discourse provided especially mothers with a framework for understanding themselves and their children. In the process of seeking advice and paradoxically also in confessing parental failures and insecurities, mothers could inscribe themselves into notions of "good" motherhood, could act according to normative understandings of motherhood and thus as culturally intelligible subjects. Nevertheless, this was not a coherent, deterministic process and parents did not always accept their ascribed role without objections.

The ways in which they rejected certain aspects of educational knowledge sheds light on an important structural characteristic of processes of subjectivation: in the process of subjecting themselves to the cultural requirements of parenthood, the letter writers could reclaim a distinct subject position which allowed them to at least partially challenge hegemonic truths (of, in this case, parental responsibility). Parental letters can be analysed as points where discursive knowledge and individual actions intersect. The further exploration of such letters and other similar sources promises to be instructive concerning the question of the relation of discourses and people's scopes of action. Moreover, by focusing on the "making" of parents, this chapter hopes to encourage greater scholarly attention in the field of childhood studies to exploring the perhaps more subtle government of parents via discourses on children and youth.

Notes

1. I would like to extend my thanks to Heather Ellis and Lily Chang as well as to Melanie Henne and Nora Kreuzenbeck for their critical and inspiring comments on this chapter. My special thanks go to Renée and George Dunham for making this research possible with their incredible hospitality and their help in so many regards.

   Agnes Maxwell-Peters to Fredric Wertham, 7 September 1948, Papers of Fredric Wertham, 1895–1981, Box 123 (Library of Congress Manuscript Division, Washington, DC).
2. See, for example, James Gilbert, *A Cycle of Outrage: America's Reaction to the Juvenile Delinquent in the 1950s* (New York/Oxford: Oxford University Press, 1986).
3. When talking about the "West", this chapter refers to the construction of a geopolitical category that was used to construct a global centre by distinguishing allegedly modern and liberal societies from those that were marked as undemocratic and underdeveloped, such as the Soviet Union and the "third world". On Cold War cultural politics on the home front, see, for example, David Halberstam, *The Fifties* (New York: Fawcett Columbine, 1994); Kyle A. Cuordileone, *Manhood and American Political Culture in the Cold War* (New York: Routledge, 2005).

4. See, for example, Anthony M. Platt, *The Child Savers: The Invention of Delinquency* (Chicago: University of Chicago Press, 1977 [1969]); Mary E. Odem, *Delinquent Daughters: Protecting and Policing Adolescent Female Sexuality in the United States, 1885–1920* (Chapel Hill: University of North Carolina Press, 1995).
5. Nina Mackert, " 'But recall the kinds of parents we have to deal with . . .' – Juvenile Delinquency, Interdependent Masculinity and the Government of Families in the Post-war U.S.", in Isabel Heinemann (ed.), *Inventing the Modern American Family. Family Values and Social Change in 20th Century United States* (Frankfurt a.M./New York: Campus, 2012), pp. 196–219. A thorough look at the US delinquency scare complicates the assumption that it was triggered primarily by experts and an alarmed media (as Gleb Tsipursky suggests in this volume). In fact, the fear of rising rates of juvenile delinquency emerged simultaneously in a range of fields and institutions and cannot easily be broken down into a specific distribution pattern, as I show in Nina Mackert, *Jugenddelinquenz. Die Produktivität eines Problems in den USA der späten 1940er bis 1960er Jahre* (Konstanz: UVK, 2014, forthcoming).
6. See, for example, William S. Bush, *Who Gets a Childhood? Race and Juvenile Justice in Twentieth-Century Texas* (Athens: The University of Georgia Press, 2010).
7. Cf., for example, Albert K. Cohen, *Delinquent Boys* (Glencoe, IL: The Free Press, 1955); Howard L. Myerhoff and Barbara G. Myerhoff, "Field Observation of Middle Class 'Gangs'", *Social Forces*, 42, 3 (1964): 328–336.
8. For a comparison of the US-American delinquency scare and similar developments in Germany, see Sebastian Kurme, *Halbstarke: Jugendprotest in den 1950er Jahren in Deutschland und den USA* (Frankfurt a. M./New York: Campus, 2006).
9. On the role of such signifiers in producing social hegemony, see Ernesto Laclau and Chantal Mouffe, *Hegemony and Socialist Strategy: Towards a Radical Democratic Politics* (London: Verso, 1985); Ernesto Laclau, *On Populist Reason* (London: Verso, 2005).
10. See, for example, Elaine Tyler May, *Homeward Bound: American Families in the Cold War Era* (New York: Basic Books, 1988); Juergen Martschukat, "Men in Gray Flannel Suits. Troubling Masculinities in 1950s America", *Gender Forum: An Internet Journal for Gender Studies*, 32 (2011), accessed 14 February 2012, http://www.genderforum.org/issues/historical-masculinities-as-an-intersectional-problem/httpwwwgenderforumorgissueshistorical-masculinities-as-an-intersectional-problemmen-in-gray-flannel-suits/.
11. Michel Foucault, *The Use of Pleasure: The History of Sexuality, Vol. 2* (New York: Vintage 1990 [Paris: Gallimard 1984]), p. 27; on the mechanisms of subjectivation, see also Nicolas Rose, *Governing the Soul: The Shaping of the Private Self* (London: Routledge, 1990).
12. Hendrickson quoted in Steven Mintz, *Huck's Raft: A History of American Childhood* (Cambridge: Harvard University Press, 2004), p. 293.
13. G. Stanley Hall, *Adolescence: Its Psychology and Its Relation to Physiology, Anthropology, Society, Sex, Crime, Religion and Education*, 2 Vols. (New York: Appleton and Co., 1904); on the cultural implications of this construction of adolescence, see Gail Bederman, *Manliness & Civilization: A Cultural History of Gender and Race in the United States, 1880–1917* (Chicago/London: University

of Chicago Press, 1995), pp. 77–120; Nancy Lesko, *Act Your Age! A Cultural Construction of Adolescence* (New York: Routledge, 2001), pp. 49–90.

14. Hall: *Adolescence*, I, xiv; on the function of this narrative as discursive legitimization of colonial and racist politics as well as its reproduction of a sexualized and gendered hegemonic order, see Ann Laura Stoler, *Race and the Education of Desire: Foucault's History of Sexuality and the Colonial Order of Things* (Durham/London: Duke University Press, 1995), pp. 151–152; Anne McClintock, *Imperial Leather: Race, Gender, and Sexuality in the Colonial Contest* (New York: Routledge, 1995), pp. 42–51.

15. Erik Erikson, *Identity: Youth and Crisis* (New York: Norton, 1968), p. 17.

16. Erik Erikson, *Childhood and Society* (New York: Norton, 1950), pp. 252–255, 261.

17. Ibid., p. 89.

18. "Age of turmoil" was the title of a movie on adolescence for psychology students: *Age of Turmoil* (1953, Crawley Films, Ltd. for McGraw-Hill), available online at http://www.archive.org/details/AgeofTur1953, accessed 12 May 2011.

19. US Congress, Senate, Committee on the Judiciary, *Juvenile Delinquency (Television Programs): Hearings before the Subcommittee to Investigate Juvenile Delinquency of the Committee on the Judiciary*, 83rd Cong., 2nd sess., 5 June, 19 and 20, October 1954, Washington, DC: Government Printing Office, 1955 (National Archives, Washington, DC, Y4.J89/2:J98/15), pp. 233–234; Harrison E. Salisbury: "Youth Outbreaks Traced to Turbulence in Family", *New York Times* (27 March 1958), p. 28.

20. Sheldon Glueck and Eleanor Glueck, *Unraveling Juvenile Delinquency* (New York: The Commonwealth Fund, 1950).

21. Mackert, "Juvenile Delinquency, Interdependent Masculinity and the Government of Families".

22. Leerom Medovoi, *Rebels: Youth and the Cold War Origins of Identity* (Durham: Duke University Press, 2005).

23. Anon, "Russians' Discipline is Severe: Pupils Subject to Strict Code", *New York Times* (11 November 1957), p. 11.

24. Andrew Hartman, *Education and the Cold War: The Battle for the American School* (New York: Palgrave Macmillan, 2008), p. 178.

25. Cf., for example, David Riesman, *The Lonely Crowd* (New Haven: Yale University Press, 1950); William Hollingsworth Whyte, *The Organization Man* (Philadelphia: University of Pennsylvania Press, 2002 [New York: Simon and Schuster, 1956].

26. Weston La Barre, "How Adolescent Are Parents?" *National Parent-Teacher*, 54, 4 (1959), p. 6.

27. Robert M. Lindner, *Must You Conform?* (New York: Rinehart, 1956), p. 11.

28. Whyte, *The Organization Man*, p. 280, see also Medovoi, *Rebels*, pp. 20–24.

29. Helen Puner, "Is it True What They Say about the Suburbs?" *Parents' Magazine*, 7 (1958), p. 97.

30. Paul Goodman, *Growing Up Absurd* (New York: Vintage Books, 1962), p. 50.

31. For the gendered and sexualized structure of this narrative, see Medovoi, *Rebels*.

32. Charles Frankel, " 'We Must Not Let Moscow Set Our Pace' ", *The New York Times Magazine* (2 October 1960), p. 98.

33. Anon., "Norman Vincent Peale Answers Your Questions", *LOOK*, 18, 24 (1954), p. 34.
34. Edward A. Richards, ed., *Proceedings of the Midcentury White House Conference on Children and Youth* (Raleigh: Health Publications Institute Inc., 1951), p. 243.
35. Lindner, *Must You Conform?*, p. 177; Robert M. Lindner, *Rebel Without a Cause: The Hypnoanalysis of a Criminal Psychopath* (New York: Grune and Strutton, 1944).
36. Lindner, *Must You Conform?*, p. 179.
37. Raymond Squires, "The Costs of Conformity", *The PTA Magazine*, 58, 7 (1964), p. 6.
38. Lindner, *Must You Conform?*, pp. 21, 177–178, 188; for a recent, power-sensitive discussion of social contract theories, see e.g. Naomi Zack, *The Ethics and Mores of Race: Equality after the History of Philosophy* (Lanham: Rowman & Littlefield, 2011).
39. On the long and complicated history of the concept of freedom in the Unites States see the classic Eric Foner, "The Meaning of Freedom in the Age of Emancipation", *The Journal of American History*, 81, 2 (1994), pp. 435–460.
40. Medovoi, *Rebels*, pp. 8ff., 22.
41. Lyn Maloney, "Letters to the Editor", *LOOK*, 22, 8 (1958), p. 12; Maloney referred to George B. Leonard, "The American Male – Why Is He Afraid to Be Different?", *LOOK*, 22, 4 (1958), pp. 95–104.
42. "Norman Vincent Peale Answers Your Questions", *LOOK*, 22, 4 (1958), p. 88.
43. Diane Strutz, "Opinions by Post", *The PTA Magazine*, 58, 10 (1964), p. 35. Discursively, the "beat generation" sometimes served alongside lower-class, non-white delinquency as a negative foil for "positive rebellion"; see for example T. Lefoy Richman, "Is There a Morals Revolt among Youth?" *National Parent-Teacher*, 54, 3 (1959), pp. 16–18.
44. US Congress, Senate, Committee on the Judiciary, *Juvenile Delinquency (National, Federal, and Youth Serving Agencies): Hearings before the Subcommittee to Investigate Juvenile Delinquency of the Committee on the Judiciary*, 83rd Cong., 1st sess., Part 1, 19, 20, 23, 24 November 1953, Washington, DC: Government Printing Office, 1954 (National Archives, Washington, DC, Y4.J89/2:J98/3/pt. 1), p. 220.
45. Lindner, *Rebel without a Cause*, p. 222.
46. For a detailed analysis of the movie and its depiction of teenage rebels and contemporary constructions of gender and sexuality, see Medovoi, *Rebels*, pp. 167–214; for further examples of how these notions of young, democratic individuality could be embraced by social movements on the left and right side of the political spectrum, see Grace Elizabeth Hale, *A Nation of Outsiders: How the White Middle Class Fell in Love with Rebellion in Post-war America* (Oxford: Oxford University Press, 2011).
47. Anders Walker, "Blackboard Jungle: Delinquency, Desegregation, and the Cultural Politics of *Brown*", *Columbia Law Review*, 110, 7 (2009), pp. 1911–1953, here pp. 1946–1948.
48. Mackert, "Juvenile Delinquency, Interdependent Masculinity and the Government of Families". On the history of black juvenile delinquency in the US more broadly, see Geoff K. Ward, *The Black Child-Savers: Racial Democracy and Juvenile Justice* (London: The University of Chicago Press, 2012).

222 *Cold War Contexts*

49. William Houseman, "Are U.S. Teenagers Rejecting Freedom?" *LOOK*, 16, 5 (1952), pp. 29–31, here p. 31.
50. Cf. Helen Leland Witmer, *Parents and Delinquency: A Report of a Conference* (Washington, DC: US Dept. of Health, Education, and Welfare, Social Security Administration, Children's Bureau, 1954), pp. 28–29.
51. Joseph K. Folsom and Jean R. Folsom, "The Promising Rebellion", *National Parent-Teacher*, 42, 7 (1947), p. 6.
52. See, for example, Dorothy W. Baruch, *How to Live with Your Teenager* (New York: McGraw-Hill, 1953); Mary Frank and Lawrence K. Frank, *Your Adolescent in Home and in School* (New York: Viking Press, 1956) and, of course, for younger children *Benjamin Spock, The Common Sense Book of Baby and Child Care* (New York: Duell, Sloan and Pearce, 1946).
53. Marianne N. Bloch, "Governing Teachers, Parents, and Children through Child Development Knowledge", *Human Development*, 43, 4/5 (2000), pp. 257–265.
54. For example, *Teamwork Can Prevent Delinquency: A Guide for Community Action to Prevent Juvenile Delinquency* [Brochure], published by New York State Youth Commission (New York, rev. ed., 1953), Records of the Judiciary Committee of the Senate, Subcommittee to Investigate Juvenile Delinquency, 1953–1961, Correspondence on Juvenile Delinquency, files by state, Box 64 (National Archives, Washington, DC).
55. For instance "Childhood and Teenage Problems", *Parents' Magazine*, 26, 1 (1951), pp. 42–43; "Family Clinic", *Parents' Magazine*, 26, 11 (1951), pp. 26, 90.
56. For example, Mollie Smart, "Group-Discussion Outlines for Parents of School-Age Children", *Parents' Magazine*, 31, 5 (1956), p. 21; R. Strang, B. Goodykoontz, R.H. Oyemann and E.H. Grant, "Personality in the Making: Study Course Guides", *National Parent-Teacher*, 48, 3 (1953), pp. 32–34. See also for a more detailed account of parent education programmes Mackert, *Jugenddelinquenz*.
57. Erikson, *Childhood and Society*, p. 258.
58. Helen L. Witmer and Ruth Kotinsky (eds), *Personality in the Making* (New York: Harper and Brothers, 1952), p. 24.
59. Erikson, *Childhood and Society*, p. 259.
60. Kathleen F. Jones, *Taming the Troublesome Child: American Families, Child Guidance, and the Limits of Psychiatric Authority* (Cambridge: Harvard University Press, 1999), p. 191.
61. On "republican motherhood" see Linda K. Kerber, *Women of the Republic: Intellect and Ideology in Revolutionary America* (Chapel Hill: University of North Carolina Press, 1980); for a more detailed account of the construction of parents as fundamentally precarious, see Ann Hulbert, *Raising America: Experts, Parents, and a Century of Advice About Children* (New York: Alfred A. Knopf, 2003), pp. 191–224.
62. May, *Homeward Bound*, p. 144.
63. On the contested constructions of motherhood in the post-war US, see especially Joanne Meyerowitz (ed.), *Not June Cleaver. Women and Gender in Post-war America, 1945–1960* (Philadelphia: Temple University Press, 1994); Ruth Feldstein, *Motherhood in Black and White: Race and Sex in American Liberalism, 1930–1965* (Ithaca: Cornell University Press, 2000).

64. See, for example, Margaret Phelps Nelson to the Senate Subcommittee, 21 April 1954, Records of the Senate Subcommittee, Box 169; anonymous letter to the radio host "Martha Deane", 16 October 1956, Wertham Papers, Box 102.
65. Mrs. Charles Muehlhausen, "Opinions by Post", *National Parent-Teacher*, 54, 7 (1960), p. 40.
66. Mrs. Roberta Goldstein, "Opinions by Post", *The PTA Magazine*, 58, 10 (1964), p. 35.
67. Mrs. Bill Stockwell to Fredric Wertham, 6 November 1954, Wertham Papers, Box 124.
68. Dorothy Conroy to Fredric Wertham, 17 June 1954, Wertham Papers, Box 124.
69. Helen Schroetter to Sheldon und Eleanor Glueck, 9 May 1955, Papers of Sheldon and Eleanor Glueck, 1911–1972, Box 58 (Harvard Law School Library, Cambridge, MA).
70. Georgann Thomas to Fredric Wertham, 19 July 1954, Wertham Papers, Box 124.
71. Mrs. Dorothy Rubens Binsky, "Letters to the Editor", *LOOK*, 22, 19 (1958), p. 14.
72. "Just a Mother", letter to *The Worcester Gazette*, 30 October 1950, Glueck Papers, Box 37.
73. Hulbert, *Raising America*, p. 193.
74. Norma Hammond, "Opinions by Post", *The PTA Magazine*, 61, 5 (1967), p. 37.
75. Herbert Lorenz to Fredric Wertham, 22 April 1954, Wertham Papers, Box 1.

Part V

Juvenile Delinquency and the Post-War State

10
Becoming Delinquent in the Post-War Welfare State: England and Wales, 1945–1965

Kate Bradley

Introduction

Before the Second World War, the majority view of academics and practitioners in the field of juvenile justice in the UK and the US was that youthful delinquency was caused by deprivation, be that in economic, physical or emotional terms.[1] These deprivations were ultimately caused by the processes of "Western modernity", namely the inequalities of capitalism, the drive to acquire material goods and the disruption of traditional family structures and social mores. The solution to this was not to physically chastise the young or to incarcerate them, but rather to prevent future bad behaviour by addressing the problems that caused it. This canonical view of the causes of juvenile delinquency is a persistent one, as the essay by Miroslava Chávez-García in this volume demonstrates.

The first juvenile court, set up in 1899 in Cook County, Chicago, established a specialist holistic model for this.[2] This concept of a juvenile court has found resonance in other parts of the world, including England and Wales.[3] The first juvenile court in England was set up in Birmingham in 1905, and a national system for England and Wales was formally introduced by the Children Act 1908.[4] Through such tools as gathering pre-hearing reports from schoolteachers and social workers and the use of probation orders, the juvenile courts aimed to prevent as well as punish.[5] The Children and Young Persons Act 1933 added further requirements in terms of the layout of the juvenile courts, banning the naming of those attending court in the press, and adjusting the upper age limit from 16 to 17 years old.[6] The Cadogan Report of

1938 recommended the cessation of corporal punishment, and birching as a penalty for juvenile males was abolished as part of the Criminal Justice Act 1948.[7] The Ingleby Report of 1958 called for the decriminalization of juvenile offenders, with rehabilitative measures instead. This report – along with others undertaken in the 1950s and 1960s – formed the backdrop for the 1969 Children and Young Persons Act, which intended to implement the measures before being scaled back by the incoming Conservative government of 1970. These developments in the realm of juvenile justice also need to be seen in the context of the movement for children's rights in the later nineteenth and early twentieth centuries, manifested most clearly in the establishment of the National Society for the Prevention of Cruelty to Children in 1884, the expansion of compulsory elementary education, the regularization of fostering and adoption, restrictions on juvenile smoking and drinking, school meals and medical inspections and the growth of the Child Study Movement.[8]

David Garland described this approach as "penal welfarist". The penal welfare state was a modernist superstructure supported by a cross-party political consensus, combining punishment with expert rehabilitation in order to achieve its ends.[9] The penal welfare state required "experts" to shape its advice, to tailor it to the precisely defined needs of individual young people, and in doing so created an army of specialists to deal with them.[10] However, the experts tended to focus their efforts on the most deprived/depraved cases, while the majority were dealt with summarily through the use of fines.[11] This was part of the middle-class grip on society as a whole and the growth of professional society in particular.[12] For Garland, this penal welfare state was disrupted by the financial crises and subsequent rethinking of the efficacy of welfare that took place in the 1970s, ushering in a far more punitive paradigm,[13] which John Pratt has termed "penal populist". The penal populist approach is driven by a public desire to see offenders punished, does not seek to understand the circumstances of the offending behaviour, to rehabilitate or to address structural inequalities, but rather seeks retribution through incarceration.[14] Garland's analysis, which, in turn, draws upon the work of Foucault, Donzelot and Habermas in terms of the creation of a middle-class, professional public sphere engaged with measuring and advising on the needs of the poor and powerless, paints a very broad-brush picture of developments in the British welfare state and attitudes toward crime and punishment.[15] Garland's chronology is problematic because it is an historical account that is not grounded in rigorous archival work, and thus is not rooted in the contours of social change in post-war Britain. While Garland's account is engaging and convincing on one level, it paints too broad a brush stroke over the historical narrative, similar to the one Selina Todd has noted in terms of perceptions of the affluence in post-war Britain and the "rediscovery of poverty" in the 1960s.[16] Although there are many historical treatments of the policy development of the welfare state, historians have only recently begun to look systematically at the social history of welfare in post-war Britain, and thus it is imperative that broad-sweep perceptions are revisited and revised in the light of fresh historical understandings.[17] As Chávez-Garcia's chapter in this volume also demonstrates, approaches to juvenile delinquency and welfare in this period need to consider the intersections of race, sex and class as a means of placing these phenomena in their broader contexts of globalization and migration. A purely "national" approach runs the risk of overlooking these factors and their very real consequences for young people and those working with them. Ideas about juvenile delinquency and its relationship to modernization and a supposedly contagious, inferior "Western" culture shaped the ways in which academics, practitioners, politicians and policy makers understood, defined and then acted upon the issue.

Through its consideration of the ways in which juvenile delinquency was seen to exist within the welfare state, this chapter offers a different account to that of Garland. As this chapter will argue, a broad-brush account overlooks some of the critical forces of change, and overstates the impact of welfare on the ground and the decline of punitive voices in public discourse before the 1970s. While Roddy Nilsson has found Garland's theory to be a satisfactory framework in terms of the Swedish situation,[18] it is not as useful as a starting point in terms of analysing the case of England and Wales. While there were agencies and institutions that did fit Garland's portrayal of a penal welfare state, and the original Children and Young Persons Act 1969 would have been its execution par excellence, the process was far more complex and contested. This chapter will explore the explanations given for delinquency and the remedies proposed for it as manifested in political discourse, the shifting location of expertise in juvenile delinquency and welfare, before looking at the Ingleby Report itself, and asking how these various aspects fit in with Garland's analysis.

The post-war paradox: Rising affluence, rising juvenile crime

Where the "penal welfarist" explanation of juvenile delinquency as the product of deprivation of one sort or another came adrift was in the decades immediately after the Second World War, when deprivation had supposedly been tackled by the provisions of the welfare state. The Labour governments of 1945–1951 introduced a welfare state that provided a financial safety net for those out of work; the National Health Service provided a healthcare programme that was free at the point of access; secondary education to age 15 and beyond was available to all, and there were major programmes of public and private house-building. Over the course of this period, work was plentiful, and employees had more disposable income in their pockets than before. Working-class teenagers in particular were seen as being particularly affluent, an assumption fuelled by Mark Abrams' market research in the later 1950s.[19] Yet the police and the Home Office noted steady increases in crime and its severity by all age groups, which followed the outbreak of war in 1939 and failed to abate in peacetime.[20] On the face of it, children and young people had more than they had ever had before, yet adults were puzzled by the persistence of bad behaviour.[21] This prompted a raft of research and policy reviews to try and find a solution to the "problem" of juvenile delinquency within the welfare state. Behind these concerns lay further anxieties about whether youthful offending might indicate more worrying shifts in the nature of British life: had the economic forces of modernity and capitalism changed Britons' morality, character and social identity to the point where these could not be rescued by affluence and the safety net of the welfare state? In particular, contemporaries worried that there was something "unBritish" or "foreign" about these supposed changes. T.R. Fyvel, the author of *The Insecure Offenders,* a book written in response to fears about the emergence of the "Teddy boys", expressed this sense that there was

> Something afoot, that there were some aspects of our materialistic, mechanized, twentieth-century society – something in the way of life, in the break-up of traditional authority, in the value of the headlines which encouraged widespread youthful cynicism in general and rather violent delinquency in particular.[22]

Contemporaries by no means saw this as an exclusively English or British problem, but one that was experienced across the world, in both East and West, throughout the British Empire, spreading along with American products. Juvenile delinquency was, on the one hand, a product of Western modernity and capitalism; it was also a signal of the decline of Britain's imperial power and the rise of the US in cultural, economic and geopolitical terms. British power had been diminished by the costs of participation in two world wars, enabling the US to take over Britain's previous role as the policeman and banker of the world. Although the US and Britain had a shared cultural heritage and language, much was made of the US being "foreign", "different" and, above all, "American". Despite the global reach of the problem, it was one for which the roots could be found in the most intimate location: parenting practices and family structures within the home, which appeared to be evolving as a result of modernization and then changing rapidly in the wake of the Second World War.[23]

Juvenile delinquency regularly occupied members of the Houses of Commons and the Lords. Members of the House of Commons, the directly elected chamber of the British parliament, were in part responding to the comments, questions and anxieties of their constituents, as well as to their own perception of media coverage and the picture presented through the annual releases of criminal statistics. The newspapers were rarely slow to latch onto tales of garrotters or battling Mods and Rockers, as the work of Pearson and Cohen has shown.[24] The use of statistics as a means of understanding complex social phenomena had grown from the mid-nineteenth century, intensifying in the mid-twentieth.[25] Crime statistics were very much a part of this world, with the first issue of criminal statistics published in 1857.[26] New possibilities in the field of computing from the mid-twentieth century onward enabled more complex statistical calculations to be carried out.[27] Criminal statistics also became news items in their own right. As with the stereotypical representations of the "juvenile delinquent", criminal statistics offered a means of trying to grasp the concrete by means of the abstract.[28] As members of both Houses were involved in drafting and ratifying laws, their perceptions of juvenile crime, its explanations and remedies were important.

This chapter will now explore some of the concerns of the MPs and Lords regarding juvenile delinquency. One set of concerns revolved around the nature of cultural products and their consumption by the young. In 1946, Cyril Dumpleton, Labour MP for St. Albans, asked James Chuter Ede, the Home Secretary, if an enquiry would be held into the impact of cinema clubs on the young. Tom Skeffington-Lodge, Labour MP for Bedford, argued that the young were being exposed "to propaganda of a most undesirable sort" during the films, while Dumpleton was concerned about the nature of the organizers. Chuter Ede was dismissive, being of the mind that "penny dreadfuls" had not hindered his own development and that the government could not usefully intervene in the matter of who would run weekend cinema clubs.[29] Dumpleton made his point with reference to the concerns of teachers and other professionals, speaking on another occasion about a headmistress in his constituency who had studied these cinema clubs, finding that the children were encouraged to passively consume the films shown.[30] Another head drew attention to the club leaders' lack of training and alleged recourse to films that would gratify and placate.[31] The headteachers presented their particular impressions of the cinema clubs, with no attempt to measure or ascertain what the children and young people had actually made of them. The voices of the young were absent. What such debates raised were the conflicts of interest between teachers who wanted to see "educational" fare being provided and the film and cinema industries, who wanted to offer products that sold.

Concerns were also raised about the specific content of these "American" products and their impact on the moral outlook of children, young people and other vulnerable groups, with the implication being that these were bringing with them a deleterious "foreign" influence. Skeffington-Lodge started a debate in the Commons in 1947 on the practice of British magazine and newspaper proprietors in buying in "American" fiction for publication. He stated that these sensational stories, full of drama, crime and divorce, were quickly adapted to suit a British audience, with his example of "St James' Park" being substituted for "Central Park" in the New York-based original. He argued that

> Their readers are unconsciously absorbing propaganda for the American way of life. I have no objection to the American way of life for Americans, but let them keep it, I suggest, in America.[32]

Such views were not typical of all members, and were rebutted accordingly – in this case, MPs spoke about Britain's own lack of moral leadership in not acting to bring rates of illegitimacy down in Barbados, as well as the way in which Britons were not compelled to buy or read such material, and the trade agreements required through Britain's participation in the Marshall Plan, the major economic recovery scheme underwritten by the US in the later 1940s and 1950s to rebuild European economies and thereby prevent the spread of Communism.[33]

Such concerns persisted. In 1952, Maurice Edelman, Labour MP for Coventry and a writer himself, raised a question in the Commons about the American-style comics. Edelman claimed that the comics had been brought into the UK by American troops during the war, but had subsequently found willing publishers and an eager market. He argued that the comics were "sadistic" and that they "introduce[d] the element of pleasure into violence". While Edelman could not prove a linkage between these comics and youth crime, he argued that this was due to a lack of enquiry.[34] The comics were not part of a gradual embracing of the "American": their arrival in the UK was a result of the war itself. In the same debate, Dr Horace King pointed to the way in which children supposedly took things on trust from adults, and that in a world of "crazy and cheap values" the state had a duty to intervene to protect the young from such deleterious influences.[35] He said:

> We want to keep our English ways. What we get from America is not the best of American life, the natural American culture that exists in a million homes in that country, but all that is worst from America both in scenes portrayed in the films and in this particularly cheap and nasty literature which is coming over.[36]

Although "America" was the label attached to these cultural products, the meaning was far from literal. What the MPs were referring to was commercialized, popular texts that were easy to access and digest, which were associated with "American" consumer culture. The "harm" side of this resulted in a campaign to ban the comics, which, as Martin Barker has shown, produced the Children and Young Persons (Harmful Publications) Act 1955, which banned such publications.[37] The "American" side of the debate continued.

Concerns about "Americanization" were one part of a cluster of anxieties that were periodically expressed by MPs in relation to the impact of the Second World War. While there were many parallels between juvenile delinquency in the First and Second World Wars, the latter had some significant differences, notably around the presence of overseas troops and prisoners of war and the level of domestic disruption and devastation. As some of the extracts above suggest, some saw the presence of GIs in Britain during the conflict as being the means by which "American" products were brought into the country and tastes established. The American cultural products were not just affordable and accessible, but spoke to an allegedly different system of values around consumption, self-gratification and a lack of regard for others. This explanation of juvenile delinquency set up a number of binary oppositions, which placed an immoral, throwaway "American" culture of serial divorces and gangsters against a moral, durable British culture. One supposed form of "Western" culture was placed in preference to another. Skeffington-Lodge's central concern about the US fiction being

"Anglicized" was the "roaring carnival of quick drinks, adolescent sex, bright lights and dimmed thinking", its location within an affluent backdrop, and the casual treatment of marriage and family life being presented as taking place within Britain, and he worried about how this would be received within Britain and the British Empire, as constituting the "British" way of life.[38] This theme would emerge in other manifestations, as part of discourse around the decline of the moral fabric of the British family and of the British nation, in the broader context of Britain's decline as an international power. Divorce was a case in point. Increasing rates of divorce through the early and mid-twentieth century were seen by some members of the Commons and Lords as being a decline in moral standards,[39] not a reflection of how the law around divorce had been liberalized in tandem with growing legal aid provision for divorce.[40] In objective terms, divorces were easier to obtain by the 1950s but there was no effective baseline for measuring how marital discord itself had changed. Parenting remained a common theme, with attention being paid to how the war had taken fathers into the forces and mothers into the factories, with daughters being tempted by troops.[41] Deficient parenting in turn formed part of wider concerns about the impact of adults, be that adults who ran cinema clubs, those who neglected their children, or many others.

As juvenile delinquency was not seen by British politicians as an exclusively British phenomenon, they were interested in juvenile delinquency around the world. This interest took two specific forms: firstly, a growing tendency for politicians to compare and contrast the behaviour of British youth and their parents with the perceived behaviour of youths in Communist countries. If the US was described in terms of being a locus of moral turpitude, then the USSR was frequently referred to as a place in which children and young people were well-behaved, and where morals were far more rigorous than those of the UK: modernity and capitalism were to blame for youth crime. Pro-Soviet attitudes in the post-war period were complex.[42] The Labour Party had an antipathetic relationship with the Communist Party of Great Britain, being opposed to any groups which sought to use revolutionary rather than parliamentary means of achieving socialism,[43] while the opposition of the Conservative Party was self-evident. On the other hand, the USSR had become a much-needed ally during the Second World War, even if relations soured early on in peacetime. In the House of Commons, Willie Gallacher, Communist MP for West Fife, waggishly told the House that the major Home Office-convened 1949 conference on juvenile delinquency should be aware that "if they can get these young people interested in Communism they will keep them away from crime".[44] Some ten years later, the Earl of Craven spoke of the horror of Communists at what he described as the pornographic qualities of the British press.[45] Some, like Kenneth Lindsay, saw Communist societies as having an in-built system of morality, in comparison with their Western, democratic counterparts:[46] a belief that was certainly more possible in the immediate aftermath of the war, before the Hungarian uprising. The idea that Communism had "values" was in sharp contrast to the portrayal of Britain as a nation in which – in England, at least – "morals" were in decline, an idea put forward by the Bishops in the House of Lords in response to the rising crime figures. As with the anxieties about "Americanization", the reality was not important. What was important in this variety of discourses was the sense that an idealized "Britain" was slipping away as its empire was dismantled. Juvenile delinquency was one signal of this.

The second arena in which an interest in international juvenile delinquency was displayed was more political than rhetorical. The creation of bodies like the League of Nations in the interwar period and the United Nations after the Second World War created new opportunities for more positive reflections on situations in other countries. Civil servants, politicians and academics alike participated in the Second United Nations Congress on Crime, held in London in 1960. The Congress involved over 1,000 delegates, and took its theme of juvenile delinquency in response to the perceived role of increased affluence, consumption and cynicism of the young in prompting an international rise in juvenile crime, while also considering the opportunities for new approaches afforded through the UN Declaration of the Rights of the Child in 1959 – and thus revealing that such understandings were rooted in the impacts of modern consumption.[47] This prompted the *Daily Mirror* to draw comparisons between crime rates in the US, Sweden and London, while considering the growing problem of children and young people forming gangs in countries in the West, comparing the Bodgies and Widgies of Australia with rioting juveniles in West Berlin and the Teddy Boys in Britain.[48] The press often ran articles on crime and particularly youth crime in other countries – often, but not exclusively the US and its gangs – so crime as a global phenomenon did exist in the public imagination.[49]

Juvenile delinquency in British colonies and British West Berlin also caused disquiet. In the case of the colonies, MPs were concerned with the variations in and efficacy of approaches toward and the treatment of juvenile delinquents across the empire. There was a perceived mismatch between attitudes and practices in the UK, and what happened in the empire, as each colony had its own legal system, which blended laws from the British legal systems with existing local practices.[50] While it meant that there was no one overarching framework, it did allow for comparisons of practice within this British world.[51] Thus, for example, although corporal punishment for young Britons was abolished through the Criminal Justice Act 1948, following the recommendations of the Cadogan Report of 1938, it persisted in the colonies, which had separate administrations, even if they all came under the imperial umbrella. In 1946, Lord Faringdon raised a question in the House of Lords about the excessive use of flogging in the colonies. Faringdon referred to Havelock Ellis' finding that flogging served to brutalize the individual rather than to deter criminality, and spoke about how the persistence of corporal punishment led to the resented subjugation of the colonies.[52] Yet there was seemingly little appetite for change; in fact Reginald Sorenson, the Labour MP for Leyton, persisted in raising questions on similar matters throughout the later 1950s, as calls for the reintroduction of corporal punishment returned in the wake of the Teddy Boy scare.[53] With decolonization gaining pace from the later 1950s, there was little impetus for serious British-led reform within the colonies, providing no answers as to whether British rule was a brutal and subjugating, or a liberating, influence, and, in turn, if the end of empire was the signal of a moral decline – or a process to be embraced.

Expertise and the juvenile delinquent

Who provided MPs in the House of Commons and members of the House of Lords with the statistics, information and insight into the nature of juvenile crime on the ground, in addition to their parliamentary constituents? Until the 1950s, expertise in juvenile delinquency and possible solutions for it had resided with a group best described as "amateur-experts". These experts were "amateur" in the sense that they lacked professional training in their areas of work, but were passionate about their cause and often had years of experience in voluntary social work: it did not mean that they were "amateur" in a pejorative sense. Indeed, many of them were active in developing and shaping professional organizations and university-based professional training and research.[54] "Amateur" and "professional" were sometimes conflated in the same way as "women" and "men", but, as Anne Logan has shown, this neat mapping did not always occur in reality.[55] Some of the male professionals had launched their careers with a period of voluntary social work in boys' clubs at settlement houses.[56] Many of these amateur-experts came from privileged backgrounds, and, while they had empathetic feelings for the young, they were not *of* the communities they served. These individuals drew their authority and sense of legitimacy from their experience in social or pastoral work. A different category of amateur-expert was the senior cleric. While the Archbishop of York and other senior clerics were professionals in terms of their theological roles, their commentary on juvenile delinquency arose from their anxieties about the disruptive impact of the Second World War on British morals, as will be seen. As Mick Ryan has noted, many of these individuals were called upon through their work or connections with such groups as the Howard League to join Home Office advisory groups or to sit on the committees of Royal Commissions. The result was a very club-like, discreet form of policy-making.[57] It did not include, however, many of those who were actively involved as professionals or paraprofessionals on the ground.[58] While there was an interest in juvenile delinquency elsewhere, it did not follow that experts from other nations were invited to take part in these groups: expertise was "British", or at least filtered through British eyes.

An example of this style of policy-making was the Central Conference on Juvenile Delinquency of 1949, which spawned a series of local conferences. The publication of the Criminal Statistics for 1947 and early figures for 1948 suggested that the apparent rise in crime during the war was not abating in peacetime. This prompted the Archbishop of York, Cyril Garbett, to instigate a debate on the matter in the House of Lords.[59] The debate led to the Central Conference, jointly run by the Home Office and the Education Department and bringing together representatives of faiths, charities, schools, universities, social workers, local government, the police, educational psychologists and the film industry in March 1949.[60] All participants came from British-based organizations. The conference concluded that the root of juvenile delinquency lay ultimately in the home, in women working, inadequate family allowances and a lack of knowledge of mothercraft; it also recommended greater investment in play and youth services, "suitable" reading material for children and better trained staff in Sunday Schools; it also felt that juvenile courts were too informal and sentimental, that too many children were "getting away" with single offences.[61] The conference was a curious mix of recommendations that could be construed as penal welfarist, insofar as the general consensus pointed to supporting the family and using civil society as a means of prevention and cure; yet these were also framed within a more conservative, anti-modern discourse of restoring the family and the church as the points of control and discipline within the community.[62] While the conference looked to the home as the site where problems began for children and young people, the broader question of juvenile delinquency was not conceived of as a purely "British" one. The war and cultural imports were external forces of exacerbation, the former through disrupting the rhythms of the home and the latter through the supposed power of films to encourage delinquent behaviour. "Bad" films were not the exclusive preserve of Hollywood; if an understanding of the film as a medium for spreading "American" values remained it formed part of a more general unease about the potential of this relatively new form of entertainment, reflected in the Wheare Report of the following year.[63]

The stranglehold of the amateur-expert began to lessen in the post-war period. This was directly related to the growth in scope and confidence of social science research in universities and within the Civil Service itself. This "scientific" approach to delineating social problems was reflected in the growing field of social science research which, by the 1930s, was increasingly the preserve of university-based researchers as opposed to privately backed individuals such as Charles Booth or Seebohm Rowntree.[64] As McClintock and Avison note, the Criminal Justice Act of 1948 enabled the government to spend money on commissioning research to be undertaken by university researchers, as well as private individuals and organizations, before the Home Office created its own Research Unit in 1957. Calls for further expansion of university social science research on behalf of the government resulted in R.A. Butler's proposal for an Institute of Criminology in the *Penal Practice in a Changing Society* White Paper of 1959: an organization which would have the capacity to undertake a deeper testing of the relationship between modernization and rising levels of juvenile delinquency.[65] This was, as Ryan notes, a direct challenge to the cosy world of the amateur-expert networks that had previously had the ear of government and marked a shift toward the use of professional research in developing policy.[66] As with the case of Latina/o youth in Spain, discussed in Chávez-Garcia's chapter in this volume, the task of delineating and defining the problem was passed to academic researchers working in tandem with professional social workers. In Britain, though, the young people functioned more as subject matter for investigation than as active agents in the research process.

In tandem with this, the demand for professionally trained social workers by the welfare state stimulated the growth of social research and teaching in universities.[67] Initiatives such as the creation of the National

College for the Training of Youth Leaders in Leicester, founded as a result of the Albemarle Report of 1960, also fuelled this demand. There was a great deal of porosity between the practitioner/policymaker and the university, particularly by the 1960s. Many of those who had experience on the ground in youth and social work went on to do research in those fields as full-time university-based researchers, such as Peter Kuenstler, while others, like Peter Townsend and Brian Abel-Smith, used their political connections to gain traction in policy development.[68] There were strong networks in some cases between practitioners and the universities. While these relationships were close, it did not follow that the academics were parochial in their reading. Many were influenced by research and practice in other countries, with the US being particularly influential, largely because of the association of the US with the supposed "modern" root causes of delinquency – the work of Thrasher, Cohen, Matza and others on youth street gangs informed much work in the UK.[69] Academics were mobile, travelling to conferences and congresses, working overseas and following publications from academics around the world.

Researching the juvenile delinquent

What of the field of research on children, young people and crime in this period? The first three examples of studies covered here were undertaken by university-trained social scientists working outside the academy at the time of the study – a point which reflects much of the porosity of the boundaries with the practitioner worlds.

A.E. Morgan's *Young Citizen* was relatively dismissive of juvenile delinquency as resulting simply from having a lack of anything more productive to do. When indulging in the same bad behaviour, middle-class children were simply naughty; the children of the poor were delinquent. Morgan favoured an economic basis to juvenile delinquency, pointing to the high wages enjoyed by boys during the Second World War, and appetites whetted by consumerism.[70] The notion of relative affluence turning the working-class boy bad was not a new one, but it was given a fresh twist toward the end of the decade by Mark Abrams, author of *The Teenage Consumer* (1959). Abrams, a market researcher, pointed out that while both the interwar and post-war teenager had "tipped up" (or passed on) most of their wages to their families, the post-war working-class teenager had far more to spend in real terms, and they were creating a "teenage market" around clothes, music and other consumer items, while their middle-class counterparts were still in school.[71]

Peter Willmott's *Adolescent Boys of East London* again focused on the role of this teenage consumer. Willmott also pointed to the importance of the kind of work that the young men went into in terms of shaping their world view and the extent of their aspirations. He likewise fixated on the normality of thieving – and who to steal from – along with the importance of being able to stand one's ground in a fight. He also pointed out how few criminal families there were.[72] These three studies all demonstrated a preoccupation with the impact of the consumer society and consumption in the post-war period. Consumption was linked with the potential for a decline in morals and cultural standards; anxiety was expressed about a culture marked by the unthinking consumption of "inferior" cultural products, a theme explored famously by Richard Hoggart in *The Uses of Literacy* (1957).[73]

The theme of families who had failed to benefit from the welfare state became a major one in the course of the 1950s and 1960s, and predated the famous "rediscovery of poverty" by Peter Townsend and Brian Abel-Smith in 1965.[74] Researchers like Pearl Jephcott and John Barron Mays pointed to the ways in which some working-class families were multiply deprived. In *Some Young People* (1954), her study of "Northbury" in East London, Jephcott revealed that families had an overwhelmingly local basis to their work and leisure lives.[75] Mays came to similar conclusions in his study of Liverpool in the mid-1960s, again finding a localized world with limited ambitions. Mays also pointed to a world in which different family norms to those of the middle classes applied,[76] something also remarked upon earlier by Terence Morris in his 1957 work on the criminal ecology of Croydon in South London. Morris painted a picture of chaotic parent(s) and families ensconced in substandard housing, with most of these families living in areas on which the welfare state spent least.[77] In 1966, David Downes again pointed to this world of families living in slum conditions and of the importance placed within these communities upon staying local.[78]

The researchers here were not directly concerned with the impact of the welfare state upon these families, but rather with the backgrounds of "delinquent youth". In their various ways, these researchers were all looking for the causes of juvenile delinquency, and, like the members of the 1949 conference, turning their attentions to the home as the source of this. Similar conclusions would be reached by education and social work professionals in Spain some decades later, as Chávez-Garcia's essay in this volume shows. What was identified as problematic in Britain was a supposedly distinctive working-class culture or subculture, which was itself conceptually rooted in US-based criminological and sociological research and a desire to find the "modern" causes of the problem. For Downes in particular, this suggested that youth delinquency was a subculture shooting off from a parent working-class culture that sat at odds with middle-class norms.[79] What the researchers did not overtly consider was how the poverty these families experienced was not a new phenomenon, but something which had existed *before* the welfare state. The welfare state had a limited impact upon such children, young people and their families. It may have improved some of their outcomes, particularly in health terms, but it did not in itself create new jobs or types of work for these families, or in any other way challenge what was an established local culture.

The Ingleby Report

The Ingleby Report of 1958 has been seen as the last hurrah of the penal welfarist regime, as it would inform policy throughout the 1960s and give shape to the only partially implemented Children and Young Persons Act of 1969.[80] The committee was set the task of looking at both criminal and civil matters relating to children and young people. They looked at the powers of the juvenile court and its workings, the institutions for young offenders, the prevention of cruelty and "moral and physical" danger to the young, as well as the provision of childcare by local authorities.[81] Their evidence was drawn from a wide range of witnesses: police, childcare and social workers, the teaching profession, leaders of local government, medics and psychologists, the legal profession, juvenile court staff and those involved in probation or running the secure estate for juveniles, as well as a range of charities, including the National Marriage Guidance Council, the NSPCC, the Family Welfare Association and the Moral Guidance Council. A radical experiment presented written evidence: the Shoreditch Project, which aimed to share information and integrate services for needy families in East London. A University of Birmingham study group also gave evidence, as did Margaret Simey, whose career straddled the boundaries of academic research, local government and juvenile justice.[82] The committee sought out expertise as widely as possible, if they did not look beyond Britain for it. They did not engage with any of the children and young people who may have used these services directly: their voices were "translated" by the professionals who spoke for them.

The main claim for the "welfarist" agenda of the Ingleby Report was its recommendation for the age of criminal responsibility to be raised from eight to twelve years of age, essentially decriminalizing the young.

However, in its place would be a fairly invasive procedure for denoting all children under 12 who committed offences as being "in need of protection or discipline".[83] This would not be a matter of simply letting children off, but rather introducing more in the way of surveillance over longer periods of time – and making parents responsible for their children's behaviour. It also located responsibility for juvenile crime not with cultural factors but specifically within a deviant family environment.[84] Otherwise, the Ingleby Report suggested no real changes to the system, but it would be a mistake to see it as being primarily concerned with a "cuddly" decriminalization of the criminal young. The committee displayed a real sympathy for the poor and the struggling, wanting greater powers for local government to intervene in family life. With its proposal to raise the age of criminal responsibility it pointed not to a rehabilitative ideal, but rather to a *preventative* one. This is an important distinction: rehabilitation speaks to the restoration of behaviour within social norms, while prevention is the eradication of non-normal behaviour in the first place. Rehabilitation was certainly part of the Ingleby Report's recommendations, but prevention pointed to a longer-term agenda of eradicating the causes of crime through changing the nature of especially working-class family life. It did not engage with the deeper structural issues that sociological researchers were at least beginning to identify, such as the localized nature of life in working-class communities and its impacts on aspirations and behaviour, and thus with the potential of more complex causes of juvenile delinquency than simply "Western" modernity.

Conclusion

A welfarist approach to juvenile delinquency was certainly evident in post-war Britain, but it does not follow that it was an uncontested paradigm. Throughout the period in question, concerns were expressed that the system was too kind or ineffectual, that the welfare state and affluence were softening up or even criminalizing the young: the processes of modernization had caused these problems, and modern approaches were failing to deal with them adequately. These concerns tied into broader issues about economic relations with other countries – the US, and thus evidence of Britain's diminished role in the world – as well as a sense that the Communist political system offered a moral framework that was increasingly lacking in the West. While those who raised these points in parliament or in the press were frequently checked by others, this was nonetheless a regularly occurring debate, a reality in itself. The location of expertise was shifting, from an "amateur-expert" group to academics and university- or college-trained professionals who worked within the framework of the welfare state and whose philosophies were part of a "social science moment", a desire to explore modernity and its relationships with social problems. This faith in expertise finds resonance in Garland's analysis, to a point. There was less faith in penal welfarism as a solution, but rather as a mechanism for finding possible solutions in a world that appeared to be shifting dramatically to contemporaries. Contemporaries did not see juvenile delinquency as being a specifically British problem, as they often perceived it as being caused by external forces, such as Americanization – even if the expertise consulted by policymakers was "British". No matter how global its reach, juvenile delinquency was seen as ultimately having its roots within the home, and specifically within the ways that modernity and the "foreign" cultural products it brought with it had disrupted older traditions.

Notes

1. H. Hendrick, *Child Welfare: England 1872–1989* (London: Routledge, 1994), pp. 9–11.
2. E. Clapp, *Mothers of All Children: Women Reformers and the Rise of the Juvenile Courts in Progressive Era America* (Philadelphia: Penn State University Press, 1998); A.M. Platt, *The Child Savers: The Invention of Delinquency* (Chicago: University of Chicago Press, 1969).
3. There are three legal jurisdictions in the UK (England and Wales, Scotland and Northern Ireland), and thus there are three different sets of legislation applicable in each of the nations. This chapter refers specifically to the English and Welsh legal system, but will on occasion refer to "Britain" as a cultural and political phenomenon.
4. A. Logan, "A Suitable Person for Suitable Cases: The Gendering of Juvenile Courts in England, c.1910–39", *Twentieth Century British History*, 16 (2005), p. 132; K. Bradley, A. Logan and S.R. Shaw, "Editorial: Youth and Crime: Centennial Reflections on the Children Act 1908", *Crimes and Misdemeanours*, 3 (2009): 1–17.
5. B.L.Q. Henriques, *The Indiscretions of a Magistrate* (London: Non-Fiction Book Club, 1950).
6. See M. Fry and C.B. Russell, *A Note Book for the Children's Court* (London: Howard League for Penal Reform, 1950), J. Watson and P. Watson, *The Modern Juvenile Court* (London: Shaw and Sons, 1973), p. 3.
7. I. Gibson, *The English Vice: Beating, Sex and Shame in Victorian England and After* (London: Duckworth, 1978), p. 144.
8. See G. Behlmer, *Friends of the Family: The English Home and Its Guardians* (Stanford: Stanford University Press, 1998) and Hendrick, *Child Welfare*.

244 Juvenile Delinquency and the Post-War State

9. D. Garland, *The Culture of Control: Crime and Social Order in Contemporary Society* (Oxford: Oxford University Press, 2002), pp. 27–28.
10. Garland, *Culture of Control*, p. 36.
11. Ibid., p. 42.
12. Ibid., pp. 47, 50.
13. Ibid.
14. J. Pratt, *Penal Populism* (Abingdon: Routledge, 2007).
15. See J. Donzelot, *The Policing of Families: Welfare versus the State* (London: Hutchinson, 1980); M. Foucault, *The Birth of the Clinic: An Archaeology of the Medical Profession* (London: Routledge, 1989); J. Habermas, *The Structural Transformation of the Public Sphere: An Inquiry into a Bourgeois Society* (Cambridge: Polity, 1989).
16. S. Todd, "Affluence, Class and Crown Street: Reinvestigating the Post-War Working Class",*Contemporary British History*, 22 (2008): 501–518.
17. On the policy development, see for example P. Thane, *Foundations of the Welfare State* (London: Longman, 1996), R. Lowe, *The Welfare State in Britain since 1945* (Basingstoke: Palgrave, 2005). For the social history, see for example K. Bradley, *Poverty, Philanthropy and the State: Charities and the Working Classes in London, 1918–1979* (Manchester: Manchester University Press, 2009), P. Thane and T. Evans, *Sinners? Scroungers? Saints? Unmarried Motherhood in Twentieth-Century England* (Oxford: Oxford University Press, 2012). The Voluntary Action History Society are highly active in promoting this area of research – see www.vahs.org.uk (correct at 25 August 2012) for more details.
18. R. Nilsson, "Creating the Swedish Juvenile Delinquent: Criminal Policy, Science and Institutionalization, c.1930–1970", *Scandinavian Journal of History*, 34 (2009): 354–375.
19. M. Abrams, *The Teenage Consumer* (London: London Press Exchange, 1959).
20. Home Office, *Summary of Statistics Relating to Crime and Criminal Proceedings for the Years 1939–1945*, Cmnd. 7227 (London: H.M. Stationery Office, 1947), pp. 7–8; R. Hood and A. Roddam, "Crime, Sentencing and Punishment", in A.H. Halsey and J. Webb (eds), *Twentieth-Century British Social Trends* (Basingstoke: Macmillan, 2000), p. 681.
21. See, for example, commentary on this in the Ministry of Education, *The Youth Service in England and Wales*, Cmnd. 929 (London: HMSO, 1960), p. 31.
22. T.R. Fyvel, *The Insecure Offenders: Rebellious Youth in the Welfare State* (Harmondsworth: Penguin, 1966), p. 24.
23. Ibid., pp. 18–21. For a US-American perspective on the relationship between parenting practices and delinquency, see the chapter in this volume by Nina Mackert.
24. G. Pearson, *Hooligan: A History of Respectable Fears* (London: Macmillan, 1983); S. Cohen, *Folk Devils and Moral Panics: The Creation of the Mods and the Rockers* (St. Albans: Paladin, 1973).
25. T. Crook and G. O'Hara (eds), *Statistics and the Public Sphere: Numbers and the People in Modern Britain, c.1800–2000* (Abingdon: Routledge, 2011), pp. 9–11.
26. Hood and Roddam, "Crime, Sentencing and Punishment", p. 675.
27. See K. Bradley, "Juvenile Delinquency and the Public Sphere: Exploring Local and National Discourses in England, c.1940–1969", *Social History*, 37 (2012): 19–35.
28. Ibid.

29. Hansard HC vol. 428 cols. 771–2 (31 October 1946).
30. Hansard HC vol. 430 col. 1959 (27 November 1946).
31. Hansard HC vol. 430 col.1659–60 (27 November 1946).
32. Hansard HC vol. 444 cols. 2357–8 (28 November 1947).
33. Hansard HC vol. 444 col. 2361–5 (28 November 1947). The trade agreements were later refined – see M. Barker, *A Haunt of Fears: The Strange History of the British Horror Comics Campaign* (Jackson, MS: University of Mississippi Press, 1992), p. 8.
34. Hansard HC vol. 504 col. 2027 (1 August 1952).
35. Hansard HC vol. 504 col. 2030 (1 August 1952).
36. Hansard HC vol. 504 col. 2031–2 (1 August 1952).
37. See Barker, *A Haunt of Fears*.
38. Hansard HC vol. 444 col. 2359 (28 November 1947).
39. See, for example: Hansard HL vol. 152 col. 1091 (3 December 1947); HL, vol. 223 col. 994 (18 May 1960).
40. See R.I. Morgan, "The Introduction of Civil Legal Aid in England and Wales, 1914–1949", *Twentieth Century British History*, 5 (1994): 38–76.
41. Hansard HC vol. 415 col. 809 (2 November 1945).
42. For a contrasting (negative) view of juvenile delinquency in the USSR from a US-American perspective, see the chapter in this volume by Nina Mackert.
43. See, for example, A. Thorpe, *The History of the British Labour Party*, (Basingstoke: Palgrave, 2008).
44. Hansard HC vol. 461 col. 527 (10 February 1949).
45. Hansard HL vol. 223 col. 994 (18 May 1960).
46. Hansard HC vol. 415 col. 829 (2 November 1945).
47. United Nations Office on Drugs and Crime, *United Nations Congresses on Crime Prevention and Criminal Justice 1955–2010* (Vienna: United Nations Information Service, 2010), http://www.un.org/en/conf/crimecongress2010/pdf/55years_ebook.pdf.
48. T. Tullett, "Teenage Hoodlums!" *Daily Mirror* Tuesday (9 August 1960), p. 9.
49. For example, "Murder for Fun", *Daily Mirror* Friday (24 August 1954), p. 2.
50. A.J. Stockwell, "Power, Authority and Freedom", in P.J. Marshall (ed.), *Cambridge Illustrated History of the British Empire* (Cambridge: Cambridge University Press, 2006), p.168.
51. Logan, "Policy Transfer".
52. Hansard HL vol. 141 col. 700–2 (4 June 1946).
53. Hansard HC vol. 501 col. 462–3 (21 May 1952), HC vol. 554 col. 97–8 (20 June 1956).
54. Basil Henriques was chair of the National Association for Boys' Clubs after 1925, while Eileen Younghusband, Pearl Jephcott and Josephine Macalister Brew straddled the worlds of social work and academia. See S. McCabe, "Henriques, Sir Basil Lucas Quixano (1890–1961)", rev. *Oxford Dictionary of National Biography* (Oxford: Oxford University Press, 2004) [http://www.oxforddnb.com/view/article/33821, accessed 24 May 2014]; K. Jones, *Eileen Younghusband: A Biography* (London: Bedford Square, 1984); A. Turnbull, 'Jephcott, (Agnes) Pearl (1900–1980)', *Oxford Dictionary of National Biography* (Oxford: Oxford University Press, 2004) [http://www.oxforddnb.com/view/article/67334, accessed 24 May 2014].

55. A. Logan "Women and the Provision of Criminal Justice Advice: Lessons from England and Wales, 1944–64", *British Journal of Criminology*, 50, 6 (2010), pp. 1077–1093.
56. V. Bailey, *Delinquency and Citizenship: Reclaiming the Young Offender, 1914–1948* (Oxford: Clarendon, 1987).
57. M. Ryan, *Penal Policy and Political Culture in England and Wales* (Winchester: Waterside Press, 2003), pp. 17–21.
58. Ryan, *Penal Policy*, pp. 22–26.
59. The National Archives (hereafter TNA) HO45/24406 Central Conference on Juvenile Delinquency. Letter A.W. Peterson to D.M. Nenk, 26 January 1949, with letter from James Chuter Ede (Home Secretary) to Alan Lascelles, Private Secretary to the King.
60. TNA HO45/24406 Invitation list to Central Conference on Juvenile Delinquency 2 March 1949.
61. TNA HO45/24406 "Causes of Juvenile Delinquency: Mainly the Home Influence", *Education* (11 March 1949), pp. 450–451.
62. See especially TNA HO45/24406 W. Murrie note to Secretary of State for meeting with Archbishop of York, 7 February 1949; Memo to Ross from W. Murrie 8 February 1949.
63. Home Department, Scottish Office and Ministry of Education *Report of the Departmental Committee on Children and the Cinema*, Cmnd. 7945 (London: HMSO, 1950) paras 137–142.
64. See M. Savage, *Identities and Social Change in Britain since 1940: The Politics of Method* (Oxford: Oxford University Press, 2011).
65. F.H. McClintock and N. Howard Avison, *Crime in England and Wales* (London: Heinemann, 1968) p. 2.
66. Ryan, *Penal Policy*, pp. 21–22.
67. Savage, *Identities*.
68. P. Kuenstler, *Learning from Community: Oxford House in Bethnal Green, 1940–48* (London: Oxford House and the Settlements Social Action Research Group, 2004), P. Townsend (1996) "Obituary: Professor Brian Abel-Smith", *Independent*, Tuesday (9 April), accessed 28 February 2012 http://www.independent.co.uk/news/obituaries/obituary-professor-brian-abelsmith-1303950.html.
69. See, for example, D. Downes, *The Delinquent Solution: A Study in Subcultural Theory* (London: Routledge and Kegan Paul, 1966).
70. A.E. Morgan, *The Young Citizen* (Harmondsworth: Penguin, 1943).
71. Abrams, *Teenage Consumer*.
72. P. Willmott, *Adolescent Boys of East London* (Harmondsworth: Penguin, 1975).
73. R. Hoggart, *The Uses of Literacy: Aspects of Working-Class Life* (London: Chatto and Windus, 1957).
74. See B. Abel-Smith and P. Townsend, *The Poor and the Poorest* (London: Bell, 1965).
75. P. Jephcott, *Some Young People* (London: George Allen and Unwin, 1954).
76. J.B. Mays, *Growing Up in the City: A Study of Juvenile Delinquency in an Urban Neighbourhood* (Liverpool: Liverpool University Press, 1954).
77. T. Morris, *The Criminal Area: A Study in Social Ecology* (London: Routledge and Kegan Paul, 1957).
78. Downes, *The Delinquent Solution*.

79. Ibid.
80. Home Office, *Report of the Committee on Children and Young Persons*, Cmnd. 1191 (London: HMSO, 1960).
81. Ibid., p. ii.
82. R. Clarke (2004) "Margaret Simey", *Guardian* (29 July) accessed 28 February 2012, http://www.guardian.co.uk/news/2004/jul/29/guardianobituaries.politics
83. Home Office, *Report of the Committee on Children and Young Persons*, p. 32.
84. Ibid., pp. 5–6.

11

Mapping the Turkish Republican Notion of Childhood and Juvenile Delinquency: The Story of Children's Courts in Turkey, 1940–1990

Nazan Çiçek

This chapter tells the story of the introduction of children's courts into the Turkish Republic in 1979. By exploring the debates surrounding the formation of a distinct and separate justice system for children, it aims to provide insights into the way juvenile delinquency as well as the conception of childhood that underpins it were understood and defined in the Turkish Republican context. After delving into the possible reasons for the reluctance of Turkish policymakers and Turkish society more broadly to establish children's courts before 1979, the chapter examines the trial and incarceration of a British child by a Turkish adult criminal court in 1972, the so-called "Timothy D. Incident", which served as a catalyst for accentuating the differences between Turkish and Western perceptions of and attitudes toward childhood in general and juvenile delinquency in particular.

As Philippe Ariès asserted in his seminal work *L'Enfant et la vie familiale sous l'ancien regime,*[1] children in medieval Europe were seen merely as adults in the making and treated casually. This situation, he suggests, changed only after the emergence of modern society which associated children firmly with the domestic sphere and hence with women and education. Thus, in modern times, children, rather than being transitory inhabitants of a Lilliputian world, came to be regarded as a *sui generis* group separate from adults deserving of special treatment and care. This modern notion of childhood as "an ontology in its own right", also assumed, inter alia, that children lived in a world of their own where innocence reigned.[2] "[Children] in this *Apollonian* image, the formaliza-tion of which occurred with the publication of Rousseau's *Emile* in 1762, were not curbed nor beaten into submission but encouraged, enabled, and facilitated."[3] They were also kept away from the adult world of vio-lence, sex, hard labour and politics. But this modern view of childhood came with something of an internal contradiction: while children came to be seen as the deserving objects of love and care with their naïve and uncorrupted nature, their pre-social, primitive and dangerous char-acter requiring supervision and control was also stressed. In this sense, from the vantage point of modernity, children shared the same basic characteristics as the masses who, many feared, could easily descend into rebellion and barbarity unless they were continuously watched and controlled. Not surprisingly those who were responsible for the estab-lishment of juvenile systems in the Western world were mostly the children of the underprivileged classes, who were believed to pose a great threat to the fragile balance of nineteenth-century society.[4] Thus the modern Western conception of childhood alternated between the images of child as savage and child as angel (or between Dionysian child and Apollonian child, as Jenks termed it[5]).

In tandem with this modern notion of childhood, a distinctive com-prehension of juvenile delinquency gradually appeared which tended to define criminal liability for children in increasingly different terms from those applied to adults.[6] As Janet Ainsworth correctly points out, the idea of a juvenile justice system was generated by "the central role of the essential otherness of the young in progressive ideology".[7] Juveniles were thought to be so intrinsically different from adults as to compel the creation of an entirely separate and independent jus-tice system for them.[8] Thus, in the Western world from the end of the nineteenth century, the institution of juvenile courts, along with some other child-related institutions, laws and norms, has come to signify the degree to which this modern Western notion of childhood that regarded children as a distinct category in the life-cycle with special needs and "physical, social and structural vulnerability"[9] had taken hold in a par-ticular culture and society. In the non-Western world where "childhood was re-discovered and became a topic of broad intellectual inquiry"[10] "at a time when the validity of traditional models appeared to have crumbled",[11] modernizing elites increasingly tended to view the child question (including juvenile delinquency) in the light of this modern Western conception of childhood which in fact was by no means mono-lithic. Yet, informed by "a post-colonial legacy", the Western world, "through the Declaration of the Rights of the Child and the work of charitable agencies and international bodies in the Third World" exported one particular vision of childhood as correct and engendered "the misguided and tacit assumption of a uniformity of childhood in Western Europe".[12]

Considering that the late Ottoman and early Republican Turkish modernizing elites frequently identified and equated civilization with the Western world, it was not surprising that they enthusiastically embraced this exported vision of "correct childhood". Thus in their eyes, just as in those of the West, "the child symbolized all that is decent and caring about a society, it was the very index of a civilization".[13] They tended to regard the way in which children were handled by a society, in the broadest sense, as a benchmark in the progress of civilization and overtly judged the success or failure of the regimes around them through the status that children acquired within those regimes. Nevertheless, the introduction of the juvenile courts (undoubtedly an essential part of this exported vision of correct childhood) into the Turkish justice system did not materialize until 1979, almost 100 years after the institution first emerged in the Western countries.[14]

In fact, the Turkish intelligentsia in general and the jurists and law practitioners in particular had been closely watching recent developments in the realm of juvenile delinquency along with the establishment of juvenile courts in other parts of the world. Hence, as early as the 1940s, just two decades after the foundation of the Turkish Republic, there were calls for the introduction of juvenile courts such as had existed in all "modern" countries for years. From 1952, there were several attempts to force parliament to pass an act regulating juvenile delinquency, yet the majority of the deputies were not convinced that the nation's delinquent children needed specialist courts. As the debate about Turkey's "undeniable lateness" with regard to measures taken to deal with juvenile delinquency in the "modern world" lingered on, parliament prepared a draft in 1965 which was to provide the groundwork for the 1979 law. The draft was severely censured by many contemporary scholars and practitioners who accused it of failing to recognize the "vulnerability" of children and thus to grasp the basic concept of both juvenile delinquency and juvenile courts. The main objection was that it treated children as miniature adults with limited skills and faculties rather than as a *sui generis* group with special needs and that it thus settled for lenient measures and sentences without any substantial notion of rehabilitation, education or correction. In other words, the institution of children's courts was devised to "try" and "punish" delinquent Turkish children through the dictates of the Turkish Penal Code[15] without any attempt to construct a separate and specialized body of laws and regulations for juvenile delinquency. The 1965 draft was transformed into the Law for the Establishment of Children's Courts in 1979 and largely failed to address any of the objections raised.

Establishing juvenile courts in the Turkish Republic

Why were Turkish children "awarded" a court of their own in the first place if they were not seen as a category in their own right? Was the introduction of children's courts regarded by the policymakers as a necessary step toward claiming a fuller membership of the "modern world" without any genuine insight into the modern notion of childhood, and hence only a facade? Or did it appear as the inevitable result of the ongoing transformation in the habitus[16] of Turkish society since the foundation of the Republic? These are the questions that will be addressed in this chapter in an attempt to explore the institutionalization of juvenile justice in the Turkish Republic.

Despite the protests of a group of intellectuals that mostly consisted of jurists, law practitioners and social workers, over several decades the Turkish Republic seemed rather reluctant to connect concerns about child welfare with crime control, which, in the Western world, had been the driving force behind the creation of juvenile courts. Instead the Republic persisted in leaving delinquent children outside the definition of "children in need of protection"[17] and, as a result, legal proceedings regarding these two different groups of children never coalesced. In 1940, a famous Turkish jurist, Faruk Erem, pointed out that the principles adopted in the Turkish Penal Code regarding juvenile delinquents belonged to another age. "This law", he remarked, "by no means believes that all children regardless of whether they committed a crime or not, equally deserve the unconditional attention, care and protection of the state." "In modern countries", he continued, "the state does not deprive some children of state protection just because they committed a crime, all children are seen and treated as children."[18] What Erem suggested was the introduction of a new child protection law that would render all children equal in terms of state protection and establish a system of juvenile courts where delinquents would be treated as part of the category of dependent and neglected children in need of protection. Nevertheless, as the Law for Children Who Need Protection of 1949 proves, the urgings of jurists like Faruk Erem fell on deaf ears in the Turkish parliament. The new law carried on placing delinquent children under the jurisdiction of the Penal Code and carefully excluded them from the definition of "children in need of protection".

As the Law of 1949 boldly revealed, the Turkish state opted to act as *parens patriae* for only a strictly defined group of children whose physical, spiritual and moral development was considered in danger, whose parents were unknown and who had not yet committed a crime.[19] With the alterations made to the Law in 1957,[20] the definition of "children in need of protection" was expanded to include children neglected by their parents and judged to be in danger of becoming prostitutes, beggars, drug addicts, alcoholics or tramps. But Turkish official resistance to mixing young offenders with law-abiding youngsters remained. Some jurists and law practitioners throughout the 1960s and 1970s stringently criticized the revised Law of 1957, urging the state to abandon its position that delinquent children should lose their right to state protection on the grounds of their criminality. At the same time, several scholars published papers in specialist legal journals where they discussed the definition as well as the treatment of "children in need of protection" in several Western countries – Britain, France, Italy and Hungary as well as the US – and examined institutions such as juvenile courts, remand homes, approved schools, borstals, attendance centres and probation hostels in these countries.[21] In 1965 the Turkish government brought in a draft bill for the establishment of juvenile courts which was neither debated nor voted on in parliament. The draft nevertheless caused a stir among the jurists, who vehemently protested that it failed to grasp the essence and true meaning of the institution of juvenile courts. Although the Draft appeared as a reforming step toward the prioritization of child welfare over punishment, it insisted on juxtaposing punishment and rehabilitative measures and on sentencing young offenders to reduced versions of adult penalties without allowing the court to assess their relative level of maturity. As Betül Taşbağ, a Turkish jurist, pointed out, "in today's legal principles with respect to juvenile delinquents, delinquent conduct is not regarded as the only determining factor, it serves as one of the factors in deciding the character of the sentence".[22]

Manuel Lopez and Rey Arrojo, United Nations observers who had been conducting research on the issue of juvenile delinquency in Turkey, castigated the draft for employing and reproducing the principles and severe penalties of the Italian Penal Code of 1889 and dismissed it as "archaic" and "unacceptable".[23] Likewise, many Turkish scholars reiterated that as long as the logic behind the treatment of juvenile delinquents remained intact the establishment of juvenile courts per se would not bring about any radical changes to the prevailing justice system.

Despite all these criticisms and protests from experts, the Law for the Establishment of Children's Courts of 1979 appeared to be a mere reproduction of the draft of 1965. The Law of 1979 accepted that children below the age of 11 had no criminal culpability and therefore could neither be held responsible for their actions nor be tried and punished for criminal conduct. Nevertheless, if their crime was normally punished with a penalty of longer than 12 months' imprisonment in the Penal Code, then a series of non-punitive sanctions such as being returned to the parents or legal guardians, being placed in a foster home or in Protectories, child care homes run by official or voluntary institutions, could be applied to those children affected even if they were under the age of 11. Delinquent children aged between 11 and 15 were to be tried by the juvenile courts and thereafter placed in reformatories in order to complete the rehabilitation process. Children who were detained would wait for the final verdict in their case in the detention centres exclusively designed for children. Although the Law of 1979 did not receive accolades from the champions of juvenile courts, it was nevertheless welcomed as a reforming step in the realm of juvenile justice. Aside from the introduction of new principles to the processes of preliminary investigation, interrogation and prosecution, social workers, psychologists, pedagogists and psychiatrists were assigned to the court as "probation and control officers" who were also responsible for the production of social inquiry reports. Moreover, it was not until 1987 that the first juvenile courts were established in the four largest cities of Turkey.

Perceptions of children and childhood among the Republican elite in 1979

Why, then, did it take the Republic almost half a century to introduce children's courts? Was this reluctance informed by a particular interpretation of the discourse of childhood innocence whereby the category of childhood is preserved through the removal of "errant" and "criminal" children who do not fit adult conceptions of "the child"? Did juvenile delinquents, in the eyes of the ruling elite, lose their claim to be considered children because of their criminal conduct? Was it a question of profitability that led the state to prioritize "non-criminal" children over juvenile delinquents, when it came to investing already scarce public funds? Was it because children's rights as well as the notion of childhood itself were situationally dependent in the Turkish case and the perceived threat to public safety overrode the interest to adhere to the norms of international children's rights including the establishment of juvenile courts? The answer to all these questions would seem in varying degrees to be affirmative; to understand why, it is necessary to take a closer look at the Republican elite's perception of childhood and children.

Keeping in mind that it is not possible to think about the institutions and structures of juvenile delinquency separately from the conceptual understandings of delinquency itself and the notions of childhood which underpin it, the following section will explore in more detail the mechanics that helped to shape the Republican elite's perception of childhood and children during the period before the introduction of children's courts in 1979.

In the early years of the debate about the institution of juvenile courts, the common conception of childhood and children held by the Turkish ruling elite, intelligentsia and policymakers was complicated by a series of tensions. The seemingly assertive and oft-repeated official discourse left no room for doubt that the Kemalist-nationalist elite was aware of the indisputable importance of children for the nation. From an examination of the undertakings of the Children's Protection Society (*Himaye-i Etfal*), one of the most publicly visible institutions of the Republican regime, it is clear that the Kemalist-nationalist cadres saw children as the future custodians of society whose needs had to be prioritized. Their beliefs about childhood can be summed up in the words of İ.H. Baltacıoğlu, a prominent author of the Republic's education policies: "Childhood is not a caricature of adulthood or an imperfect stage in human life but a flawless world in itself which has its own mind, will, reasoning and heart."[24] Since the "child" was used as a metaphor for the nation, the Kemalist elite politicized the "child question". Its resolution would prove the success of the Republic's nation-building as well as of its modernization strategies. The "child question" in this sense loomed large, ranging from the problems of high infant mortality rates, malnutrition and disease to the large groups of children who were abandoned, orphaned or forced into begging or prostitution. Other important questions concerned scientific child-rearing methods, mass education, child labour and delinquency. The particular vision of correct childhood spread across the globe by the Western world and reproduced in the official Republican discourse dictated that children should enjoy their own "innocent" and sheltered world. This, however, went against the nationalists' expectations that children should grow up rapidly and join the ranks of the regime defenders. This was one of the tensions that dominated the ruling elite's approach to the "child question".

Another, more unsettling tension stemmed from the metaphorical representations of childhood in the imagination of the ruling elite. For the Kemalist elite the concept of childhood was a discursive space in which they could reconstruct the past, present and future. From the beginning, it served as a potent vehicle[25] which represented the spontaneity, joy, purity and naturalness of the "Turkish Revolution" and had notably positive connotations. The Turkish Republic was figuratively presented as a newborn child who had no tainted and burdensome past but only a promising future. Being young or being a child in particular was romanticized and became a discursive instrument that was used to underline the supposedly energetic, vigorous and youthful qualities of Turkish society and of its newly founded nation state in contrast to the world's gerontocracies. This emphasis on the "childishness" of the Republic, in another sense, was also used to keep the self-improving revolutionary spirit alive by pointing to the importance of remaining in touch with the nation's "inner child", characterized by its capacity for unrestrained emotion, directness and self-forgetfulness.

But the idealization of the state as remaining in its infancy could also be associated with dependency and economic unproductivity; this would be incompatible with the ideals of the Republic, which wanted to catch up rapidly with the most advanced, productive and "civilized" countries in the world. The newborn Turkish Republic, in other words, was in fact struggling to "grow up", to assert its place among nations it viewed as more sophisticated and more progressive; nations, by and large, who, in turn, also saw the Republic as backward. The country's determination to "grow up" without dawdling in the phase of childhood, which in the modernist political imagination (echoing here Orientalist discourse), referred to the state of being primitive, uncivilized, backward and immature.[26] As Köksal points out,

> in sociological terms, the Turkish Revolution needed to transcend its own childhood in order to secure the Republic a place among the civilized and mature countries of the world while on the other hand it had to guard and cling to its childhood in order to reproduce its romantic ideals.[27]

This undeniable tension certainly left its imprint on the ways in which the children of the Republic were imagined, approached and treated. Two incompatible discourses were in operation. Childhood was sacralized, yet, at the same time, shunned as a stage of vulnerability and inferiority. While, on the one hand, the discourse of innocence that portrayed children as naive and vulnerable creatures was gaining ground, on the other hand, the discourse of the ideal Turkish child constructed by the new regime increasingly cast children as competent beings with a unique insight into human relationships.[28] Turkish children were asked to undertake a Sisyphean task, being required to act like small adults yet still preserve their childhood innocence. They were expected to pay their debt to the previous generation who suffered enormously to secure the future of the fatherland and to establish the Republic by displaying impeccable conduct in all areas of their lives. They not only had to prove their worth and show their appreciation for the sacrifices made for them but also had to comprehend the magnitude of their responsibility for the future of their country, society and culture.[29] As remarked by the Minister of Education, Reşit Galip, in an address to children in 1933, the glorious Turkish nation had no place for "lazy" and "immoral" children. "Those who failed to work hard and also comply with the moral values of Turkish society as they grow up would be regarded as the future enemies of the nation."[30]

By and large, Turkish children in the early Republican era had to grow up quickly, although the official discourse continued to pay lip service to their right to be children. The allegory constructed between children and the newborn Turkish nation state worked insofar as children quickly progressed toward adulthood, which, in Nandy's words, "is valued as a symbol of completeness and as an end-product of growth or development".[31] Turkish children who were equated with the nation state were expected to acknowledge their symbolic value by placing their childhood at the service of their nation's future interests. This, it seems, was an important factor that pushed the issue of juvenile delinquency to the margins of the child question and led the ruling elite not only to distinguish the category of "children in need of protection" from that of delinquent children but also to prioritize the former over the latter. In contrast with juvenile delinquents, the troubles faced by children deemed "in need of protection" were not of their own making. They neither displayed immoral behaviour nor failed to perform their duties toward the nation.

Although poverty was cited among the causes of crime, it was nevertheless maintained that unfavourable socioeconomic factors and improper familial upbringing per se did not turn children into criminals. Only children with "weak personalities" became criminals.[32] Likewise, Özge Ertem, working on children's magazines published during the early Republican era, remarks that these publications discussed "social inequalities and poverty as problems of morality rather than as issues of political value".[33] The poor child was expected to save himself from poverty by working hard, showing moral rectitude and staying away from trouble. Some medical practitioners agreed with the authors of children's magazines and books. As a neurologist from a prestigious Turkish medical school remarked in a newspaper column in 1960, "criminal children" were "morally weak and psychologically imbalanced characters" who defied the norms and values of their society. The antidote to juvenile delinquency was "reinforcement of the moral upbringing of children".[34]

When morality was placed at the centre of all social problems then criminal conduct became a matter of individual choice and responsibility. The world's first juvenile courts were established in Chicago in 1899 in a move spearheaded by Flower and Lathrop. Their establishment presented a stark challenge to "the notion that individuals make all the choices that fundamentally shape their lives"[35] and that individual responsibility was an adequate explanation for crime. By asserting state responsibility for both dependent and delinquent children the Act to Regulate the Treatment and Control of Dependent, Neglected and Delinquent Children of 1899 merged concerns about child welfare with crime control. In the Turkish case, however, well into the late 1960s, the problems of crime and poverty which had often been conceived of and discussed in similar terms in the West were dealt with separately. Poverty in itself did not denote immorality but even to use it as an excuse for criminal conduct was seen as an indication of immorality which itself was considered the root cause of crime.[36] Although poor families' living conditions and the deficiencies in their child-rearing practices were more frequently mentioned as being among the reasons for juvenile delinquency, the emphasis nevertheless was laid on dysfunctional families. As expressed by a well known Turkish jurist in 1969, as long as the child's spiritual needs were taken care of by the family, poverty was not expected to cause juvenile delinquency. Dysfunctional families that failed to provide the child with a moral upbringing and emotionally healthy environment were the central reason for delinquency.[37]

From the vantage point of Turkish policymakers, delinquent Turkish children, be they paupers or not, were, in the last analysis, responsible for their criminal behaviour and their "moral weakness" was regarded as a disgrace. By straying from the true moral path, delinquent children proved not only their ingratitude for the dedicated efforts made to help them but also their inability to comprehend their mission with regard to building the nation. What is more, delinquent children cast a dark shadow over the carefully constructed image of the ideal Turkish child. Their very existence was an infringement of the Republican zeitgeist. The issue of delinquency stood as a constant reminder that the new regime was failing to incorporate all the nation's children into the project of creating a new society composed of physically, morally and spiritually well balanced citizens. The efforts to conceal or downplay the link between poverty and delinquency also mirrored the ruling elite's concerns about growing social tensions which the official discourse had opted to deny. Largely destitute of the sort of judicial structures, economic facilities and resources normally found in a social-welfare state where the exercise of parental rights is placed under the surveillance of state institutions, the Republic looked to morality as a panacea. Amid other child-related problems, such as a high infant mortality rate, epidemics and illiteracy, delinquency largely failed to gain visibility and nationwide publicity. Therefore, it would not be completely far-fetched to suggest that in such an atmosphere the Republican elites preferred to stay aloof from an institution like juvenile courts that was generated by and in turn generated the visibility of juvenile delinquency.

Rather than recognizing children as an ontological category essentially different from adults the Republican elites approached children as adults in the making, a tendency which was mostly fashioned by the dictates of nation-building practices. This tendency to perceive children as small adults rather than physically, socially and structurally vulnerable beings with a lack of personal competence and strength led to a justice system where the notion of the essential otherness of the young which had invoked the establishment of juvenile courts in the Western world was largely unknown. This does not mean that the Turkish justice system saw no difference between adults and children in terms of culpability. The cognitive and physical limits of children were taken into account in deciding on the severity of the punishment. Yet the focus was on the crime rather than the perpetrator and the age of the perpetrator did not alter the definition or the seriousness of the crime. Since the establishment of juvenile courts is only possible where children are perceived as dependent beings led into crime, it is not particularly surprising that the Turkish justice system, which regarded children as independent agents, lacked juvenile courts.

Another factor that impeded the introduction of juvenile courts in Turkey seems to have been the gap between the perception of childhood among a section of the Turkish intelligentsia and the social imaginary of childhood among the masses in Turkish society. In Turkey, the introduction of new child-related institutions engendered by the modern notion of childhood was not demanded by civil society as a whole but rather by a small group of citizens possessing considerable cultural capital. In the case of juvenile courts, it was mostly scholars, jurists, law practitioners and social workers who urged and pressurized policymakers for the establishment of specialized courts for children. As a well-known Turkish child psychiatrist remarked in 1967, juvenile delinquents "did not attract any attention or mercy from the public". "Turkish society was by no means appalled or scandalized by the horrific scenes of young children being handcuffed and tried in criminal courts designed for adult criminals. Putting school children in adult prisons was hailed almost as a national mission."[38] Likewise, in 1989, a newspaper columnist writing on the deficiencies of the Law for the Establishment of Children's Courts of 1979 accused Turkish society of being emotionally crippled. In the article entitled "Children of a Loveless Society", Yalçın Doğan expressed his regret at being a member of a society which is incapable of showing tolerance, compassion and understanding toward children. "This society," he wrote, "by severely attacking children who committed a crime in fact projects its own violent feelings onto these children."[39] Even among jurists and law practitioners, there was no consensus on the issue of juvenile courts. The same child psychiatrist quoted above also pointed out that "the architects of the Draft of 1965 had to struggle with the strong resistance put up by their own colleagues". "It was not easy to persuade those conservative jurists with strong opinions of the necessity of establishing juvenile courts."[40] The remarks of a law professor from İstanbul University in 1972 prove that resistance was still prevalent even in the years after the completion of the Draft of 1965. In a press interview, Prof. Nevzat Gürelli opined that "under the existing circumstances the time is not ripe for us to introduce the children's courts". "It is all very easy to devise a court on paper but it is very hard to endow that court with supporting institutions that will enable the court to function properly. Therefore we should first prepare the ground on which juvenile courts can later be built."[41]

In other words, juvenile courts in Turkey do not seem to have appeared as an outcome of changing popular conceptions of childhood in Turkish society. There were no particular philanthropic organizations, pressure groups or private agencies, like the Salvation Army or Howard Association in Britain that campaigned for a separate justice system for children or vigorously kept the issue of juvenile delinquency on the public agenda throughout the years.[42]

The mainstream media did not show much interest in the category of criminal children either. A thorough analysis of a widely circulated daily paper, *Milliyet* (Nationality), between the years of 1958 and 1993 reveals the extent of public indifference toward the question of juvenile delinquency and the juvenile courts. During these 35 years the number of items that dealt with juvenile delinquents as a category or juvenile delinquency as social phenomenon or national problem amounts to only 35.

The proverbially insignificant position of civil society in the construction of the political realm in Turkey once more manifested itself in the case of juvenile courts. Since the foundation of the Republic, largely owing to the absence of a well developed civil society, bureaucratic and intellectual cadres had assumed the role of constructing the ideological-political technologies of the state and aimed at transforming the value systems of the society from above by functioning as a kind of superego.[43] A series of reforms had been carried out with a view to rehabituate the people of the Republic along Western lines. It seems that the institution of juvenile courts, when finally adopted, appeared as another novel and imported instrument used by policymakers to transform the social imaginary of childhood from above.

As the government spokesman at the time remarked, the policymakers (or modernizing politico-bureaucratic elite) of the country were attempting to complete one more task in the Republic's endeavour to catch up with the modern world by passing the Law on the Establishment, Duties and Procedures of the Juvenile Courts of 1979. The Timothy D. incident, during which the treatment of a British juvenile delinquent by the Turkish judicial system came to be regarded as the key moment that determined Turkey's commitment to (or distance from) Western civilization, offers insights into the real motivations behind the introduction of children's courts by the Turkish parliament in 1979.

A British child in a Turkish prison: The Timothy D. incident, 1971–1974

On 11 August 1971, the Narcotics Bureau of the Istanbul Security Directorate caught Timothy D. in the act of selling a substantial amount (24.2 kg) of hashish allegedly obtained in Afghanistan. He was a 14-year-old British child who had entered Turkey as a tourist on his way back from a sojourn in East Asia and the Middle East in the company of his mother, his five younger siblings and his mother's boyfriend. His mother had taken him out of school as she had decided that a journey to India and Nepal would be of much greater educational value.[44] Timothy was immediately arrested and taken before a judge. After pleading guilty he was detained and put into a prison for adults (the Sağmalcılar Prison) to await his trial, as there was no detention centre for children in Turkey. The news of a 14-year-old British child's arrest and detention in a Turkish adult prison rapidly reached Britain and attracted immense media attention. The *News of the World*, a populist conservative British tabloid, embarked on a campaign to pressure the Turkish government to free Timothy. The rather provocative slogan of the campaign was "Get this Boy out of Hell" which prompted the Turkish media to launch a counter campaign against British "conceit" and "insolence". While the *News of the World* along with some other British papers continued publishing inflammatory articles and news items claiming that Timothy was in "grave moral danger among Turkish murderers, drug-pedlars and thieves" and was maltreated by prison authorities, the Turkish media eagerly set out to refute the accusations. The portrait of Timothy painted by British tabloids as a "frightened, pale school boy who cries himself to sleep in a terrifying hell-hole of a Turkish prison constantly fearing homosexual advances and beatings"[45] did not find a sympathetic audience in Turkey. The Turkish media was furious that Britain was using a "criminal child" as a pretext to patronize Turkey and meddling with a case that was *sub judice*. British protests were received as yet another reminder of the asymmetry that had shaped the history of the power relations between the Ottoman Empire and Great Britain throughout the nineteenth and early twentieth centuries.[46]

In the social and cultural memory of Turkish society, the extraterritorial privileges known as capitulations that had allowed foreigners, including British citizens, to bypass the Ottoman courts in legal disputes for centuries were directly linked to the imperialist aspirations of Western powers. Abolishment of capitulations in 1923 was an essential part of the foundation narrative of the independent Turkish Republic. Any intervention in judicial processes in Turkish courts on behalf of a foreigner was bound to recall memories of such capitulations.

Fuelled with anger and resentment toward the Western claims of superiority over Turkey, the Turkish media and government alike were quick to perceive Orientalist and colonialist undertones in Britain's reaction to Timothy's arrest and trial. The tension reached its apogee when the Turkish court (following the Turkish Penal Code) sentenced him to six years and three months in prison on 1 March 1972. The headline of British tabloid *The Sun* was "Barbaric Turks Jail Boy of Fourteen For Six Years" which convinced Turkish public opinion that the notorious image of the Turks as the "one great anti-human specimen of humanity"[47] that had fuelled the discourse of an "anti-Turkish crusade" over past centuries was rising once more from the grave. When the exchange of letters between the Leader of the Opposition (Labour Party), Harold Wilson, and the Prime Minister, Edward Heath, in which the former had defined the Turkish court's sentence as "monstrous", was made public, the Turkish Prime Minister, Nihat Erim, cancelled his upcoming visit to London.[48] Before long, the Timothy D. case turned into a public furore peppered with jingoistic undertones on both sides that put a strain on Anglo-Turkish relations and even threatened a diplomatic rupture.

Although the widespread public sensation in Britain had largely been caused by the fact that a child of 14 years of age had been handcuffed, remanded in custody in an adult prison, tried in an adult court and sentenced to imprisonment, the Turkish public and politicians did not seem to understand why Timothy's age per se should prompt such an outrage. It was not as if the Turkish authorities had arrested an "innocent" child and subjected him to an ordeal. Neither had the Turkish court denied Timothy's young age and treated him as an adult. He was regarded as a child who had committed a serious crime and tried accordingly, which resulted in the reduction of his sentence. The Turkish media was at pains to explain that they were not discriminating against Timothy. They were treating him in the same way as they treated Turkish criminal children, according to the dictates of the Turkish Penal Code. Therefore, from the point of view of Turkish public opinion, the campaign launched in London was "unjustified" and "tendentious". As expressed by the chairman of Ankara Bar Association, British attacks on the Turkish judiciary were "nothing but a manifestation of outdated colonial mentality and illusions of grandeur".[49]

Each time the British government, politicians and media criticized the Turks for keeping a child in prison the Turkish side responded by explaining how Timothy was "granted exceptional treatment in gaol because of his youth".[50] As the Turks saw it, the idea of a child in prison was not disturbing in itself so long as the child was not ill-treated. The greatest luxury a child who committed such a serious crime could expect was not avoiding imprisonment or "a pat on the back as was the case in Britain"[51] but leniency and better treatment in prison because of his age. Throughout the trial all the British papers made a point of the fact that Timothy was handcuffed. Just before the final hearing the *Sun* said:

> His Turkish jailers are in the habit of manacling this child whenever they haul him off to court which is frequently. Yesterday he was hand-cuffed again for yet another court appearance -his seventh. […]

It is four months since the *Sun* urged his captors: Let the justice be swift and merciful. For God's sake, or Allah's, how much longer are they going to torture this schoolboy and his family?[52]

None of the Turkish papers found it necessary to mention that the child was handcuffed, as it was a well known measure routinely employed in court cases in Turkey. When the British side pointed to the harmful effects caused by close contact with adult criminals inside the prison the Turkish side maintained that Timothy was kept in a separate room with other children. In other words, the British objections were largely lost on the Turks, who insisted that their handling of the Timothy D. incident was lawful and just.

Timothy D. was caught up in the clash of two different understandings of juvenile justice, informed by different conceptions of children and childhood. The Consular Department in the British Foreign Office was quick to realize that "since there was no miscarriage of justice the only consular argument left for use in the representations was that of the boy's age which *would not impress the Turks* [emphasis mine]".[53] Likewise, the British Ambassador Roderick Sarell remarked that the only basis for representation available was the "plea that a child of barely fourteen could not be wholly responsible for a criminal act suggested to him by others".[54] The British government, however, was under enormous public and political pressure owing largely to the press clamour for action and finding it increasingly difficult to resist.[55] When the British Foreign Secretary Douglas-Home expressed to the Turkish Ambassador Kuneralp his "sense of shock at the sentence of six years imprisonment", the latter answered that

the law was very rigid and left little possibility for the judge to take into account special factors. [...] While the fact that Timothy was only fourteen made the strongest impact on British opinion, it was *not a startling fact in Turkish eyes* (emphasis mine). Already he had received special treatment in prison and a lesser sentence than if he had been older.[56]

As the public outcry in Britain grew stronger after the sentence was passed, the British Foreign Office asked the Turkish government to issue a statement of justification that they hoped could mollify those campaigning for Timothy's release.[57] The Foreign Office Permanent Undersecretary suggested to the Turkish Ambassador that the statement should explain the Turkish government's policy in regard to minors convicted of serious crimes as well as "their reasons for imprisoning them". They could also sketch out what arrangements were made for continuing young convicts' education while serving their sentences.[58] This request was countered with two statements issued by the Turkish Embassy in London and the Turkish government in Ankara. The government's statement maintained that Timothy D. was tried by a competent Turkish court and during his detention the child was "accorded the care and attention befitting his age and character". In passing the sentence the court had "taken the age of the accused and other circumstances into consideration".[59] The Embassy statement was couched in a language that emphasized the differences in the two countries' systems of juvenile justice. It mentioned that "there were no juvenile courts in Turkey but Turkish law contained special provisions for juveniles, such as the halving of sentences passed on them in appropriate cases".[60] Although it was particularly demanded by the British government, both of these statements opted not to mention Turkey's reasons for imprisoning juvenile delinquents.

The lack of juvenile courts in Turkey was in fact the crux of the matter that created a media war between the two countries out of an otherwise ordinary judicial case. The Turkish media, armed with the mission of defending the sovereignty and international prestige of Turkey, was rather reluctant to discuss what would have happened had Timothy been dealt with by a juvenile court instead of an adult criminal court. While the loud voice of the media chorus demanded respect for Turkish judicial proceedings and suggested that "the British papers should occupy themselves with some urgent measures for the prevention of tyrannical murderers of 14 and 16 years of age in Northern Ireland",[61] there were nevertheless some faint voices that raised the issue of juvenile courts and tried to make themselves heard. One of them was the Sorbonne-educated Turkish judge who passed sentence on Timothy. In a press interview after the verdict Judge Yüceöz expressed his regret that there were no children's courts in Turkey:

> If we had such courts then we could have handled this incident differently. The child could have been sent to a correctional facility where proper education for his rehabilitation is provided. Then we could return him to the society as a morally-centered citizen to pursue an honest life. [...] I am of the opinion that Timothy was not cognizant of the gravity of his crime. I wish we could pardon him or place him with a trusted family instead of sending him to jail.[62]

A law professor from Ankara Law Faculty, Bülent Nuri Esen, galloped to his support. Waiving aside all other aspects of the incident, Esen focused on the issue of juvenile courts. "I think our judicial system is considerably flawed due to the lack of children's courts" he said:

This is also the main reason that gave rise to such public outburst in Britain. A boy of fourteen cannot be regarded as criminally culpable; he is even incapable of grasping the magnitude of the crime he committed. Only children's courts can determine whether a child is fit to be tried. And what I mean by trial is to take some measures with a view to rehabilitate children and turn them into useful human beings for society. This is what modern states do. Timothy's trial is lawful according to our Penal Code. But I repeat, we need to establish children's courts.[63]

By and large, the Timothy D. incident did not lead the Turkish media to engage in an enquiry into the British juvenile justice system. There was no press coverage of the juvenile courts, remand houses or reformatories in Britain. Instead, by way of retaliation the Turkish media focused on some apparently exceptional cases such as that of 14-year-old Patricia Brown, who was awaiting trial in Holloway Prison. Comparing the gross national product and the public expenditures of the two countries in order to emphasize the economic weakness of Turkey, and hence her inability to build reformatories and detention centres for children, as well as implying that Britain as an imperialist power was among the factors that caused this weakness, was another strategy employed by the Turkish media in confronting the British campaign.[64] Many columnists also pointed out that the British were in no position to criticize the Turkish judicial system while they themselves carried out scandalous judicial proceedings in the colonies as well as in Northern Ireland before the astonished eyes of the whole world.

There were only two notable public figures that overtly instrumentalized the Timothy D. case to raise awareness about the necessity of juvenile courts. One of them was Atalay Yörükoğlu, a prominent Turkish child psychiatrist from the prestigious Hacettepe Medical School in Ankara. Yörükoğlu expressed his concern that once the media frenzy over the case diminished the question of juvenile delinquency would be forgotten again, leaving the Turkish criminal children to meet their usual destiny: complete removal from the public eye. "Our national pride is understandably hurt by the British campaign," he said, "but this should not overshadow the painful facts about our handling of juvenile delinquents."[65]

Turkey is among a handful of countries on earth where children's courts do not exist. Hundreds of Turkish children find themselves in Timothy's position every day and this saddens nobody but a few. The provisions of the Turkish Penal Code for children are extremely stern and rigid. They are only softened versions of the provisions designed for adults with no particular concern for the rehabilitation of children. Let us stop for a minute and think how we treat our children. We keep a school child in prison for days because of a homework he handed in that allegedly contains illegal political arguments. A child who is caught in the act of stealing empty soda bottles is tried in adult criminal courts and waits for the verdict for months. When we catch a child younger than 11 in an act of a sexual nature with a 12 year old we pass severe sentences on the older child assuming that he is criminally liable. Our judges and politicians do not seem to be troubled by this sort of devastating incident that occurs every day as they choose to remain aloof and inert. What is more regrettable is that we already have a Draft, albeit with some shortcomings, for the establishment of children's courts waiting to be debated in parliament.[66]

Then Yörükoğlu provided a brief description of a typical juvenile justice system operating through juvenile courts. A similar approach to the Timothy D. incident came from Abdi İpekçi, the famous editor and columnist of the widely circulated Turkish daily *Milliyet*. Although İpekçi scathingly censured the British tendency to judge everything according to their own values, habits and standards, he nevertheless seemed cognizant of the importance of juvenile courts. "In reality it is a source of sorrow for us too", İpekçi wrote, "that there are no children's courts in Turkey – as for instance in Britain." "We would all have liked to have the same possibilities and to end a harmful and worrying practice, not only for Timothy but for the hundreds of our own juvenile delinquents."[67]

While Yörükoğlu and İpekçi attempted to prompt some degree of self-criticism in Turkish public opinion, the *Daily Telegraph* in London sympathized with Turkey as a country that was fighting against illegal drug trafficking. Likewise the *Times* and the *Daily Express* published letters from their readers who condemned the British self-complacency that sparked off the vilification campaign against Turkey.[68] Yet the writers of those letters seemed motivated more by their demand for severe punishment of drug smuggling and dealing cases than by any genuine approval of Turkey's general handling of juvenile delinquency. Those dissidents aside, the majority in Britain were upset to see a child in prison. The general tone of the British approach to the incident manifested itself clearly in Prime Minister Heath's words: "A juvenile should not be sentenced to a term of imprisonment whatever the charge on which he may have been convicted."[69]

By perceiving the imprisonment of a child as a form of child abuse, Edward Heath and the British media were in fact positioning Turkey opposite to Britain on the scale of modernity, "civilization" and moral advancement. As Anneke Meyer points out, "modern society sees the treatment of children, its vulnerable members, as symbolic of the social order and indicative of its moral state". "Other countries, as well as other historical periods, can be seen as less developed in that child abuse is not even acknowledged or talked about. Such comparisons portray this country [UK] as enlightened, progressive and morally superior."[70] Throughout the Timothy D. incident Turkey was accused by the British press of being "barbarian, savage, cruel, outrageous, and acting according to the methods of the Middle Ages".[71] Acting through "a central tenet of nineteenth-century reforming liberalism which professes that one measure of a society's civilization and progress is to be found in its treatment of disadvantaged and dispossessed groups"[72] including children, British public opinion readily classified Turkey as "uncivilized" and "inhuman".[73] This strategy also worked to locate the problem of child abuse outside or with the other, which in turn helped preserve the widely cherished British (or Western) conception of the child as innately vulnerable and innocent.

Turkish policymakers and opinion leaders were only too aware that Timothy's imprisonment struck a blow at Turkey's claims to civilization and modernity. When Judge Yüceöz expressed his regret at sending Timothy to jail he did not know that the Turkish government was desperately searching for a better place where Timothy could serve his sentence without causing further damage to Turkey's image in the eyes of the "civilized" world. Because there were only four correctional schools for young offenders in Turkey, all of which were already overcrowded, and because the upper age limit to be admitted to those facilities was 15, Judge Yüceöz assumed that Timothy was destined not for a correctional school but for a children's section in an adult prison. The Turkish government, on the other hand, saw their opportunity when the British government hinted that putting Timothy into a reformatory-like institution instead of prison could work as a way of damage control for Turkey's tattered image. That is why the government statement issued in the aftermath of the verdict announced that

> in the event of the sentence being approved by the Supreme Court, Timothy D., with the aim of rehabilitating him, would benefit from a special reformatory regime and would be transferred to a Boys' Reformatory which was under the exclusive management of the civil authorities, where he would have access to educational facilities.[74]

The British Embassy reported to London that "although the normal age limit is 15 the Turks have offered privately to treat Timothy exceptionally and allow him to complete his sentence in the corrective school in Ankara.[...] Impression is that Turks are embarrassed and will welcome any chance to appear humane and lenient."[75]

Timothy was indeed placed in the Kalaba correctional school in Ankara, which the British Consul had previously visited and found to be "more than adequate with good facilities for education and recreation".[76] The events following his brief stay in the correctional school read more like a picaresque novel where Timothy escapes from the school, gets caught on the Turkish-Syrian border, is brought back to Ankara to appear in court one more time, loses his privilege to stay at the correctional school and gets sent to prison to complete the rest of his sentence. Until his release from prison at the age of 17 thanks to a general amnesty in 1974 Timothy D. continued to attract media attention in both countries, which kept Turkey's alleged "embarrassment" fresh on the agenda throughout these years.

Although the incident was never openly referred to during the parliamentary debates that led to the introduction of children's courts in Turkey in 1979, one can only be too sure that Turkish policymakers vividly remembered how the incarceration of a British child had placed Turkey at the bottom of the civilization ladder in the eyes of the Western world. The lack of a separate justice system for juveniles contributed to Turkey's image as non-Western, a quality that the founding cadres of the Republic had striven to shed for decades. It was not a coincidence that the draft of 1965 that had been collecting dust on the shelves of the Turkish National Assembly's archives was recovered and turned into the Law on the Establishment, Duties and Procedures of the Juvenile Courts after Turkey's handling of juvenile delinquents became exposed and was frowned upon by "modern" Western countries.

Concluding remarks

As emphasized through this description of the Timothy D. incident, Turkey's understanding of juvenile delinquency considerably differed from that of the Western world, which was represented by Britain in this example. The institution of juvenile courts was part and parcel of the modern conception of childhood to which Turkey had mostly paid lip service from the foundation. It was, like so many others that had been previously adopted by the Republic, an institution that was anchored in a particular culture, that is Western, with particular values and mode of thought that referred to its own genealogy. The values and perceptions attached to children by Turkish society did not spontaneously bring about the kind of mentality that had engendered juvenile courts in the Western world. Neither did Turkish society witness any large-scale (real or perceived) epidemic of juvenile delinquency that could have prompted nationwide concern such as "hooliganism" did in Britain at the turn of the twentieth century.[77]

With no discernible interest from civil society, Turkish juvenile delinquents were marginalized and left in the hands of the state, which was reluctant to mix them with non-delinquent yet dependent and neglected children. In line with the Republican zeitgeist, Turkish children were expected to put their duties toward society and nation before their own "childish" needs and desires. Those who strayed from the true path did not earn much sympathy from the state. In the Turkish case, the perceived threat to the public order whether from juvenile delinquents or criminal adults overrode an interest to adhere to international (or rather Western) norms. The ethos that governed the Turkish attitude toward crime was punitive rather than rehabilitative. Turkish society sought repression and expulsion of its criminals regardless of their age, a condition that rendered prevention and rehabilitation-oriented juvenile courts unnecessary. The exclusionary dynamics which Jenks[78] identifies in the preservation of the category of childhood in the case of children who commit acts of violence were in operation in the widest sense in Turkey's handling of juvenile delinquents. Juvenile delinquents were excluded from the category of children and relegated to another category essentialized through images of evil, immorality or pathology. By losing their innocence through crime Turkish juvenile delinquents also lost their title to childhood on which the young Republic invested its future hopes.[79] The scarcity of public funds did not help either. The Turkish state prioritized primary school buildings or milk stations over detention centres or reformatories for young offenders.

Under the circumstances it was not surprising to see that children's courts were not among the institutions most called for in Turkey. The outcry of a handful of intellectuals with law or medical degrees for the recognition of juveniles as a special status group within the penal system was systematically ignored by the Turkish parliament for decades. In the end it was the proverbial aspiration of the Turkish Republic to keep up with the "civilized", that is, Western world that cleared the way for the introduction of children's courts. The disturbing "backward" image of Turkey presented through the Timothy D. incident convinced Turkish policymakers that introducing juvenile courts was a necessity they could no longer avoid. It was also too much of a coincidence that the Turkish parliament finally turned the draft of 1965 into the Law for Children's Courts in 1979, which had been proclaimed as the International Year of the Child by UNESCO. By signing the Geneva Declaration, the first widely recognized international rights statement to specifically address children, in 1928, the Turkish Republic had underscored its intention to become a member of the League of Nations, the international sovereign community that represented the "highest civilization" of the time.[80] Half a century later, Turkey, taking its cue from the United Nations, introduced children's courts as a sort of renewed declaration of its desire to be a part of the "civilized" international community. Thus the children's courts appeared as part of Turkey's image-management project that had been under construction for decades. Soon thereafter followed the criticism that those courts in their present state neither indicated a genuine transformation in Turkey's politics of crime and punishment nor represented a radical redefinition and re-evaluation of childhood in Turkish society. They were, as the critics saw it, created as window-dressing institutions to keep up appearances. Now Turkish children had their own courts where they would appear handcuffed and be tried according to the provisions of the same Turkish Penal Code. Turkish juvenile delinquents would have to wait until 2005 when the *Law for Child Protection*[81] finally came to see them as children in need of protection whose rehabilitation should be privileged over punishment, and obviously without handcuffs.

Notes

1. Philippe Ariès, *Centuries of Childhood* (Harmansworth: Penguin, 1973).
2. Chris Jenks, *Childhood* (London: Routledge, 1996), p. 73.
3. Ibid., p. 73.
4. Harry Hendrick, "Histories of Youth Crime and Justice", in Barry Goldson and John Muncie (eds), *Youth, Crime and Justice: Critical Issues* (London:

Sage, 2006), pp. 3–16. Also See Peter Rush, "The Government of a Generation: The Subject of Juvenile Delinquency", in John Muncie, Gordon Hughes
and Eugene McLaughlin (eds), *Youth Justice: Critical Readings* (London: Sage,
2002), pp. 138–158.
5. Jenks, *Childhood*, pp. 70–78.
6. David S. Tanenhaus, *Juvenile Justice in the Making* (NC: Oxford University
Press, 2004).
7. Janet Ainsworth, "Achieving the Promise of Justice for Juveniles: A Call
for the Abolition of Juvenile Court", in Anne McGillivray (ed.), *Governing
Childhood* (Aldershot: Dartmouth, 1997), p. 87.
8. Ibid., p. 86.
9. Anneke Meyer, "The Moral Rhetoric of Childhood", *Childhood*, 14, 85 (2007),
pp. 85–104.
10. Anne Behnke Kinney, *Representations of Childhood and Youth in Early China*
(Stanford: Stanford University Press, 2004), p. 2.
11. Catherine E. Pease, "Remembering the Taste of Melons: Modern Chinese Stories of Childhood", in Anne Behnke Kinney (ed.), *Chinese Views of Childhood*
(Honolulu: University of Hawai'i Press, 1995), p. 287.
12. Jenks, *Childhood*, p. 122.
13. Ibid., p. 67.
14. In emphasizing the almost century-long time-lag in Turkey's adoption of
this modern Western institution I have no intentions of contributing to
the Eurocentric abstractions and dichotomies of history such as modernization versus late modernization. Nevertheless the ruling elites of the Turkish
Republic were staunch believers in the linear, modernist understanding of
history and the official discourse was mainly constructed on the basis of
the goal of catching up with Europe or the most modern and "civilized"
countries in the world.
15. The Turkish Penal Code of 1926 did not distinguish the child from the adult
and labelled them both as criminal, yet the punishment devised for that
crime was reduced if the perpetrator was a child. See Altan Saysel, "Suçlu
Çocukların İyileştirilmesinde Bütünlüğe Doğru" [Towards a Comprehensive
Approach in Rehabilitation of Juvenile Delinquents], *Adalet Dergisi*, 63, 1
(January 1972), pp. 29–39.
16. "Habitus" in a Bourdieuan sense refers to socially acquired, embodied systems of dispositions that generate perception, appreciation, thought and
action. See Pierre Bourdieu, *In Other Words: Essays toward a Reflexive Sociology*,
trans. M. Adamson (Stanford: Stanford University Press, 1990), p. 190.
17. The term "children in need of protection" found its roots in the context
of orphaned and abandoned children that became an increasingly pressing matter for the Ottoman Empire amidst the many wars, insurrections
and displacements which marked the end of the nineteenth century and
the beginning of the twentieth. The problem of children living and working on the streets of big cities became extremely acute when the Turkish
economy faced an enormous economic crisis during and after the Second
World War. Several ad hoc committees that were set up by the Turkish
parliament to inquire into the problem of "children in need of protection" during the 1940s conducted research and prepared reports. In some
of these reports criminal children, along with orphaned, abandoned, poor,

illegitimate, truant and idle children were included in the target group and the state was called to devise a new bureau under the aegis of the Health Ministry to deal with "the children in need of protection".

For further reading on the issue of social work and child welfare in Turkey see Turgay Çavuşoğlu, *Sosyal Hizmetlerin Yakın Tarihinden Sayfalar 1917–1983* [Some Pages from the History of Social Work] (Ankara: SABEV, 2005); Makbule Sarıkaya, "Cumhuriyetin İlk Yıllarında Bir Sosyal Hizmet Kurumu: Türkiye Himaye-i Etfal Cemiyeti" [A Social Work Institution circa the Foundation of the Republic: Turkish Children's Protection Society], *A.Ü. Türkiyat Araştırmaları Enstitüsü Dergisi*, 34 (2007), pp. 321–338.

18. Faruk Erem, *Ceza Hukuku Önünde Suçlu Çocuklar* [Criminal Children in the Penal Law] (İstanbul: Hukuk İlmini Yayma Kurumu Yayınları, 1940).

19. 5387 Sayılı Korunmaya Muhtaç Çocuklar Hakkında Kanun, Türkiye Büyük Millet Meclisi, 23 Mayıs 1949 [Law for Children Who Need Protection, Turkish Grand National Assembly, 23 May 1949].

20. 6972 Sayılı Korunmaya Muhtaç Çocuklar Hakkında Kanun, Türkiye Büyük Millet Meclisi, 15 Mayıs 1957 [Law for Children Who Need Protection, Turkish Grand National Assembly, 15 May 1957].

21. See, for example, Hasan Altürk, "İngiltere ve Gal'de Çocuk Mahkemeleri" [Juvenile Courts in England and Wales], *Adalet Dergisi* 52-11/12 (1961): 1149–1158; Veli İnanç, "İngiltere'de Çocuk Mahkemeleri" [Juvenile Courts in Britain], *Adalet Dergisi* 56-1 (1965): 23–38; Arif Aybar, "Fransa'da Çocuk Mahkemeleri ve Suçlu Çocukların Usulü Mahkemesi" [Juvenile Courts and Court Procedures for Juvenile Delinquents in France], *Adalet Dergisi* 57-12 (1966), pp. 864–880.

22. Betül Taşbağ, "17 Kasım 1965 Tarihli Çocuk Mahkemelerinin Kuruluş ve Yargılama Usulleri Hakkındaki Kanun Teklifi Üzerine Mütalaalar" [Comments on the Draft of the Law on the Establishment, Duties and Procedures of the Juvenile Courts], *Ankara Barosu Dergisi* 23–2 (1966), pp. 248–250.

23. Manuel Lopez and Rey Arrojo, *Türkiye'de Suçluların Islahı* [Rehabilitation of Convicts in Turkey], (Ankara: Yarı Açık Cezaevi Matbaası, 1967), quoted in Sevda Uluğtekin, *Çocuk Mahkemeleri ve Sosyal İnceleme Raporları* [Children's Courts and Social Inquiry Reports], 2nd edition, (Ankara: Ankara Barolar Birliği Yayınları, 2004) [1994], pp. 56–57.

24. İsmayıl Hakkı Baltacıoğlu, *İçtimai Mektep* [Social School], (İstanbul: Sühulet Kütüphanesi, 1932), 34. Also See Güven Gürkan Öztan, *Türkiye'de Çocukluğun Politik İnşası* [Political Construction of Childhood in Turkey] (İstanbul: İstanbul Bilgi Üniversitesi Yayınları, 2011), p. 157.

25. Jacqueline Rose, *The Case of Peter Pan: Or the Impossibility of Children's Fiction* (Basingstoke: Macmillan, 1994), p. 43.

26. Ashis Nandy, "Reconstructing Childhood: A Critique of the Ideology of Adulthood", in *Traditions, Tyranny and Utopias: Essays in the Politics of Awareness* (Delhi: Oxford University Press, 1992), pp. 57–63.

27. Duygu Köksal, "Ulusun Çocukluğu" [Childhood of the Nation], *Toplumsal Tarih* 40 (1997), p. 9.

28. For a discussion of the image of the "ideal child" in Britain, see Stephanie Olsen's chapter in this volume.

29. See the Address Delivered by Hasan Ali Yücel, the Minister of Education, at the Celebrations of Youth and Sports Day in 1939 in which he says: "Turkish

Youth, you must always remember the sacrifices made by us, namely the previous generation, for the sake of the fatherland. We have no doubt that you will follow our example and selflessly work for the nation." Speech by Hasan Ali Yücel, *Ulus*, Mayıs 20 [May] 1939.

30. "23 Nisan Çocuk Bayramında Ankara'daki Merasimde Maarif Vekili Doktor Reşit Galip Beyin Nutku" [The Address by Dr. Reşit Galip, the Minister of Education, delivered at the Celebrations of the Children's Day of 23 April], *Çocuk Sesi* 174 (1933) quoted in Özge Ertem, "The Republic's Children and Their Burdens in 1930s and 1940s Turkey: The Idealized Middle-Class Children as the Future of the Nation and the Image of 'Poor' Children in Children's Periodicals" (Unpublished MA Thesis, Boğaziçi University, 2005), p. 44.

31. Nandy, "Reconstructing Childhood", p. 59.

32. Özgür Sevgi Göral, "The Child Question and Juvenile Delinquency During Early Republican Era" (Unpublished MA Thesis, Boğaziçi University, 2003), p. 122.

33. Ertem, "The Republic's Children", p. 12.

34. Ercüment Baktır MD, "Tıbbi Bahisler: Suçlu Çocuklar" [Medical Issues: Criminal Children], *Milliyet*, Şubat 16 [February], 1960.

35. Tanenhaus, *Juvenile Justice in the Making*, p. 35.

36. Bengü Kurtege, "The Historical Politics of the Juvenile Justice System and the Operation of Law in the Juvenile Court in İstanbul in Regard to Property Crimes" (Unpublished MA Thesis, Boğaziçi University, 2009), p. 33.

37. "Feyyaz Gölcüklü'nün Konuşması" [Speech by Feyyaz Gölcüklü], Korunmaya Muhtaç Çocuklar Paneli 22 Kasım 1969 [Panel on the Children in Need of Protection 22 November 1969] (İstanbul: İstanbul İktisadi Araştırmalar Vakfı, 1970), p. 58, quoted in Kurtege, "The Historical Politics", p. 33.

38. Atalay Yörükoğlu MD, "Çocuk Suçluluğu" [Juvenile Delinquency], *Milliyet*, Ekim (27 October 1967).

39. Yalçın Doğan, "Sevgisiz Toplumun Çocukları" [Children of a Loveless Society], *Milliyet*, Ekim (8 October 1989).

40. Yörükoğlu, "Çocuk Suçluluğu" [Juvenile Delinquency], *Milliyet*, Ekim (27 October 1967).

41. Nevzat Gürelli, "Adalet Yılı Açılırken Hukuk Reformu" [On the Judicial Reform], *Milliyet*, Eylül (3 September 1972).

42. Ian Michael Livie, "Curing Hooliganism: Moral Panic, Juvenile Delinquency, and the Political Culture of Moral Reform in Britain, 1898–1908" (Unpublished PhD Diss, University of Southern California, 2010), p. vi.

43. Fethi Açıkel, "Devletin Manevi Şahsiyeti ve Ulusun Pedagojisi" [The Spiritual Identity of the State and the Pedagogy of the Nation], in Tanıl Bora (ed.), *Modern Türkiye'de Siyasi Düşünce: Milliyetçilik* [Political Thought in Modern Turkey: Nationalism] (İstanbul: İletişim Yayınları, 2002), pp. 117–139.

44. *Milliyet*, "Türk Makamları Dürüst Hareket Etmişlerdir" [Daily Telegraph Says: Turkish Authorities Act Righteously], Mart 5 [March], 1972; *Milliyet*, "Başımıza Ne Geldiyse" [All Our Troubles], Mart 7 [March], 1972.

45. *News of the World*, "Get This Boy Out of Hell", 30 January 1972.

46. Until the last quarter of the nineteenth century Great Britain as the leading actor in the 'Eastern Question' sought to maintain the territorial integrity and political independence of the Ottoman Empire in order to protect her economic and military interests in the Eastern Mediterranean and backed the

crumbling empire against Russia. Yet when the Ottoman finances foundered in 1875 the British foreign policy toward the Ottoman Empire underwent a substantial transformation. Great Britain ceased to support the Ottoman Empire and later joined forces with Russia in the First World War that culminated in the dismemberment of the Ottoman Empire, which caused feelings of anger and humiliation for the Ottomans. See Nazan Çiçek, *The Young Ottomans Turkish Critics of the Eastern Question in the Late Nineteenth Century* (London: I.B.Tauris, 2010).

47. William E. Gladstone, *Bulgarian Horrors and the Question of the East* (London: John Murray, 1876), p. 13.
48. Public Record Office [PRO] FCO 9/1620, from Ankara (Sarell) to FCO 061500Z, tel no 472 of 6 March 1972. Quoting the semi-official Anatolian Agency, British Ambassador Sarell reported that Turkish Prime Minister reached this decision "because of the cheap and dirty campaign which the British press opened against Turkey and Turkish justice, using as an excuse the verdict on the child called Timothy [...]". Also See *Daily Telegraph*, "Turkish Premier Drops London Visit Over D. Case"(6 March 1972).
49. *Cumhuriyet*, "İngilizler'in Kampanyası Bütün Yurtta Tepki Yarattı" [Campaign Launched by the British Caused Backlashes Throughout the Country], Mart 6 [March], 1972; *Daily Telegraph*, "Turkish Premier Drops London Visit Over D. Case", 6 March 1972.
50. Prosecutor Nedim Demirel's statement to the press in *The Guardian*, "Boy 'not ill-treated' In Prison", 3 February 1972.
51. Yaşar Aysev, "Anglosakson Egoizmi" [AngloSaxon Egotizm], *Barış*, Mart 5 [March], 1972. Also See PRO FCO 9/1620 Ankara to FCO, ME/3933/C/5, Turkish Comment on Reaction to Timothy D. Case, Ankara Home Service in Turkish on 05 March1972, 7 March 1972.
52. *The Sun*, "The Sun Says: Free Timothy Now", 24 February 1972.
53. PRO FCO 9/1620, Dr. Grace Thornton (Consular Department) to A. Brooke (Southern European Department), 29 February 1972.
54. PRO FCO 9/1620, Sarell to FCO, 291620Z, tel no 431 of 29 February 1972.
55. PRO FCO 9/1620, Douglas-Home (Foreign Secretary) to Ankara and İstanbul, 261201Z, tel no 247 of 25 February 1972.
56. PRO FCO 9/1620, Douglas-Home to Ankara, 012000Z, tel no 272 of 1 March 1972.
57. In assessing British reactions to Turkey's handling of the Timothy D. case it should be borne in mind that two years before, Britain had enacted the Children and Young Persons Act 1969, which sought to substitute non-criminal proceedings in place of criminal procedures for the 10–14 age group, to encourage a more liberal use of non-criminalized care proceedings for those aged 14–17, and to involve parents with social workers in deciding on a course of treatment in order to avoid court appearance. See Hendrick, "Histories of Youth", p. 11.
58. PRO FCO 9/1620, Douglas-Home to Ankara, 012000Z, tel no 272 of 1 March 1972; PRO FCO 9/1620, Dr. Grace Thornton (Consular Department), Circular, 2 March 1972.
59. PRO FCO 9/1620, Statement by the Turkish Authorities, 1 March 1972.
60. PRO FCO 9/1620, Statement by the Turkish Embassy, 1 March 1972.

61. *Cumhuriyet*, "İngiliz Basını" [British Press], Mart 6 [March], 1972. Also Quoted in *Daily Telegraph*, "Turkish Premier Drops London Visit over D. Case", 6 March 1972.
62. Judge Uluer Yüceöz's Statement to the Press, *Milliyet*, "Üzülsek Bile Kanunun Vaz Ettiği Cezayı Veririz" [We Execute the Law No Matter How Sorry We Are For the Accused], Mart 5 [March], 1972.
63. Bülent Nuri Esen's statement to the press, *Cumhuriyet*, "İngilizler'in Kampanyası Bütün Yurtta Tepki Yarattı" [Campaign Launched by the British Caused Backlashes throughout the Country], Mart 6 [March] 1972.
64. Cihad Baban, "Bu Kadarı Biraz Fazla Değil mi İngiliz Basını?" [The British Media, Are You Not Crossing a Line?], *Cumhuriyet*, Mart 7 [March] 7, 1972.
65. Yörükoğlu, "Çocuk Mahkemeleri ve Suçlu Çocuklar" [Children's Courts and Criminal Children], *Milliyet*, Mart 14 [March] 1972.
66. Ibid.
67. Abdi İpekçi, "Bir Mahkumiyet Dolayısıyla" [On the Occasion of a Prison Sentence], *Milliyet*, Mart 3 [March] 1972.
68. Those letters were translated into Turkish and published in Turkish dailies. For examples See Hasan Pulur, "İngiltere'de Böyle İnsanlar da Yaşar" [These People Live in England Too], *Milliyet*, Mart 25 [March], 1972; *Milliyet*, "Türk Makamları Dürüst Hareket Etmişlerdir" [Daily Telegraph Says: Turkish Authorities Act Righteously], Mart 5 [March] 1972.
69. PRO FCO 9/1620 Edward Heath to Harold Wilson, 2 March 1972.
70. Meyer, "The Moral Rhetoric", p. 100.
71. PRO FCO 9/1620 Sarell to FCO, 041230Z, tel no 460 of 4 March 1972; *Hürriyet*, "İngilizler Türkiye'ye Hakaret Kampanyası Açtı" [The British Have Opened a Campaign of Insults against Turkey], Mart 4 [March] 1972.
72. Carolyn Steedman, *Childhood, Culture and Class in Britain: Margaret McMillan 1860–1931* (London: Virago, 1990), pp. 63–64.
73. *The Sun*, "The Sun Says: Free Timothy Now", 24 February 1972.
74. PRO FCO 9/1620, Statement by the Turkish Authorities, 1 March 1972.
75. PRO FCO 9/1620, Sarell to FCO, 021725Z, tel no 9 of 2 March 1972.
76. PRO FCO 9/1620, Sarell to FCO, E042108, tel no 491 of 8 March 1972.
77. Livie, "Curing Hooliganism", p. 14.
78. Jenks, *Childhood*, pp. 127–133.
79. Ashley Lauren Taylor, "From Dennis-the Menace to Billy-the-Kid: The Evolving Social Construction of Juvenile Offenders in the United States from 1899–2007" (Unpublished PhD Diss, Duke University, 2010), p. 22.
80. Kathryn Libal, "Children's Rights in Turkey", *Human Rights Review*, 3, 1 (2001), p. 38.
81. 5395 Sayılı Çocuk Koruma Kanunu, Türkiye Büyük Millet Meclisi, 3 Temmuz 2005 (Law for Child Protection, Turkish Grand National Assembly, 3 July 2005).

Index

Note: Locators followed by the letter 'n' refer to notes.

276

CPSIA information can be obtained at www.ICGtesting.com
Printed in the USA
LVOW05*0456251014

410479LV00008B/70/P